Dialectical Materialism
An Introduction

Dialectical Materialism
An Introduction

Maurice Cornforth

Complete Edition
Three Volumes in One

DIALECTICAL MATERIALISM: AN INTRODUCTION
Maurice Cornforth

First Aakar Edition 2015
Reprinted 2017

ISBN 978-93-5002-340-2

Published in agreement with Lawrence and Wishart Limited, London for publication and sale only in the Indian Subcontinent (India, Pakistan, Bangladesh, Nepal, Maldives, Bhutan and Sri Lanka).

Published by
AAKAR BOOKS
28 E Pocket IV, Mayur Vihar Phase I, Delhi 110 091
Phones: 011 2279 5505, 011 2279 5641
Email: aakarbooks@gmail.com

Printed at
Sapra Brothers, Noida

CONTENTS

VOLUME III: THEORY OF KNOWLEDGE

Part I: The Nature and Origin of the Mind

Part II: The Development of Ideas

Part III: Truth and Freedom

VOLUME I
MATERIALISM AND THE DIALECTICAL METHOD

PART ONE

MATERIALISM

Chapter One

PARTY PHILOSOPHY

Party Philosophy and Class Philosophy

Dialectical materialism is the revolutionary philosophy of the working class. It is the philosophy of the revolutionary working-class party.

This definition must appear a strange one, both to many politicians and to many philosophers. But we will not begin to understand dialectical materialism unless we can grasp the thought which lies behind this definition.

Let us ask, first of all, what conception of philosophy lies behind the idea expressed in this definition of party or—since a party is always the political representative of a class—class philosophy.

By philosophy is usually meant our most general account of the nature of the world and of mankind's place and destiny in it—our world outlook.

That being understood, it is evident that everybody has some kind of philosophy, even though he has never learned to discuss it. Everybody is influenced by philosophical views, even though he has not thought them out for himself and cannot formulate them.

Some people, for example, think that this world is nothing but "a vale of tears" and that our life in it is the preparation for a better life in another and better world. They accordingly believe that we should suffer whatever befalls us with fortitude, not struggling against it, but trying to do whatever good we can to our fellow creatures. This is one kind of philosophy, one kind of world outlook.

Other people think that the world is a place to grow rich in, and that each should look out for himself. This is another kind of philosophy.

But granted that our philosophy is our world outlook, the task arises of working out this world outlook systematically and in detail, turning it into a well-formulated and coherent theory, turning vaguely held popular beliefs and attitudes into more or less systematic doctrines. This is what the philosophers do.

By the time the philosophers have worked out their theories, they have often produced something very complicated, very abstract and very hard to understand. But even though only a comparatively few people may read and digest the actual productions of philosophers, these productions may and do have a very wide influence. For the fact that philosophers have systematised certain beliefs reinforces those beliefs, and helps to impose them upon wide masses of ordinary people. Hence, everyone is influenced in one way or another by philosophers, even though they have never read the works of those philosophers.

And if this is the case, then we cannot regard the systems of the philosophers as being wholly products of the brain-work of the individual philosophers. Of course, the formulation of views, the peculiar ways in which they are worked out and written down, is the work of the particular philosopher. But the views themselves, in their most general aspect, have a social basis in ideas which reflect the social activities and social relations of the time, and which, therefore, do not spring ready-made out of the heads of philosophers.

From this we may proceed a step further.

When society is divided into classes—and society always has been divided into classes ever since the dissolution of the primitive communes, that is to say, throughout the entire historical period to which the history of philosophy belongs—then the various views which are current in society always express the outlooks of various classes. We may conclude, therefore, that the various systems of the philosophers also always express a class outlook. They are, in fact, nothing but the systematic working out and theoretical formulation of a class outlook, or, if you prefer, of the ideology of definite classes.

Philosophy is and always has been class philosophy. Philosophers may not realise this, but that does not alter the fact.

For people do not and cannot think in isolation from society, and therefore from the class interests and class struggles which pervade society, any more than they can live and act in such isolation. A philosophy is a world outlook, an attempt to understand the world, mankind and man's place in the world. Such an outlook cannot be anything but the outlook of a class, and the philosopher functions as the thinking representative of a class. How can it be otherwise? Philosophies are not imported from some other planet, but are produced here on earth, by people involved, whether they like it or not, in existing class relations and class struggles. Therefore, whatever philosophers say about themselves, there is no philosophy which does not embody a class outlook, or which is impartial, as opposed to partisan, in relation to class struggles. Search as we may, we shall not find any impartial, non-partisan, non-class philosophy.

Bearing this in mind, then, we shall find that the philosophies of the past have all, in one way or another, expressed the outlook of the so-called "educated" classes, that is to say, of the exploiting classes. In general, it is the leaders of society who express and propagate their ideas in the form of systematic philosophies. And up to the appearance of the modern working class, which is the peculiar product of capitalism, these leaders have always been the exploiting classes. It is their outlook which has dominated philosophy, just as they have dominated society.

We can only conclude from this that the working class, if today it intends to take over leadership of society, needs to express its own class outlook in philosophical form, and to oppose this philosophy to the philosophies which express the outlook and defend the interests of the exploiters.

"The services rendered by Marx and Engels to the working class may be expressed in a few words thus: they taught the working class to know itself and be conscious of itself, and they substituted science for dreams," wrote Lenin in his obituary on Fredrick Engels. Marx and Engels founded and established the revolutionary theory of working-class struggle, which illumines the road by which the working class can throw off capitalist exploitation, can take the leadership of all the masses of the people, and so free the whole of society once and for all of all oppression and exploitation of man by man. They taught that without its own party, independent of all bourgeois parties, the working class certainly could not win victory over capitalism, could not lead the whole of society forward to the abolition of capitalism and the establishment of socialism. Lenin further developed the Marxist teachings about the party. He showed that the party must act as the vanguard of its class, the most conscious section of its class, and that it is the instrument for winning and wielding political power.

To fulfil such a rôle, the party must evidently have knowledge, understanding and vision; in other words, it must be equipped with revolutionary theory, on which its policies are based and by which its activities are guided.

This theory is the theory of Marxism-Leninism. And it is not just an economic theory, nor yet exclusively a political theory, but a world outlook—a philosophy. Economic and political views are not and never can be independent of a general world outlook. Specific economic and political views express the world outlook of those who hold such views, and conversely, philosophical views find expression in views on economics and politics.

Recognising all this, the revolutionary party of the working class cannot but formulate, and having formulated, hold fast to, develop and treasure, its party philosophy. In this philosophy—dialectical materialism—are embodied the general ideas by means of which the party understands the world which it is seeking to change and in terms of which it defines its aims and works out how to fight for them. In this philosophy are embodied the general ideas by means of which the party seeks to enlighten and organise the whole class, and to influence, guide and win over all the masses of working people, showing the conclusions which must be drawn from each stage of the struggle, helping people to learn from their own experience how to go forward towards socialism.

And so we see why it is that in our times a philosophy has arisen which expresses the revolutionary world outlook of the working class.

Experience itself has taught the party the need for philosophy. For experience shows that if we do not have our own revolutionary socialist philosophy, then inevitably we borrow our ideas from hostile, anti-socialist sources. If we do not adopt today the outlook of the working class and of the struggle for socialism, then we adopt—or slip into, without meaning to do so—that of the capitalists and of the struggle against socialism. This is why the working-class party—if it is to be the genuine revolutionary leadership of its class, and is not to mislead its class by the importation of hostile capitalist ideas, and of policies corresponding to such ideas—must be concerned to formulate, defend and propagate its own revolutionary philosophy.

Class Philosophy and Truth

Against what has just been said about a class and party philosophy, the objection is bound to be raised that such a conception is a complete travesty of the whole idea of philosophy.

Class interests may incline us to believe one thing rather than another, some will say, but should not philosophy be above this? Should not philosophy be objective and impartial, and teach us to set class and party interests aside, and to seek only for the truth? For surely what is true is true, whether this suits some or other class interests or not? If philosophy is partisan—party philosophy—how can it be objective, how can it be true philosophy?

In reply to such objections, we may say that the working-class standpoint in philosophy is very far indeed from having no concern for truth.

Is there no such thing as truth? Of course there is—and

men are getting nearer to it. For different outlooks, partisan as they may be, are not on a level so far as nearness to truth is concerned. Every philosophy embodies a class outlook. Yes, but just as one class differs from another class in its social rôle and in its contribution to the development of society, so one philosophy embodies positive achievements in comparison with another in the working out of the truth about the world and society.

People are prone to believe that if we adopt a partisan, class standpoint, then we turn our backs on truth; and that, on the other hand, if we genuinely seek for truth, then we must be strictly impartial and non-partisan. But the contrary is the case. It is only when we adopt the partisan standpoint of historically the most progressive class that we are able to get nearer to truth.

The definition of dialectical materialism, therefore, as the philosophy of the revolutionary working-class party, is in no way incompatible with the claim of dialectical materialism to express truth, and to be a means of arriving at truth. On the contrary. We have every right to make this claim, in view of the actual historical position and rôle of the working class.

Except for the working class, all other classes which have aspired to take the leadership of society have been exploiting classes. But every exploiting class, whatever its achievements, has always to find some way of *disguising* its real position and aims, both from itself and from the exploited, and of making out that its rule is just and permanent. For such a class can never recognise its real position and aims as an exploiting class, or the temporary character of its own system.

For example, in ancient slave society, Aristotle, the greatest philosopher of antiquity, made out that the institution of slavery was decreed by nature, since some men were by nature slaves.

In the heyday of feudal society the greatest philosopher of the middle ages, Thomas Aquinas, represented the entire universe as being a kind of feudal system. Everything was arranged in a feudal hierarchy, with God surrounded by the chief archangels at the top. Everything depended on what was next above it in the system, and nothing could exist without God.

As for capitalism, it dissolves all feudal ties and, as Marx and Engels observed in *The Communist Manifesto*, "has left remaining no other nexus between man and man than naked self-interest, than callous cash payment". This was reflected in the beginnings of capitalist philosophy, especially in Britain.

This philosophy saw the world as consisting of independent atoms, each complete in itself, concerned only with itself, and all interacting. This was a mirror of capitalist society, as seen by the rising bourgeoisie. And by means of such ideas they succeeded, too, in disguising their own aims of domination and profit. Worker and capitalist were "on a level", each was a free human atom, and they entered into a free contract, the one to work, the other to provide capital and pay wages.

But the working class does not need any such "false consciousness" as is contained in such philosophies. It does not want to set up a new system of exploitation, but to abolish all exploitation of man by man. For this reason, it has no interest whatever in disguising anything, but rather in understanding things just as they really are. For the better it understands the truth, the more is it strengthened in its struggle.

Moreover, other classes have always wanted to perpetuate themselves and to last out for as long as they could. And so they have favoured philosophical "systems" which give themselves a permanent place in the universe. Such systems attempt to define the nature of the universe so as to represent certain things and certain relations as being necessary, eternal and unchangeable. And then they make it appear that a particular social system is a necessary part of the whole.

But the working class does not need to perpetuate itself. On the contrary, it needs to do away with its own existence as a class as quickly as possible, and to establish a classless society. Therefore, the working class has no use at all for any philosophical "system" which establishes any false permanence. Its class position and aims are such that it can afford to and needs to recognise and trace out the change, coming into being and ceasing to be of *everything* in existence.

Our party philosophy, then, has a right to lay claim to truth. For it is the only philosophy which is based on a standpoint which demands that we should always seek to understand things just as they are, in all their manifold changes and interconnections, without disguises and without fantasy.

A Revolution in Philosophy

"The Marxian doctrine is omnipotent because it is true," wrote Lenin. "It is complete and harmonious, and provides men with an integral world conception which is irreconcilable with any form of superstition, reaction or defence of bourgeois oppression" (*The Three Sources and Three Component Parts of Marxism*).

And he further wrote:

"There is nothing resembling 'sectarianism' in Marxism, in the sense of its being a hidebound, petrified doctrine, a doctrine which arose *away from* the highroad of development of world civilisation. On the contrary, the genius of Marx consists precisely in the fact that he furnished answers to questions the foremost minds of mankind had already raised. His teachings arose as the direct and immediate *continuation* of the teachings of the greatest representatives of philosophy, political economy and socialism. . . ."

In its philosophical aspect, Marxism appears as the culmination of a whole great development of philosophical thought, in which the problems of philosophy were posed and took shape in the course of a series of revolutions, its highest point being reached in the classical German philosophy of the early nineteenth century.

But if Marxism is thus the continuation and culmination of the past achievements of philosophy, it is a continuation which puts an end to an epoch and constitutes a new point of departure. For in comparison with past philosophies, it launches out on new lines. It constitutes a revolution in philosophy, an end to the "systems" of the past, a philosophy of an entirely new kind.

Marxism-Leninism is no longer a philosophy which expresses the world outlook of an exploiting class, of a minority, striving to impose its rule and its ideas upon the masses of the people, in order to keep them in subjection; but it is a philosophy which serves the common people in their struggle to throw off all exploitation and to build a classless society.

Marxism-Leninism is a philosophy which seeks to understand the world in order to change it. "The philosophers have only interpreted the world in various ways," wrote Marx. "The point, however, is to change it." Therefore, if we could say of past philosophy that it has been an attempt to understand the world and man's place and destiny in it—an attempt necessarily conditioned by the class outlook, prejudices and illusions of the various exploiting class philosophers—we have to say of Marxist-Leninist philosophy that it is an attempt to understand the world in order to change the world and to shape and realise man's destiny in it. Dialectical materialism is a theoretical instrument in the hands of the people for use in changing the world.

Marxism-Leninism, therefore, seeks to base our ideas of things on nothing but the actual investigation of them, arising from and tested by experience and practice. It does not invent a "system" as previous philosophies have done, and then try to make everything fit into it.

Thus dialectical materialism is in the truest sense a popular philosophy, a scientific philosophy and a philosophy of practice.

The revolutionary characteristics of dialectical materialism are embodied in the two features of Marxist-Leninist philosophy which give it its name—dialectics and materialism.

In order to understand things so as to change them we must study them, not according to the dictates of any abstract system, but in their real changes and interconnections—and that is what is meant by dialectics.

We must set aside preconceived ideas and fancies about things, and strive to make our theories correspond to the real conditions of material existence—and that means that our outlook and theory is materialistic.

In dialectical materialism, wrote Engels, in his book *Ludwig Feuerbach*, "the materialist world outlook was taken really seriously for the first time and was carried through consistently. . . ." For "it was resolved to comprehend the real world—nature and history—just as it presents itself to everyone who approaches it free from preconceived idealist fancies. It was decided relentlessly to sacrifice every idealist fancy which could not be brought into harmony with the facts conceived in their own and not in a fantastic connection. And materialism means nothing more than this."

Chapter Two

MATERIALISM AND IDEALISM

Materialism and Idealism—Opposed Ways of Interpreting Every Question

Materialism is not a dogmatic system. It is rather a way of interpreting, conceiving of, explaining every question.

The materialist way of interpreting events, of conceiving of things and their interconnections, is opposed to the idealist way of interpreting and conceiving of them. Materialism is opposed to idealism. On every question, there are materialist and idealist ways of interpreting it, materialist and idealist ways of trying to understand it.

Thus materialism and idealism are not two opposed abstract theories about the nature of the world, of small concern to ordinary practical folk. They are opposed ways of interpreting and understanding every question, and, consequently, they express opposite approaches in practice and lead to very different conclusions in terms of practical activity.

Nor are they, as some use the terms, opposite moral attitudes —the one high-minded, the other base and self-seeking. If we use the terms like this, we will never understand the opposition between idealist and materialist conceptions; for this way of speaking is, as Engels said, nothing but

> "an unpardonable concession to the traditional philistine prejudice against the word materialism resulting from the long-continued defamation by the priests. By the word materialism the philistine understands gluttony, drunkenness, lust of the eye, lust of the flesh, arrogance, cupidity, miserliness, profit-hunting and stock-exchange swindling—

in short, all the filthy vices in which he himself indulges in private. By the word idealism he understands the belief in virtue, universal philanthropy and in a general way a 'better world', of which he boasts before others" (*Ludwig Feuerbach*).

Before trying to define materialism and idealism in general terms, let us consider how these two ways of understanding things are expressed in relation to certain simple and familiar questions. This will help us to grasp the significance of the distinction between a materialist and an idealist interpretation.

First let us consider a very familiar natural phenomenon—a thunderstorm. What causes thunderstorms?

An idealist way of answering this question is to say that thunderstorms are due to the anger of God. Being angry, he arranges for lightning and thunderbolts to descend upon mankind.

The materialist way of understanding thunderstorms is opposed to this. The materialist will try to explain and understand thunderstorms as being solely due to what we call natural forces. For example, ancient materialists suggested that far from thunderstorms being due to the anger of the gods, they were caused by material particles in the clouds banging against one another. That this particular explanation was wrong, is not the point: the point is that it was an attempt at materialist as opposed to idealist explanation. Nowadays a great deal more is known about thunderstorms arising from the scientific investigation of the natural forces involved. Knowledge remains very incomplete, but at all events enough is known to make it quite clear that the explanation must be on materialist lines, so that the idealist explanation has become thoroughly discredited.

It will be seen that while the idealist explanation tries to relate the phenomenon to be explained to some *spiritual* cause—in this case the anger of God—the materialist explanation relates it to *material* causes.

In this example, most educated people today would agree in accepting the materialist interpretation. This is because they generally accept the *scientific* explanation of natural phenomena, and every advance of natural science is an advance in the *materialist* understanding of nature.

Let us take a second example, this time one arising out of social life. For instance: Why are there rich and poor? This is a question which many people ask, especially poor people.

The most straightforward idealist answer to this question is to say simply—it is because God made them so. It is the will of God that some should be rich and others poor.

But other less straightforward idealist explanations are more in vogue. For example: it is because some men are careful and farsighted, and these husband their resources and grow rich, while others are thriftless and stupid, and these remain poor. Those who favour this type of explanation say that it is all due to eternal "human nature". The nature of man and of society is such that the distinction of rich and poor necessarily arises.

Just as in the case of the thunderstorm, so in the case of the rich and poor, the idealist seeks for some spiritual cause—if not in the will of God, the divine mind, then in certain innate characteristics of the human mind.

The materialist, on the other hand, seeks the reason in the material, economic conditions of social life. If society is divided into rich and poor, it is because the production of the material means of life is so ordered that some have possession of the land and other means of production while the rest have to work for them. However hard they may work and however much they may scrape and save, the non-possessors will remain poor, while the possessors grow rich on the fruits of their labour.

On such questions, therefore, the difference between a materialist and an idealist conception can be very important. And the difference is important not merely in a theoretical but in a practical sense.

A materialist conception of thunderstorms, for example, helps us to take precautions against them, such as fitting buildings with lightning conductors. But if our explanation of thunderstorms is idealist, all we can do is to watch and pray. If we accept an idealist account of the existence of rich and poor, all we can do is to accept the existing state of affairs—rejoicing in our superior status and bestowing a little charity if we are rich, and cursing our fate if we are poor. But armed with a materialist understanding of society we can begin to see the way to change society.

It is clear, therefore, that while some may have a vested interest in idealism, it is in the interests of the great majority to learn to think and to understand things in the materialist way.

How, then, can we define materialism and idealism, and the difference between them, in general terms, so as to define the essence of the question? This was done by Engels in the book on *Ludwig Feuerbach.*

> "The great basic question of all philosophy, especially of modern philosophy, is that concerning the relation of thinking and being. . . . The answers which the philosophers have given to this question split them into two great camps. Those who asserted the primacy of spirit to nature and therefore in the last instance assumed world creation in some form or another . . . comprised the camp of idealism. The others, who regarded nature as primary, belong to the various schools of materialism."

Idealism is the way of interpreting things which regards the spiritual as prior to the material, whereas materialism regards the material as prior. Idealism supposes that everything material is dependent on and determined by something spiritual, whereas materialism recognises that everything spiritual is dependent on and determined by something material. And this difference manifests itself both in general philosophical conceptions of the world as a whole, and in conceptions of particular things and events.

Idealism and the Supernatural

At bottom, idealism is religion, theology. "Idealism is clericalism," wrote Lenin in his *Philosophical Notebooks.* All idealism is a continuation of the religious approach to questions, even though particular idealist theories have shed their religious skin. Idealism is inseparable from superstition, belief in the supernatural, the mysterious and unknowable.

Materialism, on the other hand, seeks for explanations in terms belonging to the material world, in terms of factors which we can verify, understand and control.

The roots of the idealist conception of things are, then, the same as those of religion.

To believers, the conceptions of religion, that is to say, conceptions of supernatural spiritual beings, generally seem to have their justification, not, of course, in any evidence of the senses, but in something which lies deep within the spiritual nature of man. And, indeed, it is true that these conceptions do have very deep roots in the historical development of human consciousness. But what is their origin, how did such conceptions arise in the first place? We can certainly not regard such conceptions as being the products, as religion itself tells us, of divine revelation, or as arising from any other supernatural cause, if we find that they themselves have a natural origin. And such an origin can in fact be traced.

Conceptions of the supernatural, and religious ideas in general, owe their origin first of all to the helplessness and ignorance of men in face of the forces of nature. Forces which men cannot understand are personified—they are represented as manifestations of the activity of spirits.

For example, such alarming events as thunderstorms were, as we have seen, explained fantastically as due to the anger of gods. Again, such important phenomena as the growth of crops were put down to the activity of a spirit: it was believed that it was the corn spirit that made the corn grow.

From the most primitive times men personified natural forces in this way. With the birth of class society, when men were impelled to act by social relations which dominated them and which they did not understand, they further invented supernatural agencies doubling, as it were, the state of society. The gods were invented superior to mankind, just as the kings and lords were superior to the common people.

All religion, and all idealism, has at its heart this kind of *doubling of the world*. It is dualistic, and invents a dominating ideal or supernatural world over against the real material world.

Very characteristic of idealism are such antitheses as: soul and body; god and man; the heavenly kingdom and the earthly kingdom; the forms and ideas of things, grasped by the intellect, and the world of material reality, perceptible by the senses.

For idealism, there is always a higher, more real, non-material world—which is prior to the material world, is its ultimate source and cause, and to which the material world is subject. For materialism, on the other hand, there is *one* world, the material world.

By idealism in philosophy we mean any doctrine which says that beyond material reality there is a higher, spiritual reality, in terms of which the material reality is in the last analysis to be explained.

Some Varieties of Present-day Idealist Philosophy

At this point a few observations may be useful concerning some characteristic doctrines of modern bourgeois philosophy.

For nearly three hundred years there has been put forward a variety of philosophy known as "subjective idealism". This teaches that the material world does not exist at all. Nothing exists but the sensations and ideas in our minds, and there is no external material reality corresponding to them.

And then again, this subjective idealism is put forward in the form of a doctrine concerning knowledge: it denies that we can know anything about objective reality outside ourselves, and says that we can have knowledge of appearances only and not of "things in themselves".

This sort of idealism has become very fashionable today. It even parades as extremely "scientific". When capitalism was still a progressive force, bourgeois thinkers used to believe that we could know more and more about the real world, and so control natural forces and improve the lot of mankind indefinitely. Now they are saying that the real world is unknowable, the arena of mysterious forces which pass our comprehension.

We have seen that, at bottom, idealism always believes in *two worlds*, the ideal and the material, and it places the ideal prior to and above the material. Materialism, on the other hand, knows one world only, the material world, and refuses to invent a second, imaginary, superior ideal world.

Materialism and idealism are irreconcilably opposed. But this does not stop many philosophers from trying to reconcile and combine them. In philosophy there are also various attempted compromises between idealism and materialism.

One such attempted compromise is often known as "dualism". Such a compromise philosophy asserts the existence of the spiritual as separate and distinct from the material—but it tries to place the two on a level. Thus it treats the world of non-living matter in a thoroughly materialist way: this, it says, is the sphere of activity of natural forces, and spiritual factors do not enter into it and have nothing to do with it in any way. But when it comes to mind and society, here, says this philosophy, is the sphere of activity of spirit. Here, it maintains, we must seek explanations in idealist and not in materialist terms.

Such a compromise between materialism and idealism, therefore, amounts to this—that with regard to all the most important questions concerning men, society and history we are to continue to adopt idealist conceptions and to oppose materialism.

Another compromise philosophy is known as "realism". In its modern form, this philosophy has arisen in opposition to subjective idealism.

The "realist" philosophers say that the external material world really exists independent of our perceptions and is in some way reflected by our perceptions. In this the "realists" agree with the materialists in opposition to *subjective* idealism; indeed, you cannot be a materialist unless you are a thoroughgoing realist on the question of the real existence of the material world.

But merely to assert that the external world exists independent of our perceiving it, is not to be a materialist. For example, the great Catholic philosopher of the middle ages, Thomas

Aquinas, was in this sense a "realist". And to this day most Catholic theologians regard it as a heresy to be anything but a "realist" in philosophy. But at the same time they assert that the material world, which really exists, was created by God, and is sustained and ruled all the time by the power of God, by a spiritual power. So far from being materialists, they are idealists.

Moreover, the word "realism" is much abused by philosophers. So long as you believe that something or other is "real", you may call yourself a "realist". Some philosophers think that not only is the world of material things real, but that there is also, outside space and time, a real world of "universals", of the abstract essences of things: so these call themselves "realists". Others say that, although nothing exists but the perceptions in our minds, nevertheless these perceptions are real: so these call themselves "realists" too. All of which goes to show that some philosophers are very tricky in their use of words.

The Basic Teachings of Materialism in Opposition to Idealism

In opposition to all the forms of idealism, and of tricky compromises between materialism and idealism, the basic teachings of materialism can be formulated very simply and clearly.

To grasp the essence of these teachings we should also understand what are the main assertions made in every form of idealism. There are three such main assertions of idealism.

1. Idealism asserts that the material world is dependent on the spiritual.
2. Idealism asserts that spirit, or mind, or idea, can and does exist in separation from matter. (The most extreme form of this assertion is subjective idealism, which asserts that matter does not exist at all but is pure illusion.)
3. Idealism asserts that there exists a realm of the mysterious and unknowable, "above", or "beyond", or "behind" what can be ascertained and known by perception, experience and science.

The basic teachings of materialism stand in opposition to these three assertions of idealism.

1. Materialism teaches that the world is by its very nature material, that everything which exists comes into being on the basis of material causes, arises and develops in accordance with the laws of motion of matter.
2. Materialism teaches that matter is objective reality existing outside and independent of the mind; and that far from the mental existing in separation from the material, everything mental or spiritual is a product of material processes.
3. Materialism teaches that the world and its laws are knowable, and that while much in the material world may not be known there is no unknowable sphere of reality which lies outside the material world.

The Marxist-Leninist philosophy is characterised by its absolutely consistent materialism all along the line, by its making no concessions whatever at any point to idealism.

Materialism and Idealism in Practice

As was pointed out above, the opposition of materialism and idealism—which has now been stated in its most general terms—is not an opposition between abstract theories of the nature of the world, but is an opposition between different ways of understanding and interpreting every question. That is why it is of such profound importance.

Let us consider some of the very practical ways in which the opposition of materialism and idealism is manifested.

Idealists tell us, for example, not to place "too much" reliance on science. They tell us that the most important truths are beyond the reach of science. Hence they encourage us not to believe things on the basis of evidence, experience, practice, but to take them on trust from those who pretend to know best and to have some "higher" source of information.

In this way idealism is a very good friend and standby of every form of reactionary propaganda. It is the philosophy of the capitalist press and the B.B.C. It favours superstitions of all sorts, prevents us from thinking for ourselves and making a scientific approach to moral and social problems.

Again, idealists tell us that what is most important for us all is the inner life of the soul. They tell us that we shall never solve our human problems except by some inner regeneration. This is a favourite theme in the speeches of well-fed persons. But many workers fall for it too—in factories, for example, where a "Moral Rearmament" group is active. They tell you not to fight for better conditions, but to improve your soul. They do not tell you that the best way to improve yourself both materially and morally is to join in the fight for peace and socialism.

Again, an idealist approach is common amongst many socialists. Many sincere socialists, for example, think that what is essentially wrong with capitalism is that goods are unfairly distributed, and that if only we could get everyone, including the capitalists, to accept a new conception of fairness and justice, then we could do away with the evils of capitalism. Socialism to them is nothing but the realisation of an abstract idea of justice.

The idealism of this belief lies in its assumption that it is simply the *ideas* which we hold that determine the way we live and the way society is organised. Those who think in this way forget to look for the *material* causes. For what in fact determines the way goods are distributed in capitalist society —the wealth enjoyed by one part of society, while the other and greater part lives in poverty—is not the ideas which men hold about the distribution of wealth, but the material fact that the mode of production rests on the exploitation of the worker by the capitalist. So long as this mode of production remains in existence, so long will extremes of wealth and poverty remain, and so long will socialist ideas of justice be opposed by capitalist ideas of justice. The task of socialists, therefore, is to organise and lead the struggle of the working class against the capitalist class to the point where the working class takes power from the capitalist class.

If we do not understand this, then we cannot find the way to fight effectively for socialism. We shall find that our socialist ideals are constantly disappointed and betrayed. Such, indeed, has been the experience of British socialism.

It can be seen from these examples how idealism serves as a weapon of reaction; and how when socialists embrace idealism they are being influenced by the ideology of the capitalists. We can no more take over and use capitalist ideas for the purposes of socialist theory than we can take over and use the capitalist state machine, with all its institutions and officials, for the purposes of building socialism.

Right through history, indeed, idealism has been a weapon of reaction. Whatever fine systems of philosophy have been invented, idealism has been used as a means of justifying the rule of an exploiting class and deceiving the exploited.

This is not to say that truths have not been expressed in an idealist guise. Of course they have. For idealism has very deep roots in our ways of thinking, and so men often clothe their thoughts and aspirations in idealist dress. But the idealist form is always an impediment, a hindrance in the expression of truth—a source of confusion and error.

Again, progressive movements in the past have adopted and fought under an idealist ideology. But this has shown only that they contained in themselves the seeds of future reaction—inasmuch as they represented the striving of a new exploiting class to come to power; or that they were themselves influenced by ideas of reaction; or it has been a mark of their weakness and immaturity.

For example, the great revolutionary movement of the English bourgeoisie in the seventeenth century fought under idealist, religious slogans. But the same appeal to God which justified Cromwell in the execution of the King justified him also in stamping out the Levellers.

Early democrats and socialists had many idealist notions. But in their case this demonstrated the *immaturity* and *weakness* of the movement. The idealist illusions had to be overcome if the revolutionary working-class movement was to arise and triumph. As the movement grew strong, the continuance within it of idealist notions represented an alien, reactionary influence.

We can truly say that idealism is essentially a conservative force—an ideology helping the defence of things as they are, and the preservation of illusions in men's minds about their true condition.

On the other hand, every real social advance—every increase in the productive forces, every advance of science—generates materialism and is helped along by materialist ideas. And the whole history of human thought has been the history of the fight of materialism against idealism, of the overcoming of idealist illusions and fantasies.

Materialism teaches us to have confidence in ourselves, in the working class—in people. It teaches us that there are no mysteries beyond our understanding, that we need not accept that which is as being the will of God, that we should contemptuously reject the "authoritative" teachings of those who set up to be our masters, and that we can ourselves understand nature and society so as to be able to change them.

Chapter Three

MECHANISTIC MATERIALISM

The Changing World and How to Understand It

Before Marx, materialism was predominantly *mechanistic.*

We often hear people complain that the materialists seek to reduce everything in the world, including life and mind, to a system of soulless mechanism, to a mere mechanical interaction of bodies. This refers to mechanistic materialism. Marxist materialism is, however, not mechanistic but dialectical. To understand what this means we need first to understand something about mechanistic materialism itself.

We can approach this problem by asking how materialists have sought to understand the various processes of change which are observed everywhere in the world.

The world is full of change. Night follows day and day night; the seasons succeed each other; people are born, grow old and die. Every philosophy recognises that change is an omnipresent fact. The question is: how are we to understand the change which we observe everywhere?

Change may be understood, in the first place, in an idealist way or in a materialist way.

Idealism traces back all change to some idea or intention—if not human, then divine. Thus for idealism, changes in the material world are, in the last analysis, initiated and brought about by something outside matter, not material, not subject to the laws of the material world.

But materialism traces back all change to material causes. In other words, it seeks to explain what happens in the material world from the material world itself.

But while the occurrence of change has been recognised by everyone, since none can ignore it, philosophers have nevertheless sought to find something which does not change—something permanent, something changeless, behind or within the change.

This is generally an essential part of the ideology of an exploiting class. They are afraid of change, because they are afraid that they, too, may be swept away. So they always seek for something fixed and stable, not subject to change. They try to hitch themselves on to this, as it were.

The earlier materialists, too, sought for this. Behind all the changing appearances they looked for something which never changes. But while idealists looked for the eternal and changeless in the realm of spirit, these materialists looked for it in the material world itself. And they found it in the ultimate material particle—the eternal and indestructible atom.

For such materialists, then, all *changes* were produced by the movement and interaction of *unchanging* atoms.

This is a very ancient theory, put forward over two thousand years ago in Greece, and earlier still in India.

In its day it was a very progressive theory, a great weapon against idealism and superstition. The Roman poet Lucretius, for example, explained in his philosophical poem *On the Nature of Things* that the purpose of the atomistic theory of the Greek philosopher Epicurus was to demonstrate "what are the elements out of which everything is formed, and how everything comes to pass without the intervention of the gods".

Thus there was born a materialism which saw the world as consisting of hard, impenetrable material particles, and which understood all change as arising from nothing but the motion and interaction of such particles.

This theory was revived in modern times. In the sixteenth and seventeenth centuries philosophers and scientists turned to it in their fight against feudal, Catholic philosophy. But this modern materialism proved to be much richer in content than the ancient. For it tried to work out what were the laws of interaction of material particles, and so to present a picture of how all phenomena, from merely physical changes to the life of man, resulted from the motion and interaction of the separate parts of matter. In this way, by the eighteenth century, there had appeared the characteristic modern theories of mechanistic materialism.

A Bourgeois Philosophy

Mechanistic materialism was in essence an ideology, a mode of theorising, of the rising bourgeoisie. In order to understand it we must understand, first of all, that it arose and developed in opposition to feudal ideology—that its critical edge was directed against feudal ideas, that it was in fact the most radical of all bourgeois forms of opposition against the feudal outlook.

In the period of the rise of the bourgeoisie, the feudal social relations were shattered, and so were the feudal ideas, embodied in the Catholic philosophy, in which those social relations were enshrined.

The feudal system, whose economic basis lay in the exploitation of the serfs by the feudal proprietors, involved complex social relationships of dependence, subordination and allegiance. All this was reflected, not only in social and political philosophy, but also in the philosophy of nature.

It was typical of the natural philosophy of the feudal period that everything in nature was explained in terms of its proper place in the system of the universe, in terms of its supposed position of dependence and subordination in that system, and of the end or purpose which it existed to serve.

The bourgeois philosophers and scientists destroyed these feudal ideas about nature. They regarded nature as a system of bodies in interaction, and, rejecting all the feudal dogmas, they called for the investigation of nature in order to discover how nature really worked.

The investigation of nature advanced hand in hand with the geographical discoveries, the development of trade and transport, the improvement of machinery and manufactures. The greatest strides were made in the mechanical sciences, closely connected as they were with the needs of technology. So it came about that materialist theory was enriched as the result of the scientific investigation of nature, and in particular by the mechanical sciences.

This determined at once the strength and the weakness, the achievement and the limitation, of the materialist theory.

What pushed that theory forward was, so Engels writes in *Ludwig Feuerbach*, "the powerful and ever more rapidly onrushing progress of science and industry". But it remained "predominantly mechanical", because only the mechanical sciences had attained any high degree of development. Its "specific, but at that time inevitable limitation" was its "exclusive application of the standards of mechanics".

The mechanistic way of understanding nature did not arise, however, simply from the fact that at that time it was only the mechanical sciences which had made any great progress. It was deeply rooted in the class outlook of the most progressive bourgeois philosophers, and this led to their turning exclusively to the mechanical sciences for their inspiration.

Just as the bourgeoisie, overthrowing feudal society, stood for individual liberty, equality and the development of a free market, so the most progressive philosophers of the bourgeoisie—the materialists—overthrowing the feudal ideas, proclaimed that the world consisted of separate material particles interacting with one another in accordance with the laws of mechanics.

This theory of nature reflected bourgeois social relations no less than the theories it replaced had reflected feudal social relations. But just as the new bourgeois social relations broke the feudal fetters and enabled a great new development of the forces of production to begin, so the corresponding bourgeois theory of nature broke down the barriers which feudal ideas had placed in the way of scientific research and enabled a great new development of scientific research to begin.

The philosophical outlook seemed to find its confirmation in science, and science provided materials for the development and working out in detail of the philosophical outlook.

The World and the Machine

The world—so thought the mechanistic materialists—consists of nothing but particles of matter in interaction. Each particle has an existence separate and distinct from every other; in their totality they form the world; the totality of their interactions forms the totality of everything that happens in the world; and these interactions are of the mechanical type, that is to say, they consist simply of the external influence of one particle upon another.

Such a theory is equivalent to regarding the whole world as nothing but a complex piece of machinery, a mechanism.

From this standpoint, the question always posed about any part of nature is the question we ask about a machine: what is its mechanism, how does it work?

This was exemplified in Newton's account of the solar system. Newton adopted the same general view as the Greek materialist, Epicurus, in as much as he thought that the material world consisted of particles moving about in empty space. But faced with any particular natural phenomenon, such as the movements of the sun and planets, Epicurus was not in the least concerned to give any exact account of it. With regard to the apparent movement of the sun across the heavens from east to west, for example, Epicurus said that the important thing was to understand that the sun was not a god but was simply a collection of atoms: no account of the actual machinery of its motions was necessary. Perhaps, he said, the sun goes round and round the earth; but perhaps it disintegrates and its atoms separate every night, so that it is "a new sun" which we see the next morning: to him such questions were simply unimportant. Newton, on the other hand, was concerned to show exactly how the solar system worked, to demonstrate the mechanics of it, in terms of gravity and mechanical forces.

But just as Epicurus was not interested in how the solar system worked, so Newton was not interested in how it originated and developed. He took it for granted as a stable piece of machinery—created, presumably, by God. Not how it originated, not how it developed, but how it worked, was the question which he dealt with.

The same mechanistic approach was manifested in Harvey's discovery of the circulation of the blood. The essence of his discovery was that he demonstrated the mechanism of circulation, regarding the heart as a pump, which pumps the blood out along the arteries so that it flows back through the veins, the whole system being regulated by valves.

To understand the mechanistic outlook better, let us ask: what is a mechanism? what is characteristic of a mechanism?

(*a*) A mechanism consists of permanent parts, which fit together.

(*b*) It requires a motive force to set it going.

(*c*) Once set going, the parts interact and results are produced according to laws which can be exactly stated.

Consider, for example, such a mechanism as a watch. (*a*) It consists of a number of different parts—cogs, levers and so on—fitted neatly together. (*b*) It has to be wound up. (*c*) Then, as the spring uncoils, the parts interact according to laws exactly known to watchmakers, resulting in the regular movements of the hands on the dial.

Further, to know how a mechanism, such as a watch, works, you must take it to bits, find out what its parts are, how they fit together and how, by their interactions, once the mechanism is set in motion by the application of the required motive force, they produce the total motion characteristic of the mechanism in working order.

This is just how the mechanistic materialists regarded nature. They sought to take nature to bits, to find its ultimate component parts, how they fitted together and how their interactions produced all the changes we perceive, all the phenomena of the world. And moreover, finding out how the mechanism worked, they sought to find out how to repair it, how to improve it, how to change it and to make it produce new results corresponding to the requirements of man.

The Strength and Achievement of Mechanistic Materialism

Mechanistic materialism was an important milestone in our understanding of nature. And it was a great progressive step of bourgeois thinkers, a blow against idealism.

The mechanists were thorough-going in their materialism. For they waged a progressive fight against idealism and clericalism by trying to extend to the realm of mind and society the same mechanistic conceptions which were used in the scientific investigation of nature. They sought to include man and all his spiritual activities in the mechanistic system of the natural world.

The most radical mechanists regarded not merely physical processes, and not merely plant and animal life, but man himself as a machine. Already in the seventeenth century the great French philosopher Descartes had said that all animals were complicated machines—automata: but man was different, since he had a soul. But in the eighteenth century a follower of Descartes, the physician Lamettrie, wrote a book with the provocative title *Man a Machine.* Men, too, were machines, he said, though very complicated ones.

This doctrine was looked upon as exceptionally shocking, and as a terrible insult to human nature, not to mention God. Yet it was in its time a progressive view of man. The view that men are machines was an advance in the understanding of human nature as compared with the view that they are wretched pieces of clay inhabited by immortal souls. And it was, comparatively speaking, a more humane view.

For example, the great English materialist and utopian socialist Robert Owen, in his *New View of Society,* told the pious industrialists of his time:

> "Experience has shown you the difference of the results between mechanism which is neat, clean, well-arranged and always in a high state of repair, and that which is allowed to be dirty, in disorder, and which therefore becomes much out of repair. . . . If, then, due care as to the state of your inanimate machines can produce such beneficial results, what may not be expected if you devote equal attention to your *vital* machines, which are far more wonderfully constructed?"

This humanitarianism was, however, at the best bourgeois humanitarianism. Like all mechanistic materialism, it was rooted in the class outlook of the bourgeoisie. The view that man is a machine is rooted in the view that in production man is a mere appendage of the machine. And if on the one hand this implies that the human machine ought to be well tended and kept in good condition, on the other hand it equally implies that no more should be expended for this purpose than is strictly necessary to keep the human machine in bare working order.

The Weakness and Limitations of Mechanistic Materialism

Mechanistic materialism had grave weaknesses.

(1) It could not sustain the materialist standpoint consistently and all the way.

For if the world is like a machine, who made it, who started it up? There was necessary, in any system of mechanistic materialism, a "Supreme Being", outside the material world —even if he no longer continuously interfered in the world and kept things moving, but did no more than start things up and then watch what happened.

Such a "Supreme Being" was postulated by nearly all the mechanistic materialists; for example, by Voltaire and Tom Paine. But this opens the door to idealism.

(2) Mechanistic materialism sees change everywhere. Yet because it always tries to *reduce* all phenomena to the same system of mechanical interactions, it sees this change as nothing but the eternal *repetition* of the same kinds of mechanical processes, an eternal cycle of the same changes.

This limitation is inseparable from the view of the world as a machine. For just as a machine has to be started up, so it can never do anything except what it was made to do. It cannot change itself or produce anything radically new. Mechanistic theory, therefore, always breaks down when it is a question of accounting for the emergence of *new quality*. It sees change everywhere—but nothing *new*, no *development*.

The various processes of nature—chemical processes and the processes of living matter, for example—cannot in fact be all reduced to one and the same kind of mechanical interaction of material particles.

Chemical interactions differ from mechanical interactions

in as much as the changes which take place as a result of chemical interaction involve a change of quality. For example, if we consider the mechanical interaction of two particles which collide, then their qualitative characteristics are irrelevant and the result is expressed as a change in the quantity and direction of motion of each. But if two chemical substances come together and combine chemically, then there results a new substance qualitatively different from either. Similarly, from the point of view of mechanics heat is nothing but an increase in the quantity of motion of the particles of matter. But in chemistry, the application of heat leads to qualitative changes.

Nor do the processes of nature consist in the repetition of the same cycle of mechanical interactions, but in nature there is continual development and evolution, producing ever new forms of the existence or, what is the same thing, motion of matter. Hence the more widely and consistently the mechanistic categories are applied in the interpretation of nature, the more is their essential limitation exposed.

(3) Still less can mechanistic materialism explain *social* development.

Mechanistic materialism expresses the radical bourgeois conception of society as consisting of social atoms, interacting together. The real economic and social causes of the development of society cannot be discovered from this point of view. And so great social changes seem to spring from quite accidental causes. Human activity itself appears to be either the mechanical result of external causes, or else it is treated—and here mechanistic materialism collapses into idealism—as purely spontaneous and uncaused.

In a word, mechanistic materialism cannot give an account of men's social activity.

Mechanistic Materialism and Utopian Socialism

The mechanistic view treated men quite abstractly, each man being regarded as a social atom endowed by nature with certain inherent properties, attributes and rights.

This was expressed in the bourgeois conception of "the

rights of man", and in the bourgeois revolutionary slogan: "All men are equal".

But the conception of human rights cannot be deduced from the abstract nature of man, but is determined by the stage of society in which men are living. Nor are men what they are "by nature", but they become what they are, and change, as a result of their social activity. Nor are all men "by nature" equal. In opposition to the bourgeois conception of abstract equality, which amounted to mere formal equality of rights as citizens, equality before the law, Marx and Engels declared that:

> "the real content of the proletarian demand for equality is the demand for the abolition of classes. Any demand for equality which goes beyond that of necessity passes into absurdity" (Engels: *Anti-Dühring*, Part I, Chapter X).

Adopting their abstract, mechanistic view of men as social atoms, the progressive mechanists tried to work out, in an abstract way, what form of society would be best for mankind —what would best suit abstract human nature, as they conceived of it.

This way of thinking was taken over by the socialist thinkers who immediately preceded Marx, the utopian socialists. The utopian socialists were mechanistic materialists. They put forward socialism as an ideal society. They did not see it as necessitated by the development of the contradictions of capitalism—it could have been put forward and realised at any time, if only men had had the wit to do so. They did not see it as having to be won by working-class struggle against capitalism—it would be realised when everyone was convinced that it was just and best adapted to the requirements of human nature. (For this reason Robert Owen appealed to both the Archbishop of Canterbury and Queen Victoria to support his socialist programme.)

Again, the mechanistic materialists—and this applied above all to the utopian socialists—thought that what a man was, his character and his activities, was determined by his environment and education. Therefore they proclaimed that to make men better, happier and more rational it was simply necessary to place them in better conditions and to give them a better education.

But to this Marx replied in his *Theses on Feuerbach*:

> "The materialist doctrine that men are products of circumstances and upbringing and that, therefore, changed men are produced by changed circumstances and changed upbringing, forgets that circumstances are changed precisely by men and that the educator must himself be educated."

If men are simply the products of circumstances, then they are at the mercy of circumstances. But on the contrary, men can themselves change their circumstances. And men themselves are changed, not as a mechanical result of changed circumstances, but in the course of and as a result of their own activity in changing their circumstances.

So what are the real material social causes at work in human society, which give rise to new activities, new ideas and therefore to changed circumstances and changed men?

Mechanistic materialism could not answer this question. It could not explain the laws of social development nor show how to change society.

Therefore while it was a progressive and revolutionary doctrine in its time, it could not serve to guide the struggle of the working class in striving to change society.

Chapter Four

FROM MECHANISTIC TO DIALECTICAL MATERIALISM

Things and Processes

In order to find how the limitations of the mechanist approach can be overcome we may consider first of all certain extremely dogmatic assumptions which are made by mechanistic materialism. These mechanistic assumptions are none of them justified. And by bringing them to the light of day and pointing out what is wrong with them, we can see how to advance beyond mechanistic materialism.

(1) Mechanism sees all change as having at its basis permanent and stable things with definite, fixed properties.

Thus for the mechanists the world consists of indivisible, indestructible material particles, which in their interaction manifest such properties as position, mass, velocity.

According to mechanism, if you could state the position, mass and velocity of every particle at a given instant of time, then you would have said everything that could be said about the world at that time, and could, by applying the laws of mechanics, predict everything that was going to happen afterwards.

This is the first dogmatic assumption of mechanism. But we need to reject it. For the world does not consist of *things* but of *processes*, in which things come into being and pass away.

> "The world is not to be comprehended as a complex of ready-made things," wrote Engels, "but as a complex of processes, in which things apparently stable, no less than their mind-images in our heads, the concepts, go through

an uninterrupted change of coming into being and passing away" (*Ludwig Feuerbach*).

This, indeed, is what science in its latest developments teaches us. Thus the atom, once thought to be eternal and indivisible, has been dissolved into electrons, protons and neutrons; and these themselves are not "fundamental particles" in any absolute sense, i.e. they are not eternal and indestructible, any more than the atom; but science more and more shows that they, too, come into being, pass away and go through many transformations.

What is fundamental is not the "thing", the "particle", but the unending *processes* of nature, in which *things* go through "an uninterrupted change of coming into being and passing away". And nature's process is, moreover, infinite: there will always be fresh aspects to be revealed, and it cannot be reduced to any *ultimate* constituents. "The electron is as inexhaustible as the atom, nature is infinite," wrote Lenin (*Materialism and Empirio-Criticism*).

Just so in considering society, we cannot understand a given society simply in terms of some set of institutions in and through which individual men and women are organised, but we must study the social processes which are going on, in the course of which both institutions and people are transformed.

Matter and Motion

(2) The second dogmatic assumption of mechanism is the assumption that no change can ever happen except by the action of some external cause.

Just as no part of a machine moves unless another part acts on it and makes it move, so mechanism sees matter as being inert—without motion, or rather without self-motion. For mechanism, nothing ever moves unless something else pushes or pulls it, it never changes unless something else interferes with it.

No wonder that, regarding matter in this way, the mechanists had to believe in a Supreme Being to give the "initial impulse".

But we need to reject this lifeless, dead theory about matter. This theory separates matter and motion: it thinks of matter as just a dead mass, so that motion always has to be impressed on matter from outside. But, on the contrary, you cannot separate matter and motion. Motion, said Engels, is the mode of existence of matter.

"Motion is the mode of existence of matter. Never anywhere has there been matter without motion, nor can there be. Motion in cosmic space, mechanical motion of smaller masses on the various celestial bodies, the motion of molecules as heat or as electrical or magnetic currents, chemical combination or disintegration, organic life—at each given moment each individual atom of matter in the world is in one or other of these forms of motion, or in several forms of them at once. All rest, all equilibrium is only relative, and only has meaning in relation to one or other definite form of motion. A body, for example, may be on the ground in mechanical equilibrium, may be mechanically at rest; but this in no way prevents it from participating in the motion of the earth and in that of the whole solar system, just as little as it prevents its most minute parts from carrying out the oscillations determined by its temperature, or its atoms from passing through a chemical process. Matter without motion is just as unthinkable as motion without matter" (*Anti-Dühring*).

Far from being dead, lifeless, inert, it is the very nature of matter to be in process of continual change, of motion. Once we realise this, then there is an end of appeal to the "initial impulse". Motion, like matter, never had a beginning.

The conception of the inseparability of matter and motion, the understanding that "motion is the mode of existence of matter", provides the way to answering a number of perplexing questions which usually haunt people's minds when they think about materialism and which lead them to desert materialism and to run to the priests for an explanation of the "ultimate" truth about the universe.

Was the world created by a Supreme Being? What was the origin of matter? What was the origin of motion? What was the very beginning of everything? What was the first cause? These are the sort of questions which puzzle people.

It is possible to answer these questions.

No, the world was not created by a Supreme Being. Any particular organisation of matter, any particular process of matter in motion, has an origin and a beginning—it originated out of some previous organisation of matter, out of some previous process of matter in motion. But matter in motion had no origin, no beginning.

Science teaches us the inseparability of matter and motion. However static some things may seem to be, there is in them continual motion. The atom, for instance, maintains itself as the same only by means of a continual movement of its parts.

So in studying the causes of change, we should not merely seek for external causes of change, but should above all seek for the source of the change within the process itself, in its own self-movement, in the inner impulses to development contained within things themselves.

Thus in seeking the causes of social development and its laws, we should not see social changes as being brought about by the actions of great men, who impressed their superior ideas and will on the inert mass of society—nor as being brought about by accidents and external factors—but as being brought about by the development of the internal forces of society itself; and that means, by the development of the social forces of production.

Thus unlike the utopians, we see socialism as the result, not of the dreams of reformers, but of the development of capitalist society itself—which contains within itself causes which must inevitably bring it to an end and lead to the socialist revolution.

The Forms of Motion of Matter

(3) The third dogmatic assumption of mechanism is the assumption that the mechanical motion of particles, i.e. the simple change of place of particles as the result of the action on them of external forces, is the ultimate, basic form of

motion of matter; and that all changes, all happenings whatsoever can be reduced to and explained by such mechanical motion of particles.

Thus all the motion of matter is reduced to simple mechanical motion. All the changing qualities which we recognise in matter are nothing but the appearances of the basic mechanical motion of matter. However varied the appearances may be, whatever new and higher forms of development may appear to arise, they are all to be reduced to one and the same thing—the eternal repetition of the mechanical interaction of the separate parts of matter.

It is difficult to find any justification for such an assumption. In the material world there are many different types of process, which all constitute different forms of the motion of matter. But they can by no means be all reduced to one and the same form of (mechanical) motion.

> "Motion in the most general sense," wrote Engels, "conceived as the mode of existence, the inherent attribute, of matter, comprehends all changes and processes occurring in the universe, from mere change of place right to thinking. The investigation of the nature of motion had as a matter of course to start from the lowest, simplest forms of this motion and to learn to grasp these before it could achieve anything in the way of explanation of the higher and more complicated forms" (*Dialectics of Nature*).

The simplest form of motion is the simple change of place of bodies, the laws of which are studied by mechanics. But that does not mean that all motion can be reduced to this simplest form of motion. It rather means that we need to study how, from the simplest form of motion, all the higher forms of motion arise and develop—"from mere change of place right to thinking".

One form of motion is transformed into another and arises from another. The higher, more complex form of motion cannot exist without the lower and simpler form: but that is not to say that it can be reduced to that simpler form. It is inseparable from the simpler form, but its nature is not exhausted thereby. For example, the thinking which goes on in our heads is inseparable from the chemical, electrical etc. motion which goes on in the grey matter of the brain; but it cannot be reduced to that motion, its nature is not exhausted thereby.

The *materialist* standpoint, however, which rejects the mechanistic idea that all forms of motion of matter can be reduced to mechanical motion, must not be confused with the *idealist* notion that the higher forms of motion cannot be explained as arising from the lower forms. For example, idealists assert that life, as a form of motion of matter, cannot possibly be derived from any processes characteristic of non-living matter. For them, life can only arise through the introduction into a material system of a mysterious something from outside—a "vital force". But to say that a higher form of motion cannot be reduced to a lower form is not to say that it cannot be derived from the lower form in the course of the latter's development. Thus materialists will always affirm that life, for example, appears at a certain stage in the development of more complex forms of non-living matter, and arises as a result of that development, not as a result of the introduction into non-living matter of a mysterious "vital force". The task of science in this sphere remains to demonstrate experimentally how the transition from non-living to living matter takes place.

Thus the mechanistic programme of reducing all the motion of matter to simple, mechanical motion must be rejected. We need rather to study all the infinitely various forms of motion of matter, in their transformations one into another, and as they arise one from another, the complex from the simple, the higher from the lower.

In the case of society, no one has yet tried to show how social changes can be explained by the mechanical interactions of the atoms composing the bodies of the various members of society—though to do so would be the logical culmination of the mechanistic programme. But the next best thing is attempted by the mechanistic theory known as "economic determinism". According to this theory, the whole motion of society is to be explained by the economic changes taking place in society, all the determinants of social change have been exhausted when the economic process has been described. This is an example of the mechanistic programme of reducing a complex motion to a single simple form—the process of social change, including all the political, cultural and ideological developments, to a simple economic process. But the task of explaining social development cannot be fulfilled by trying to reduce the whole development to an economic process. The task is rather to show how, on the basis of the economic process, all the various forms of social activity arise and play their part in the complex movement of society.

Things and their Interconnection

(4) The last dogmatic assumption of mechanism to be mentioned is that each of the things or particles, whose interactions are said to make up the totality of events in the universe, has its own fixed nature quite independent of everything else. In other words, each thing can be considered as existing in separation from other things, as an independent unit.

Proceeding on this assumption it follows that all relations between things are merely external relations. That is to say, things enter into various relationships one with another, but these relationships are accidental and make no difference to the nature of the things related.

And regarding each thing as a separate unit entering into external relations with other things, it further follows that mechanism regards the whole as no more than the sum of its separate parts. According to this view, the properties and laws of development of the whole are uniquely determined by the properties of all its parts.

Not one of these assumptions is correct. Nothing exists or can exist in splendid isolation, separate from its conditions of existence, independent of its relationships with other things. Things come into being, exist and cease to exist, not each independent of all other things, but each in its relationship with other things. The very nature of a thing is modified and transformed by its relationships with other things. When things enter into such relationships that they become parts of a whole, the whole cannot be regarded as nothing more than the sum total of the parts. True, the whole is nothing apart from and independent of its parts. But the mutual relations which the parts enter into in constituting the whole modify their own properties, so that while it may be said that the whole is determined by the parts it may equally be said that the parts are determined by the whole.

Once again, the development of science itself shows the inadmissibility of the old mechanistic assumptions. These assumptions have force only in the very limited sphere of the study of the mechanical interactions of discrete particles. In physics they were already shattered with the development of the study of the electro-magnetic field. Still less are they admissible in biology, in the study of living matter. And still less are they admissible in the study of men and society. We cannot understand social processes, as mechanists always try to do, as resulting simply from a set of fixed characteristics of "human nature". For "human nature" is always conditioned by and in various respects changes with changes in men's social relations.

The Correction of Mechanistic Materialism

When we bring into the open and reject these assumptions of mechanistic materialism, then we begin to see the need for a materialist doctrine of a different, of a new type—a materialism which overcomes the weaknesses and narrow, dogmatic assumptions of mechanism.

This is dialectical materialism.

Dialectical materialism understands the world, not as a complex of ready-made things, but as a complex of processes, in which all things go through an uninterrupted change of coming into being and passing away.

Dialectical materialism considers that matter is always in motion, that motion is the mode of existence of matter, so that there can no more be matter without motion than motion without matter. Motion does not have to be impressed upon matter by some outside force, but above all it is necessary to look for the inner impulses of development, the self-motion, inherent in all processes.

Dialectical materialism understands the motion of matter as comprehending all changes and processes in the universe, from mere change of place right to thinking. It recognises, therefore, the infinite diversity of the forms of motion of matter, the transformation of one form into another, the development of the forms of motion of matter from the simple to the complex, from the lower to the higher.

Dialectical materialism considers that, in the manifold processes taking place in the universe, things come into being, change and pass out of being, not as separate individual units, but in essential relation and interconnection, so that they cannot be understood each separately and by itself but only in their relation and interconnection.

In dialectical materialism, therefore, there is established a materialist conception far richer in content and more comprehensive than the former mechanistic materialism.

Chapter Five

THE DIALECTICAL CONCEPTION OF DEVELOPMENT

The Idea of Evolution

We have seen that the corrections of the mechanistic standpoint made by dialectical materialism are fully justified by and have a basis in the advance of science. Indeed, the advance of science itself has shattered the whole conception of the universe held by the older, mechanistic materialists.

According to that conception, the universe always remained much the same. It was a huge machine which always did the same things, kept grinding out the same products, went on and on in a perpetual cycle of the same processes.

Thus it used to be thought that the stars and the solar system always remained the same—and that the earth, with its continents and oceans and the plants and animals inhabiting them, likewise always remained the same.

But this conception has given way to the conception of evolution, which has invaded all spheres of investigation without exception. Science, however, does not advance in isolation from society as a whole, and the widespread application of the idea of evolution was due not simply to its verification in scientific theory but also to its popularity with the new, rising forces of industrial capitalism, themselves the patrons of science.

> "The bourgeoisie cannot exist without constantly revolutionising the instruments of production, and thereby the relations of production, and with them the whole relations of society. Conservation of the old modes of production in

unaltered form was, on the contrary, the first condition of existence of all earlier industrial classes. Constant revolutionising of production, uninterrupted disturbance of all social conditions, everlasting uncertainty and agitation, distinguish the bourgeois epoch from all earlier ones" (Marx and Engels: *Manifesto of the Communist Party*).

The industrial capitalists saw themselves as the bearers of progress. And as they thought progress was the law of capitalism, so they saw it as the law of the whole universe.

So there was made possible a great advance in the scientific picture of the universe. We find developing a picture of the universe, not as static, as always the same, but as in continual progressive development.

The stars did not always exist—they were formed out of masses of dispersed gas.

Once formed, the whole stellar system, with all the stars in it, goes through an evolutionary process, stage by stage.

Some stars, like our sun, acquire planets—a solar system. Thus the earth was born. As its surface cooled, so chemical compounds were formed, impossible in the high temperatures of the stars.

Thus matter began to manifest new properties, non-existent before—the properties of chemical combination.

Then organic compounds were formed out of the complex linking of carbon atoms. And from organic matter the first bodies arose which began to manifest the properties of life, of living matter. Still new properties of matter emerged—the properties of living matter.

Living organisms went through a long evolution, leading eventually to man. With man, human society was born. And still new processes, with new laws, arose—the laws of society, and the laws of thought.

What comes next?

Capitalist science can go no further. Here it ends, since capitalist science cannot contemplate the ending of capitalism. But socialist science shows that man himself is about to embark on a new phase of evolution—communist society, in which the whole social process will be brought under his own conscious, planned direction.

All this is the evolutionary history of the material universe.

Apart from the last point, it may be said this is all common knowledge. Bourgeois thinkers know this as well as Marxists, though they often forget it. But Marxism does not only stress the fact that everything in the world goes through a process of development. What Marxism found out was how to understand and explain this development in a materialist way.

The discovery of Marxism was the discovery of the laws of materialist dialectics. And that is why Marxism alone is able to give a fully scientific account of development and to point out the future path.

This is the meaning of Marx's great discovery—how to understand change and development in a materialist way, and therefore how to become masters of the future.

Idealist Conceptions of Change and Development

How did bourgeois thinkers try to account for the universal change and development which they discovered?

Let us consider what some of them have had to say over a period of more than a century.

Hegel said that the whole process of development taking place in history was due to the Absolute Idea realising itself in history. Herbert Spencer said that all development was a process of increasing "integration of matter", and he put this down to what he called an "Incomprehensible and Omnipresent Power". Henri Bergson said that everything was in process of evolution, due to the activity of "the Life Force". Fairly recently, a school of British philosophers has coined the phrase "emergent evolution". They pointed out that in the course of development new qualities of matter are continually emerging, one after the other. But as to why this should happen, one of the leaders of this school, Professor Samuel Alexander, said that it was inexplicable and must be accepted "with natural piety", while another of its leaders, Professor C. Lloyd Morgan, said that it must be due to some immanent force at work in the world, which he identified with God.

Thus in every case some fantasy, something inexplicable and unpredictable, was conjured up to explain development. And so, when they thought about the future, all these bourgeois philosophers of evolution either thought, like Hegel, that development had now finished (Hegel taught that the Absolute Idea was fully realised in the Prussian State of which he was a distinguished employee), or else regarded the future as unfathomable.

Nowadays they begin to give up hope altogether and regard everything—past, present and future—as incomprehensible, the result of forces no one can ever understand or control.

A second defect in the evolutionary ideas of most bourgeois thinkers is that they regard the process of evolution as a smooth, continuous and unbroken process. They see the process of transition from one evolutionary stage to another as taking place through a series of gradations, without conflict and without any break in continuity.

But continuity is not the law of development. On the contrary, periods of smooth, continuous evolutionary development are interrupted by sudden and abrupt changes. The emergence of the new stage in development takes place, when the conditions for it have matured, by a break in continuity, by the leap from one state to another.

Hegel was the first to point this out.

With every period of transition, he observed:

> "it is as in the case of the birth of a child; after a long period of nutrition in silence, the continuity of the gradual growth in size, of quantitative change, is suddenly cut short by the first breath drawn—there is a break in the process, a qualitative change—and the child is born" (*Phenomenology of Mind*).

But Marx alone followed up this profound observation of Hegel. As for the ensuing bourgeois thinkers, although the investigations of science, and common experience itself, clearly demonstrate that development cannot take place without discontinuity, without abrupt transitions and the leap from one state to another, they have nevertheless in their general theories tried to make unbroken continuity the law of evolution.

This prejudice in favour of a smooth line of evolution has gone hand in hand with the liberal belief that capitalist society will evolve smoothly—through orderly bourgeois progress broadening down "from precedent to precedent", as Tennyson once expressed it. To have thought differently about evolution in general would have implied that we would have to think differently about social evolution in particular.

The Dialectical Materialist Conception of Development

The problem of understanding and explaining development in a materialist way—that is, "in harmony with the facts conceived in their own and not in a fantastic connection"—is answered by dialectical materialism.

Dialectical materialism considers the universe, not as static, not as unchanging, but as in continual process of development. It considers this development, not as a smooth, continuous and unbroken process, but as a process in which phases of gradual evolutionary change are interrupted by breaks in continuity, by the sudden leap from one state to another. And it seeks for the explanation, the driving force, of this universal movement, not in inventions of idealist fantasy, but within material processes themselves—in the inner contradictions, the opposite conflicting tendencies, which are in operation in every process of nature and society.

The main ideas of materialist dialectics, which are applied in dealing with the laws of development of the real material world, including society, will be the subject of the following chapters. But this is how Lenin summed them up in his *Philosophical Notebooks*.

The essential idea of materialist dialectics is:

> "the recognition of the contradictory, mutually exclusive, opposite tendencies in all phenomena and processes of nature. . . . This alone furnishes the key to the self-movement of everything in existence. It alone furnishes the key

to the leaps, to the break in continuity, to the transformation into the opposite, to the destruction of the old and emergence of the new. . . .

In its proper meaning, dialectics is the study of the contradiction within the very essence of things.

Development is the struggle of opposites."

Where contradiction is at work, there is the force of development.

This materialist understanding of dialectics is the key to understanding the forces of development within the material world itself, without recourse to outside causes.

This discovery arises from the whole advance of science and philosophy.

But above all it arises from the investigation of the laws of society, an investigation made imperative thanks to the very development of society—from the discovery of the contradictions of capitalism, explaining the forces of social development, and thereby showing the way forward from capitalism to socialism.

That is why bourgeois thinkers could not answer the problem of explaining the real material forces of development in nature and society. To answer this problem was to condemn the capitalist system. And here they had a blind spot. Only the revolutionary philosophy of the vanguard of the revolutionary class, the working class, could do it.

Marx's discovery of the laws of materialist dialectics showed us how to understand the dialectical development of nature. But above all it showed us how to understand social change and how to wage the working-class struggle for socialism.

This discovery revolutionised philosophy.

It signalised the triumph of materialism over idealism, by doing away with the limitations of the merely mechanistic materialism of the past.

It likewise spelled the end of all "systems" of philosophy.

It made philosophy into a revolutionary weapon of the working people, an instrument, a method for understanding the world so as to change it.

PART TWO

DIALECTICS

Chapter Six

DIALECTICS AND METAPHYSICS

The Metaphysical Way of Thinking

We have seen how materialist explanation is opposed to idealist explanation. And then we saw how materialists formerly interpreted things in a mechanist way, but how mechanistic materialism proved inadequate to explain real processes of change and development. For this we need materialist dialectics. We need to study and understand things dialectically.

The dialectical method is, indeed, nothing but the method of studying and understanding things in their real change and development.

As such, it stands opposed to *metaphysics*.

What is metaphysics? Or more exactly, what is the metaphysical way of thinking, which is opposed by the dialectical way of thinking?

Metaphysics is essentially an abstract way of thinking. In a sense all thinking is "abstract", since it works with general concepts and cannot but disregard a great deal of particular and unessential detail. For example, if we say that "men have two legs", we are thinking of the two-leggedness of men in abstraction from their other properties, such as having a head, two arms and so on; and similarly we are thinking of all men in general, disregarding the individuality of particular men. But there is abstraction and abstraction. Metaphysics is distinguished by the fact that it makes false, misleading abstractions. The art of right thinking involves learning how to avoid metaphysical abstraction.

Suppose, for example, we are thinking about men, about

"human nature". Then we should think about human nature in such a way that we recognise that men live in society and that their human nature cannot be independent of their living in society but develops and changes with the development of society. We shall then form ideas about human nature which correspond to the actual conditions of men's existence and to their change and development. But yet people often think about "human nature" in a very different way, as though there were such a thing as "human nature" which manifested itself quite independent of the actual conditions of human existence and which was always and everywhere exactly the same. To think in such a way is obviously to make a false, misleading abstraction. And it is just such an abstract way of thinking that we call "metaphysics".

The concept of fixed, unchanging "human nature" is an example of metaphysical abstraction, of the metaphysical way of thinking.

The metaphysician does not think in terms of real *men*, but of "Man" in the abstract.

Metaphysics, or the metaphysical way of thinking, is, then, that way of thinking which thinks of things (1) in abstraction from their conditions of existence, and (2) in abstraction from their change and development. It thinks of things (1) in separation one from another, ignoring their interconnections, and (2) as fixed and frozen, ignoring their change and development.

One example of metaphysics has already been given. It is not difficult to find plenty more. Indeed, the metaphysical way of thinking is so widespread, and has become so much part and parcel of current bourgeois ideology, that there is hardly an article in a journal, a talk on the radio, or a book by a learned professor, in which examples of metaphysical fallacy are not to be found.

A good deal is said and written, for example, about democracy. But the speakers and writers usually refer to some pure or absolute democracy, which they seek to define in abstraction from the actual development of society, of classes and of class struggle. But there can be no such pure democracy; it is a metaphysical abstraction. If we want to understand democracy we have always to ask: democracy for whom, for the exploiters or the exploited? We have to understand that since democracy is a form of government, there is no democracy which is not associated with the rule of some particular class, and that the democracy which is established when the working class is the ruling class is a higher form of democracy than capitalist democracy, just as capitalist democracy is a higher form of democracy than, say, the slave-owners' democracy of ancient Greece. In other words, we should not try to think of democracy in abstraction from real social relations and from the real change and development of society.

Again, in many British schools the children are regularly subjected to "intelligence tests". It is alleged that each child possesses a certain fixed quantity of "intelligence", which can be estimated without regard to the actual conditions of the child's existence and which determines his capabilities throughout the whole of his life regardless of whatever conditions for change and development may subsequently come his way. This is another example of metaphysics. In this case the metaphysical conception of "intelligence" is used as an excuse for denying educational opportunities to the majority of children on the grounds that their intelligence is too low for them to benefit from such opportunities.

In general, metaphysics is a way of thinking which tries to fix the nature, properties and potentialities of everything it considers once and for all: it presupposes that each thing has a fixed nature and fixed properties.

And it thinks in terms of "things" rather than "processes". It tries to sum up everything in a formula, which says that the whole world, or any part of the world which is under consideration, consists of just such and such things with such and such properties. Such a formula we may call a "metaphysical" formula.

In philosophy, metaphysics often means the search for the "ultimate constituents of the universe". Thus the materialists who said that the ultimate constituents were small, solid, material particles were just as much metaphysicians as the idealists who said that the ultimate constituents were spirits. All such philosophers thought they could sum up "the ultimate nature of the universe" in some formula. Some have had this formula, some that, but all have been metaphysicians. Yet it has been a hopeless quest. We cannot sum up the whole infinite changing universe in any such formula. And the more we find out about it, the more is this evident.

It should now be clear that the mechanistic materialism which we discussed in the preceding chapters can equally well be called *metaphysical* materialism.

We may also note, in passing, that certain philosophers today, the so-called positivists, who say we have no right to assert that anything exists except our own sense-perceptions, claim to be against "metaphysics" because they claim to reject any philosophy which seeks for "the ultimate constituents of the universe". For them, "metaphysics" means any theory which deals with "ultimates" not verifiable in sense-experience. By using the term in this way, they conceal the fact that they themselves are, if anything, more metaphysical than any other philosophers. For their own mode of thinking reaches extremes of metaphysical abstraction. What could be more metaphysical than to imagine, as the positivist philosophers do, that our sense-experience exists in abstraction from the real material world outside us? Indeed, they themselves make "sense-experience" into a metaphysical "ultimate".

In opposition to the abstract, metaphysical way of thinking, dialectics teaches us to think of things in their real changes and interconnections. To think dialectically is to think concretely, and to think concretely is to think dialectically. When we oppose the dialectical method to metaphysics, then we show up the inadequacy, one-sidedness or falsity of the abstractions of metaphysics.

This consideration enables us to understand the original meaning of the term "dialectics". The word is derived from the Greek *dialego*, meaning to discuss or debate. It was considered that to discuss a question from all sides, and from all angles, allowing different one-sided points of view to oppose and contradict each other during the debate, was the best method of arriving at the truth. Such was the dialectics employed, for example, by Socrates. When anyone claimed to have a formula which answered some question once and for all, Socrates would enter into discussion with him and, by forcing him to consider the question from different angles, would compel him to contradict himself and so to admit that his formula was false. By this method Socrates considered that it was possible to arrive at more adequate ideas about things.

The Marxist dialectical method develops from and includes dialectics in the sense in which it was understood by the Greeks. But it is far richer in content, far wider in its scope. As a result, it becomes something qualitatively *new* as compared with pre-Marxist dialectics—a new revolutionary method. For it is combined with a consistent materialism, and ceases to be a mere method of argument, becoming a method of investigation applicable to both nature and society, a method of materialist understanding of the world which grows out of and guides the activity of changing the world.

The Metaphysical "Either-Or"

Metaphysics presupposes that each thing has its own fixed nature, its own fixed properties, and considers each thing by itself, in isolation. It tries to settle the nature and properties of each thing as a given, separate object of investigation, not considering things in their interconnection and in their change and development.

Because of this, metaphysics thinks of things in terms of hard and fast antitheses. It opposes things of one sort to things of another sort: if a thing is of one sort, it has one set of properties; if of another sort, it has another set of properties; the one excludes the other, and each is thought of in separation from the other.

Thus Engels writes in his introduction to *Anti-Dühring*:

"To the metaphysician, things and their mental images, ideas, are isolated, to be considered one after the other, apart from each other, rigid fixed objects of investigation given once and for all. He thinks in absolutely irreconcilable antitheses. 'His communication is Yea, yea, Nay, nay, for whatever is more than these cometh of evil.' For him a thing either exists or it does not exist; it is equally impossible for a thing to be itself and at the same time something else."

Philosophers have expressed the essence of this metaphysical way of thinking in the formula: "Each thing is what it is, and not another thing." This may sound no more than plain common sense. But that only shows that so-called common sense itself conceals misleading ideas which need to be brought into the open. This way of thinking prevents us from studying things in their real changes and interconnections—in all their contradictory aspects and relationships, in their process of changing from "one thing" into "another thing".

It is not only philosophers who are metaphysicians.

There are left-wing trade unionists, for example, who are as metaphysical as any school of philosophers. For them everyone at their trade union branch meeting is either a class-conscious militant or else he is a right-wing opportunist. Everyone must fit into one or other category, and once he is down as "right wing" he is finished so far as they are concerned. That some worker who has been their opponent in the past and on some issues may yet prove an ally in the future and on other issues is not allowed for in their metaphysical outlook on life.

In one of Molière's plays there is a man who learns for the first time about prose. When they explain to him what prose is, he exclaims: "Why, I've been speaking prose all my life!"

Similarly, there are many workers who may well say: "Why, I've been a metaphysician all my life!"

The metaphysician has his formula ready for everything. He says—either this formula fits or it does not. If it does, that settles it. If it does not, then he has some alternative formula ready. "Either-or, but not both" is his motto. A thing is either this or that; it has either this set of properties or that set of properties; two things stand to one another either in this relationship or in that.

The use of the metaphysical "either-or" leads people into countless difficulties.

For example, difficulties are felt in understanding the relations between American and British imperialism today. For it is argued: either they are working together, or else they are not. If they are working together, then there is no rift between them; if there is a rift between them, then they are not working together. But on the contrary, they are working together and yet there are rifts between them; and we cannot understand the way they work together nor fight them effectively unless we understand the rifts which divide them.

Again, difficulties are felt in understanding the possibility of the peaceful co-existence of capitalist and socialist states. For it is argued: either they can co-exist peacefully, in which case antagonism between capitalism and socialism must cease; or else the antagonism remains, in which case they cannot co-exist peacefully. But on the contrary, the antagonism remains, and yet the striving of the socialist states and of millions of people in all countries for peace can lead to peaceful relations between capitalist and socialist states.

It is often difficult to avoid a metaphysical way of thinking. And this is because, misleading as it is, it yet has its roots in something very necessary and useful.

It is necessary for us to classify things—to have some system of classifying them and assigning their properties and relations. That is a prerequisite of clear thinking. We have to work out what different kinds of things there are in the world, to say that these have these properties as distinct from those which have those other properties, and to say what are their relations.

But when we go on to consider these things and properties and relations each in isolation, as fixed constants, as mutually exclusive terms, then we begin to go wrong. For everything in the world has many different and indeed contradictory aspects, exists in intimate relationship with other things and not in isolation, and is subject to change. And so it frequently happens that when we classify something as "A" and not "B" then this formula is upset by its changing from "A" to "B", or by its being "A" in some relationships and "B" in others, or by its having a contradictory nature, part "A" and part "B".

For example, we all know the difference between birds and mammals, and that while birds lay eggs mammals, in general, produce their young alive and suckle them. Naturalists used to believe that mammals were rigidly distinguished from birds because, amongst other things, mammals do not lay eggs. But this formula was completely upset when an animal called the platypus was discovered, for while the platypus is undoubtedly a mammal, it is a mammal which lays eggs. What is the explanation of this irregular behaviour of the platypus? It is to be found in the evolutionary relationship of birds and mammals, which are both descended from original egg-laying animals. The birds have continued to lay eggs while the mammals stopped doing so—except for a few conservative animals like the platypus. If we think of animals in their evolution, their development, this appears very natural. But if we try, as the older naturalists tried, to make them fit into some rigid, fixed scheme of classification, then the products of evolution upset that classification.

Again, an idea or a theory which was progressive in one set of circumstances, when it first arose, cannot for that reason be labelled "progressive" in an absolute sense, since it may later become reactionary in new circumstances. For instance, mechanisitc materialism when it first arose was a progressive theory. But we cannot say that it is still progressive today. On the contrary, under the new circumstances which have arisen mechanistic theory has become retrograde, reactionary. Mechanism, which was progressive in the rising phase of capitalism, goes hand in hand with idealism as part of the ideology of capitalism in decay.

Common sense, too, recognises the limitations of the metaphysical way of thinking.

For example: When is a man bald? Common sense recognises that though we can distinguish bald men from non-bald men, nevertheless baldness develops through a process of losing one's hair, and therefore men in the midst of this process enter into a phase in which we cannot say absolutely either that they are bald or that they are not: they are in process of becoming bald. The metaphysical "either-or" breaks down.

In all these examples we are confronted with the distinction between an *objective process*, in which something undergoes change, and the *concepts* in terms of which we try to sum up the characteristics of the things involved in the process. Such concepts never do and never can always and in all respects correspond to their objects, precisely because the objects are undergoing change.

Engels explained this in a letter (March 12, 1895) to a certain Mr. C. Schmidt, who was puzzled by it:

> "Are the concepts that prevail in natural science fictions because they by no means always coincide with reality? From the moment we accept the theory of evolution all our concepts of organic life correspond only approximately to reality. Otherwise there would be no change; on the day that concept and reality absolutely coincide in the organic world, development is at an end."

And he pointed out that similar considerations apply to all concepts without exception.

The Unity and Struggle of Opposites

When we think of the properties of things, their relationships, their modes of action and interaction, the processes into which they enter, then we find that, generally speaking, all these properties, relationships, interactions and processes divide into *fundamental opposites*.

For example, if we think of the simplest ways in which two bodies can act on one another, then we find that this action is either repulsion or attraction.

If we consider the electical properties of bodies, then there is positive and negative electricity.

In organic life, there is the building up of organic compounds and the breaking of them down.

Again, in mathematics, there is addition and subtraction, plus and minus.

And in general, whatever sphere of inquiry we may be considering, we find that it involves such fundamental opposites. We find ourselves considering, not just a number of *different* things, *different* properties, *different* relations, *different* processes, but pairs of *opposites*, fundamental *oppositions*. As Hegel put it: "In opposition, the different is not confronted by any other, but by *its* other" (*Encyclopaedia of Philosophical Sciences: Logic*, Section 119).

Thus if we think of the forces acting between two bodies, there are not just a number of different forces, but they divide into attractive and repulsive forces; if we think of electric charges, there are not just a number of different charges, but they divide into positive and negative; and so on. Attraction stands opposed to repulsion, positive electricity to negative electricity.

Such fundamental oppositions are not understood by the metaphysical way of thinking.

In the first place, the metaphysical way of thinking tries to ignore and discount opposition. It seeks to understand a given subject-matter simply in terms of a whole number of different properties and different relations of things, ignoring the fundamental oppositions which are manifested in these properties and relations. Thus those who think in metaphysical terms about class-divided societies, for example, try to understand society as consisting merely of a large number of different individuals connected together by all kinds of different social relations—but they ignore the fundamental opposition of exploiters and exploited, manifested in all those social relations.

In the second place, when the metaphysical way of thinking does nevertheless come upon the fundamental oppositions and cannot ignore them, then—true to its habit of thinking of each thing in isolation, as a fixed constant—it considers these opposites each in isolation from the other, understands them separately and as each excluding the other. Thus, for example, the older physicists used to think of positive and negative electricity just simply as two different "electrical fluids".

But contrary to metaphysics, not only are fundamental

opposites involved in every subject-matter, but these opposites mutually imply each other, are inseparably connected together, and, far from being exclusive, neither can exist or be understood except in relation to the other.

This characteristic of opposition is known as polarity: fundamental opposites are polar opposites. A magnet, for example, has two poles, a north pole and a south pole. But these poles, opposite and distinct, cannot exist in separation. If the magnet is cut in two, there is not a north pole in one half and a south pole in the other, but north and south poles recur in each half. The north pole exists only as the opposite of the south, and vice versa; the one can be defined only as the opposite of the other.

In general, fundamental opposition has to be understood as polar opposition, and every subject-matter has to be understood in terms of the polar opposition involved in it.

Thus in physics we find that attraction and repulsion are involved in every physical process in such a way that they cannot be separated or isolated the one from the other. In considering living bodies, we do not find in some cases the building up of organic compounds and in other cases their breaking down, but every life process involves both the building up and the breaking down of organic compounds. In capitalist society the increasing socialisation of labour is inseparable from its opposite, the increasing centralisation of capital.

This unity of opposites—the fact that opposites cannot be understood in separation one from another, but only in their inseparable connection in every field of investigation—is strikingly exemplified in mathematics. Here the fundamental operations are the two oppositions, addition and subtraction. And so far is it from being the case that addition and subtraction can be understood each apart from the other, that addition can be represented as subtraction and vice versa; thus the operation of subtraction $(a-b)$ can be represented as an addition $(-b+a)$. Similarly a division a/b can be represented as a multiplication $a \times (1/b)$ (Engels: *Dialectics of Nature*, "Note on Mathematics").

The unity of opposites, their inseparable connection, is by

no means to be understood as a harmonious and stable relationship, as a state of equilibrium. On the contrary. "The unity of opposites is conditional, temporary, transitory, relative. The struggle of mutually exclusive opposites is absolute, just as development and motion are absolute" (Lenin: *Philosophical Notebooks*).

The existence of fundamental polar oppositions, manifesting themselves in every department of nature and society, expresses itself in the *conflict* and *struggle* of opposed tendencies, which, despite phases of temporary equilibrium, lead to continual motion and development, to a perpetual coming into being and passing away of everything in existence, to sharp changes of state and transformations.

Thus, for example, the equilibrium of attractive and repulsive forces in the physical world is never more than conditional and temporary; the conflict and struggle of attraction and repulsion always asserts itself, issuing in physical changes and transformations, whether transformations on an atomic scale, chemical changes or, on a grand scale, in the explosion of stars.

Dialectics and Metaphysics

To sum up.

Metaphysics thinks in terms of "ready-made" things, whose properties and potentialities it seeks to fix and determine once and for all. It considers each thing by itself, in isolation from every other, in terms of irreconcilable antitheses—"either-or". It contrasts one thing to another, one property to another, one relationship to another, not considering things in their real movement and interconnection, and not considering that every subject-matter represents a unity of opposites—opposed but inseparably connected together.

Contrary to metaphysics, dialectics refuses to think of things each by itself, as having a fixed nature and fixed properties—"either-or"—but it recognises that things come into being, exist and cease to be in a process of unending change and development, in a process of complicated and ever-changing inter-relationship, in which each thing exists only in its connection with other things and goes through a series of transformations, and in which is always manifested the unity, inseparable interconnection and struggle of the opposite properties, aspects, tendencies characteristic of every phenomenon of nature and society.

Contrary to metaphysics, the aim of dialectics is to trace the real changes and interconnections in the world and to think of things always in their motion and interconnection.

Thus Engels writes in *Ludwig Feuerbach*:

> "The world is not to be comprehended as a complex of ready-made things but as a complex of processes. . . . One no longer permits oneself to be imposed upon by the antitheses insuperable for the old metaphysics. . . ."

And in *Anti-Dühring*:

> "The old rigid antitheses, the sharp impassible dividing lines are more and more disappearing. . . . The recognition that these antitheses and distinctions are in fact to be found in nature but only with relative validity, and that on the other hand their imagined rigidity and absoluteness have been introduced into nature only by our minds—this recognition is the kernel of the dialectical conception of nature.
>
> Dialectics . . . grasps things and their images, ideas, essentially in their inter-connection, in their sequence, their movement, their birth and death. . . ."

Lenin wrote in his *Philosophical Notebooks* that the understanding of the "contradictory parts" of every phenomenon was "the essence of dialectics". It consists in "the recognition (discovery) of the contradictory, mutually exclusive, opposite tendencies in all phenomena and processes of nature, including mind and society".

Lastly, Marx in the Preface to *Capital* wrote that:

> "dialectic . . . in its rational form is a scandal and abomination to bourgeoisdom and its doctrinaire professors, because

it includes in its comprehension and affirmative recognition of the existing state of things, at the same time also, the recognition of the negation of that state, of its inevitable breaking up; because it regards every historically developed social form as in fluid movement, and therefore takes into account its transient nature not less than its momentary existence; because it lets nothing impose upon it, and is in its essence critical and revolutionary."

Chapter Seven

CHANGE AND INTERCONNECTION

Four Principal Features of the Marxist Dialectical Method

In his *Dialectical and Historical Materialism* Stalin said that there are four principal features of the Marxist dialectical method.

(1) Contrary to metaphysics, dialectics does not regard nature as just an agglomeration of things, each existing independently of the others, but it considers things as "connected with, dependent on and determined by each other". Hence it considers that nothing can be understood taken by itself, in isolation, but must always be understood "in its inseparable connection with other things, and as conditioned by them".

(2) Contrary to metaphysics, dialectics considers everything as in "a state of continuous movement and change, of renewal and development, where something is always arising and developing and something always disintegrating and dying away". Hence it considers things "not only from the standpoint of their interconnection and interdependence, but also from the standpoint of their movement, their change, their development, their coming into being and going out of being".

(3) Contrary to metaphysics, dialectics does not regard the process of development as "a simple process of growth", but as "a development which passes from . . . quantitative changes to open, fundamental changes, to qualitative changes", which occur "abruptly, taking the form of a leap from one state to another". Hence it considers development as "an onward and upward movement, as a transition from an old qualitative state to a new qualitative state, as a development from the simple to the complex, from the lower to the higher".

(4) Contrary to metaphysics, dialectics "holds that the process of development from the lower to the higher takes

place . . . as a disclosure of the contradictions inherent in things . . . as a struggle of opposite tendencies which operate on the basis of these contradictions".

We shall postpone until the next chapter consideration of the latter two features, which concern the process of development from one qualitative state to another, from the lower to the higher. In this chapter we shall consider the first two features of the dialectical method, namely, that it considers things always in their interconnection and in their movement and change.

Considering Things in Their Interconnection and Circumstances

The dialectical method demands, first, that we should consider things, not each by itself, but always in their interconnection with other things.

This sounds "obvious". Nevertheless it is an "obvious" principle which is very often ignored and is extremely important to remember. We have already considered it and some examples of its application in discussing metaphysics, since the very essence of metaphysics is to think of things in an abstract way, isolated from their relations with other things and from the concrete circumstances in which they exist.

The principle of considering things in relation to actual conditions and circumstances, and not apart from those actual conditions and circumstances, is always of fundamental importance for the working-class movement in deciding the most elementary questions of policy.

For example, there was a time when the British workers were fighting for a ten-hour day. They were right at that time not to make their immediate demand an eight-hour day, since this was not yet a realisable demand. They were equally right, when they got a ten-hour day, not to be satisfied with it.

There are times when it is correct for a section of workers to come out on strike, and there are times when it is not correct. Such matters have to be judged according to the actual circumstances of the case. Similarly there are times when it is correct to go on prolonging and extending a strike, and there are times when it is correct to call it off.

No working-class leader can be of very much use if he tries to decide questions of policy in terms of "general principle" alone, without taking into account the actual circumstances in relation to which policy has to be operated, without understanding that the same policy can be right in one case and wrong in another, depending on the concrete circumstances of each case.

Thus in *Left-Wing Communism* Lenin wrote:

> "Of course, in politics, in which sometimes extremely complicated—national and international—relationships between classes and parties have to be dealt with . . . it would be absurd to concoct a recipe, or general rule . . . that would serve in all cases. One must have the brains to analyse the situation in each separate case."

This readiness on the part of Marxists to adapt policy to circumstances and to change policy with circumstances is sometimes called Communist "opportunism". But it is nothing of the kind—or rather, it is the very opposite. It is the application in practice of the science of the strategy and tactics of working-class struggle. Indeed, what is meant by opportunism in relation to working-class policy? It means subordinating the long-term interests of the working class as a whole to the temporary interests of a section, sacrificing the interests of the class to defence of the temporary privileges of some particular group. Communists are guided by the principle stated in *The Communist Manifesto*, that "they always and everywhere represent the interests of the movement as a whole". And this requires that, in the interests of the movement as a whole, one must analyse the situation in each separate case, deciding what policy to pursue in each case in the light of the concrete circumstances.

On general questions, too, the greatest confusion can arise from forgetting the dialectical principle that things must not be considered in isolation but in their inseparable interconnection.

For example, the British Labour leaders once said, and

many members of the Labour Party continue to say, that nationalisation is an instalment of socialism. They consider nationalisation by itself, in isolation, out of connection with the state and with the social structure in relation to which nationalisation measures are introduced. They overlook the fact that if the public power, the state, remains in the hands of the exploiters, and if their representatives sit on and control the boards of the nationalised industries, which continue to be run on the basis of exploiting the labour of one class for the profit of another class, then nationalisation is not socialism. Socialist nationalisation can come into being only when the public power, the state, is in the hands of the workers.

Again, in political arguments people very often appeal to a concept of "fairness" which leads them to judge events without the slightest consideration of the real meaning of those events, of the circumstances in which they occur. What's sauce for the goose is sauce for the gander: that is the principle employed in such arguments.

Thus it is argued that if we defend the democratic right of the workers in a capitalist country to agitate for the ending of capitalism and the introduction of socialism, then we cannot deny to others in a socialist country the right to agitate for the ending of socialism and the reintroduction of capitalism. Those who argue like this throw up their hands in horror when they find that former groupings in the U.S.S.R., who sought to restore capitalism in that country, were deprived of the possibility of carrying out their aims, and that later the same thing happened to groupings with similar aims in Hungary. Why, they exclaim, this is undemocratic, this is tyranny! Such an argument overlooks the difference between fighting in the interests of the vast majority of the people to end exploitation, and fighting in the interests of a small section to preserve or reintroduce exploitation; it overlooks the difference between defending the right of the vast majority to run their affairs in their own interests, and defending the right of a small minority to keep the majority in bondage; in other words, it overlooks the difference between moving forwards and backwards, between putting the clock on and putting it back, between revolution and counter-revolution. Of course, if we fight to achieve socialism, and if we achieve it, then we shall defend what we have achieved and shall not allow the slightest possibility of any group destroying that achievement. Let the capitalists and their hangers-on shout about democracy "in general". If, as Lenin said, we "have the brains to analyse the situation", we shall not be deceived by them.

The "liberal" concept of "fairness" has, indeed, often served as a favourite weapon of reaction. In 1949 and again in 1950, when the fascists decided to hold a demonstration in London on May Day, the Home Secretary promptly banned the workers' May Day demonstration. If I ban one, I must ban the other, he blandly explained. How scrupulously "fair" he was!

The principle of understanding things in their circumstances and interconnections is likewise a very important principle in science. Yet scientists, who take things to bits and consider their various properties, very often forget that things which they may consider in isolation do not exist in isolation. And this leads to serious misunderstandings.

Soviet biologists, for example, guided by this first principle of dialectics, have stressed the unity of the organism and its environment. They have pointed out that you cannot consider the organism as having a nature of its own, isolated from its environment: that is metaphysics. Thus there is no such thing as a plant, for instance, isolated from its environment: such a plant is a mere museum piece, a dead plant artificially preserved. Living plants grow in a soil, in a climate, in an environment, and they grow and develop by assimilating that environment. Thus Lysenko defined the heredity, or nature, of an organism as its requirement of certain conditions for its life and development, and its responding to various conditions in a certain way. This understanding of the unity of organism and environment had important consequences. For it led to the expectation that by compelling an organism to adapt itself to and assimilate changed conditions, its nature could be changed. And this expectation has been verified in practice.

Some biologists, on the other hand, wished to treat the

organism abstractly, metaphysically, as isolated from its real conditions of life. They conceived of the "nature" of the organism as quite independent of its conditions of life. Hence they concluded, in true metaphysical style, that the heredity of an organism "is what it is", and that it was no use trying to change it in the ways in which Soviet biologists *have* changed the heredity of organisms.

Considering Things in Their Movement, Their Coming into Being and Going out of Being

Let us now consider some examples of the second principle of dialectics, which demands that we should consider things in their movement, their change, their coming into being and going out of being.

This principle, too, is of great importance in science.

Soviet biologists, for example, guided by this principle of dialectics, considered the organism in its growth and development. Thus at a certain stage of growth, the nature of the organism is still plastic; if you can modify it at that state, you can often change its nature, give it a changed heredity. Something is newly coming into being in the organism, and that is the time to foster it and to give it a desired direction. But if that stage is passed, then its nature becomes fixed and you cannot change it. You must find just the right stage of growth if you wish to modify the heredity of the organism.

This second principle of dialectics teaches us always to pay attention to what is new, to what is rising and growing—not just to what exists at the moment, but to what is coming into being.

This principle is of paramount importance for revolutionary understanding, for revolutionary practice.

The Russian Bolsheviks, for example, saw from the very beginning how Russian society was moving—what was new in it, what was coming into being. They looked for what was rising and growing, though it was still weak—the working class. While others discounted the importance of the working class and finished by entering into compromises with the forces of the old society, the Bolsheviks concluded that the working class was the new, rising force, and led it to victory.

Similarly today, when Press and radio are full of the boasts and threats of the American imperialists and their followers, we stress that which is rising and growing all over the world, the people's camp of peace, which is bound to continue to grow and to overwhelm the imperialists in shameful disaster.

Again, in the fight for unity of the working-class movement, in relation to the British Labour Party and the affiliated trade unions, we pay attention above all to that which is arising and growing in the movement. Therefore we see a great deal more than the policy of the right-wing leaders and their influence. The right wing has its basis in the past, though it is still strong. But there are arising the forces of the future, determined to fight against capitalism and war.

Similarly in relation to individual people—we should foster and build on what is coming to birth in them, what is rising and moving ahead. This is what a good secretary or organiser does.

Such examples as these show that the basis of the dialectical method, its most essential principle, is to study and understand things in their concrete interconnection and movement.

Against "Ready-made Schemes"—"Truth is Always Concrete"

Sometimes people imagine that dialectics is a preconceived scheme, into the pattern of which everything is supposed to fit. This is the very opposite of the truth about dialectics. The employment of the Marxist dialectical method does not mean that we apply a preconceived scheme and try to make everything fit into it. No, it means that we study things as they really are, in their real interconnection and movement. "The most essential thing in Marxism," Lenin wrote, "is the concrete analysis of concrete conditions" (quoted by Mao Tse-tung in *On Contradiction*).

This is something which Lenin insisted on again and again. Indeed, in his pamphlet *One Step Forward, Two Steps Back*, he proclaimed it as "the fundamental thesis of dialectics".

"Genuine dialectics," Lenin wrote, proceeds "by means of a thorough, detailed analysis of a process in all its concreteness. The fundamental thesis of dialectics is: there is no such thing as abstract truth, truth is always concrete."

What did he mean by "truth is always concrete"? Just that we will not get at the truth about things, either about nature or society, by thinking up some general scheme, some abstract formula; but only by trying to work out as regards each process just what are the forces at work, how they are related, which are rising and growing and which are decaying and dying away, and on this basis reaching an estimate of the process as a whole.

So Engels said: "There could be no question of building the laws of dialectics into nature, but of discovering them in it and evolving them from it. . . . Nature is the test of dialectics" (*Anti-Dühring*).

As regards the study of society, and the estimate we make of real social changes on which we base our political strategy, Lenin ridiculed those who took some abstract, preconceived scheme as their guide.

According to some "authorities", the Marxist dialectics laid it down that all development must proceed through "triads"—thesis, antithesis, synthesis. Lenin ridiculed this.

> "It is clear to everybody that the main burden of Engels' argument is that materialists must depict the historical process correctly and accurately, and that insistence on . . . selection of examples which demonstrate the correctness of the triad is nothing but a relic of Hegelianism. . . . And, indeed, once it has been categorically declared that to attempt to 'prove' anything by triads is absurd, what significance can examples of 'dialectical' process have? . . . Anyone who reads the definition and description of the dialectical method given by Engels will see that the Hegelian triads are not even mentioned, and that it all amounts to regarding social evolution as a natural-historical process of development. . . .

What Marx and Engels called the dialectical method is nothing more nor less than the scientific method in sociology, which consists in regarding society as a living organism in a constant state of development, the study of which requires an objective analysis of the relations of production which constitute the given social formation and an investigation of its laws of functioning and development" (*What the "Friends of the People" Are and How They Fight the Social Democrats*, Part I).

Let us consider some examples of what the "analysis of a process in all its concreteness" and the principle that "truth is always concrete" mean, in contrast to the method of trying to lay down some preconceived scheme of social development and of appealing to such a scheme as a basis for policy.

In Tsarist Russia the Mensheviks used to say: "We must have capitalism before socialism." First capitalism must go through its full development, then socialism will follow: that was their scheme. Consequently they supported the liberals in politics and enjoined the workers to do no more than fight for better conditions in the capitalist factories.

Lenin repudiated this silly scheme. He showed that the liberals, frightened by the workers, would compromise with the Tsar; but that the alliance of workers with peasants could take the lead from them, overthrow the Tsar, and then go on to overthrow the capitalists and build socialism before ever capitalism was able to develop fully.

After the proletarian revolution was successful, another scheme was propounded—this time by Trotsky. "You can't build socialism in one country. Unless the revolution takes place in the advanced capitalist countries, socialism cannot come in Russia." Lenin and Stalin showed that this scheme, too, was false. For even if the revolution did not take place in the advanced capitalist countries, the alliance of workers and peasants in the Soviet Union had still the forces to build socialism.

In Western European countries it used often to be said:

"We must have fascism before communism." First the capitalists will abandon democracy and introduce the fascist dictatorship, and then the workers will overthrow the fascist dictatorship. But the Communists replied, no, we will fight together with all the democratic forces to preserve bourgeois democracy and to defeat the fascists, and that will create the best conditions for going forward to win working-class power and to commence to build socialism.

Lastly, today we sometimes hear the argument: "Capitalism means war; therefore war is inevitable." No, this scheme is false as well. The imperialists have tried to stake their policy on wars of conquest. But they cannot make war without the people. The more they prepare for war, the more open their aggressiveness becomes, the more one power attempts to impose its domination on another and the more hardships they impose on the people, the more can the people be rallied to oppose their war. Therefore peace can be preserved. And by fighting to preserve peace we can lay the basis for ending the conditions which create the danger of war. So war is not inevitable: the imperialist plans can be defeated. They can be defeated if the working class rallies all the peace-loving forces around itself. And if we defeat the imperialist war plans, that will be the best road towards the ending of capitalism itself and the building of socialism. Imperialism will not be ended by waiting for it to wreck itself in inevitable wars, but by uniting to prevent the realisation of its war plans.

In all these examples it will be seen that the acceptance of some ready-made scheme, some abstract formula, means passivity, support for capitalism, betrayal of the working class and of socialism. But the dialectical approach which understands things in their concrete interconnection and movement, shows us how to forge ahead—how to fight, what allies to draw in. That is the inestimable value of the Marxist dialectical method to the working-class movement.

Chapter Eight

THE LAWS OF DEVELOPMENT

What Do We Mean by "Development"?

In stressing the need to study real processes in their movement and in all their interconnections, Stalin pointed out that in the processes of nature and history there is always "renewal and development, where something is always arising and developing and something always disintegrating and dying away" (*Dialectical and Historical Materialism*).

When that which is arising and developing comes to fruition, and that which is disintegrating and dying away finally disappears, there emerges something *new*.

For as we saw in criticising mechanistic materialism, processes do not always keep repeating the same cycle of changes, but advance from stage to stage as something new continually emerges.

This is the real meaning of the word "development". We speak of "development" where stage by stage something new keeps emerging.

Thus there is a difference between mere *change* and development. Development is change proceeding according to its own internal laws from stage to stage.

And there is equally a difference between *growth* and development. This difference is familiar to biologists, for example. Thus growth means getting bigger—merely quantitative change. But development means, not getting bigger, but passing into a qualitatively new stage, becoming qualitatively different. For example, a caterpillar grows longer and fatter; then it spins itself a cocoon, and finally emerges as a butterfly. This is development. A caterpillar *grows* into a bigger caterpillar; it *develops* into a butterfly.

Processes of nature and history exemplify, not merely change, not merely growth, but development. Can we, then, reach any conclusions about the general laws of development? This is the further task of materialist dialectics—to find what general laws are manifested in all development, and to give us, therefore, the *method of approach* for understanding, explaining and controlling development.

Quantity and Quality; The Law of the Transformation of Quantitative into Qualitative Changes

This brings us to the two latter features of the Marxist dialectical method. The first of these may be called "the law of the transformation of quantitative into qualitative change". What does this mean?

All change has a quantitative aspect, that is, an aspect of mere increase or decrease which does not alter the nature of that which changes. But quantitative change, increase or decrease, cannot go on indefinitely. At a certain point it always leads to a qualitative change; and at that critical point (or "nodal point", as Hegel called it) the qualitative change takes place relatively suddenly, by a leap, as it were.

For example, if water is being heated, it does not go on getting hotter and hotter indefinitely; at a certain critical temperature, it begins to turn into steam, undergoing a qualitative change from liquid to gas. A cord used to lift a weight may have a greater and greater load attached to it, but no cord can lift a load indefinitely great: at a certain point, the cord is bound to break. A boiler may withstand a greater and greater pressure of steam—up to the point where it bursts.

This law of the transformation of quantitative into qualitative change is also met with in society. Thus before the system of industrial capitalism comes into being there takes place a process of the accumulation of wealth in money form in a few private hands (largely by colonial plunder), and of the formation of a propertyless proletariat (by enclosures and the driving of peasants off the land). At a certain point in this process, when *enough* money is accumulated to provide capital for industrial undertakings, when *enough* people have been proletarianised to provide the labour required, the conditions have matured for the development of industrial capitalism. At this point an accumulation of quantitative changes gives rise to a new qualitative stage in the development of society.

In general, qualitative changes happen with relative suddenness—by a leap. Something new is suddenly born, though its potentiality was already contained in the gradual evolutionary process of continuous quantitative change which went before.

Thus we find that continuous, gradual quantitative change leads at a certain point to discontinuous, sudden qualitative change. We have already remarked in an earlier chapter that most of those who have considered the laws of development in nature and society have conceived of this development only in its continuous aspect. This means that they have considered it only from the aspect of a process of growth, of quantitative change, and have not considered its qualitative aspect, the fact that at a certain point in the gradual process of growth a new quality suddenly arises, a transformation takes place.

Yet this is what always happens. If you are boiling a kettle, the water suddenly begins to boil when boiling point is reached. If you are scrambling eggs, the mixture in the pan suddenly "scrambles". And it is the same if you are engaged in changing society. We will only change capitalist society into socialist society when the rule of one class is replaced by the rule of another class—and this is a radical transformation, a leap to a new state of society, a revolution.

If, on the other hand, we consider quality itself, then qualitative change always arises as a result of an accumulation of quantitative changes, and differences in quality have their basis in differences of quantity.

Thus just as quantitative change must at a certain point give rise to qualitative change, so if we wish to bring about qualitative change we must study its quantitative basis, and know what must be increased and what diminished if the required chance is to be brought about.

Natural science teaches us how purely quantitative difference—addition or subtraction—makes a qualitative difference in nature. For example, the addition of one proton in the nucleus of an atom makes the transition from one element to another. The atoms of all the elements are formed out of combinations of the same protons and electrons, but a purely quantitative difference between the numbers combined in the atom gives different kinds of atoms, atoms of different elements with different chemical properties. Thus an atom consisting of one proton and one electron is a hydrogen atom, but if another proton and another electron are added it is an atom of helium, and so on. Similarly in chemical compounds, the addition of one atom to a molecule makes the difference between substances with different chemical properties. In general, different qualities have their basis in quantitative difference.

As Engels put it in his *Dialectics of Nature*:

> "In nature, in a manner exactly fixed for each individual case, qualitative changes can only occur by the quantitative addition or subtraction of matter or motion. . . .
>
> All qualitative differences in nature rest on differences of chemical composition or on different quantities or forms of motion or, as is almost always the case, on both. Hence it is impossible to alter the quality of a body without addition or subtraction of matter or motion, i.e. without quantitative alteration of the body concerned."

This feature of the dialectical law connecting quality and quantity is familiar to readers of the popular literature about atomic bombs. To make a uranium bomb it is necessary to have the isotope, uranium-235; the more common isotope, uranium-238, will not do. The difference between these two is merely quantitative, a difference in atomic weight, depending on the number of neutrons present in each case. But this quantitative difference of atomic weight, 235 and 238, makes the qualitative difference between a substance with the properties required for the bomb and a substance without those properties. Further, having got a quantity of uranium-235, a certain "critical mass" of it is required before it will explode. If there is not enough, the chain reaction which constitutes the explosion will not occur; when the "critical mass" is reached, the reaction does occur.

The hydrogen bomb likewise depends on definite quantitative conditions to make it go off. The thermo-nuclear reaction which constitutes the explosion takes place only when a sufficient degree of heat is present. So this heat has to be generated, e.g. by an atomic explosion, in order to explode the hydrogen bomb.

Thus we see that quantitative changes are transformed at a certain point into qualitative changes, and qualitative differences rest on quantitative differences. This is a universal feature of development. What makes such development happen?

Development Takes Place Through the Unity and Struggle of Opposites

In general, the reason why in any particular case a quantitative change leads to a qualitative change lies in the very nature, in the content, of the particular processes involved. Therefore in each case we can, if we only know enough, explain just why a qualitative change is inevitable, and why it takes place at the point it does.

To explain this we have to study the facts of the case. We cannot invent an explanation with the aid of dialectics alone; where an understanding of dialectics helps is that it gives us the clue as to where to look. In a particular case we may not yet know how and why the change takes place. In that case we have the task of finding out, by investigating the facts of the case. For there is no mystery concealed behind the emergence of the qualitatively new.

Let us consider, for example, the case of the qualitative change which takes place when water boils.

When heat is applied to a mass of water contained in a kettle, then the effect is to increase the motion of the molecules composing the water. So long as the water remains in its liquid state, the forces of attraction between the molecules are sufficient to ensure that, though some of the surface molecules are continually escaping, the whole mass coheres together as a mass of water inside the kettle. At boiling point, however, the motion of the molecules has become sufficiently violent for large numbers of them to begin jumping clear of the mass. A qualitative change is therefore observed. The water begins to bubble and the whole mass is rapidly transformed into steam. This change evidently occurs as a result of the oppositions operating within the mass of water—the tendency of the molecules to move apart and jump free versus the forces of attraction between them. The former tendency is reinforced to the point where it overcomes the latter as a result, in this case, of the external application of heat.

Another example we have considered is that of a cord which breaks when its load becomes too great. Here again, the qualitative change takes place as a result of the opposition set up between the tensile strength of the cord and the pull of the load.

These examples prepare us for the general conclusion that, as Stalin puts it, "the internal content of the process of development, the internal content of the transformation of quantitative changes into qualitative changes" consists in the struggle of opposites—opposite tendencies, opposite forces—within the things and process concerned.

Thus the law that quantitative changes are transformed into qualitative changes, and that differences in quality are based on differences in quantity, leads us to the law of the unity and struggle of opposites.

Here is the way Stalin formulates this law, this feature of dialectics, in his *Dialectical and Historical Materialism*:

> "Contrary to metaphysics, dialectics holds that internal contradictions are inherent in all things and phenomena of nature, for all have their negative and positive sides, a past and a future, something dying away and something developing; and that the struggle between these opposites, the struggle between the old and the new, between that which is dying away and that which is being born, between that which is disappearing and that which is developing, constitutes the internal content of the process of development,

the internal content of the transformation of quantitative changes into qualitative changes.

The dialectical method therefore holds that the process of development from the lower to the higher takes place not as a harmonious unfolding of phenomena, but as a disclosure of the contradictions inherent in things and phenomena, as a 'struggle' of opposite tendencies which operate on the basis of these contradictions."

To understand development, to understand how and why quantitative changes lead to qualitative changes, to understand how and why the transition takes place from an old qualitative state to a new qualitative state, we have to understand the contradictions inherent in each thing and process we are considering, and how a "struggle" of opposite tendencies arises on the basis of these contradictions.

We have to understand this concretely, in each case, bearing in mind Lenin's warning that "the fundamental thesis of dialectics is: truth is always concrete". We cannot deduce the laws of development in the concrete case from the general principles of dialectics: we have to discover them by actual investigation in each case. But dialectics tells us what to look for.

Dialectics of Social Development—The Contradictions of Capitalism

The dialectics of development—the unity and struggle of opposites—has been most thoroughly worked out in the Marxist science of society. Here, from the standpoint of the working-class struggle, on the basis of working-class experience, we can work out the dialectic of the contradictions of capitalism and of their development very exactly.

But the principles involved in the development of society are not opposed to but are in essence the same as those involved in the development of nature, though different in their form of manifestation in each case. Thus Engels said in *Anti-Dühring*:

"I was not in doubt that amid the welter of innumerable changes taking place in nature the same dialectical laws of motion are in operation as those which in history govern the apparent fortuitousness of events."

How Marxism understands the contradictions of capitalism and their development, this crowning triumph of the dialectical method, was explained in general terms by Engels in *Socialism, Utopian and Scientific.*

The basic contradiction of capitalism is not simply the conflict of two classes, which confront one another as two external forces which come into conflict. No, it is the contradiction within the social system itself, on the basis of which the class conflict arises and operates.

Capitalism brought about:

> "the concentration of the means of production in large workshops and manufactories, their transformation into means of production which were in fact social. But the social means of production and the social products were treated as if they were still, as they had been before, the means of production and the products of individuals. Hitherto, the owner of the instruments of labour had appropriated the product because it was as a rule his own product, the auxiliary labour of other persons being the exception; now, the owner of the instruments of production continued to appropriate the product, although it was no longer *his* product, but exclusively the product of *others' labour.* Thus, therefore, the products, now socially produced, were not appropriated by those who had really set the means of production in motion and really produced the products, but by the *capitalists.*"

The basic contradiction of capitalism is, therefore, the contradiction between socialised production and capitalist appropriation. It is on the basis of this contradiction that the struggle between the classes develops.

> "In this contradiction . . . the whole conflict of today is already present in germ. . . . The contradiction between

social production and capitalist appropriation became manifest as the antagonism between proletariat and bourgeoisie."

And the contradiction can only be resolved by the victory of the working class, when the working class sets up its own dictatorship and initiates social ownership and appropriation to correspond to social production.

This example very exactly illustrates the point of what Stalin said about "struggle of opposite tendencies which operate on the basis of these contradictions". The class struggle exists and operates on the basis of the contradictions inherent in the social system itself.

It is from the struggle of opposite tendencies, opposing forces, arising on the basis of the contradictions inherent in the social system, that social transformation, the leap to a qualitatively new stage of social development, takes place.

In this way the laws of dialectical development, summarised in the principles of the transformation of quantitative into qualitative change and of the unity and struggle of opposites, are found at work in the development of society. To carry into effect the socialist transformation of society, therefore, the working class must learn to understand the social situation in the light of the laws of dialectics. Guided by that understanding, it must base the tactics and strategy of its class struggle on the concrete analysis of the actual situation at each stage of the struggle.

Chapter Nine

CONTRADICTION

Contradictions Inherent in Processes

In the last chapter we considered how qualitative change is brought about by the struggle of opposed forces. This was exemplified equally in the change of state of a body from liquid to solid or gas, and in the change of society from capitalism to socialism. In each case there are "opposite tendencies" at work, whose "struggle" eventuates in some fundamental transformation, a qualitative change.

This "struggle" is not external and accidental. It is not adequately understood if we suppose that it is a question of forces or tendencies arising quite independently the one of the other, which happen to meet, to bump up against each other and come into conflict.

No. The struggle is internal and necessary; for it arises and follows from the nature of the process as a whole. The opposite tendencies are not independent the one of the other, but are inseparably connected as parts or aspects of a single whole. And they operate and come into conflict on the basis of the contradiction inherent in the process as a whole.

Movement and change result from causes *inherent* in things and processes, from *internal* contradictions.

Thus, for example, the old mechanist conception of movement was that it only happened when one body bumped into another: there were no internal causes of movement, that is, no "self-movement", but only external causes. But on the contrary, the opposed tendencies which operate in the course of the change of state of a body operate on the basis of the contradictory unity of attractive and repulsive forces inherent in all physical phenomena.

Again, the class struggle in capitalist society arises on the basis of the contradictory unity of socialised labour and private appropriation inherent in that society. It does not arise as a result of external causes, but as a result of the contradictions within the very essence of the capitalist system. On the other hand, Tory and right-wing Labour theoreticians make out that the class struggle is stirred up by external interference—by "Communist agitators" and "Soviet agents". And they believe that if only this external interference could be stopped, the system could get along very well as it is.

The internal necessity of the struggle of opposed forces, and of its outcome, based on the contradictions inherent in the process as a whole, is no mere refinement of philosophical analysis. It is of very great practical importance.

Bourgeois theorists, for example, are well able to recognise the fact of class conflicts in capitalist society. What they do not recognise is the necessity of this conflict; that it is based on contradictions inherent in the very nature of the capitalist system and that, therefore, the struggle can only culminate in and end with the destruction of the system itself and its replacement by a new, higher system of society. So they seek to mitigate the class conflict, to tone it down and reconcile the opposing classes, or to stamp it out, and so to preserve the system intact. Precisely this bourgeois view of the class conflict is brought into the labour movement by social democracy.

It was in opposition to such a shallow, metaphysical way of understanding class conflict that Lenin pointed out in *The State and Revolution*:

> "It is often said and written that the core of Marx's theory is the class struggle; but it is not true. . . . To limit Marxism to the theory of the class struggle means curtailing Marxism, distorting it, reducing it to something which is acceptable to the bourgeoisie. A Marxist is one who extends the acceptance of the class struggle to the acceptance of the dictatorship of the proletariat. This is where the profound difference lies between a Marxist and an ordinary petty (or even big) bourgeois. This is the touchstone on

which the real understanding and acceptance of Marxism should be tested."

In general, contradiction is inherent in a given process. The struggle which is characteristic of the process is not an external clash of accidentally opposed factors, but is the working out of contradictions belonging to the very nature of the process. And this conditions the outcome of the process.

Contradiction Consists of the Unity and Struggle of Opposites

The key conception of dialectics is this conception of contradiction inherent in the very nature of things—that the motive force of qualitative change lies in the contradictions contained within all processes of nature and society, and that in order to understand, control and master things in practice we must proceed from the concrete analysis of their contradictions.

What exactly do we mean by "contradiction"?

According to the common, metaphysical conception, contradictions occur in our ideas about things, but not in things. We can assert contradictory propositions about a thing, and then there is a contradiction in what we say about it; but there can be no contradiction in the thing. This point of view regards contradiction simply and solely as a logical relation between propositions, but does not consider it as a real relation between things. Such a point of view is based on considering things statically, as "fixed and frozen", disregarding their motions and dynamic interconnections.

If we consider the real, complex movements and interconnections of real, complex things, then we find that contradictory tendencies can and do exist in them. For example, if the forces operating in a body combine tendencies of attraction and of repulsion, that it is a real contradiction. And if the movement of society combines the tendency to socialise production with the tendency to preserve private appropriation of the products, that is a real contradiction too.

The existence of contradictions in things is a very familiar state of affairs. There is nothing in the least abstruse about it, and it is often referred to in everyday conversations. For example, we speak of a man as having a "contradictory" character, or as being "a mass of contradictions". This means that he evinces opposed tendencies in his behaviour, such as gentleness and brutality, recklessness and cowardice, selfishness and self-sacrifice. Or again, contradictory relations are the subject of everyday gossip when we talk about married couples who are always quarrelling but never happy apart.

Such examples show that when we speak in Marxist philosophy about "contradictions in things", we are not inventing some far-fetched philosophical theory, but are referring to something which is familiar to everyone. Nor are we using the word "contradiction" in some new and strange sense of our own, but are using the word in its ordinary, everyday sense.

A real contradiction is a *unity* of opposites. There is a real contradiction inherent, as we say, in the very nature of a thing or process or relationship when in that thing or process or relationship opposite tendencies are combined together in such a way that neither can exist without the other. In the unity of opposites, the opposites are held together in a relation of mutual dependence, where each is the condition of existence of the other.

For example, the class contradiction between workers and capitalists in capitalist society is just such a unity of opposites, because in that society neither can the workers exist without the capitalists nor the capitalists without the workers. The nature of the society is such that these opposites are held together in it in inseparable unity. This unity of opposites belongs to the very essence of the social system. Capitalism is a system in which capitalists exploit workers and workers are exploited by capitalists.

It is the unity of opposites in a contradiction which makes inescapable and necessary the *struggle* of opposites. Since the opposed terms are inseparably united, there is no getting out of the struggle. Thus, for example, because opposed classes are united in capitalist society, the development of that society proceeds, and cannot but proceed, in the form of a class struggle.

We may also speak of the *interpenetration* of opposites in a contradiction. For being united in struggle, each opposed tendency is in its actual character and operation at any phase of the struggle influenced, modified or penetrated by the other in many ways. Each side is always affected by its relation with the other.

The Working Out of Contradictions

We can only understand, and can only control and master, the processes of nature and of society by understanding their contradictions, and the consequences of those contradictions—the way they work out.

Contradiction is the driving force of change. So if we want to understand how things change, and to control and utilise their changes, then we must understand their contradictions.

Why should we say that contradiction is the driving force of change? It is because it is only the presence of contradictions in a process which provides the internal conditions making change necessary. A process which contained no contradictions would simply go on and on in the same way until some external force stopped it or modified it. A movement without contradictions would be continuous repetition of the same movement. It is the presence of contradictions, that is, of contradictory tendencies of movement, or of a unity and struggle of opposites, which brings about *changes* of movement in the course of a process.

Imagine, if you can, a society without contradictions. This would be a society in which by continuing to do the same things in the same ways people would satisfy all their needs. Such a society would never change. There would continually be movement in it, in as much as people would be doing things all the time; but the movement would always be the same. There would be a process, but a process of repetition.

However, no such society exists or ever could exist, because from the very nature of the conditions of human life there must always be contradictions in society. By satisfying their needs people create new unsatisfied needs, and by advancing their forces of production they bring about a state of affairs in which they need to change their social relations and institutions correspondingly. This is why changes happen in society. The social process is not a process of repetition but a process in which new things happen.

Again, some metaphysical materialists tried to represent the universe as a system of particles bumping into and bouncing off one another. Such a universe would be a universe of the continuous motion of particles, but it would be a universe of the continuous repetition of the same motion. The real universe is not like this, because it is full of contradictions—the contradictions of attraction and repulsion studied by physics, of the association and dissociation of atoms studied by chemistry, of the processes of life and of the relationship of organism with environment studied by biology. It is the working out of these contradictions (in their specific forms in specific processes) which makes up the real changing processes of the real changing world.

This shows that where contradictions exist, there follows the working out of those contradictions—the working out of the struggle of opposites which arises from the unity of opposites. A process is the working out of its own essential contradictions.

The Universality and Particularity of Contradictions

Contradiction is a universal feature of all processes. But each particular kind of process has its own particular contradictions, which are characteristic of it and different from those of other processes.

This point was underlined by Mao Tse-tung in his essay *On Contradiction*, where he made the most thorough analysis of the conception yet contributed to Marxist literature. He called it the distinction between "the universality" and "the particularity" of contradiction.

We can never deduce what will happen in any particular case, or how a particular process can be controlled, from the universal idea of contradiction. As has already been stressed, the dialectical method does not consist in applying some preconceived scheme to the interpretation of everything, but consists in basing conclusions only on the "concrete analysis of concrete conditions".

Each kind of process has its own dialectic, which can be grasped only by the detailed study of that particular process. The dialectic of the sub-atomic world is not the same as that of the bodies directly perceptible to our senses. The dialectic of living organisms is not the same as that of the processes of inorganic matter. The dialectic of human society is a new law of motion. And each phase of human society brings with it again its own particular dialectic.

Thus, for example, the contradiction between tendencies of attraction and repulsion in physical motion, and between the interests of classes in society, are both contradictions. This is evidence of the universality of contradiction. But each has its own distinctive character, different from that of the other. This is evidence of the particularity of contradiction.

We cannot learn either the laws of physics or the laws of society if we try to deduce them from the universal idea of contradiction. We can learn them only by investigating physical and social processes. Physical movements and the movement of people in society are quite different forms of movement, and so the contradictions studied by social science are different, and work out in a different way, from those studied by physics. Social and physical processes are similar in that each contains contradictions, but dissimilar in the contradictions each contains.

The contradictions characteristic of each kind of process may be called the essential contradictions of that kind of process. For instance, contradictions between attractive and repulsive forces are essential contradictions of physical processes, and contradictions between forces of production and relations of production are essential contradictions of social processes.

If we further consider the essential contradictions characteristic of different kinds of process, then we can further say that these are manifested in specific ways in specific instances of processes of a given kind.

For example, the essential contradictions of social processes are manifested in specific ways in each specific social formation. The contradiction between forces of production and relations of production takes specific forms in different formations of society. Thus in capitalist society it takes the specific capitalist form of the contradiction between the increasingly social character of production and the retention of private appropriation.

Again, the relations between any species of living organism and its environment are contradictory. The organism lives only by means of its environment, and at the same time its environment contains threats to its life which it has continually to overcome. In the case of man, this contradiction takes the form of the specific contradictory relation between man and nature; and this relation itself takes even more specific forms with each stage of man's social development. Man is a part of nature and lives by means of nature, and man lives by opposing himself to nature and subduing nature to his will. This contradictory relation itself develops, and takes specific forms, as man develops. It is present in both primitive communism and in communism, for example, but presents a different aspect in the latter from the former.

In order to understand a process, then, and to learn how to control and master it, we must get to know its essential contradictions and investigate the specific forms they take in specific instances.

The Outcome of Contradictions

The unity of opposites in a contradiction is characterised by a definite relation of superiority-inferiority, or of domination, between the opposites. For example, in a physical unity of attraction and repulsion, certain elements of attraction or repulsion may be dominant in relation to others. The unity is such that one side dominates the other—or, in certain cases, they may be equal.

Any qualitative state of a process corresponds to a definite relation of domination. Thus, the solid, liquid and gaseous states of bodies correspond to different domination-relationships in the unity of attraction and repulsion characteristic of the molecules of bodies. Similarly, in the contradictions of capitalist society, the element of private appropriation plays a dominant rôle in relation to its opposite, social production, and the capitalist class dominates over the working class. If these domination relationships become reversed, then that marks a qualitative change, the ending of the capitalist state of society, the beginning of a new state.

Domination relationships are obviously, by their very nature, impermanent and apt to change, even though in some cases they remain unchanged for a long time. If the relationship takes the form of equality or balance, such balance is by nature unstable, for there is a struggle of opposites within it which is apt to lead to the domination of one over the other. And then if one dominates over the other, the struggle of opposites contains the possibility of the position being reversed.

"The unity of opposites," said Lenin, "is conditional, temporary, transitory, relative. The struggle of opposites is absolute." That is obviously true. Whatever the domination relationship in the unity of opposites may be, it is always apt to change, as a result of which the former unity of opposites will be dissolved and a new unity of opposites take its place.

The outcome of the working out of contradictions is, then, a change in the domination relation characteristic of the initial unity of opposites. Such a change constitutes a change in the nature of a thing, a change from one state to another, a change from one thing to another, a change entailing not merely some external alteration but a change in the internal character and laws of motion of a thing.

It is precisely such a change that we mean by a "qualitative" change.

For instance, if a piece of iron is painted black and instead we paint it red, that is merely an external alteration (affecting the way it reflects light and so its appearance to a seeing eye), but it is not a qualitative change in the sense we are here defining. On the other hand, if the iron is heated to melting point, then this *is* such a qualitative change. And it comes about precisely as a change in the attraction-repulsion relationship characteristic of the internal molecular state of the metal. The metal passes from the solid to liquid state, its internal character and laws of motion become different in certain ways, it undergoes a qualitative change.

Qualitative change is the result of a change in the balance of opposites. Such a change is prepared by a series of quantitative changes affecting the domination relation in the unity of opposites. As the domination relation changes, quantitative change passes into qualitative change.

When such a fundamental or qualitative change comes about as a result of the dissolution of an old form of unity of opposites and the coming into being of a new one, then the opposites themselves change. The side which passes from being dominated over to being dominant is changed in that process, and so is the other side, which passes from being dominant to being dominated over. Hence in the new qualitative state there are not the same old opposites in a changed relation, but because the relation is changed the opposites, held together in that relation, are changed too. There is a new unity of opposites, a new contradiction.

When, for instance, the working class becomes stronger than the capitalist class and from being dominated over becomes dominant, then in the new qualitative state of society the capitalist class disappears (for the dominant working class deprives it of its conditions of existence), and the working class, existing in completely new conditions, becomes virtually a new class. The contradictions of society therefore change; the particular contradictions of the old state disappear and new contradictions are born. The struggle between the working class and the capitalists comes to an end, and new kinds of struggle begin.

External and Internal Causes of Qualitative Change

How far is the passage from quantitative to qualitative change determined by the working out of the contradiction inherent in the process itself, or by internal causes, and how far is it determined by external or accidental causes?

It is determined by both, but in different ways.

Both in nature and society different things are always interacting and influencing each other. Hence external causes must always play a part in the changes which happen to things. At the same time, the character of the changes always depends on internal causes.

This problem was discussed by Mao Tse-tung in his essay *On Contradiction.* He concluded:

> "Contradiction within a thing is the basic cause of its development, while the relationship of a thing with other things—their interconnection and interaction—is a secondary cause. . . . External causes are the condition of change and internal causes the basis of change, external causes becoming operative through internal causes."

Consider, for example, such an event as the hatching of a chicken. The chicken does not develop inside the egg unless heat is applied from outside. But what develops in the egg, what hatches out, depends on what is inside the egg. As Mao remarks: "In a suitable temperature an egg changes into a chicken, but there is no temperature which can change a stone into a chicken, the fundamentals of the two things being different."

Again, water does not boil unless it is heated. But the boiling process resulting from the application of heat comes about on the basis of the internal contradiction of attraction and repulsion characteristic of the molecules of water.

Similarly in society, a revolution does not proceed without the intervention of external causes, but its character and outcome, and indeed the fact that it happens at all, depend on internal causes. Thus the basis of the Russian Revolution lay in the contradictions within Russian society. These made the revolution inevitable and determined its character. But what actually set off the revolution in 1917 was something external, the conditions brought about by the imperialist war.

In general, if we consider qualitative changes, then their qualitative character can be explained only by the operation of internal causes; the particular contradictions on which the old quality was based determine what new quality emerges. The external causes affect only the quantitative changes of things—the times and places of their beginning, and the rate at which they proceed.

"Purely external causes can only lead . . . to changes in size and quantity, but cannot explain why things are qualitatively different in a thousand and one ways and why things change into one another" (Mao Tse-tung, *On Contradiction*).

Thus, for example, the class struggle in capitalist society may be speeded up or slowed down by a variety of particular external causes. But the existence of the class struggle, its continuation, its direction and its final outcome are determined by the contradictions inherent in the capitalist system.

The Suddenness and Gradualness of Qualitative Change

Qualitative change being the outcome of the working out of contradictions, it follows that the whole process of the struggle of opposites may be regarded as a process of the replacement of one quality by another, of an old quality by a new one. The old quality corresponds to the dominance of one element in the unity of opposites. The reversal of this dominance leads to the replacement of the old quality by the new. In this sense each element in a unity of opposites is the bearer of a distinct quality. The struggle of the one to maintain its dominance is what maintains the old quality, the struggle of the other to reverse this dominance is what brings into being the new quality replacing the old.

For instance, all life is a unity of opposites, of processes of the building up and breaking down of living matter. So long as the building up maintains itself within this unity, life remains. When, however, the opposite begins to dominate, then death commences.

Again, if we consider the contradictions of capitalist society, then it is evident that the capitalist state of society depends on private appropriation dominating social production, and the capitalist class dominating the working class. It is the struggle of the working class against the capitalist class, and the struggle to free social production from the fetters of private appropriation, which, when the reversal of the old state happens, brings about a new socialist state of society.

It has already been pointed out that every contradiction has its own specific character. And so the struggle of opposites has in every case also its own specific character, according to the particular contradiction from which it arises. It follows that processes of qualitative change, replacements of old by new qualities, have also each their own specific character, according to the qualities concerned. What is *universally* true is simply that qualitative change comes about as the working out of contradictions, as an outcome of quantitative change. But this universal truth does not tell us how any *particular* change will work out. We can only discover that by knowing each particular case.

Thus considering the workings out of different kinds of social contradictions, which result in qualitative changes in society, each works out differently. For example, the contradiction between the great mass of the people and the feudal lords was worked out in the struggle for the democratic revolution; that between the working class and the capitalist class is worked out in the struggle for socialist revolution; that between the colonies and imperialism is worked out in the national liberation struggle; and that between the working class and peasantry in socialist society, in the collectivisation and mechanisation of agriculture.

Whatever the method by which different contradictions work out, a point is always reached where the quantitative aspect of the struggle of opposites within the contradiction has been sufficiently modified for the new quality to emerge. This is the point where qualitative change *begins*. How it *continues* depends entirely on the particular character of the contradiction of which it is the outcome, on the particular way the struggle of opposites continues.

Qualitative change is always sudden, and cannot but be sudden, in the sense that at a certain point of quantitative change a new quality emerges which was not present before. That is to say, at this point new things begin to happen, new causes operate and new effects are produced, new laws of motion come into operation.

This is the so-called qualitative "leap", the first appearance of the new which was not there before.

Thus qualitative change is preceded by a process of working up to the emergence of new quality. During this process contradictions are working out, so to speak, unseen—without manifestation in qualitative change. At the termination of this phase, the phase of the emergence of new quality begins abruptly or suddenly, and cannot but do so.

For example, when water is heated a movement takes place which suddenly turns into a boiling process. When a child is growing in the womb a movement takes place which suddenly turns into the process of birth. In society movement takes place amongst the classes, conflicts are sharpened, opinions mature, and suddenly there begins a decisive revolutionary change.

After that, how qualitative change proceeds, the swiftness or slowness and, in general, the manner of its completion, depends entirely on the circumstances of particular cases. Once a new quality emerges—once it has leaped into being—then a process of new qualitative character beings, in which the new quality gradually supplants the old.

While, therefore, qualitative change begins suddenly, it continues gradually. How quickly or how slowly the new supplants the old depends on the nature of the process and the conditions under which it occurs.

For instance, physical changes of state, such as water coming to the boil, are sudden, because a point is suddenly reached when a new thing, steam, begins to be formed: but the conversion of water into steam is a gradual process. It is the same with chemical changes. And it is the same again with qualitative changes in society. A point is reached in the working out of social contradictions where the qualitative change begins—the change from the power of one class to the power of another class, from one system of production relations to another: after that, this change may take a longer or shorter time to be completed.

Take, for example, the political aspect of social revolutions, that is, the conquest of state power. In the Russian socialist revolution this took place by a single blow—which means, comparatively quickly. In a few days all the decisive positions of power passed into the hands of the working class. In the next round of socialist revolutions—those in the present people's democracies—it took place over a longer period, by a series of steps in which first one and then another position of power was conquered. If we look back to the revolutions through which the bourgeoisie formerly won power from the feudal lords, then these took place over a longer period still—often extending over many years.

Or if we consider economic changes, these tend to be comparatively slow, taking place through a series of steps. For instance, capitalist relations, once they emerged in feudal society, extended their scope step by step over a long period. Again, the displacement of capitalism by socialism, once begun, is another gradual process, though it takes place more rapidly than the displacement of feudalism by capitalism. (It takes place more rapidly for a definite reason, namely, that socialism cannot begin to displace capitalism until after the working class has won state power, and then the power of the state operates to direct and speed up economic change. The change from feudalism to capitalism, on the other hand, generally begins long before state power passes into the hands of the capitalist class, and meanwhile the feudal state acts rather to slow down than to speed up the change.)

These examples show that there is a quantitative side to qualitative change, namely, the power and speed with which it completes itself. And naturally, under certain unfavourable circumstances it may never be completed at all. In certain cases it is possible for the change to begin, and then be turned back again and disappear.

The dialectical materialist conception of contradiction includes both the suddenness and gradualness of qualitative change. The difference between this conception of change and that of many other philosophies is not that dialectical materialism lays it down that all qualitative changes are sudden, whereas the others say they are gradual. It is that dialectical materialism understands change as coming from the struggle of opposites, from the working out of contradictions, whereas the others overlook or deny this. They suppose that change comes in a smooth way, without conflicts, or else by merely external conflicts.

Antagonism and Non-antagonism in Contradictions

The working out of contradictions always involves one side struggling with and overcoming the other. But according to the nature of the contradiction, this process may take place in different ways. And in society in particular, a distinction must be drawn between contradictions the solution of which involves the forcible suppression or destruction of one side by the other, and those whose solution does not require such methods.

The change from capitalism to socialism, for example, takes place through the forcible suppression of the capitalist class by the working class. But the ensuing change from socialism to communism does not require the forcible suppression of anyone. The former change is effected by means of a struggle between mutually antagonistic forces, whereas no such antagonisms have to be fought out to effect the latter change.

In general, social contradictions are antagonistic when they involve conflicts of economic interest. In such cases one group imposes its own interests on another, and one group suppresses another by forcible methods. But when conflicts of economic interest are not involved, there is no antagonism and therefore no need for the forcible suppression of any group by any other. Once class antagonisms are done away with in socialist society, all social questions can be settled by discussion and argument, by criticism and self-criticism, by persuasion, conviction and agreement.

Antagonism, therefore, is not the same thing as contradiction. Nor is it the same thing as the struggle of opposites within a contradiction. The struggle of opposites is a universal, necessary feature of every contradiction, and it may take an antagonistic form or it may not, depending on the particular nature of the particular contradiction.

So Lenin remarked that "antagonism and contradiction are utterly different. Under socialism antagonism disappears, but contradiction remains" (*Critical Notes on Bukharin's "Economics of the Transition Period"*).

As Mao Tse-tung put it: "Antagonism is only one form of struggle within a contradiction, but not its universal form."

The distinction between antagonism and non-antagonism in the contradictions of society is of great practical importance. There are many contradictions in society, and it is practically important to distinguish which are antagonistic and which are not, in order to find the right method of dealing with them. If a contradiction of the one kind is mistaken for a contradiction of the other kind, then wrong action is taken which cannot lead to the desired results.

For example, reformist socialists think there is no need for the working class to take power and use it to suppress the capitalist class, whereas Marxists recognise that capitalism can be ended and socialism achieved by no other method. But when socialism is established classes and class antagonisms disappear, and so methods of struggle right for the fighting out of class antagonisms are wrong for the ensuing struggle to pass from socialism to communism. Contradictions remain, but since they no longer take the form of antagonism of interest they do not require for their solution forcible measures to impose the interests of one section upon another.

The distinction between antagonism and non-antagonism in contradictions within society is a distinction between those contradictions which can work out only by the use of material force by one side against the other, and those which can work out entirely as a result of discussions among the members of society and agreed decisions taken after such discussion. Contradictions of this last kind are a special kind of contradiction which can arise only among rational human beings, and among them only when they are united in co-operation for a common interest and not divided by antagonistic interests. In such contradictions there appears the new element of the rational, purposive, consciously controlled working out of contradictions, as opposed to the blind working out of contradictions in nature—the new element of human freedom as opposed to natural necessity.

When all means of production are brought fully under planned social direction, then it may be expected that men's mastery over nature will enormously increase, and the conquest and transformation of nature by man will in turn mean profound changes in men's mode of life. For instance, ability to produce an absolute abundance of products with a minimum expenditure of labour, and abolition of the antithesis between manual and intellectual labour clearly imply profound changes in social organisation, in outlook, in habits, in mode of life generally. The effecting of such changes cannot but involve, at each stage, the overcoming of forms of social organisation, of outlooks and habits, belonging to the past. Development, therefore, will continue to take place through the disclosure of contradictions, the struggle between the new and the old. New needs and new tendencies will arise out of the existing conditions at each stage, which will come into contradiction with the existing forms of social organisation and social life, and hence lead to their passing and giving way to new forms. But there is no reason to expect that this development will take place, as hitherto, through violent conflicts and social upheavals. On the contrary, when men understand the laws of their own social organisation and have it under their own co-operative control, then it is possible to do away with old conditions and create new conditions in an agreed and planned way, without violent conflict or upheaval. Contradiction and the overcoming of the old by the new remains; but the element of antagonism and conflict between men in society disappears and gives way to the properly human method of deciding affairs—by scientific appraisal of conditions, needs and courses of action.

Chapter Ten

DEVELOPMENT AND NEGATION

The Forward Movement of Development

In many processes the working out of their contradictions results in a directed or forward movement, in which the process moves forward from stage to stage, each stage being an advance to something new, not a falling back to some stage already past.

Other processes, however, are not characterised by such a forward movement.

For instance, water when cooled or heated undergoes a qualitative change, passes into a new state (ice or steam), but the movement is without direction and cannot be called either progressive or retrogressive. If, for example, we are making tea, then we might call it a move forward to turn water into steam; if we are making iced drinks, then ice is a move forward. The fact is that ice can turn into water and water into steam, and back again, and this movement has no direction of its own. When, however, we consider such a movement as that of society, we find that it has a direction of its own: society moves forward from primitive communism to slavery, from slavery to feudalism, from feudalism to capitalism, from capitalism to communism. This is a movement with a direction, a "forward" movement.

Hegel used to think that natural processes were all of the undirected kind (like ice-water-steam-water-ice), and that a direction could only come into processes when "spirit" or "consciousness" was at work in them.

"The changes that take place in nature," he wrote in the Introduction to his *Philosophy of History*, "however infinitely various they may be, exhibit only a perpetually repeating cycle; in nature there takes place 'nothing new under the sun' . . . only in those changes which take place in the region of Spirit does anything new arise."

But the distinction does not in fact depend on any difference between "nature" and "spirit". A movement can have a direction without any consciousness being present to direct it. Spirit or consciousness itself is a product of nature; biological changes, leading up to man, have a direction; so have geological changes; so have processes in the evolution of stars; and so on. In general, direction in processes has a "natural" explanation. If some processes have direction and others have not, this depends solely on the particular character of the processes themselves and of the conditions under which they happen.

In general, since qualitative change in a process is always consequent upon quantitative change, it has a direction when those quantitative changes arise from conditions permanently operating within the process itself, and otherwise it has no direction. It has a direction when (however conditioned by external factors) it is impelled forward by internal causes. In that case the direction it takes is "its own" just because it arises from internal causes.

What, then, is the basis of direction in processes, of the internal causes of a forward movement of development? It is to be found in the existence and long-term operation in those processes of essential contradictions which work out by taking a series of specific forms. This is what gives rise to a directed series of stages, a long-term process of development in a definite direction.

Thus, for example, if social development has a direction this arises because man exists in a permanent contradictory relationship with nature. The permanent existence of this contradiction gives rise to a permanent tendency of man to improve his forces of production, and as this tendency operates so stage by stage contradictions arise between the social forces of production and the relations of production. The direction of man's social evolution is the direction of man's mastery over nature, and the movement of society takes this direction simply because of the natural conditions of human life, the impulses to change and development which people experience because of the necessity to satisfy their needs.

Similarly, if such things as stars pass through a series of evolutionary stages, this is because the contradictory conditions of their existence give rise to continuous processes, such as radiation, the continuation of which brings about a series of qualitative stages in their history.

We certainly should not say, as some philosophers have said, that throughout infinite time the infinite universe develops from stage to stage in a predetermined direction. There is no evidence for any such assertion—indeed, there is no sense in it. We cannot speak about the direction taken by everything, but only about the direction of the development of particular things in which we are interested. The directed development of things is not due to God or Spirit working in them, nor is it the manifestation of some mysterious cosmic law, but it arises and flows from the particular contradictions of particular things. Particular things are characterised by particular contradictions, as a result of which their movement takes a particular direction.

The Contradiction between Old and New, Past and Future

When there is a forward movement of development in a process, then stage by stage there occurs, as Stalin put it, "a transition from an old qualitative state to a new qualitative state", the supplanting of an old quality by a new one.

The new stage of development comes into being from the working out of the contradiction inherent in the old. And the new stage itself contains a new contradiction, since it comes into being containing something of the past from which it springs and of the future to which it leads. It has, therefore, its "negative and positive sides, a past and a future, something dying away and something developing". On this basis there once again arises within it "the struggle between the old and the new, between that which is dying away and that which is being born, between that which is disappearing and that which is developing".

Thus the forward movement of development is the continuous working out of a series of contradictions. Development continually drives forward to new development. The whole process at each stage is in essence the struggle between the old and the new, that which is dying and that which is being born.

To understand the laws of development of anything we must therefore understand its contradictions and how they work out.

A process usually contains not one but many contradictions. It is a knot of contradictions. And so to understand the course of a process we must take into account all its contradictions and understand their inter-relationship.

This generally means, first of all, that we must grasp the *basic* contradiction of a process, in its general character and in the specific form it takes at each stage. The basic contradiction is that contradiction inherent in the very nature of the process which determines its direction.

Thus in society, for instance, the basic contradiction is that between the forces of production and the relations of production, and this takes a specific form at each stage of society. In capitalist society it is the contradiction between social production and private appropriation. This basic contradiction is what determines the direction of development, namely, from capitalism to socialism—to social appropriation to match social production.

Given the basic contradiction, then a process is characterised by a number of big and small consequential contradictions, the character and effects of which are conditioned by the basic contradiction. The operation and working out of these constitutes the total process of the working out of the basic contradiction towards the emergence of a new stage of the process, a new quality.

The basic contradiction works out by the instrumentality of all the struggle arising from all the consequential contradictions. In this, however, one particular contradiction generally plays the key or *principal* rôle. In other words, of all the elements, tendencies or forces entering into various forms of struggle in a knot of contradictions, there is generally one which plays the *principal* rôle in working out the basic contradiction to its solution in the realisation of a new stage and the supplanting of an old quality by a new one.

Within any capitalist country, for example, there are many contradictions. Besides the contradiction between the working class and the capitalist class, there are other contradictions between other classes—the urban petty bourgeoisie, the peasants, the landlords, etc.—as well as contradictions within the capitalist class itself. There are also contradictions of an international kind, such as those between a given capitalist country and others, and between imperialists and colonial peoples. But within all this knot of contradictions, it is the struggle of the working class with the capitalist class which, in the given country, plays the key or principal rôle in carrying society forward from capitalism to socialism. For this is the one contradiction which can work out in such a change from the dominance of one side to that of the other as will bring about a fundamental change in the quality of the whole.

Thus, for example, the contradiction between the big capitalists and the petty bourgeoisie always takes the form of domination by the big capitalists, who keep on growing stronger in relation to the petty bourgeoisie who, for their part, keep on being pressed back and growing weaker. Hence the petty bourgeoisie cannot be the principal revolutionary force in a capitalist country, and their contradiction with the big capitalists cannot be the principal contradiction. The working class, on the other hand, grows stronger as capitalism develops, and is the force which, dominated over by the capitalists, can eventually overthrow this domination. That is why the working class is the principal revolutionary force, and why the contradiction between this class and the capitalists is the principal contradiction.

To understand the laws of development of a process, therefore, one must not only understand the basic contradiction of the process at each stage, but also what is the principal force for working out the basic contradiction and carrying the process forward to the next stage.

Mao Tse-tung pointed out that "in studying any process . . . we must do our utmost to discover its principal contradiction". This may be a complex task, since what is the principal contradiction in certain circumstances may not be so in others. "Once the principal contradiction is grasped, any problem can be readily solved," whereas if we do not grasp the principal contradiction we "cannot find the crux of a problem and naturally cannot find the method of solving contradictions".

"This is the method Marx taught us when he studied capitalist society," wrote Mao. Marx showed how in its struggle with the capitalist class the working class could find allies and take advantage of circumstances arising from all the knot of social contradictions, in order to lead society forward from capitalism to communism.

The Rôle of Negation in Development

The forward movement of development, complex as it may be in each particular case, always takes place through the struggle of the new and the old and the overcoming of the old and dying by the new and rising.

Thus in social development, in the transition from capitalism to socialism, what is new and rising in the economic life of capitalist society—social production—contradicts what is old and carried over from the past—private appropriation, and a new force arises, the working class, whose struggle against the capitalist class is a struggle for the realisation of the new stage against the defenders of the old.

This dialectical conception of development is opposed to the older liberal conception favoured by bourgeois theoreticians. The liberals recognise development and assert that progress is a universal law of nature and society. But they see it as a smooth process; and, if they have at times to recognise the existence of struggle, they see it mainly as an unfortunate interruption, more likely to impede development than to help it forward. For them, what exists has not to be supplanted by what is coming into existence, the old has not to be overcome by the new, but it has to be preserved, so that it can gradually improve itself and become a higher existence.

True to this philosophy, which they took over from the capitalists, the social democrats strove to preserve capitalism, with the idea that it could grow into socialism. And thus striving to preserve capitalism, they ended by fighting not for socialism but against it. These exponents of no struggle and class collaboration cannot avoid struggle: they simply enter into it on the other side.

Comparing the dialectical materialist, or revolutionary, conception of development with this liberal, reformist conception, we may say that the one recognises and embraces, while the other fails to recognise and shrinks from, the rôle of *negation* in development. Dialectics teaches us to understand that the new must struggle with and overcome the old, that the old must give way to and be supplanted by the new—in other words, that the old must be negated by the new.

The liberal, who thinks metaphysically, understands negation simply as saying: "No". To him negation is merely the end to something. Far from meaning advance, it means retreat; far from meaning gain, it means loss. Dialectics, on the other hand, teaches us not to be afraid of negation, but to understand how it becomes a condition of progress, a means to positive advance.

The Positive Character of Negation

"Negation in dialectics does not mean simply saying no," wrote Engels in *Anti-Dühring*.

When in the process of development the old stage is negated by the new, then, in the first place, that new stage could not have come about except as arising from and in opposition to the old. The conditions for the existence of the new arose and matured within the old. The negation is a positive advance, brought about only by the development of that which is negated. The old is not simply abolished, leaving things as though it had never existed: it is abolished only after it has itself given rise to the conditions for the new stage of advance.

In the second place, the old stage, which is negated, itself constitutes a stage of advance in the forward-moving process of development as a whole. It is negated, but the advance which took place in it is not negated. On the contrary, this advance is carried forward to the new stage, which takes into itself and carries forward all the past achievement.

For example: socialism replaces capitalism—it negates it. But the conditions for the rise and victory of socialism were born of capitalism, and socialism comes into existence as the next stage of social development after capitalism. Every achievement, every advance in the forces of production, and likewise every cultural achievement, which took place under capitalism, is not destroyed when capitalism is destroyed, but, on the contrary, is preserved and carried further.

This positive content of negation is not understood by liberals, for whom negation is "simply saying no". Moreover, they think of negation as coming only from outside, externally. Something is developing very well, and then something else comes from outside and negates it—destroys it. That is their conception. That something by its own development leads to its own negation, and thereby to a higher stage of development, lies outside their comprehension.

Thus the liberals conceive of social revolution not only as a catastrophe, as an end to ordered progress, but they believe that such a catastrophe can be brought about only by outside forces. If a revolution threatens to upset the capitalist system, that is not because of the development of the contradictions of that system itself, but is due to "agitators".

Of course, there *is* negation which takes the form simply of a blow from outside which destroys something. For instance, if I am walking along the road and am knocked down by a car, I suffer negation of a purely negative sort. Such occurrences are frequent both in nature and in society. But this is not how we must understand negation if we are to understand the *positive* rôle of negation in the process of development.

At each stage in the process of development there arises the struggle of the new with the old. The new arises and grows strong within the old conditions, and when it is strong enough it overcomes and destroys the old. This is the negation of the past stage of development, of the old qualitative state; and it means the coming into being of the new and higher stage of development, the new qualitative state.

Negation of Negation

This brings us to a further dialectical feature of development—the negation of negation.

According to the liberal idea that negation "means simply saying no", if the negation is negated then the original position is restored once more without change. According to this idea, negation is simply a negative, a taking away. Hence if the negation, the taking away, is itself negated, that merely means putting back again what was taken away. If a thief takes my watch, and then I take it away from him, we are back where we started—I have the watch again. Similarly, if I say, "It's going to be a fine day", and you say, "No, it's going to be a wet day", to which I reply, "No, it's not going to be a wet day", I have simply, by negating your negation, re-stated my original proposition.

This is enshrined in the principle of formal logic, "not not-A equals A". According to this principle, negation of negation is a fruitless proceeding. It just takes you back where you started.

Let us, however, consider a real process of development and the dialectical negation which takes place in it.

Society develops from primitive communism to the slave system. The next stage is feudalism. The next stage is capitalism. Each stage arises from the previous one, and negates it. So far we have simply a succession of stages, each following as the negation of the other and constituting a higher stage of development. But what comes next? Communism. Here there is a return to the beginning, but at a higher level of development. In place of primitive communism, based on extremely primitive forces of production, comes communism based on extremely advanced forces of production and containing within itself tremendous new potentialities of development. The old, primitive classless society has become the new and higher classless society. It has been raised, as it were, to a higher power, has reappeared on a higher level. But this has happened only because the old classless society was negated by the appearance of classes and the development of class society, and because finally class society, when it had gone through its whole development, was itself negated by the working class taking power, ending exploitation of man by man, and establishing a new classless society on the foundation of all the achievements of the whole previous development.

This is the negation of negation. But it does not take us back to the original starting point. It takes us forward to a new starting point, which is the original one raised, through its negation and the negation of the negation, to a higher level.

Thus we see that in the course of development, as a result of a double negation, a later stage can repeat an earlier stage, but repeat it on a higher level of development.

The importance of this conception of negation of negation does not lie in its supposedly expressing the necessary pattern of all development. All development takes place through the working out of contradictions—that is a necessary universal law; but specific contradictions do not necessarily work out in such a way that an earlier stage of development is repeated at a later stage—sometimes that may happen and sometimes not, depending on the specific character of the processes of development.

Yet the repetition of an earlier stage *is* a notable feature of some processes of development and, moreover, to bring it about is often an important aim of practice. The importance of the conception of negation of negation lies in what it says about the conditions for such repetition. If features of an earlier stage are to be repeated at a later stage, that cannot take place by a simple return to the earlier stage—for that stage is past and cannot come back. It can only take place by their being reproduced at a later stage, in which case they are inevitably changed and modified in accordance with the character of that later stage. Thus features of the past can reappear in the future only as changed and transformed by the process of negation of negation and not by a simple return to the past.

This principle, like other principles of dialectics, has a quality of obviousness which is often overlooked. It is an obvious truth—but it is overlooked by all those who express a hankering to return to the past. Such hankerings must always be vain. It is in practice vitally important to realise that what is past *cannot* be restored when forward development is in operation. Nevertheless some features of the past may be restored, but only by carrying forward the process of development to a new stage, in which those features reappear in new ways—"on a higher level", as a negation of negation, enriched and transformed as a result of the first negation.

We have already seen how the negation of negation occurs in history in the development from primitive communism to communism. The second appearance of communism is only possible after going through the whole development of class-society—the first negation; and it embodies all that has been achieved during that development.

Again, in the history of thought, the "primitive, natural materialism" of the earliest philosophers was negated by philosophical idealism, and modern materialism arises only as the negation of that negation.

> "This modern materialism," wrote Engels in *Anti-Dühring*, "is not the mere re-establishment of the old, but adds to the permanent foundations of this old materialism the whole thought content of two thousand years of development of philosophy and natural science."

The practical importance of the negation of the negation can be seen most clearly if we take the example of the development of individual property, where it again occurs.

Marx, in the first volume of *Capital*, pointed out that the pre-capitalist "individual private property founded on the labours of the proprietor" is negated—destroyed—by capitalist private property. For capitalist private property arises only on the ruin and expropriation of the pre-capitalist individual producers. The individual producer used to own his instruments of production and his product—both were taken away from him by the capitalists. But when capitalist private property is itself negated—when "the expropriators are expropriated"—then the individual property of the producers is restored once more, but in a new form, on a higher level.

> "This does not re-establish private property for the producer, but gives him individual property based on the acquisitions of the capitalist era, i.e. on co-operation and the possession in common of the land and means of production."

The producer, as a participant in socialised production, then enjoys, as his individual property, a share of the social product—"according to his work" in the first stage of communist society, and "according to his needs" in the fully developed communist society.

When capitalism arose, the *only* way forward was through this negation of negation. Some of the British Chartists put forward in their land policy demands aimed at arresting the new capitalist process and restoring the *old* individual private property of the producer. This was vain. The only road forward for the producers was by the struggle against capitalism and for socialism—not to restore the *old* individual property which capitalism had destroyed, but to destroy capitalism and so re-create individual property on a *new*, socialist basis.

Similarly the Russian Narodniki, against whom Lenin fought in the 1890s, wanted somehow to arrest the process of capitalist development and restore the old peasant communes. Lenin's fight against them was based on showing that this was impossible.

The principle of negation of negation is thus an expression of the simple truth that one cannot put the clock back and reconstitute the past. One can only move forward into the future through the working out of all the contradictions contained within the given stage of development and through the negations consequent on them.

Chapter Eleven

A SCIENTIFIC WORLD OUTLOOK

Science and Materialism

Dialectical materialism, the world outlook of the Marxist-Leninist Party, is a truly scientific world outlook. For it is based on considering things as they are, without arbitrary, preconceived assumptions (idealist fantasies); it insists that our conceptions of things must be based on actual investigation and experience, and must be constantly tested and re-tested in the light of practice and further experience.

Indeed, "dialectical materialism" means: understanding things just as they are ("materialism"), in their actual interconnection and movement ("dialectics").

The same cannot be said about other philosophies. They all make arbitrary assumptions of one kind or another, and try to erect a "system" on the basis of those assumptions. But such assumptions are arbitrary only in appearance; in fact they express the various prejudices and illusions of definite classes.

Dialectical materialism is in no sense a philosophy "above science".

Others have set philosophy "above science", in the sense that they have thought they could discover what the world was like just by thinking about it, without relying on the data of the sciences, on practice and experience. And then, from this lofty standpoint, they have tried to dictate to the scientists, to tell them where they were wrong, what their discoveries "really meant" and so on.

But Marxism makes an end of the old philosophy which claimed to stand above science and to explain "the world as a whole".

"Modern materialism . . . no longer needs any philosophy standing above the sciences," wrote Engels in *Anti-Dühring*. "As soon as each separate science is required to get clarity as to its position in the great totality of things and of our knowledge of things a special science dealing with this totality is superfluous."

Dialectical materialism, he further wrote:

"is in fact no longer a philosophy, but a simple conception of the world which has to establish its validity and be applied not in a science of sciences standing apart, but within the positive sciences. . . . Philosophy is therefore . . . both abolished and preserved; abolished as regards its form, and preserved as regards its real content."

Our picture of the world about us, of nature, of natural objects and processes, their interconnections and laws of motion, is not to be derived from philosophical speculation, but from the investigations of the natural sciences.

The scientific picture of the world and its development is not complete, and never will be. But it has advanced far enough for us to realise that philosophical speculation is superfluous. And we should refuse to fill in gaps in scientific knowledge by speculation.

The growing picture of the world which natural science unfolds is a materialist picture—despite the many efforts of philosophers to make out the contrary. For step by step as science advances it shows how the rich variety of things and processes and changes to be found in the real world can be explained and understood in terms of material causes, without bringing in God or spirit or any supernatural agency.

Every advance of science is an advance of materialism against idealism, a conquest for materialism—although when driven out of one position idealism has always taken up another position and manifested itself again in new forms, so that in the past the sciences have never been consistently materialist.

For every advance of science means showing the order and development of the material world "from the material world itself".

Science and Socialism

The scientific character of Marxism is manifested especially in this, that it makes *socialism* into a science.

We do not base our socialism, as the utopians did, on a conception of abstract human nature. The utopians worked out schemes for an ideal society, but could not show how to achieve socialism in practice. Marxism made socialism into a science by basing it on an analysis of the actual movement of history, of the economic law of motion of capitalist society in particular, thus showing how socialism arises as the necessary next stage in the evolution of society, and how it can come about only by the waging of the working-class struggle, through the defeat of the capitalist class and the institution of the dictatorship of the proletariat.

Thus Marxism treats man himself, society and history, scientifically.

> "Socialism, since it has become a science, demands that it be pursued as a science," wrote Engels in his *Prefatory Note to "Peasant War in Germany"*, "that is, that it be studied. The task will be to spread with increased zeal among the masses of the workers the ever more clarified understanding thus acquired, to knit together ever more firmly the organisation both of the party and of the trade unions."

Scientific study of society shows that human history develops from stage to stage according to definite laws. Men themselves are the active force in this development. By understanding the laws of development of society, therefore, we can guide our own struggles and create our own socialist future.

Thus scientific socialism is the greatest and most important of all the sciences.

The practitioners of the natural sciences have been getting

worried because they feel that governments do not know how to put their discoveries to proper use. They have good cause to worry about this. Science is discovering the secrets of nuclear energy, for example; but its discoveries are being used to create weapons of destruction. Many people are even coming to believe that it would be better if we had no science, since its discoveries open up such terrifying possibilities of disaster.

How can we ensure that the discoveries of science are put to proper use for the benefit of mankind? It is scientific socialism, Marxism-Leninism, alone which answers this problem. It teaches us what are the forces which make history and thereby shows us how we can make our own history today, change society and determine our own future. It teaches us, therefore, how to develop the sciences in the service of mankind, how to carry them forward in today's crisis. Physics can teach us how to release nuclear energy, it cannot teach us how to control the social use of that energy. For this there is required, not the science of the atom, but the science of society.

Conclusions

We have now briefly surveyed the principal features of the Marxist materialist conception of the world and of the Marxist dialectical method. What conclusions can we draw at this stage?

(1) The world outlook of dialectical materialism is a consistent and reasoned outlook, which derives its strength from the fact that it arises directly from the attempt to solve the outstanding problems of our time.

The epoch of capitalism is an epoch of stormy development in society. It is marked by revolutionary advances of the forces of production and of scientific discovery, and by consequent uninterrupted disturbance of all social conditions. This sets one theoretical task above all, and that is to arrive at an adequate conception of the laws of change and development in nature and society.

To this theoretical task dialectical materialism addresses itself.

(2) This is not the task of working out a philosophical

system, in the old sense. What is required is not any system of ideas spun out of the heads of philosophers, which we can then admire and contemplate as a system of "absolute truth".

Capitalist society is a society rent with contradictions, and the more it has developed the more menacing and intolerable for the working people have the consequences of these contradictions become. The new powers of production are not utilised for the benefit of society as a whole but for the profit of an exploiting minority. Instead of leading to universal plenty, the growth of the powers of production leads to recurrent economic crises, to unemployment, to poverty and to hideously destructive wars.

Therefore the philosophical problem of arriving at a true conception of the laws of change and development in nature and society becomes, for the working people, a practical political problem of finding how to change society, so that the vast new forces of production can be used in the service of humanity. For the first time in history the possibility of a full and rich life for everyone exists. The task is to find how to make that possibility a reality.

It is to the solution of this practical task that the theory of dialectical materialism is devoted.

(3) Addressing itself to this task, dialectical materialism is and can only be a partisan philosophy, the philosophy of a party, namely, of the party of the working class, whose object is to lead the millions of working people to the socialist revolution and the building of communist society.

(4) Dialectical materialism cannot but stand out in sharp contrast to the various contemporary schools of bourgeois philosophy.

What have these various schools of philosophy to offer at the present time? Systems and arguments by the bucketful—most of them neither original nor cogent, if one takes the trouble to analyse them closely. But no solution to the problems pressing upon the people of the capitalist countries and the colonies. How to end poverty? How to end war? How to utilise production for the benefit of all? How to end the oppression of one nation by another? How to end the exploitation of man by man? How to establish the brotherhood of men? These are our problems. We must judge philosophies by whether or not they show how to solve them. By that criterion, the philosophical schools of capitalism must one and all be judged—"weighed in the balance and found wanting".

The prevailing bourgeois philosophies, with all their differences, have in common a retreat from the great positive ideas which inspired progressive movements in the past. True, there remain within the ranks of bourgeois philosophy those who continue, according to their lights, trying to preserve and carry forward some of these positive ideas. For they are ideas which cannot by any manner of means be extinguished. But the prevailing philosophies emphasize men's helplessness and limitations; they speak of a mysterious universe; and they counsel either trust in God or else hopeless resignation to fate or blind chance. Why is this? It is because all these philosophies are rooted in acceptance of capitalism and cannot see beyond capitalism. From start to finish they reflect the insoluble crisis of the capitalist world.

(5) Dialectical materialism asks to be judged and will be judged by whether it serves as an effective instrument to show the way out of capitalist crisis and war, to show the way for the working people to win and wield political power, to show the way to build a socialist society in which there is no more exploitation of man by man and in which men win increasing mastery over nature.

Dialectical materialism is a philosophy of practice, indissolubly united with the practice of the struggle for socialism.

It is the philosophy born out of the great movement of our times—the movement of the people who labour, who "create all the good things of life and feed and clothe the world", to rise at last to their full stature. It is wholly, entirely dedicated to the service of that movement. This is the source of all its teachings, and in that service its conclusions are continually tried, tested and developed. Without such a philosophy, the movement cannot achieve consciousness of itself and of its tasks, cannot achieve unity, cannot win its battles.

Since the greatest task facing us is that of ending capitalist society and building socialism, it follows that the chief problem to which dialectical materialism addresses itself, and on the solution of which the whole philosophy of dialectical materialism turns, is the problem of understanding the forces of development of society. The chief problem is to reach such an understanding of society, of men's social activity and of the development of human consciousness, as will show us how to achieve and build the new socialist society and the new socialist consciousness. The materialist conception and dialectical method with which we have been concerned in this volume are applied to this task in the materialist conception of history.

READING LIST

The following are the principal original works setting forth the philosophy of dialectical materialism. Those marked with an asterisk are the best for beginners.

MARX AND ENGELS:
The German Ideology, Part I

ENGELS:
*Socialism, Utopian and Scientific**
*Ludwig Feuerbach**
Anti-Dühring
The Dialectics of Nature

LENIN:
*The Teachings of Karl Marx**
Materialism and Empirio-Criticism
Philosophical Notebooks

STALIN:
*Dialectical and Historical Materialism**
Anarchism or Socialism?

MAO:
On Contradiction

VOLUME II

HISTORICAL MATERIALISM

PREFACE TO THE SECOND EDITION

This volume has been so much revised and changed in this new edition as to be virtually a new book. These extensive changes have been made in the attempt to eradicate any kind of dogmatism, and to bring theory into closer accord with practice and with the actual course of events.

The second chapter is in part based on an article on "Marxism as Science" which appeared in *Marxism Today*, April, 1960.

M. C.

London,

May, 1962

Chapter One

SCIENTIFIC SOCIALISM

Capitalism and Socialism

The idea of socialism arose and gripped men's minds in modern society because of discontent with the evils of capitalism, and the perception that only by a radical transformation of the entire economic basis of society could these evils be done away with.

In capitalist society the means of production—the land, factories, mills, mines, transport—belong to the capitalists, and production is carried on for capitalist profit. But the essence of socialism is that the means of production become social property, and that, on the basis of social ownership, production is carried on for the benefit of the whole of society.

From its very beginning, capitalism meant a previously undreamed of increase in the powers of producing wealth. But this wealth went to swell the profits of a few, while the mass of the working people were condemned to toil and poverty. To use the new powers of producing wealth, not to enrich a few but to enrich the whole of society, is the aim of socialism.

Great new productive forces have been created in modern society as witness the discoveries of science and the growth of industry. But it becomes ever more evident that the capitalist owners and managers cannot direct the development and use of these forces for the benefit of the majority of the people.

Today the means exist, in modern technique and science, to feed and clothe the whole world; to provide education, culture, opportunity for everyone; to provide all with a high standard of living. If all the discoveries at our disposal were used, and if supplies were directed where they are most needed, this could undoubtedly be done. Nuclear energy can provide almost unlimited power, automation can lighten labour and turn out goods in profusion, medical science can relieve or stamp out diseases, the biological and agricultural sciences can ensure enough food for a bigger population than the world at present supports. Instead, resources both human and technical remain unemployed. For if all this were done, where would be the profit for the great capitalist monopolies? Meantime, while people still suffer and die from shortages, vast resources are squandered on weapons of destruction. People have even come to fear new knowledge and higher techniques, because they fear that the result of higher techniques may only be crisis and unemployment, and that the result of more knowledge may only be the invention of even more fearful weapons of destruction. The profit system has converted men's highest achievements into threats to their livelihood and very existence. This is the final sign that that system has outlived its time and must be replaced by another.

Socialism means that the vast resources of modern technique are developed and used to meet the needs of the people. Production is not carried on for profit but to satisfy the material and cultural requirements of society. And this is ensured because the means of production, all the means of creating wealth, are taken out of the control of a capitalist minority, whose concern is its own profit, and come under the control of the working people themselves.

Socialist Theory and the Working-Class Movement

But in order to achieve socialism, we need something more than a general idea of socialism as a better order of society than capitalism. We need to understand what social forces must be organised and what opponents they will have to defeat.

The first conceptions of socialism were utopian. The first socialists had the vision of a better order of society, gave it form and colour, and proclaimed it far and wide. But it remained merely a vision. They could not say how to realise it in practice.

The utopians criticised the capitalist order of society as unreasonable and unjust. For them, socialism was based simply on reason and justice; and because they considered that the light of reason belonged equally to all men, they appealed to everyone—and first of all to the rulers of society, as being the best educated and most influential—to embrace the truth of socialism and put it into practice.

They contributed the first exposure and condemnation of capitalism, and the first vision of socialism—a society based on common ownership of the means of production—as the alternative to capitalism. But this vision was spun out of the heads of reformers. The utopians could not show the way to achieve socialism, because they had no conception of the laws of social change and could not point to the real social force capable of creating a new society.

That force is the working class. The capitalist class is bound to resist socialism, because the end of the profit system means the end of the capitalist class. For the working class, on the other hand, socialism means its emancipation from exploitation. Socialism means the end of poverty and insecurity. It means that workers work for themselves and not for the profit of others.

The achievement of socialism depends on the mobilisation of the working class in the fight for socialism, and on its overpowering the resistance of the capitalist class. And in this struggle the working class must seek to unite with itself all those sections—and together they constitute the majority of society—who in one way or another are fleeced by the greed for profits of the ruling capitalist minority.

But more than that. If socialism is to be won, if working-class emancipation from capitalism is to be achieved, then the working-class movement must become conscious of its socialist aim. But this consciousness does not spontaneously arise of itself. It requires the scientific working out of socialist theory, the introduction of this theory into the working-class movement, and the fight for it inside that movement.

The very conditions of life of the workers lead them to combine to defend their standards of life from capitalist attack, and to improve them. But the trade union struggle to defend and improve working-class standards does not get rid of capitalism. On the contrary, so long as working-class struggle is limited to such purely economic aims, its utmost stretch is to gain concessions from capitalism while continuing to accept the existence of the system. And the movement can pass beyond this phase of fighting for no more than reforms within capitalism only when it equips itself with socialist theory. Only then can it become conscious of its long-term aim of getting rid of capitalism altogether, and work out the strategy and tactics of the class struggle for achieving this aim.

In the history of the working-class movement there have been many leaders concerned with nothing beyond winning concessions from capitalism. They have in effect sought merely temporary gains for different sections of the working class at the expense of the long-term interests of the whole class. This is known as "opportunism". And the root of opportunism in the working-class movement consists in accepting the spontaneous struggle for concessions and reforms as the be-all and end-all of the movement.

If socialism is to be achieved, the working-class movement must not rely only on the spontaneous development of the mass struggle for better conditions. It must equip itself with socialist theory, with the scientific understanding of capitalism and of the position of the different classes under capitalism, with the scientific understanding that emancipation can be achieved only by uniting all forces for the overthrow of capitalism and the establishment of socialism.

Without the guiding and organising force of scientific socialist theory, the working class cannot win victory over capitalism. The union of socialist theory with the mass working-class movement is a condition for the advance from capitalism to socialism.

The Marxist Science of Society

The great contribution of Marxism was to develop scientific socialist theory and to introduce it into the working-class movement.

Marx and Engels based socialism on a scientific understanding of the laws of development of society and of the class struggle. And so they were able to show how socialism could be won, and to arm the working class with knowledge of its historical mission.

Marx did not arrive at his conclusions as a pure research worker, though he did conduct profound research. In the 1840's Marx was engaged as a revolutionary republican and democrat in the movement which led up to the revolutionary year 1848. And he arrived at his conclusions as an active politician, striving to understand the movement in which he participated in order to help guide it to the goal of the people's emancipation from oppression, superstition and exploitation.

These conclusions were formulated in *The Manifesto of the Communist Party* which Marx wrote, in collaboration with Engels, in 1848.

They saw the whole social movement as a struggle between classes; they saw the contending classes themselves as products of the economic development of society; they saw politics as the reflection of the economic movement and of the class struggle; they saw that the bourgeois revolution then in progress, the task of which was to remove the vestiges of feudal rule and establish democracy, was preparing the way for the proletarian, socialist revolution; and they saw that this revolution could only be consummated by the working class conquering political power.

It was only because they espoused the cause of the working class and saw in it the new, rising, revolutionising force in history, that Marx and Engels were able to discover the laws of social change, which those who adopted the standpoint of the exploiting classes could never do.

"Certain historical facts occurred which led to a decisive change in the conception of history," wrote Engels in *Socialism, Utopian and Scientific*. "In 1831 the first working-class rising had taken place at Lyons; between 1838 and 1848 the first national workers' movement, that of the English Chartists, reached its height. The class struggle between proletariat and bourgeoisie came to the front. . . . But the old idealist conception of history . . . knew nothing of class struggle based on material interests, in fact knew nothing at all of material interests. . . . The new facts made imperative a new examination of all past history."

From this new situation, Engels continued, it became clear: "that all past history was the history of class struggles; that these warring classes are always the product of conditions of production and exchange, in a word, of the economic conditions of their time; that therefore the economic structure of society always forms the real basis from which, in the last analysis, is always to be explained the whole superstructure of legal and political institutions, as well as of the religious, philosophical and other conceptions of each historical period."

From the recognition of the significance of the class struggle in capitalist society came the realisation that the class struggle was likewise waged in previous epochs and that, in fact, the whole of past history since the break-up of the primitive communes was the history of class struggles.

But on what was the class struggle based? On the clash of the material interests of the different classes. Realising this, the key to historical development as a whole had to be sought in the sphere of these material interests. The different classes with their different interests were seen to be "the product of the conditions of production and exchange", of the economic conditions prevailing in society.

Marx, in *Wage-Labour and Capital*, pointed out that "in production men not only act on nature but also on one another. They produce only by co-operating in a certain way and mutually exchanging their activities. In order to produce, they enter into definite connections and relations with one another, and only within these social connections and relations does their action on nature, does production, take place."

Marx and Engels discovered the key to understanding the whole development of society in the investigation of these production relations, i.e., the economic conditions of production and exchange, and of the struggle between classes produced by these economic conditions.

Thus understanding the laws of historical development,

Marx and Engels showed that socialism was not a utopian dream but the necessary outcome of the development of capitalist society and of the working-class struggle against capitalism. They taught the working class to be conscious of its own strength and of its own class interests, and to unite for a determined struggle against the capitalist class, rallying around itself all the forces discontented with capitalism. They showed that it was impossible to get rid of capitalism and establish socialism unless the working class won political power, deprived the capitalist class of all power and stamped out its resistance. And they showed that in order to emerge from the old world and create a new, classless society, the working class must have its own party, which they called the Communist Party.

Chapter Two

MATERIALISM AND THE SCIENCE OF SOCIETY

The Materialist Conception of History

The general theory of the motive forces and laws of social change, developed on the basis of Marx's discoveries, is known as the materialist conception of history, or historical materialism. It was arrived at by applying the materialist world outlook to the solution of social problems. And because he made this application, materialism was with Marx no longer simply a theory aimed at interpreting the world, but a guide to the practice of changing the world, of building a society without exploitation of man by man.

Above all, historical materialism has a contemporary significance. It is applicable here and now. It leads to conclusions not only about the causes of past events but about the causes of events now taking place, and therefore about what to do, about what policy to fight for, in order to satisfy the real needs of the people.

When modern industry was created there were created the means to produce enough to satisfy fully the needs of every human being, and therefore to realise the age-old dream of universal plenty. The means exist to do it; and the materialist conception of history, by explaining how social relations change and how modern industry came about, shows how it can be done.

It is precisely in this contemporary application that historical materialism demonstrates its scientific character. For the final test of social science, as of all other science, is in its practical application. If historical materialism makes history into a science, this is because it is not only a theory about how to interpret history but also a theory about how to make history, and therefore the basis for the practical policy of the revolutionary class which is making history today.

Social Relations and the Laws of Social Development

Materialism means explaining what takes place in the material world from the material world itself. The materialist approach to explaining processes of nature means investigating those processes themselves in order to discover their laws of operation. And because human affairs are part of the material world, the materialist approach to explaining social events means likewise investigating social processes in order to discover their laws of operation.

Such investigation must be empirical and scientific. It is not a question of deducing anything about society from the general philosophical principles of materialism, but of applying the normal methods of science—the framing and testing of theories or hypotheses—to the study of society. This is the foundation on which the theory of historical materialism rests. As Engels put it in his speech at Marx's graveside: "Just as Darwin discovered the law of development of organic nature, so Marx discovered the law of development of human history." It is a discovery of science, made and verified by applying scientific methods differing not at all from those applied with equal success in other branches of science.

In the opening pages of *The German Ideology* Marx and Engels remarked that "the first premise of all human history is the existence of living human individuals. Thus the first fact to be established is the physical organisation of these individuals and their consequent relation to the rest of nature". But the subject matter of social science is not the physiology and psychology of human individuals, their individual activities and reactions. That is taken for granted. Human individuals create and sustain society and the typical products of society by entering into social relations with one another; and it is these social relations which are the subject matter of social science.

In the last analysis, when we say that certain social relations have been formed and certain social phenomena produced, we are referring to what numbers of unspecified human individuals do in association. For instance, if we speak of commodity production we are referring to how they organise their productive activity and distribute its products; if we say that a certain idea has arisen, we are referring to how they speak and act; if we say that certain institutions have been set up, we are referring to how they regulate their affairs. Social science abstracts from the individuals and deals with the social relations. It is not concerned with individual but with aggregate humanity.

Of course, some individuals do occupy a special individual position within social relations. For many social relations depend on placing individuals in special positions—kings, chairmen of boards, presidents, popes and archbishops, leaders of movements, and so on. The individual decisions and actions of those individuals may have wide social repercussions. The character and extent of these must depend, however, upon the social relations within which they are acting. The key problems which social science has to unravel are not problems of the actions and motivations of individuals but problems of the interdependence of social relations. Social relations change and develop. The problem of how such change and development is brought about and of the laws which govern it—the main problem of the scientific understanding of society and its history—is the problem of analysing and sorting out the interdependence of social relations. What are called "laws" regulating society and its development are simply generalised statements of such interdependence.

For instance, what is the famous "law of supply and demand" in economics but a statement of the dependence of the terms of sale upon the relations of sellers and buyers? The sellers bring certain goods to market and the buyers come there with certain requirements and means of paying: that is a social relation between people as sellers and buyers. When the sale is effected and money changes hands, that is also a social relation. The "law of supply and demand" states the dependence of the latter relationship on the former. It is entirely and exclusively concerned with the interdependence of certain social relations.

No one would deny that *some* social relations are regulated by laws. In particular, when products are produced as commodities economic laws are discoverable regulating their production and exchange. But it has been and still is strenuously denied that there are invariable laws of social development operating throughout human history, in terms of which we can explain how and why social development in general takes place.

In support of this denial it is argued that because each event in human history is unique, and exactly the same circumstances are never repeated, therefore there is no basis for the discovery of invariable laws governing social changes. We can speak, for instance, of the laws of mechanics governing the motions of bodies, because the same mechanical interaction is repeated over and over again; but not so with the events of human history.

This argument rests on an obvious confusion. Of course every event, whether in nature or society, is unique. But in society, as in nature, the same *kind* of event—for instance, a revolution—is often repeated; and *variants* of the same social relations are repeated over and over again. All the conditions are present, therefore, for the discovery of laws. Despite all the manifold changes of society there are certain general relations which are always present in varying forms, because these are basic relations without which no society at all can exist; and from the study of such relations general laws always applicable to the development of any society emerge.

The Foundations of Social Science

It is evident that social relations cannot, like many relations in nature, be studied experimentally. The social scientist cannot set up social relations experimentally in order to discover how they operate; nor can he experimentally separate some social relations from others, for purposes of study. He is himself a member of society, and has to take it as he finds it, in all its baffling complexity. Marx remarked on this difficulty in the

Preface to *Capital*, where he contrasted the investigation of social changes with that of, say, chemical changes. In social analysis, he wrote, "neither microscopes nor chemical reagents are of use. The force of abstraction must replace both". That is to say, where it is not possible to separate certain relations experimentally, they must be separated in the mind of the investigator.

Marx's discovery of the fundamental laws of social development was reached by asking whether any relations can be distinguished which must always be present in any form of society, because they are the condition for any form of social life whatever. Once such relations are abstracted, then hypotheses can be put forward about their interdependencies and these can be checked against the actual social record. The whole development of society is then explained as regulated by the laws of interdependence so formulated. Such was Marx's method.

When the key question is asked the answer becomes strikingly obvious. The necessary condition for any society is that men should associate to produce their material means of subsistence. Without this collective action of men on nature there is no human life, it constitutes the very essential of the human mode of life. The process of social production is, therefore, the primary process of all social life. It is "primary" in this precise sense: that social life begins with it, that it is present continuously throughout all social life, and that no other social activity or social relation can occur unless this primary activity, this primary social relation, sustains it.

From this beginning, Marx went on to frame a general hypothesis, consisting of several interconnected propositions, which together may be said to constitute a general law of social development. The theory will be stated here only in barest outline; it will be reviewed in more detail, and its more important consequences discussed, in the ensuing chapters.

(1) In order to carry on production people must enter into relations of production. These are concerned with property in means of production, and with the mode of distribution of the product, and in their totality they define the economic

structure of society.

(2) People enter into relations of production, and so associate in an economic organisation, independent of any conscious decision but corresponding to the character of their productive forces. That is to say, people who depend for their subsistence on certain production techniques evolve property relations—and eventually class relations—appropriate to those techniques. For instance, a primitive hunting tribe will live the social life of primitive communism. When animals are domesticated, the herds will tend to become the property of particular families within the community. When power-driven machinery is first introduced, it is as the property of capitalists who employ wage-labour. And so on.

(3) Social institutions, and with them prevailing systems of ideas, will then arise corresponding to the economic structure of society. They will be such as to serve the carrying on of the prevailing mode of production. For instance, a primitive tribe could hardly possess a legislative assembly, or a standing army and police force, or universities; on the other hand, such institutions are required for carrying on a modern capitalist society. Only when a certain economic basis exists do such institutions, with their corresponding ideologies, arise.

These three propositions make up the key to explaining how social development proceeds and how the various historical features of society arise and change. Corresponding to certain forces of production certain relations of production come into being. Within these production relations new forces of production eventually develop. Then the situation arises when, in Marx's words, the old production relations begin to act as "fetters" upon the further development of production. The relations of production have then to be changed, and the whole "superstructure" of ideas and institutions is changed with them.

The theory thus postulates a law of interdependence between production, the relations of production, and the social superstructure of institutions and ideas. And it is a hypothesis which can be checked against the known facts and is verified by them. Indeed, it is hard to imagine how anything different could arise in society. Could production relations arise which were inappropriate to the given forces of production? Or when they become fetters on production, would it be possible to avoid a struggle for new production relations? Again, could a society survive, the institutions of which failed to serve its basic economic processes? Could such institutions possibly be formed? And when such institutions grow outmoded, would it be possible to avoid a struggle to change them? If we ask such questions as these the laws formulated by Marx begin to have the same obvious and compelling look as, for instance, the laws of thermodynamics. One might as well ask whether a physical system could create energy from nothing. If an engine were built which ran without fuel, or could do more work without more fuel, that would falsify the laws of thermodynamics. And if a society were created which kept going without production, or in which economic structure was not adapted to production and social superstructure to economic basis, that would falsify historical materialism. But there is no such engine, and no such society. Such fundamental laws of science are always verified by all the relevant facts, and no instances which would falsify them are ever to be found.

Historical materialism supplies a foundation for social science in much the same way as the theory of evolution by natural selection supplies a foundation for biological science. Whatever species may be considered, it evolved by natural selection and that conditions its entire character. Similarly, whatever society may be considered, it came to be what it is by adaptation of production relations to production, and of ideas and institutions to production relations.

Indeed, Darwin arrived at the theory of natural selection by very much the same "method of abstraction" as Marx—more or less simultaneously—employed in the theory of historical materialism. Darwin's theory grew from the fundamental consideration that every species lives by adaptation to an environment, just as Marx's theory grew from the consideration that every society lives by a mode of production. But this same type of abstraction is employed in *all* fundamental scientific theory. Newton, for example, employed it in arriving at his formulation of the laws of motion: the condition of existence of any body at any instant is that it has a certain motion of its own and is acted on by external forces. Marx employed it a second time in his special investigation, in *Capital*, of commodity production. He began that investigation with the consideration that the one thing all commodities have in common is that they are products of human labour, and that therefore what people are doing when they exchange commodities is to exchange the products of definite quantities of socially-necessary labour-time.

General Laws and Particular Events

All fundamental scientific theory is very general in character and, consequently, very flexible. It can show the same general connections holding in circumstances so widely different that there appear to be no such connections. It can explain the operations of a large variety of particular causes, and recognise in particular instances the operation of particular causes which could not have been forecast in terms of the general laws alone.

Historical materialism shares this breadth and flexibility. Just as Darwinism can account for many odd features of species in terms of particular causes operating within the general process of natural selection, so Marxism can account for the most varied social phenomena in terms of particular causes operating within the general process of adaptation of relations of production to production. It is no objection to the theory to say that it is incapable of predicting such particular causes. The point is that it is capable of explaining them and their effects within the general process of social evolution.

For example, in the development of English society under the Tudors it so happened that a particular quarrel arose between Henry VIII and the Pope, because Henry wanted to divorce his wife and the Pope refused permission. Henry broke with the Pope, and this gave him an excuse to confiscate the Church lands and divide them amongst his cronies—an action which had very far-reaching economic and political consequences. There is no law of social development in accordance with which Henry was bound to become dissatisfied with his wife and quarrel with the Pope about it. On the contrary, these particular events which had such large effects arose from particular causes which could not be deduced from any general laws and were relatively accidental. But the fact that Henry was able to take advantage of these events, that he could get away with the confiscation of Church lands, and that these actions brought about changes within class relations—all that is explicable only through the contradictory social relations which had come into being at that particular period. Moreover, in other places where similar social contradictions existed similar economic and political changes were effected. Other European monarchs, who had no trouble with their wives, were making the same break with the Church and its institutions, as a result of the same deep-seated and general causes, though the individual circumstances and causes varied greatly in different cases.

The laws which regulate the development of social relations operate through the relatively accidental circumstances and actions of the individuals who live within those social relations. But the laws are not some kind of "fate" externally imposed upon human individuals. It is the very life-process of the individuals—the fact that they are human—which leads to their entering into relations which exhibit those laws. Just as the attractions and repulsions of the elements of a physical system lead to their entering into various combinations, so the dependence of human individuals one upon another, and of all on their joint action on nature, leads to their entering into social relations and to the development of those social relations.

Thus human society develops through a succession of relatively accidental events, all of which can be traced to their particular causes and have their particular effects, and which in their totality present a law-governed process of the development of social relations.

Human Intentions and Objective Law

Society consists of human beings, and there is therefore an essential distinction between social processes and natural processes. "In nature there are only blind, unconscious agencies acting upon one another," wrote Engels in *Ludwig Feuerbach* (chap. 4). "In the history of society, on the other hand, the actors are all endowed with consciousness, are men acting with deliberation or passion, working towards definite goals; nothing happens without a conscious purpose, without an intended aim."

Social effects are brought about by the conscious, intentional activity of human beings, who choose what they will do. And this circumstance has sometimes been held to be incompatible with the view that social development is regulated by objective laws. If, it is argued, social development depends upon human intelligence, choice and will, it cannot be regulated by laws. Yet the conclusion does not follow. For the fact that people change their social relations by their own voluntary actions does not imply that in these changes there are no general laws of the interdependence of social relations. On the contrary, whenever people enter into certain relations this fact influences other of their relations; within the totality of changing social relations there are laws of interdependence, and people cannot establish or change their relations just as they like.

When we consider people's desires and intentions, in their social context, we should ask: what influences their intentions and their choices, and what determines the outcome of their intentional actions? For people do not set aims before themselves regardless of their circumstances; and when people choose what to do and act with certain intentions the results of their actions are often not what they intended. Clearly, therefore, it is not possible to explain the actual development of society simply from the intentions in the minds of the members of society.

The ideas in men's minds, the aims they set themselves, and the emotions they feel, arise in response to their material conditions of existence, which include relationship with nature and relationship with one another in society. The forces bringing about social change are not "ideas" or "aims" in the abstract, nor abstract individuals each of whom decides independently what he will do, but, as Marx and Engels put it in *The German Ideology*, "real, active men, as they are conditioned by a definite development of their productive forces and of the intercourse corresponding to these"; and they form their ideas and aims "on the basis of their real life-process". It is the necessary condition of any human life that people should produce their means of subsistence, and that they should enter into production relations corresponding with their productive forces. This happens independent of anyone's idea or intention or choice. But possessing certain productive forces and living within certain production relations, people then form their ideas and intentions corresponding to these real-life conditions in which they find themselves.

From these conditions arise definite interests, contradictions of interest, aims and ambitions. Ideas, passions, plans and intentions arise in the minds of individuals accordingly, in response to those conditions of life. And so social life proceeds.

In a primitive hunting tribe, for instance, it is natural that the people's plans should be mostly confined to hunting, and that the height of any individual's ambition should be to become a chief. If, perhaps through some change of environment, they get an interest in cultivation or domestication of animals, then other plans, other ambitions arise. The people keep their society going by their own initiative and efforts; but the direction of their efforts is conditioned by their material mode of life.

In a modern capitalist society, of course, conditions are far more complex and include profound social contradictions. When wage-labour is employed, for instance, the workers have a common interest in improving their standards of life; the intention of doing so is born in their minds, and trade unions are organised to do it. Obviously, this is bound to happen. Trade union organisation is as inevitable in capitalist society as it is inevitable that water will seek its own level. But trade unions are created by nothing but the workers' own efforts, by their acting on their own initiative, in a conscious intentional way, with each one choosing whether to join a trade union or not. The point is that the direction of the efforts is determined by the material conditions of life. At the same time, the capitalists will also be pursuing their own interests, some well-meaning people will be making proposals to reconcile conflicting interests, some of the workers will be conceiving ambitions to raise their individual status by using trade union positions, some of the capitalists will understand this and set about buying them out, and so on, and so on. A vast complex of differing and conflicting aims and ideas is born from the given conditions, and eventually the conditions are changed by the social activities of the people so motivated.

What, then, determines the character of the changes? Not simply the socially-conditioned intentions of the makers of change. For, as Engels wrote in *Ludwig Feuerbach* (chap. 4), "numerous desired ends cross and conflict with one another, or these ends themselves are from the outset incapable of realisation, or the means of attaining them are insufficient. Thus the conflict of innumerable individual wills and individual actions in the domain of history produces a state of affairs entirely analogous to that in the realm of unconscious nature. . . . The many individual wills active in history for the most part produce results quite other than those they intended—often quite the opposite".

Just as the material mode of production is the foundation for the various different motivations which develop within society, so it also determines which ends are practical and which are not, and what the eventual outcome of the conflicting motivations will be.

The French Revolution, for example, was the explosive result of contradictions within the old society. From the position they occupied within the economic structure of that society, the peasants, town workers and rising bourgeoisie were all frustrated in the pursuit of their material interests, and all consequently oppressed under the rule of the nobility. They rose for "liberty, equality and fraternity", and smashed the feudal fetters. But what resulted was something not intended by the majority of those taking part in the revolution. As soon as the feudal fetters were smashed, free scope was afforded to the economic activity of the bourgeoisie—and the result was the development of capitalism. Fighting for liberty, what they did was to give nascent capitalism the chance to consolidate itself. This happened thanks to the initiative and efforts of the revolutionaries; but the final results of that initiative and those efforts depended on the sum total of social relations in French society.

Thus while society is composed of individuals who together make their own history by their own conscious activity, we must look behind people's conscious aims, intentions and motives to the economic development of society in order to find the laws of historical development. It is there that we discover the laws which regulate the changes in the circumstances conditioning people's actions, the transformations of material interests into conscious motives in their heads, and the final outcome of their activity.

"Men make their own history," wrote Marx in *The Eighteenth Brumaire of Louis Bonaparte* (chap. 1). "But they do not make it just as they please. They do not make it under circumstances chosen by themselves, but under circumstances directly encountered, given and transmitted from the past."

Like many other laws now known to science, the fundamental laws of social development, which regulate how these circumstances come into being and how they are changed, do not deal with the determination of individual events but with the consequences over a period of time of a large number of individual interactions. They state the consequences of individuals living in society. The intercourse of individuals in society must always lead to their using such productive forces as are to hand, to their entering into production relations corresponding to those productive forces, and to motivations and conflicts, based on those production relations, through which production relations are eventually changed corresponding to the development of new productive forces.

The Law of Progress

The fundamental law of social development is that of the adaptation of relations of production to production. The social relations of production have to be adapted to the social action of men on nature whereby men produce their means of life. The operation of this law brings about, with time, the progressive development of human society—that is, an irreversible progression from an earlier stage to a later stage. And that is because, from time to time, people are able to develop their forces of production. Given the actual physical, chemical and biological processes of the earth's surface, and the presence of men, employing brain and hand to use those processes for their own ends, there exists the possibility of a progressive development of techniques, each of which is sooner or later explored, though a long time may pass before favourable conditions arise for such exploration. And from this development of forces of production follow corresponding modifications and changes in relations of production and in the entire superstructure of social relations based on the relations of production. Thus human societies develop from formations based on lower production techniques to those based on higher production techniques. The distance traversed from stone tools to the automated factory and the nuclear reactor is the measure of human progress to date.

Progress, as so defined, cannot be due—as Hegel supposed human development was due—to any universal spirit mysteriously working itself out in human destinies and guiding them towards some end, any more than particular misfortunes and catastrophes that befall people are due to a malign fate manipulating human puppets towards their destruction. The whole conception of an external influence at work in human affairs—whether it is called the Absolute Spirit, God, Fate, or merely the influence of the stars, makes very little difference—is an idealist conception, totally foreign to science and therefore to Marxism. The only agency which determines human affairs is the agency of people themselves, wresting their livelihood from nature and entering into social relations to do so.

Thus determined, progress is naturally neither steady nor uniform. Important new techniques—such as the wheel, iron working, the use of water power, and so on—are introduced only at times and places where there occurs a coincidence of circumstances favourable to their discovery and application. But once introduced, new techniques bring power and benefits to their users which mean that they are not likely to be given up. Once introduced, new techniques are not lost again, but go on being used and eventually serve as the basis for still higher techniques. Moreover, big changes in production and consequently in production relations tend to be localised, to occur at long intervals, and to spread from a given locality.

In the history of mankind to date there have been two great changes in production of decisive importance. The first, which occurred only after hundreds of thousands of years of primitive techniques practised by scattered tribes after the birth of the human species, was the introduction of agriculture. This led to the division of society into classes and to the stormy, though comparatively short, period of man's evolution in which man was exploited by man and his history became the history of class struggles. The second was the introduction of modern industry, based on the general use of sources of energy other than human or animal muscle-power. This led to the extreme polarisation of class relations under capitalism and the birth among the exploited of the irresistible movement towards communism. The production relations adapted to modern industry, once it has developed sufficiently, are those of communism. Thanks to modern techniques, which include means of transport and communication, and to the capitalist drive for profit, once capitalism became established in one region it very quickly reached out until it brought the whole world under its sway. Thus modern industry meant the end of the process in which social development was localised and progress confined to separate regions, and the beginning of a world process of the advance of all humanity to classless communist society based on a uniformly high level of technique.

Scientific Theory and Social Practice

Knowledge of the laws of social development brings knowledge of the real forces at work in contemporary society and of how that society can and must be changed.

When production is outstripping production relations, there arises a historical necessity of changing those relations in order that people can carry forward production and enjoy the benefits it is capable of bringing them. To effect this change is a historical task. Such historical necessity and the corresponding historical task is an objective fact, completely independent of anyone's desires or intentions. To speak of it expresses not simply an aspiration or political programme, clothed in grand words, but an actually existing set-up of human relations.

Capitalism contains such a necessity and such a task—the necessity and task of advancing to socialism. And within the capitalist relations, one class, the working class, is by virtue of its position within those relations the social force to carry out the job. In this sense we may speak of its having a historical mission. This is a fact, whether anyone knows it or not, and whether anyone does anything about it or not. Marxism did not invent the historical mission of the working class, but discovered it.

In a similar way, in the bourgeois revolution a necessity and a task existed, and the nascent bourgeoisie had the mission of establishing a new order of society—which they successfully did. In the course of time tasks are fulfilled, because the existence of the task means that circumstances conspire to impel people towards its fulfilment. If one generation fails, it remains for the next generation. "Mankind sets itself only such tasks as it can solve," wrote Marx in the Preface to *Critique of Political Economy*, "since . . . the task itself arises only when the material conditions for its solution already exist or are at least in the process of formation."

The subject matter of social science is man's own social activity, whereas natural science deals with the object of that activity, the materials and forces of nature. Hence social science differs from natural science in that, by its discovery of the laws of development of social activity, it defines the historical task facing mankind at a given time and, therefore, the social end or goal of activity. Natural science, on the other hand, is concerned solely with means: it shows how natural forces can be used, and that is all. Physics, for example, by discovering the laws of physical processes, enables us to use those processes for our own purposes, as means to our own ends: it does not define those ends.

To define the historical task in contemporary society is, of course, at the same time to make a prediction, namely, that that task is likely eventually to be fulfilled. Thus Marxism does make a definite prediction: that capitalism will not continue indefinitely, and that—barring the possible catastrophe of mankind using the recent discovery of nuclear energy to destroy itself—it will be superseded by world communist society. But prediction is never the main function of either natural or social science. It is only secondary to the main function, which is to enable us to regulate our social activity, in production and in other spheres, in the light of discovery of the objective properties and laws of nature and society. So while the discovery of the laws of social development does imply a prediction about the future development of society, its primary significance is that it defines practical goals and practical policies towards realising them. Those who fail to grasp this are confusing Marx with Old Moore. In social activity, knowledge of the laws of development becomes itself a force in that development, and is enlarged and clarified as the development proceeds.

Another peculiarity of social science as compared with natural science is that it discovers and defines its own reasons for existence. The very definition of the contemporary task explains why scientific knowledge—a scientific theory—is needed to enable the task to be fulfilled. All earlier social formations came into being through members of society spontaneously pursuing their own immediate interests, as these arose from an existing mode of production. Capitalism, for instance, was not created by people acting on any scientific theory of capitalism, but by people following their noses in circumstances favourable to the development of capitalist relations, as a result of which the members of the rising bourgeois class seized any opportunity for profit and acted in combination against anyone and anything that blocked them. With the working class in capitalist society, on the other hand, spontaneous action leads no further than organisation to secure higher wages, shorter hours and better living conditions. To advance to socialism requires deliberate measures to change the relations of production, and the prior conquest of political power by the working class in order to be able to institute such measures. To do that requires theoretical knowledge of what is to be done, based on the scientific investigation of social processes, and a mass movement informed by scientific theory.

Every revolutionising discovery in history has been made only when conditions were ripe for it and the need for it existed. Thus the great discoveries of modern natural science were made only when the development of the mode of production had created the conditions and the need for them. The same is true of the social discoveries of Marx.

The Theory of the Working-Class Movement

The establishment of fundamental scientific theory in any field has always meant the overthrow of old prejudices, and so has run up against the opposition of definite interests. This applies still more with the science of society. Marx's discovery showed how men form societies, and frame their ideas and principles, on the basis of the material process of production. This threw down the last stronghold of idealism—the conception of human consciousness as having its ultimate source in something other than the material world; and with it the whole idea of the sanctity, rationality and permanence of any human institutions. In particular, Marx's discovery demonstrated the contradictions of capitalism and the necessity of replacing it by socialism. Obviously, if social science demonstrates these conclusions then not only does it meet with opposition but it simply cannot be accepted at all within the capitalist order.

Marxism arose as the theory of the working-class movement, which alone needed such a theory, and within the ranks of which alone could it be worked out, accepted and used; and after socialism was victorious in some countries, it was developed further as the theory of socialism and communism. The so-called social science of the bourgeois establishment has of course had to admit—by the back door, as it were, and usually without acknowledgement—some selected Marxist ideas; but the fundamental theory is consistently repudiated. In consequence, bourgeois social science remains at a primitive, descriptive level, without fundamental theory. And as for the definition of social goals, these are treated as the subject of morals or religion or politics, as distinct from science.

The use of Marxist theory to the working-class movement is threefold. It arms the movement with scientific knowledge of the actual position of the working class. It enables the movement scientifically to formulate practical aims. And it guides the movement in working out the necessary strategy and tactics for achieving those aims.

The working-class movement cannot transform society without the benefit of fundamental theory. And this theory teaches it to keep practical goals in sight rather than dream of utopian ideals, and to base its policies not on general precepts and exhortations but on recognition of the real material conditions and needs of the people.

In the application of science in the politics of class struggle a distinction must be made between certain general and invariable principles, on the one hand, and particular policies framed to cope with particular situations and phases of struggle on the other.

It is necessary to pursue a policy of working-class struggle against the capitalist class, uniting always the maximum forces to defeat the main enemy; this struggle must be carried to the point where the working class, with its allies, is able to gain political power to establish socialism and overcome all resistance against it; and to achieve this position of power, the working class must be led by a political party dedicated to the aim of socialism and guided by scientific socialist theory. These are inviolable principles to abandon which amounts in practice to abandoning the goal of socialism and the means to realise it.

Within the framework of general principles there is then the problem of finding the right policies to meet each eventuality that arises. And here, it must be allowed, a large element of variation and improvisation comes in. Those dogmatists have a strange idea of applying social science, who imagine that it is possible to state in advance everything that is going to happen, and to lay down hard and fast rules for determining correct policies.

In the working-class struggle it is possible and necessary to make an analysis of the salient facts of a given situation, to forecast the probable behaviour of individuals, groups and classes in such a situation, and in the light of that to arrive at a plan of action. But at the same time, control is lacking over nearly all these factors; even the way in which decisions taken within the movement are carried out depends on the tightness or looseness of organisation, the waging of internal controversies, and all manner of subjective factors influencing individuals. Hence the contingent and the unforeseen always play a large part in the politics of class struggle, and a wise leadership is one which has no illusions of infallibility and is always on the alert to draw conclusions from new experiences.

Social Science and Communism

The consolidation of socialism, followed by the evolution of socialism into communism, means the end of exploitation of man by man and with that the end of class struggles. Evidently, therefore, the future conditions of human social activity will, in that event, be very different from the past. So different will they be that Marx, in the Preface to *Critique of Political Economy*, wrote that the transition to socialism "brings the prehistory of human society to a close".

With communism, as the *Communist Manifesto* put it, "all production has been concentrated in the hands of a vast association of the whole nation". And then, to quote Engels in *Socialism, Utopian and Scientific*, "man's own social organisation, hitherto confronting him as a necessity imposed by nature and history, becomes the result of his own free action. The extraneous objective forces which have hitherto governed history pass under the control of man himself". It is then no longer a question of waging class struggle in conditions under which many factors determining the outcome are beyond control, but of planning the basic processes of social life for the satisfaction of human needs.

This implies that the whole mode of application of social science is changed. Its application becomes a matter of estimating the material needs of society, and the current material and human resources available, and of planning production and distribution accordingly. Thus in its application social science becomes an exact, mathematical and quantitative discipline, like the natural sciences applied in the techniques of production.

This change corresponds to the situation in which, as Engels also puts it, "the government of persons has been replaced by the administration of things". The task of social science under communism is not to work out ways and means of manipulating human beings so as to force or cajole them into some predetermined pattern of social activity. The task is to work out the plan of production and distribution for the whole community, to be undertaken with the minimum of labour, so that people may on that basis freely enjoy that blossoming forth of human energy which is for man an end in itself.

Writing of the tasks of science in his early *Economic and Philosophical Manuscripts*, Marx concluded: "Natural science will in time subsume under itself the science of man, just as the science of man will subsume under itself natural science; there will be *one* science." The subject of science will be the laws of development of nature and human society, and the ways and means of man's securing the continuous satisfaction in his social life of all his needs. The discovery of the fundamental laws of man's social activity was an essential step towards this unification of the sciences which is necessary as a means to securing the flowering of human life.

Chapter Three

THE MODE OF PRODUCTION

Production of the Means of Life

Historical materialism finds the key to the laws of development of society in "the simple fact that mankind must first of all eat, drink, have shelter and clothing, before it can pursue politics, science, art, religion, etc." (Engels, *Speech at the Graveside of Karl Marx.*)

Before people can do anything else, they must obtain the means of life—food, clothing and shelter. And they obtain the means of life, not as a free gift from nature, but by associating together to produce their necessities of life and to exchange the things produced. Only on the basis of associating to produce and exchange the means of life can they develop and pursue any of their other social interests.

Hence "the production of the means to support human life and, next to production, the exchange of things produced . . . is the basis of every social order. . . . In every society that has appeared in history, the distribution of the products and with it the division of society into classes, is determined by what is produced and how it is produced and how the product is exchanged." (Engels, *Socialism, Utopian and Scientific*, chap. 3.)

In this way historical materialism traces back the ultimate cause of the whole movement of society to the social activity of men in the production and exchange of the means of life—that is, to the conditions of material life of society and to changes in the conditions of material life.

The way in which people produce and exchange their means of life is known as the *mode of production.* Every society is based on a mode of production, which is what ultimately determines the character of all social activities and institutions.

Production and Property

The mode of production is always social, because each individual does not produce the whole of his material needs for himself, solely by his own labour, independent of other individuals. The material goods required by the community are produced by the labour of many individuals, who thus carry on, as Marx put it, a "mutual exchange of activities" in producing the social product which is distributed among the community.

So in considering the mode of production we must distinguish first of all the forces which people bring into operation in order to produce the products—the actual material means by which production is undertaken; and secondly, the mutual relations into which people enter in producing and exchanging the products.

We must distinguish the *forces of production* and the *relations of production*. These together define the mode of production. Thus a given mode of production consists of entering into certain relations of production in order to employ certain forces of production. And different modes of production are distinguished by differences in the forces of production and the relations of production.

What exactly do we denote by *forces of production?*

In order to produce, instruments of production are necessary, that is, tools, machines, means of transport, and so on. But these do not produce anything by themselves. It is people who make and use them. Without people with the skill to make and use the instruments of production, no production is possible.

The forces of production, therefore, consist of the instruments of production, and people, with their production experience and skill, who use these instruments. A labour force, with its experience and skill, is part of the forces of production; and the greater its experience and the greater its skill, the more potent a force of production it is.

Later, science becomes a major ingredient of the forces of production.

And what do we mean by the *relations of production?*

These relations are partly simple and direct relations which people enter into with one another in the actual production process itself—simple and direct relations between people engaged in a common productive task.

But when people carry on production they must needs enter into social relations, not only with one another, but also with the *means of production* which they are utilising.

By the "means of production" we denote something more than the instruments of production. We denote all those means which are necessary to produce the finished product—including not only the instruments (which are part of the forces of production), but also land, raw materials, buildings in which production is undertaken, and so on.

In undertaking production, then, it is necessary for people socially to regulate their mutual relations to the means of production. And this is how *property* relations arise. In social production, the means of production become the property of various people or groups of people. For in carrying on production and exchange it is necessary that some arrangement should be made, binding on the members of society, by which it is known who is entitled to dispose of the various means of production and of the product which is produced by working with them.

This regulation of people's mutual relations to the means of production, and consequently of their share of the product, is not undertaken as a result of any one collective and deliberate act—of any general decision or "social contract". It comes about by an unconscious or spontaneous process. People come to regulate their mutual relations to the means of production, and so also to regulate the disposal of the social product, in a way adapted to the forces of production—since otherwise they could not carry on production. And entering into these relations in the process of production, they become conscious of them as property relations which are socially obligatory and legally binding.

In the very primitive production carried on by a tribe of hunters, the hunters enter into simple, direct relations with one another as fellow hunters, fellow tribesmen; and the land they hunt over and the beasts they hunt are not regarded as the property of any particular individuals or groups. The whole tribe organises hunting expeditions, and what they bring back from the hunt is common property and is shared out among the tribesmen.

But when division of labour arises, and one person specialises in producing this and another in producing that, then the instruments used begin to be regarded as the property of particular persons, and so does the product produced become the property of the producer, to be disposed of by himself. Similarly, when animals are domesticated and herds are raised, herds become the property of particular families, and of the head of the family. At a later stage, land becomes private property.

Thus as a result of the development of the forces of production—for the development of agriculture, handicrafts, and so on, is precisely a development of the forces of production—and as a result of the division of labour which accompanies this development, there gradually arises ownership of means of production by individual people or groups of people. In other words, private property arises.

Here it can already be seen that the driving force in social development is the development of the forces of production.

Property relations are essentially social relations between people, arising out of production. At first sight, property relations look like simple two-term relations between individual people and things, between individual property-owners and the property they own. This is not so, however. The appearance is illusory. Robinson Crusoe on his island was not a property-owner but simply a man on an island. Property relations are complex social relations between people in society—complex relations between men in society, not simple relations between men and things. In the production which they carry on, men establish social relations, or relations of production, between one another whereby the means of production which they utilise are the property of this or that individual, or of this or that group, and similarly with the product produced.

Property relations, therefore, are ways of regulating people's mutual relationships in the process of utilising the means of production and disposing of the product.

To speak of property is simply a way of giving legal expression to these mutual relations of people in society. As property relations, these appear as obligatory relations, binding on society and all the members of society.

Now, therefore, we can define the relations of production as the mutual relations into which people enter in the process of production and disposal of the product, and of which they become conscious as property relations.

The relations of production obtaining in any particular society are said to constitute the *economic structure* of that society.

Exploitation

The products of productive activity are appropriated in various different ways and so differently distributed among the members of society, according to the type of economic structure prevailing.

What determines the way in which, in different societies, the product is appropriated?

In general, it is the form of ownership of the means of production, the nature of the property relations, which determines the form of appropriation and the way in which the means of life are distributed.

In the most primitive communities the means of production are communally owned, they are held in common by the producers. This is a consequence of the very primitive character of the instruments of production. With only very primitive tools and implements, division of labour has hardly developed, people have to work in common in order to survive, and work in common leads to the common ownership of the means of production. The fruits of production, such as they are, are accordingly shared by the whole community. Just as the means of production are not the property of any particular individual or group, so the product is not appropriated by any individual or group. This primitive mode of life is neither comfortable nor cultured nor secure, but it does exhibit within the tribe brotherhood and communal solidarity.

In socialist society, again, the means of production are socially owned. And then once more the product is socially appropriated, being distributed "to each according to his labour" in the first stage of socialist society, and "to each according to his needs" in the stage of fully developed communist society.

But in all the communities known to history between primitive communism and socialism—between primitive production and modern large-scale social production—means of production are not socially owned but are the property of individuals or groups, and means of production of crucial importance are the property of a minority of the community. As a result, those who own these means of production are able, by virtue of their position as owners, to appropriate the lion's share of the product. And so it becomes possible for them to live on the fruits of the labour of others, in other words, to exploit others. Those who do not own means of production are compelled to work for the benefit of those who do.

How does such a state of affairs come about?

In the first place, the division of labour breaks up the primitive system of communal production by a whole tribe and results in ownership of means of production gradually passing into the hands of particular individuals and groups. With this comes the private appropriation of the product, for the product is appropriated by whoever owns the means of production. As herds pass out of the common possession of the tribe into the ownership of individual heads of families, as cultivated land is allotted to the use of single families, as handicrafts appear, so the corresponding product ceases to be a communal possession and is privately appropriated.

Further, with private property there begins also the transformation of the product into a commodity—a process which is finally completed in capitalist society, when practically the whole product takes the form of commodities.

It is when products are exchanged for other products that

we call them "commodities": commodities are products produced for the purpose of exchanging them for other products. "The rise of private property in herds and articles of luxury," wrote Engels in his *Origin of the Family, Private Property and the State* (chap. 5), "led to exchange between individuals, to the transformation of products into commodities." For while in a communal mode of production people share out their products amongst themselves, thus carrying on "a mutual exchange of activities" but not an exchange of products, when private property develops the owner does not necessarily require the product he has appropriated for himself but exchanges it for other products.

And this has far-reaching effects. "When the producers no longer directly consumed their products themselves, but let it pass out of their hands in the act of exchange, they lost control of it," Engels continued. "They no longer knew what became of it; the possibility was there that one day it would be used against the producer to exploit and oppress him."

As commodity exchange grows and, with it, the use of money, it acts as a powerful force in further breaking up all former communal modes of production, concentrating the ownership of property into the hands of some, while others are dispossessed. The inevitable result of the growth of private property is the division of the community into "haves" and "have-nots", those with property and those without it, possessors and dispossessed.

In the second place, the division of labour, from which these results follow, is linked with a growth of the productivity of labour. Where formerly the productive labour of a whole tribe could scarcely produce enough to satisfy the minimum requirements of all the producers, now labour produces a surplus. Those who work can produce enough to satisfy their own essential needs, and more besides. Hence there arises the possibility that those who own means of production may appropriate to themselves, without labour, the surplus from the labour of others. And once this possibility has come into being, it is soon taken advantage of.

An early result is slavery. Once the producer can produce

by his labour more than he himself consumes, it becomes worth while for some people to enslave others. Thus there appear masters and slaves, the masters appropriating to themselves the whole product of the slaves' labour and allowing the slaves only as much as is necessary to keep them alive.

Slavery is the simplest and most direct form of exploitation of man by man. That does not imply that it was necessarily the first; various ways in which a chief or proprietor extracted services and tribute from others reduced to various degrees of dependence on him are probably at least as ancient. Another simple form of exploitation is the feudal, the exploitation of serfs by feudal proprietors such as was widely practised in Europe during the Middle Ages. Here the lord does not own the serf as the master does the slave, but he owns the land and the serf is effectively tied to the land, whether by law or by force of circumstances: the serf is then permitted to get his living from the land on condition that he renders up to the lord as his due a part of the produce. A third form of exploitation is the capitalist, the exploitation of wage-workers by capitalists. Here the workers are legally free, in the sense that they can go where they like and work for whom they like, but are deprived of means of production and can make a living only by selling their labour-power to the capitalists. The latter, as owners of the means of production, appropriate the product.

But whatever the form of exploitation, the substance is always the same: the producers produce a surplus over and above their own essential requirements, and this surplus is appropriated by non-producers by virtue of their ownership of some form of property.

For the producers, exploitation therefore means that only a part of their total labour is used by them for themselves, to produce their own requirements, and the rest is taken and used by another. When the productivity of labour has risen so that producers can produce a surplus above what they need for themselves, a part of their labour becomes surplus labour—and exploitation means that this surplus labour is taken and its product appropriated by another, by virtue of ownership of property. By taking other people's labour, the exploiters can live well without having to work themselves.

"The essential difference," wrote Marx in *Capital* (vol. I, chap. 9, sect. 1), "between the various economic forms of society, between, for instance, a society based on slave labour and one based on wage labour, lies only in the mode in which this surplus labour is in each case extracted from the actual producer, the labourer."

It is the development of production and the development of property which give rise to exploitation. Exploitation means that some people, the minority of society, are by virtue of their ownership of property living without labour on the fruits of the labour of others, of the majority.

It follows that in every mode of production which involves the exploitation of man by man, the social product is so distributed that the majority of the people, the people who labour, are condemned to toil for no more than the barest necessities of life. Sometimes, it is true, favourable circumstances arise when they can win more, but more often they get the barest minimum—and at times not even that. On the other hand, a minority, the owners of the means of production, the property owners, enjoy leisure and luxury. Society is divided into rich and poor.

It further follows that if we are ever to do away with the extremes of poverty and wealth, then this can never be achieved simply by calling for a new mode of distribution of the social product. Capitalist society, for example, cannot be reformed simply by decreeing a more equal distribution of products, as is envisaged in the reformist slogans of "fair distribution of the proceeds of labour" or "fair shares for all". For the distribution of the means of consumption is based on the ownership of the means of production. It is the latter which must be attacked.

"The so-called distribution relations," wrote Marx in *Capital* (vol. III, chap. 51), "correspond to and arise from historically determined specific forms of the process of production and mutual relations entered into by men in the production process of human life. The historical character of these distribution relations is the historical character of production relations, of which they express merely one aspect. Capitalist distribution differs from those forms of distribution which arise from other modes of production, and every form of distribution disappears with the specific form of production from which it is descended and to which it corresponds."

Classes and Class Struggles

With the development of social production beyond the primitive commune, the community is divided into groups occupying different places in social production as a whole, with different relationships to the means of production and therefore different methods of acquiring their share of the product. Such groups constitute the social *classes*, and their relations constitute the class relations or class structure of a given society.

The existence of classes is a consequence of the division of labour in social production. From the division of labour follow forms of private property, and thence the division of society into classes. "The various stages of development in the division of labour are just so many different forms of ownership," wrote Marx and Engels in *The German Ideology*. "That is, the existing stage in the division of labour determines also the relations of individuals to one another with reference to the materials, instruments and products of labour."

What constitutes and distinguishes classes, therefore, is not primarily differences in income, mentality or habits, as is vulgarly supposed, but the places they occupy in social production and the relations in which they stand to the means of production. This is what determines their differences in income, habits, mentality, and so on.

"The fundamental feature that distinguishes classes," Lenin explained in an article on *Vulgar Socialism and Narodism*, "is the place they occupy in social production and, consequently, the relation in which they stand to the means of production."

In *A Great Beginning* Lenin proposed the following more exhaustive definition of classes:

"Classes are large groups of people which differ from each other by the place they occupy in a historically definite system of social production, by their relation (in most cases fixed and formulated in laws) to the means of production, by their role in the social organisation of labour, and, consequently, by the dimensions of the social wealth that they obtain and their method of acquiring their share of it. Classes are groups of people one of which may appropriate the labour of another, owing to the different places they occupy in the definite system of social economy."

With classes there arise class antagonisms and class struggles.

Classes are antagonistic when the places they occupy in the system of social production are such that one class obtains and augments its share of social wealth only at the expense of another. Thus the relations between exploiters and exploited are inevitably antagonistic. And so are the relations between one exploiting class and another when their methods of exploitation come into conflict, that is, when the extraction of surplus labour by the one gets in the way of the extraction of surplus labour by the other. Thus the relations between rising bourgeoisie and feudal lords, for example, were antagonistic, since the one could maintain and the other develop its method of exploitation only at the expense of the other. Again, in nineteenth century England there was a certain antagonism between the industrial capitalists and the landowners.

"These warring classes," wrote Engels in *Socialism, Utopian and Scientific* (chap. 1), "are always the product of the conditions of production and exchange, in a word, of the economic conditions of their time."

Society based on exploitation is inevitably divided into antagonistic classes. Such a society is torn by class conflicts—always between exploiters and exploited, and sometimes between rival exploiters.

For this reason, as *The Communist Manifesto* began by stating: "the history of all hitherto existing society is the history of class struggles."

These class struggles are rooted in conflicts of material interest between the different classes—conflicting economic interests arising from the different places occupied by different classes in social production, their different relations to the means of production, and their different methods of obtaining and augmenting their share of social wealth.

Of course, not all class relations are antagonistic. If more than one method of exploitation is used to extract surplus labour, that means that society is founded on more than one form of property and has a complex class structure containing more than one exploiting class and more than one exploited class. In that case, there is no basic antagonism between the different classes of the exploited. On the contrary, these classes are potential allies against the exploiters—even though differences in their habits and mentality and aims, arising from differences in their relations to the means of production, may prevent them acting together and may sometimes be used by the exploiters to set one class against the other. Thus, for example, in a country with capitalist industry and peasant agriculture, the relations between the urban working class and the exploited peasantry are not antagonistic.

Again, in the socialist society of the U.S.S.R. there still remain today two distinct classes, the Soviet workers and peasants—though the distinction between them is becoming blurred. Like all class distinctions, this one is rooted in the different places the classes occupy in social production. The Soviet workers are engaged in state enterprises socially owned by the whole society in the person of the socialist state; the collective farm peasants are engaged in group, co-operative enterprises—collective farms. The class distinction is based on the distinction between public and group property. But neither class exploits the other, neither acquires and augments its share of social wealth at the expense of the other, and so there is no antagonism between them.

Social-Economic Formations

We have seen that the mode of production involves two factors—the forces of production, consisting of instruments of production and people with production experience and skill, and the relations of production. The latter in their totality constitute the economic structure of society. Different economic structures represent so many economic formations which have come into being and then been superseded in the history of mankind. Economic structures are not bestowed on man in society ready-made by Providence, tailored to last him for ever, but evolve as men change their relationship with nature in production and so change their relationships with one another. "My standpoint," wrote Marx in the Preface to the first German edition of *Capital*, views "the economic formation of society as a process of natural history."

What constitutes difference of economic formation, and how are different types of social-economic formation to be classified?

Differences of economic formation are differences of production relations, and different types of social-economic formation are defined in terms of different kinds of production relations. People always depend for their livelihood on certain definite means of production. The relationships which people set up with one another which determine who performs productive labour, who owns means of production, and who has what claim on the product, are the production relations in terms of which the differences of social-economic formation which occur in the course of history are defined.

In classifying different types of historically constituted social-economic formation, there is a fundamental distinction, in the first place, between those with social ownership of means of production and those with private ownership, or private property.

With their first emergence from the animal world people were associated in small groups in which all the able-bodied contributed to production, the means of production were held in common, and the product was shared out amongst the group, all of whom had an equal claim on it. The evidence for this consists of inferences from what we know about surviving primitive peoples, together with the consideration that very primitive people could not well have lived in any other way. This type of economy has been called "primitive communism". There is very little doubt that such was the economy of men for a very long time—more controversial are secondary questions, about kinship relations, social customs and beliefs, and so on.

Modern socialism, once more, presents an economic formation in which means of production are socially owned. The great difference between this and primitive communism is due to the fact that the instruments of production are of a very powerful and advanced kind, and production is on a very large scale. People are no longer members of clans, bound together and to the land, their principal means of production, by close communal ties. Land and means of production are no longer parcelled out amongst small communes, each of which is thereby subordinate to its means of production; means of production are socially owned on a grand scale and the whole of production is planned for the benefit of society as a whole. As production approaches the point of absolute abundance, this economic formation is carried from the stage when the claim on the product is determined by labour performed to the stage when it is determined simply by need.

In some regions the primitive communist way of life was eventually disturbed by improvements of techniques leading to division of labour, the production of a surplus, commodity exchange, and the formation of private property. These events took place in the distant past, they were never recorded, and so we today can draw only more or less probable inferences as to where they took place and the exact course they followed. What they quite evidently led to, and that only after a very long process, was economic formations in which society was divided into classes and man was exploited by man. But the precise character of the production relations of early class-divided societies is a matter of somewhat dubious inference. There are few written records—in many cases, none at all. And while archaeologists can dig up relics of productive forces, production relations do not leave such material relics. The most that can be done is to draw inferences from variations in the size and equipment of houses, grave furniture, and so on.

The fundamental criterion distinguishing the different economic formations of class-divided society is the method of exploitation, or the method of extracting surplus labour from the producers and claiming the product of that labour. The definition of the method of exploitation at the same time defines the property and class relations of society.

When production is mainly agricultural, as was the case with all societies until a comparatively late period of history, the main method of exploitation must consist of extracting surplus labour from the agricultural producers. The main means of production is land, and to understand the method of exploitation it is therefore necessary to know how the primary producers worked the land and how they were related to it.

It would appear that in the early class-divided societies—and these, it should be remembered, existed for a period of many thousands of years before written history begins with classical Greece and Rome—surplus labour was extracted from the primary producers in various ways, sometimes by forced labour, always by exacting some form of tribute. Tribute has been exacted by central rulers, often claiming to be gods and owing their power to the fact that they had a monopoly over rare metals and often managed the water supply and irrigation works; by royal conquerors or their appointed representatives or satraps, in kind or in taxes; or by local magnates.

Such tribute was originally imposed upon communities of producers amongst whom there still remained strong survivals of primitive communism. Describing the method of exploitation in India, characteristic of the "oriental" or "asiatic" model of production prevailing there prior to the British conquest, Marx wrote of "village communities built upon the common ownership of land" which were "ground down by taxation". The producers in these communes, engaged not only in agricultural but also in various forms of primitive industrial labour, were "not confronted by private land-owners" but rather by "a state which stands over them as their landlord and simultaneously as their sovereign." (*Capital*, vol. III, in chapters 20, 23 and 47.)

Wherever commodity exchange became more developed,

and with it the power of money, the original commune or clan system, which survived within earlier modes of exploitation, was increasingly broken up. Land then became liable to be bought, sold and mortgaged. Communal holdings were expropriated, and land become private property with the inevitable appearance of large landholdings. Producers parted with surplus labour also as interest on debts, and while most were impoverished a few became rich and turned into exploiters themselves.

The peculiarity of slavery, as a distinct and ancient method of exploitation, is that the person of the slave is owned by the master, who also owns land and other means of production and sets the slave to work as he sees fit. Evidently, slaves were primarily obtained by capture. But where commodity exchange developed, they became commodities to be bought and sold, so that slaves represented an investment of money and a source of income; and furthermore, many people became enslaved for debt.

It is probable that slavery was a feature of the earliest class-divided society, so that the exploitation of slaves began as soon as exploitation began, and existed alongside the exploitation of non-slave agricultural producers as a source of additional wealth and power to a part of the owning classes. Thus there were temple slaves, household slaves, slaves engaged in working metals, and so on. But a specifically slave economic formation arises only when, with development of commodity exchange and private ownership of land, it has become profitable to buy slaves for use in extractive and other industries; or when a large part of the peasantry has become impoverished by debt or other exactions, and has been expropriated and replaced by slaves—in short, when slavery becomes the major or predominant method of extracting surplus labour, as was the case with the great slave estates of ancient Rome.

Incidentally, the purest slave system that ever existed was that of the plantations of the Southern States of America, which ended less than a century ago. This was a commodity-producing economy, depending on trade with industrial capitalist economies which presently overwhelmed it; and the slaves were acquired for cash from the slave-traders who played so big a part in the primitive accumulation of capital. This illustrates the fact that slavery by itself does not suffice to define one single and unique social-economic formation, and is not peculiar to one particular stage of economic development. In fact, slavery has been a feature of many economic formations from very ancient times to very recently, just as wage-labour has also been. There is no economic formation of class-divided society which contains only one method of exploitation, and which is therefore of a "pure" type. Each formation that historically comes into existence must be defined as a specific historically constituted complex of different methods of exploitation, applied to specific technically-defined types of labour, with one method predominating.

The specific type of economic formation known as feudalism arises when land is owned by a hereditary nobility and when peasants, who possess their own instruments of production, have the use of land—to which they may be legally tied as serfs—on condition of paying dues in kind or in money or both to the nobility; and when likewise handicrafts and small manufactures exist in dependence on the nobility whose land they occupy, paying dues to them.

Feudalism can arise in a fairly obvious way from a system of slave estates by the replacement of slaves by serfs and of slave-owning landowners by feudal landowners. And there is no doubt that historically the feudal system in Europe did arise from the decline and wreck of the former Roman slave system, when enterprises based on slavery had either ceased to pay or had been broken up by invasions. There has perhaps not yet been enough investigation of what has been called the feudal economy in China and elsewhere to define it with exactitude or to know from what exactly it arose.

Be that as it may, it is certain that capitalism arose historically only from economic development within a feudal society. It arose when improvements in manufacture and agricultural techniques had created conditions in which the bulk of products could be produced as commodities; when landowners, eager to get more money, had expropriated large numbers of agricultural producers and left them to their own devices without enslaving them (this happened in England, for example, first by expropriations by landowners turning their estates into sheep runs to sell wool to the wool merchants, and then by enclosures for the sake of developing capitalist methods of farming); and when in mercantile centres large sums of money, accumulated by looting less developed areas, piracy, slave trading, and so on, were available as capital in the hands of individuals.

With capitalism, the producer is expropriated from all means of production and can live only by selling his labour-power to the capitalist owner of means of production, who thus extracts his surplus labour in the form of surplus value, or "unpaid labour". The value of the commodities produced in a day's work is greater than that of the worker's own labour-power, which he sells to the capitalist; and this difference is the surplus value which the capitalist appropriates, and which he realises in cash and to his profit when he sells the goods produced.

The historical sequence of social-economic formations is a natural history or evolutionary process in this sense—that production relations are always adapted to given forces of production, so that those that arise in adaptation to more advanced forces of production represent a higher stage of development of the economic formation of society than those adapted to less advanced forces of production. The stage of development that a given society has attained is objectively decided by the level of the forces of production and by how far its economic structure permits people to extract the maximum powers from those forces of production.

Thus evidently, primitive communism is the first and lowest social-economic formation, and socialism the highest. Socialism is a higher, more developed formation than capitalism, capitalism than feudalism, feudalism than the other formations that succeeded primitive communism, and all of them than primitive communism. The ancient Greeks and Romans reached a more developed stage than their barbarian neighbours, the Chinese or the Europeans of the Middle Ages than the Romans, Western capitalism than medieval feudalism. And now Soviet communism is rapidly reaching a more developed stage than Western capitalism.

In a famous passage of the Preface to *Critique of Political Economy*, Marx wrote: "In broad outlines, asiatic, ancient, feudal and modern bourgeois modes of production can be designated as progressive epochs in the economic formation of society. The bourgeois relations of production are the last antagonistic form of the social process of production . . . the productive forces developing in the womb of bourgeois society create the material conditions for the solution of that antagonism."

It would appear that the progress here referred to is that in which (1) commodity production has not yet reached the point where the communal ownership of land and sharing out of land amongst members of communes has been disrupted, and private ownership of land is not yet widely established (the "asiatic" epoch); (2) private ownership of land and other means of production is highly developed and a major part of commodity production is carried on by slave labour (the "ancient" epoch); (3) slaves cease to be widely used and their labour is replaced by that of serfs and others owing dues to feudal landowners (the "feudal" epoch); (4) the greater part of the social product is produced as commodities, and workers in major productive enterprises are completely expropriated from means of production and converted into wage-labourers selling their labour-power to capitalists (the "bourgeois" epoch).

Finally, in examining the typical corresponding economic formations that came into being in various regions, it also appears that as in the economic development the productive forces of primitive communism are surpassed, so society becomes emancipated from primitive production relations—and consequently also from the ideologies that correspond to them. The higher the stage of economic development, the more have the primitive communal relations binding the producers to the means of production been dissipated. These remain strong in all early class-divided societies, and the principal economic agency responsible for their dissolution is commodity exchange. This grows with production itself, and is a strong force impoverishing the primary producers and leading to their expropriation from the land: slavery, wherever it is widely introduced, plays a big part here. As communal production relations among primary producers are dissipated, so also are clan ties and clan authority undermined, and the authority of a state power exerted over a territory takes their place. Industrial capitalism, which finally accomplishes the complete expropriation of workers from their means of production, is then the prelude to socialism and the foundation of fully developed communist society—for then the whole means of production can be taken into social ownership by the whole of society.

Chapter Four

THE FUNDAMENTAL LAW OF SOCIAL DEVELOPMENT

Development of the Forces of Production

We have defined the mode of production and the types of production relations—economic and class structures—through which production develops. This development of production is the basis of the entire development of society. We shall now consider the causes of this economic development, the laws which govern the transition from one economic formation to another, and the forces which effect the transition.

People develop their forces of production. They change their relations of production, and with these changes new classes come to the fore. Changes in relations of production are consequent upon development of the forces of production, being made in adaptation to new forces of production so as to make possible their full or fuller employment, and these changes are effected through class struggles and by the agency of definite classes—such is the fundamental law of social development in accordance with which people effect the historical development of one mode of production after another.

First we shall consider the development of the forces of production.

In the course of history, the instruments of production have been developed from crude stone tools up to modern machinery. Each technical invention has been dependent on previous ones and could not have been made had the earlier techniques not been already available. The history of technology thus follows a sequence determined by the objective properties of the materials and forces in the physical, chemical and biological environment available for employment by man. This development of techniques was effected by people, who designed and used the instruments of production. Consequently, the development of the instruments of production was also a development of people—of their experience, skill, knowledge, and ability to make and handle the instruments of production.

This development of the forces of production, including the development of the experience, skills, knowledge and abilities of people themselves, is the root cause of the whole of social development.

From what does it arise?

It arises from men's constant striving to master nature. And this striving is not some divine gift but the natural consequence of the fundamental opposition or contradiction between men and their natural environment, which is present from the first moment when men began to fashion tools and to co-operate in their use—that is, from the birth of mankind.

"Man," wrote Marx in *Capital* (vol. I, chap. 7, sect. 1), "opposes himself to nature as one of her own forces, setting in motion arms and legs, head and hands, the natural forces of his body, in order to appropriate nature's productions in a form adapted to his own wants. By thus acting on the external world and changing it, he at the same time changes his own nature. He develops his slumbering powers and compels them to act in obedience to his will."

Men, seeking to satisfy their wants, manage to improve their technique, their tools and their skill—in other words, their productive forces. And it is only when new productive forces present them with new possibilities and so arouse in them the feeling of new needs, that men begin to feel the necessity of a change in production relations.

The development of productive forces is, however, far from being a steady, continuous process throughout the history of society. If every generation had always improved upon the productive forces inherited from the previous generation, history would have moved a great deal faster and a great deal more evenly than has in fact been the case. On the contrary, it has frequently happened that, having once acquired certain techniques, people have made do with them for a very long time. And then their production relations have remained basically the same for a very long time, too. Again, acquirements have been regional. While some have forged ahead with new techniques, those living in some other region have remained stuck with old techniques.

Thus, for example, production remained at the level of the old stone age for hundreds of thousands of years, and all those generations continued to live the life of primitive communism. Some scarcely moved at all until colonisers arrived from outside. Again, in some regions methods of agriculture remained unchanged for thousands of years, and for all that time production relations remained virtually unchanged. But when, for whatever reasons, new productive forces are acquired, then a process begins resulting eventually in changes of production relations amongst those who have acquired those productive forces. New techniques are introduced within the existing production relations, but at a certain stage their employment leads to people changing their production relations.

Very rapid development of productive forces is a feature of capitalist society. But it was not the case in modern history that first capitalist relations of production were introduced and only after that did development of productive forces begin. On the contrary, this development began within the feudal system, and it was only afterwards that capitalist relations of production supplanted the feudal relations. A whole series of inventions during the middle ages (new applications of water power, the modern type of plough, new methods of navigation, the spinning-wheel, new mining methods, lathes, cast iron, etc.) provided the conditions for the development of capitalism.

In carrying on production, people necessarily enter into definite relations of production. And in the long run, they always bring these relations of production into correspondence with their productive forces.

"Social relations are closely bound up with productive

forces," wrote Marx in *The Poverty of Philosophy*. "In acquiring new productive forces men change their mode of production. . . . The hand-mill gives you society with the feudal lord; the steam-mill, society with the industrial capitalist."

Spontaneous or Unplanned Development

To understand the causes of this development of productive forces and of corresponding production relations it is necessary to premise that in the past people have not brought new productive forces into employment, nor set up new production relations, as a result of any plan or intention.

In developing new tools and techniques people have always been seeking some immediate advantage, but have been far from planning or intending the revolutionary social results which have in fact followed from such development.

For example, when manufacture first started, the manufacturers who started it had no plan of creating gigantic new productive forces; they were simply seeking their own immediate advantage. To carry on manufacture they began to hire wage-labour, in other words, to initiate capitalist relations of production. They did not do this because they had an ambitious and far-seeing plan for building capitalism; they did it because that turned out to be the way in which manufacture could best be carried on.

In this way the development of new productive forces—in our example, those brought into operation by manufacture—was never decided upon but happened spontaneously, without any plan, as a result of certain people seeking their own immediate advantage. And similarly, the development of these productive forces led to the institution of new relations of production—once more, spontaneously, by economic necessity, and without any plan. This is what Marx expressed by saying that the development of production relations happened "independent of men's will".

"In the social production which men carry on," he wrote in the Preface to *Critique of Political Economy*, "they enter into definite relations that are indispensable and independent of their will; these relations correspond to a definite stage of development of their material forces of production."

The relations of production into which people enter in the course of their social production are "indispensable"—because they cannot carry on production without entering into definite relations of production; and also "independent of their will"—because they do not decide beforehand to institute certain definite relations of production, but enter into these relations independent of any such plan.

Hence, first the development of productive forces and then the change of production relations is caused by social economic activities which people perform because of the necessity of living—spontaneously, without any deliberate decision or plan, independent of their will. This is a feature of social development right up to the socialist revolution. Only with the victory of the socialist revolution does it happen that production relations are changed as a result of deliberate decision and that thereafter the development of production is also regulated by a plan.

Changes of Relations of Production

Changes of the relations of production depend on development of the forces of production. Such is the law of social development. For it is a requirement of all social production that the relations which people enter into in carrying on production must be suitable to the type of production they are carrying on. Hence, it is a general law of economic development that the relations of production must necessarily be adapted to the character of the forces of production.

As we have seen, the very nature of production as a contradictory relationship between men and nature implies a tendency for new techniques to be discovered from time to time. But as for production relations, on the other hand, once established they tend to remain fixed—the economic structure, the forms of property, the social system, is a conservative factor which resists change.

The invention and employment of new productive forces introduces, as is obvious, new division of labour and creates a greater quantity and variety of products. But this new division of labour itself gives rise to new forms of property, through which the new division of labour is organised and which regulate the appropriation and distribution of the greatly increased product. The property relations and mode of exchange of economic activities and products which arose from and corresponded to the earlier productive forces no longer suffice for the organisation of a new division of labour and the distribution of its products.

For this reason, the relation between production relations and productive forces is a contradictory one. The same production relations which were well suited for the productive forces in use at one time are not well suited to new productive forces, and so come to hinder their development and to act as a fetter on it. When this happens, it is clear that instead of production relations being in conformity with productive forces there is an active contradiction between them. And because production relations tend to resist change, because there are always people whose material interests are bound up with certain production relations and who therefore resist any change, this contradiction issues in deep social conflicts.

For example, as we have just seen, the development of manufacture—and, we should add, the development also of new techniques in agriculture—required and led to the employment of wage-labour. Only with capitalist relations could the newly-developed forces of production be more fully employed. But the existing feudal relations, which tied the labourer to the land and to the service of his lord, were a barrier to the development of the new productive forces. Hence these relations, within which production had once flourished, now began to act as a fetter. A contradiction arose between the old production relations and new productive forces.

So long as production relations are in conformity with productive forces, they remain relatively unchanged. And in some regions it has come about that certain production relations, once established, have proved so extraordinarily conservative that no impulse to improve productive forces has arisen within them—or if it did arise, it was strangled at birth, and the employment of new techniques was discouraged and put down. But wherever any people do develop new productive forces, this development eventually reaches a point where it is hindered by the existing relations of production. And it is at that point that a change in the relations of production becomes necessary, and is carried into effect.

The development of productive forces is a law of human history, which asserts itself despite all pauses and setbacks. Anything which opposes this irresistible development is bound, sooner or later, to be swept away. So when relations of production begin to hinder the use of new productive forces, the time is approaching when the social system based on them will fall.

What has taken place, up to the appearance of the capitalist economic formation, is that whenever people have developed new forces of production they have, in doing so, begun to enter into new relations of production; and then those new production relations have supplanted former ones and been consolidated into a new social-economic formation.

Thus the communal system of primitive communism corresponded to a very primitive level of development of production. When the cultivation of crops and domestication of animals appeared, the beginnings of private property and commodity exchange arose, and the old communal relations began to be changed. A new kind of community of separate households emerged, with "some more equal than others". When the use of metals was acquired, then society became further and more deeply divided.

The people who first settled in river valleys and began irrigation works could not organise those works except by means of some form of property in which they were centrally controlled by a single authority. A new type of property was eventually superimposed upon the old property of the members of the communes. A new type of social-economic formation arose and superseded the old, which was incapable of developing the new type of production. The land was said to belong to the gods, and those who supervised production and got the main share of the product were called gods or servants of gods: this was evidently an imaginative way of describing an economic arrangement, a form of property and of the exploitation of man by man, which had come into being because it was capable of organising production in a way older forms of property were not.

Those peoples who acquired the use of iron acquired thereby many advantages over those who had not done so. They were able to cultivate new lands, and to set up small industries; commodity exchange and the use of money increased and brought to the fore new landed and financial interests which broke and displaced former aristocracies. Where, as in Greece and Rome, a social-economic formation with slavery as the dominant mode of exploitation arose, this took place because large-scale agricultural enterprises, extractive industries and building could more effectively be carried on by slave labour than by clansmen paying tribute. The former labourers and proprietors were ruined, and the old production relations were replaced by the specific economic formation of the slave system of "classical" times.

Engels remarked (in part II, chap. 4, of *Anti-Dühring*) that this development of slavery thoroughly undermined the remnants of primitive communal relations which had survived throughout all former systems. "It was slavery," he wrote, "that first made possible the division of labour between agriculture and industry on a considerable scale. . . . We should never forget that our whole economic, political and intellectual development has as its presupposition a state of things in which slavery was as necessary as it was universally recognised. In this sense we may say: Without the slavery of antiquity, no modern socialism."—In China and other countries of the East, the ancient economic development of which is still imperfectly understood, communal relations among producers seem to have survived in a way that inhibited any internal development towards a capitalist mode of production, and to have proved a strongly conservative force until very recently when, the power of former landowners having been abolished, they could be transformed into the socialist relations of the people's commune.

So long as slavery remained in force in Europe as the main method of exploiting labour, improvements in production techniques—especially those making use of natural forces other than human muscle-power—were inhibited. But when, with invasions and the weakening of the central slave-owning power, the supply of slaves began to dry up, improvements associated with the fuller use of water power, improved harness for draught animals, improved ploughs, and so on, began to be effected. Slavery was never abolished at a single stroke; slave-labour remained alongside free labour. But the improved techniques were not easily workable by slave labour, and could be used to advantage within the feudal rather than the old slave relations. Feudal methods of exploitation then came to replace slavery.

Later still, feudalism in its turn came to hinder the development of the productive forces. Feudal ownership, feudal dues and restrictions on trade hampered the development of agriculture and manufacture employing new inventions which demanded a source of wage-labour. Feudalism then gave way to capitalism and capitalist relations of production.

The capitalist relations brought about a development of productive forces on a scale and at a speed unknown before. This was because scientific research now came to be a powerful force of production, and the drive for profit and accumulation of capital led the capitalist owners continually to develop new techniques. But the fuller use and development of the forces of production is now being blocked by capitalism.

The fundamental feature of the increase of the forces of production brought about within capitalism is the socialisation of labour. Petty, individual production has been replaced by the power of social labour, in which men co-operate together in great productive enterprises using power-driven machinery. Social labour is capable of immense achievements, miracles of construction for the welfare of all mankind. But it is fettered by the capitalist production relations, which make the product the property of the capitalists and compel social production to serve private profit.

Social production is in contradiction with private capitalist appropriation, and must needs break the fetter of the capitalist production relations. When social ownership and social appropriation is established to match social production, not only are all the brakes taken off technical advance, but the great productive forces of social labour are set free—people are their own masters and are working for themselves.

The general picture which emerges of social development from one formation of production relations to another is, then, as follows.

First, relations of production arise in conformity with the development of the productive forces. But a time comes when further development of new productive forces is hindered by old relations of production. From forms of development of the social forces of production, these relations turn into their fetters. Then comes a period of revolutionary change, when one type of production relations is replaced by another.

How, then, by what means, by what forces, are such changes brought about?

Class Struggle as the Motive Force of Social Change

Society develops through a series of stages, in each of which a definite type of property predominates. This development is far from being a smooth, gradual process of evolution, working itself out through a series of imperceptible changes and adjustments, without conflict. On the contrary, property relations are changed through a series of revolutions. And after the first establishment of private property, these are brought about by people pursuing class interests and by the struggle of one class against another.

As we have seen, whenever people develop new forces of production they begin to enter into new relations of production. Forms of property in means of production come into existence appropriate to the organisation of those forces of production. A method of exploitation, or of extraction of surplus labour from the producers, goes with those forms of property. And so, with the development of new forces of production, new classes arise, and new class divisions and antagonisms within society.

These antagonisms include, first of all, the antagonism between exploiters and exploited. The exploiters, as a class, seek all means to consolidate their property, to extract more surplus labour and to increase their wealth. Unless utterly beaten down and enslaved, the exploited resist this, and take whatever action they can to keep more of their labour for themselves. Moreover, those exploited classes which retain forms of property of their own—such as members of communes who have land in common or, later, serfs and free peasants—together with small independent producers or petty traders, seek to hang on to their property, to enlarge it if they can, and to resist encroachments from big exploiting property interests.

Thus there have been, for example, many peasant risings, slave revolts, and so on, aimed at getting free from at least some exactions and at winning security of tenure or resettlement on the land. Again, small men have resisted impoverishment and expropriation—sometimes for a time successfully, as with the big movements in ancient Greece and Rome which gained such demands as cancellation of debts.

Further, throughout history great exploiting classes have established empires. They have by armed force extended their sway over wide territories, subjecting the economically less developed people there to exploitation—exacting tribute, catching slaves, looting their resources. Modern imperialism, in essence the division of the world between great monopoly capitalist interests for purposes of exporting capital and obtaining raw materials and markets for metropolitan industries, is but the modern form of an imperialism which has thousands of years of history. Imperial conquest has always encountered the resistance of the conquered. And time and time again, this resistance has eventually contributed to the downfall of exploiting classes. When in the distant past great exploiting classes, with their empires, have been overthrown by barbarian invasions, these invasions were seldom simply invasions by nomads or other migrating peoples who were only after land or plunder. They were invasions by people who had the choice of either submitting to exploitation by ancient imperialists, or else attacking and overthrowing their empires. Modern imperialism does not face any invasion by "barbarians"—but the modern liberation movement of colonial peoples is none the less fatal to it.

Secondly, there are antagonisms between exploiting classes. In particular, the exploiting class whose property and method of exploitation is associated with the organisation of new and improved forces of production always comes into antagonism against older exploiting classes. Consolidating their property, struggling by all means, including armed force, to increase their wealth by extending their own method of exploitation, they come into collision with the older exploiters. And it is when circumstances favour them—as they generally do, because new forces of production are more powerful than old—that the older forms of property are overwhelmed, and the older exploiting classes are either eliminated altogether, by being ruined or perhaps killed off, or forced into a merely subsidiary place in the new economy.

With the rise of private property and exploitation, and the division of society into antagonistic classes, social life becomes a scene of violence, cruelty and war. However dark his superstitions and miserable his condition, there is no doubt that primitive man was comparatively peaceable. His life may have been, as Thomas Hobbes put it, "nasty, brutish and short", but it was not filled with war and civil strife. But the material interests of exploiting classes drive them into oppression and violence—into imposing by force their exaction of surplus labour, violent struggle against other classes, and aggressive wars. The specific character and aims of war depend on the method of obtaining wealth which motivates the war, whether to conquer new lands, catch slaves, secure new markets and raw materials, or find outlets for investment of capital.

Thus it has been through class struggles and wars that revolutionary social changes have been effected.

The waging of class struggles has always, as *The Communist Manifesto* put it, "ended, either in a revolutionary reconstitution of society at large, or in the common ruin of the contending classes". This "common ruin" seems often to have overtaken social organisms in earlier times, consummated often by invasions by barbarians. It was, by the way, this frequent phenomenon in history which apparently led Professor Arnold Toynbee, for example, to formulate a theory about the law of the rise and inevitable fall of all civilisations: he made a sweeping generalisation from numerous but insufficiently analysed data. But it is also possible that this could be the fate of our own civilisation, if antagonisms between old and new social formations end in nuclear warfare.

Every economic formation came into existence, overcame an older one and was consolidated under the lead of a definite class—namely, the class whose material interests were served by the mode of disposing of surplus labour peculiar to that formation. And since this new class appears as the opponent of the older exploiting class and of the existing system of exploitation and oppression, "the class making a revolution appears from the very start . . . as the representative of the whole of society" (Marx and Engels, *The German Ideology*, part I). It is thus able to mobilise the support of other classes opposed to its own main enemy, and this contributes to its victory. Afterwards, when a new method of exploitation becomes dominant in society, antagonisms break out afresh.

The bourgeoisie, in its battle against feudalism, was in this way able to mobilise the greater part of society against its feudal enemy. But when capitalism was under way, new class antagonisms broke out.

It is a peculiarity of capitalism that it simplifies class contradictions by bringing to the fore the one great antagonism between capitalist class and working class. The exploiting class is now faced with no rival exploiting class but only with the class of the exploited. But this is now an exploited class organised and educated by the very socialisation of labour which capitalism itself brings into existence. It is an exploited class for the first time able itself to take over leadership of the whole of society, not looking backwards to some older form of petty property but forward to social ownership of the means of production.

At the same time, capitalism greatly sharpens *all* class

contradictions. The first socialist revolution did not in fact take place where capitalism was already most highly developed. It took place in Russia, where the capitalist class was still comparatively weak but where all class contradictions had reached their sharpest expression—between workers and capitalists, peasants and landowners, national minorities and their oppressors. The Russian working class was able to take the lead of all the exploited, in order to overthrow all the exploiters and finally end the exploitation of man by man.

Individuals and Classes

The theory of class struggle enables us to understand the role of prominent individuals in history.

No class plays a role in history without leaders, so that the activities of public men play an essential part in getting things done—whether the leaders are heading revolutionary movements, consolidating gains, merely keeping things going, or defending lost causes. The authority and power of the historical personage, of the man whose actions seem, unlike those of historically anonymous people, to shape society for good or ill and to make history, is derived from a class. And unless he enjoys the support of a class whose interests and tendencies he represents, he is impotent and can exert no decisive influence.

Hence there arise in different historical periods prominent men of different types, varying with the task their class calls on them to fulfill. The barbarian conqueror, the tyrant, the prudent or vicious emperor, the good or bad king, the wily politician, the fiery agitator, the scientific socialist—all are products of the social conditions in which they play their parts. For the same reason, the type of personality that comes to the top is the one suited to the job in hand, while others, perhaps more gifted in other ways, remain obscure. Similarly, it is natural that in times of revolutionary change great and dynamic personalities come to the fore, while at other times only mediocrities show their faces.

Historical development is not determined by the personal decisions of public men, but by the movement of classes. The prominent men of a class affect its fortunes by the wisdom or otherwise of their actions, but they do not make or break a class. Moreover, where a leader is evidently failing, he tends to be deposed and someone more able to be substituted.

It is the same with cultural and intellectual leaders. Those who make their mark are those whose work reflects the needs of their times.

"When it is a question of investigating the driving powers which lie behind the motives of men who act in history," wrote Engels in *Ludwig Feuerbach* (chap. 4), "it is not a question so much of the motives of single individuals, however eminent, as of those motives which set in motion great masses, whole peoples, and again whole classes. To ascertain the driving causes which are reflected as conscious motives in the minds of acting masses and their leaders . . . is the only path which can put us on the track of the laws holding sway both in history as a whole and at particular periods in particular lands."

Those historians who fail to grasp the determining role of economic development and the class struggle in history find themselves in difficulties when trying to explain historical events—and even in deciding which events are worthy of being classed as "historical". If it is a matter of the personalities and motives of individuals accounting for what happens, then the historian is faced with the practical impossibility of finding sufficient evidence to know their personalities and their motives with any degree of certainty. Indeed, as it is usually hard enough to know the personal motives of one's own acquaintances, and even sometimes of oneself, it is evident that still less can be ascertained about individuals long dead, for whose characters only obviously biased testimonials are available. The historian has to fill in his lack of knowledge from his own bias and imagination: the innocent Miss Catherine Morland in *Northanger Abbey* can be excused for saying of history: "I often think it odd that it should be so dull, for a great deal of it must be invention."

But historians have only themselves to thank if they are thus driven into scepticism about the discovery of historical causes, and into the conclusion that what is actually "important" in history can be decided only by the subjective interest of the historian himself. While the details of individual motives must necessarily remain hidden, the social causes of historical development are open to historical knowledge; and what is "important" is objectively decided by its bearing on the development of the mode of production.

The State and Revolution

How has it been possible, in societies divided into exploiters and exploited, for an exploiting minority to preserve its domination over the majority, and for the social organism not to fall in pieces under stress of class struggle?

It has been possible only because the minority possessed and had control over a special organisation for coercing the rest of society and at the same time preserving the unity of society. That organisation is the state.

The state is not an organisation of the whole of society, but a special organisation within society, armed with power to repress and coerce. Whatever the form of the state—whether it be an autocracy, a military dictatorship, a democracy, etc. —its most essential components are the means to exercise compulsion over the members of society. Such compulsion is exercised by means of special bodies of armed men—soldiers, police and so on. It is enforced by physical means—by the possession of arms; by the possession of strong buildings, prisons, with locks and bars; by the possession of instruments to inflict pain and death. The state must also include a machinery of administration, a corps of state officials. It also develops a legal system, an authority for making laws and judges to interpret and administer them. And it also develops means not only of coercing men physically, but mentally, by various types of ideological and propaganda agencies.

Such a special organisation became necessary only when society was divided into antagonistic classes. From that time onwards, the state became necessary as a special power to prevent the social antagonisms from disrupting and destroying society.

"The state has not existed from all eternity," wrote Engels in *The Origin of the Family, the State and Private Property* (chap. 9). "At a definite stage of economic development, which involved the cleavage of society into classes, the state became a necessity because of this cleavage."

"As the state arose from the need to keep class antagonisms in check, but also in the thick of the fight between classes," he continued, "it is normally the state of the most powerful, economically ruling class, which by its means becomes also the politically ruling class, and so acquires new means of holding down and exploiting the oppressed class."

The state, wrote Lenin the *The State and Revolution* (chap. 1), is "an organ of class rule, an organ for the repression of one class by another".

At each stage of development, as we have seen, a particular type of production relations becomes predominant in the social economy, and the corresponding class assumes the dominant place in social production. It can gain and maintain that place only in so far as it can enforce its own interests upon the rest of society. And it can do that only in so far as it can gain and maintain control over the state. In every epoch, therefore, so long as society is divided into antagonistic classes, a particular class holds the state power and thereby establishes itself as the ruling class. In a slave society it is the slave-owners, in feudal society the feudal lords, in capitalist society the capitalists, and when capitalism is overthrown the working class becomes the ruling class.

When the working class becomes the ruling class, then there is no longer the rule of the minority of the exploiters over the majority of the exploited, but the rule of the majority. In this, working-class power differs from all previous state power. Previous state power has, as Marx expressed it in *The Eighteenth Brumaire of Louis Bonaparte* (chap. 7) perfected an "enormous bureaucratic and military organisation". The task of the working class is to smash it. When eventually all exploitation is eliminated, the coercive powers of the state will no longer be needed and the state itself will finally disappear.

In the history of class struggles every ruling exploiting class has always defended to the last the property relations on which depended its wealth and influence and, indeed, its very existence as a class. It has done so by its control over the state. And so all classes which stand in antagonism to the ruling class are inevitably driven into political action, if not to destroy the state power of the ruling class and wrest control of the state away from it, then at least to modify and influence that state power in their own interests.

"Every class struggle is a political struggle," wrote Marx and Engels in *The Communist Manifesto*. Just as, in the last analysis, every major political struggle is a struggle of classes, so the class struggle becomes a struggle to influence state, that is, political affairs and, in revolutionary periods, a struggle for state power.

Decisive revolutionary changes in the economic structure of society are necessitated, and the way is prepared for them, by an economic process which develops independently of men's will—by the growth of productive forces and the consequent incompatibility of old production relations with new productive forces. But such changes are actually carried through by political actions, very often taking the form of war. For whatever are the issues raised, and whatever forms the struggle takes, these are in the last analysis the ways in which men become conscious of the economic and class conflicts and fight them out.

Social revolution is, therefore, the transfer of state or political power from one class to another class. "The question of power is the fundamental question of every revolution," wrote Lenin, in an article *On Slogans*.

Revolution means the overthrow of a ruling class which defends existing relations of production, and the conquest of state power by a class which is interested in establishing new relations of production.

Every revolution, therefore, makes forcible inroads into existing property relations, and destroys one form of property in favour of another form of property.

"The abolition of existing property relations is not at all a distinctive feature of communism," said *The Communist*

Manifesto. "All property relations in the past have continually been subject to historical change consequent upon the change in historical conditions. The French Revolution, for example, abolished feudal property in favour of bourgeois property. The distinguishing feature of communism is not the abolition of property generally, but the abolition of bourgeois property."

Progress and Exploitation

The great revolutionary changes of the past have seen the replacement of one exploiting class by another exploiting class, and thus the replacement of one method of exploitation by another method of exploitation.

In this process, the revolutionary energy of the exploited masses in their struggle against the exploiters has helped to destroy one exploiting class—in order to replace it by another exploiting class. Their struggle has served to break up the old system and to replace it by a new and higher system, but still a system of class exploitation.

Thus the revolts of slaves against slaveowners helped to break up the slave system—but to replace it by the feudal system. And the revolts of serfs against their lords helped to break up the feudal system—but to replace it by the capitalist system.

The whole of human progress is rooted in the increasing mastery of men over nature, in the increase of the social forces of production. In advancing their mastery over nature, men not only obtain their material needs, but enlarge their ideas, perfect their knowledge, develop their various capacities.

But yet this progress has borne a contradictory character. As man has mastered nature, so has man oppressed and exploited man. The benefits of progress belonged at one pole of society, the toil and sweat at the other. Each new stage of advance brought only new methods of exploitation; and with each step, more people were exploited.

"Since civilisation is founded on the exploitation of one class by another class," wrote Engels in *The Origin of the Family etc.* (chap. 9), "its whole development proceeds in a constant contradiction. Every step forward in production is at the same time a step backwards in the position of the oppressed class—that is, of the great majority. Whatever benefits some necessarily injures others; every fresh emancipation of one class is necessarily a new oppression for another class."

Thus every step of progress has been made at the expense of the working people. The great advances of "classical" civilisation brought slavery in their train, and could only be carried through by means of slavery. The birth and growth of modern industry involved the wholesale ruin of small producers, the expropriation of masses of peasants from the land, the plunder of colonies, enormous increase of exploitation.

The growth of modern industry, however, has increased the powers of production to an extent unknown before. The power now exists, and for the first time, to produce plenty for everyone, without anyone wearing himself out with manual labour. In the past the forces of production were so limited that it was impossible to create conditions of leisure for any but a privileged minority of society. As Christ is reported to have said: "The poor ye have always with you." But this is no longer necessary today.

For just this reason, it is only now that the working people have arrived at a position when they themselves can rule and can take over the general management and direction of society. The slaves and serfs in the past could revolt time and again against their rulers, but were not themselves capable of taking command over production. They always had to look to someone else to manage social affairs. They always looked for a saviour, appealing to kings and other unlikely people to bring them justice. For the very character of the productive system meant that they were necessarily engrossed in manual labour, and so had to look to some privileged and educated minority to carry out the work of government.

We saw earlier that the division of society into exploiting and exploited classes was a result of the division of labour. And the division into rulers and ruled was a further consequence. With the development of production, a number of functions concerned with safeguarding the general interests of the community necessarily became the province of a special group within the community.

"This independence of social functions in relation to society increased with time," wrote Engels in *Anti-Dühring* (part II, chap. 4), "until it developed into domination over society." Consequently, the majority of the people were relegated to the position where they were wholly occupied with toil, and the general functions of social management were assumed by a master class.

"So long as the working population was so much occupied in their necessary labour that they had no time left for looking after the common affairs of society—the direction of labour, affairs of state, legal matters, art, science, etc.—so long was it necessary that there should exist a special class, freed from actual labour, to manage these affairs." And then this class "never failed to impose a greater and greater burden of labour, for their own advantage, on the working masses.

"Only the immense increase of the productive forces attained through large-scale industry makes it possible to limit the labour time of each individual to such an extent that all have enough free time to take part in the general—both theoretical and practical—affairs of society. It is only now, therefore, that any ruling and exploiting class has become superfluous."

It is not the case, then, that throughout history all ruling classes have been parasites upon the body of society. They have performed a necessary social function. But as production has advanced, a larger part of the ruling classes has become parasitical, until now they perform no necessary function whatever.

By the beginning of the present century capitalism had developed to the stage of imperialism, when a few giant monopolies divided up the entire world among themselves. All the peoples were subject to them. There was an enormous accession of wealth and power into a few hands. Never before was the contrast between the wealth and power of the few and the poverty and subjection of the many so glaring, nor had it existed on such a world scale. But this was also the time for the people themselves to take over. The epoch of imperialism is the epoch of socialist revolution—a revolution of an altogether new kind, which abolishes all exploitation and lays the foundations of a society without class antagonisms.

By creating the socialised production of modern large-scale industry, capitalism has created conditions in which for the first time there exists the possibility of securing for all members of society not only continually improving material standards but also the completely unrestricted development of all their faculties. And it has created in the working class an exploited class which, by its very position as the product of large-scale industry, is fully capable of taking over the management of society. The very advance of industry creates the conditions in which the working class not only grows in numbers and organisation, but trains itself for the task of taking command of production.

Thus "the history of class struggles forms a series of evolutions in which, nowadays, a stage has been reached where the exploited and oppressed class—the proletariat—cannot attain its emancipation from the sway of the exploiting and ruling class—the bourgeoisie—without, at the same time, and once and for all, emancipating society at large from all exploitation, oppression, class distinction and class struggles" (Engels, Preface to the 1888 English edition of *The Communist Manifesto*).

The Socialist Revolution

The principal conclusion of the scientific investigation of social development is, then, that of the historical necessity of the socialist revolution. And the materialist conception of history reveals on what forces socialism must rely, and how its victory can be won.

The socialist revolution is different in kind from every previous revolutionary change in human society.

In every revolution the economic structure of society is transformed. Every previous transformation has meant the birth and consolidation of a new system of exploitation. The socialist revolution, on the other hand, once and for all ends all exploitation of man by man.

In every revolution a new class comes to power, as ruling

class. In every previous revolution power was transferred into the hands of an exploiting class, a tiny minority of society. In the socialist revolution, on the other hand, power passes into the hands of the working class, at the head of all the working people—that is, into the hands of the vast majority. And this power is used, not to uphold the privileges of an exploiting class, but to destroy all such privileges and to end all class antagonisms.

Every revolution, since class society began, has been an act of liberation, inasmuch as it has achieved the emancipation of society from some form of class oppression. To this extent, every revolution has had a popular character. But in every previous revolution one form of oppression has been thrown off only to be replaced by another. The energy of the masses has been devoted to destroying the oppression of the old system. But the new system which replaced the old was built under the direction of new exploiters, who invariably made it their business to impose new forms of oppression on the people. In the socialist revolution, on the other hand, the people not only destroy the old system, they are themselves the builders of the new.

The condition of the transition from capitalism to socialism is the conquest of power by the working class—in other words, the ending of capitalist class rule and the establishment of the dictatorship of the proletariat.

In order that the working people may build socialism, in order that capitalist property may be abolished in favour of socialist property, the capitalist state must be replaced by a workers' socialist state.

Led by the working class, and with power in their own hands, the task of the working people is then to confiscate capitalist property in the principal means of production and to make them social property, suppress the resistance of the defeated capitalist class, organise planned production for the benefit of society as a whole, and finally abolish all exploitation of man by man.

Summing up the principal lessons of historical materialism, in a letter to J. Weydemeyer (March 5th, 1852), Marx wrote:

"No credit is due to me for discovering the existence of classes in modern society, nor yet the struggle between them. Long before me bourgeois historians had described the historical development of this struggle of the classes, and bourgeois economists the economic anatomy of the classes. What I did new was to prove:

(1) that the existence of classes is only bound up with particular historical phases of the development of production;

(2) that the class struggle necessarily leads to the dictatorship of the proletariat;

(3) that this dictatorship itself only constitutes the transition to the abolition of all classes and to a classless society."

Chapter Five

THE SOCIAL SUPERSTRUCTURE

The Ideas and Institutions of Society

The materialist conception of history, wrote Engels in the introduction to *Socialism, Utopian and Scientific*, "seeks the ultimate cause and great moving power of all important historical events in the economic development of society, in the changes in the mode of production and exchange, in the consequent division of society into distinct classes, and in the struggle of these classes against one another".

The fundamental law of social change is the law which governs the changes in the mode of production. The growth of the forces of production comes into conflict with the existing relations of production, leading to social revolution, to the fall of the old system of relations of production and the creation of a new system, to the overthrow of the old ruling class and the coming to power of a new class.

But "in considering such transformations," wrote Marx (Preface to *Critique of Political Economy*), "a distinction should always be made between the material transformations of the economic conditions of production, which can be determined with the precision of natural science, and the legal, political, religious, aesthetic and philosophic—in short, ideological—forms in which men become conscious of the conflict and fight it out. Just as our opinion of an individual is not based on what he thinks of himself, so can we not judge of such a period of transformation by its own consciousness; on the contrary, this consciousness must be explained rather from the contradictions of material life, from the existing conflict between the social forces of production and the relations of production."

For instance, at the close of the Middle Ages many people were prepared to die for the sake of the new Protestant religion, and fierce religious wars took place. But were they really fighting only for religion? Out of the religious wars arose new states and ultimately the establishment and consolidation of capitalist society. The urge to new ideas arose as a result of the formation of new relations of production and new classes, and people became conscious of conflicts based on economic contradictions as conflicts of new ideas and ideals against old ones.

Again, in Britain the new bourgeoisie at the time of the civil war fought for parliamentary institutions against the king. The civil war was fought as a war for parliament against royalty, and likewise as a war of puritans against churchmen. But the real content of the war was a fight of the bourgeoisie for power. The bourgeoisie controlled parliament, it was their institution, used by them in the fight against royalty. And when they did establish parliamentary government, it led to the creation of conditions for the unfettered development of manufacture and commerce.

In general, struggles about ideas and institutions are struggles through which people become conscious of their economic conflicts and fight them out—through which people on the one side defend and on the other side attack a given system of production relations. Such conflicts arise from contradictions between the social forces of production and the relations of production, which necessitate the development of new relations of production. It is through struggles about institutions and ideas that the conflicts are fought out and economic development effected.

Hence in considering the development of society we have not only to consider the basic development of the mode of production and the economic contradictions which in the last analysis determine that development. We have also to consider the way in which people, in their conscious social activity, "become conscious of conflict and fight it out". We have to consider, in short, the development of the ideas and institutions of society. For ideas and institutions play an active role in social development, and it is through them that people carry on their social life and fight out the conflicts arising from it.

Social Being and Social Consciousness

According to idealist conceptions of history, as opposed to the materialist conception, the primary, determining factor in social development is to be found in the ideas and institutions of society. According to the idealists, men first develop certain ideas, then they create institutions corresponding to those ideas, and on that basis they carry on their economic life. In this way they place things exactly upside down. They put everything on its head. For instead of ideas and institutions developing on the basis of the material life of society, they say that material life develops on the basis of ideas and institutions.

"The whole previous view of history," said Engels in his speech at Marx's graveside, "was based on the conception that the ultimate causes of all historical changes are to be looked for in the changing ideas of human beings. . . . But the question was not asked as to whence the ideas come into men's minds."

Once this question is asked, he went on to explain, "the ideas of each historical period are most simply to be explained from the economic conditions of life, and from the social and political relations of the period which are in turn determined by these economic conditions."

Let us take an example.

It is often supposed that our forefathers overthrew the former feudal relations of subordination because the idea was born in their minds that men were equal. But why should this idea have suddenly become so influential? Why should the feudal relations of subordination, which for centuries had been held to be natural and just, suddenly begin to appear unnatural and unjust? These questions lead us from the sphere of ideas to the sphere of the conditions of material life. It was because material, economic conditions were changing that influential classes of people began to think in a new way, and to condemn institutions which up to then few had questioned. The existing feudal relations were no longer in keeping with developing economic conditions. It was the development of economic activity and economic relations which created the forces which overthrew feudalism and laid the foundations of capitalism. And so the rise and spread of the idea of equality, as opposed to feudal inequality, followed upon and reflected the changes in material conditions of life.

Again, why should the idea of socialism have suddenly grown so influential once capitalism was under way? For centuries private property had been regarded as natural and just, and even as the necessary basis for any civilisation. But now, on the contrary, it began to appear unnecessary and oppressive. Once more, this new way of thinking, and the profound influence which socialist ideas began to exert, arose from new economic conditions. Under capitalism production was ceasing to be an individual matter and was becoming a social matter, and private property and private appropriation based on it were no longer in keeping with the new character of production.

In general, the rise of new ideas can never be regarded as a sufficient explanation of social changes, since the origin of ideas and the source of their social influence must always itself be explained. And this explanation is to be sought in the conditions of material life of society.

We shall find accordingly that corresponding to the different conditions of material life of society at different periods quite different ideas are current, and that the differences in the ideas of different classes in different periods—and likewise in the organisations and institutions which they support and set up—are always in the last analysis to be explained in terms of differences in conditions of material life.

"Does it require deep intuition," asked Marx and Engels in *The Communist Manifesto*, "to comprehend that man's ideas, views and conceptions, in a word, man's consciousness, changes with every change in the conditions of his material existence, in his social relations and in his social life?"

Summing up in the Preface to *Critique of Political Economy*, Marx wrote: "It is not the consciousness of men that determines their being, but, on the contrary, their social being that determines their consciousness."

Basis and Superstructure

In entering into relations of production and carrying on the economic activities of production and distribution people acquire definite interests and requirements of life, and become involved in conflicts arising from contradictory interests and requirements. All these are objective, material facts, which exist independently of what people may think about them. But people act consciously, have ideas about themselves and their aims in life, and in their conscious activity are organised within all kinds of institutions to serve all kinds of consciously conceived purposes.

In considering, therefore, the totality of social life we have to distinguish, on the one hand, the economic structure and economic development of society, which exists quite independently of what people think and may be determined with the precision of natural science; and, on the other hand, the ideas and conscious aims which arise in people's minds, and the institutions which are developed in accordance with those ideas and aims.

Hence in the study of society we should distinguish two distinct aspects, or interconnected strands of social development: on the one hand, the development of production relations and the conflicts arising from it; on the other hand, the whole intellectual, political and institutional development of society. On the one hand, there is the development of productive forces and of relations of production—the passage from one mode of production to another, of one social-economic formation to another. On the other hand, there is the development of religion, politics, art, philosophy, and of churches, states, parties, organisations and movements, and institutions of all kinds.

What is the relation between these two strands of development? Marx called it the relation of "basis" to "superstructure". At whatever stage of social evolution, people are engaged together in a mode of production; on the basis of their production relations they work out ideas and associate in institutions, through which they represent to themselves their various interests and organise themselves in pursuit of their interests. These are said to develop as a superstructure upon the basis.

Thus people conceive and adopt religious, political, philosophical, moral or aesthetic ideas, and associate in institutions intended to embody them and propagate them. But they do not do this as it were in a vacuum. They are members of a society kept going by a certain mode of production, linked together by definite production relations. Such relations constitute the necessary basis for any social life; without such relations there can be no social life at all, and therefore no ideas or institutions. These relations, therefore, always constitute the basis on which people come together for any social purpose—the basis of all ideologies and institutions.

It follows that the ideas and institutions people adopt are always conditioned by their basic social relations, the relations of production. And the ideas which gain currency and the institutions through which people carry on their social life change with changes in the basic production relations. Aims, outlooks and beliefs, and likewise organisations and institutions, are created answering to the opportunities, needs and interests—including, of course, conflicting interests—which are inherent in the relations of production.

The distinction of "basis" and "superstructure", as two strands or levels of social development, is a distinction between those social processes which are the most obvious and open to investigation, and most immediately affect the members of society and strike the attention of historians, and those which are less immediately obvious and the details of which can only be uncovered by patient researches. What is most obvious is the ideas which people are proclaiming, the institutions they are organised in, the arguments they are engaging in, the speeches they are making and the epithets they are throwing at each other, and the political battles and wars they are fighting. Less obvious and, as it were, buried beneath all this but nevertheless sustaining it, are the economic relations and economic processes of society. All the hurly-burly on the surface is conditioned by the underlying economic relationships, and serves a social function relative to their development.

In carrying on production and entering into production relations adapted to their forces of production, people require, first of all, what may be called institutions of management, and institutions of rule or state institutions. In so far as production is managed and society is ruled in the interests of a particular class, with management and rule serving the purpose of furthering a particular mode of exploitation, there also take shape forms of organised self-protection and resistance, or of revolutionary struggle, on the part of the non-ruling or exploited classes.

In feudal Europe, for instance, the manorial institutions and guilds, and in later capitalist societies the firms, limited liability companies, chambers of commerce, government departments, trade unions, and so on, are all institutional forms through which production is managed and basic economic conflicts carried on. These forms have their own development, and may vary greatly according to circumstances. For instance, in Britain today the light engineering industry is managed through the competition of numerous firms, the chemical industry is managed mainly by a single great monopoly, the railways are managed by a nationalised public authority. Similarly, forms of management of socialist industries may differ in different circumstances, according to the degree of centralisation or decentralisation of management, and so on. Further, just as the different forms of management and rule take shape historically and, by their form, influence the course of historical development, the same applies to the organisation of opposition and resistance. For instance, the peculiar historically-constituted structure of the British labour movement as compared with that of other Western European countries or of the U.S.A. has its effects in the contemporary social struggles in Britain.

Political and economic ideas, programmes and modes of thought take shape in connection with the functions of management and rule, either to promote or to resist the particular form of management and rule. This is the most immediate or direct way in which institutional and ideological processes are connected with the basic economic structure. More remotely connected with the economic basis, and more directly related to the current institutional and political conflicts, there arise further ideological processes—religious, legal, philosophical, artistic, and so on—and the institutions associated with them.

It is worth noting, further, that the relation of "basis" and "superstructure" is essentially a dynamic and not a static relation. It is essentially a relation between inseparable aspects of the total social process, one of which develops on the basis of the other and serves a social function relative to the other—the ideological and institutional process on the basis of the economic structure, and serving a social function relative to economic development. Words can be misleading, especially when they make use of analogies, as do the words "basis" and "superstructure". Thus if you think of society as like a building, which has a "basis" or "foundation" buried in the earth, and a "superstructure" consisting of the various storeys erected on the foundation, that is misleading—for society, unlike a building, is continually changing and developing. Of what does society consist? It is not at all like a building, made of bricks or of a steel framework with slabs of concrete fixed on to it. Society consists of individual people engaged in social activities. The precondition of all their activities is production, in doing which they enter into social relations of production corresponding to their forces of production; they engage in all other social activities and enter into all other social relations on the basis of these relations of production. It is in this sense that the ideological and institutional development of society takes place on the basis of economic development. It is in this sense that the ideas which are current in any society at any time, the institutions, and likewise the ideological controversies and institutional rivalries, develop as a superstructure on the basis of the production relations.

The Methodology of Historical Explanation

We saw above that idealist conceptions of history, according to which ideas and institutions are the determining factors in social development, are defective because they fail to answer the question "whence the ideas come into men's minds".

On the other hand, the strand of economic development is self-explanatory. If you ask "why did certain economic relations arise?"—why did private property come into being, why did products become commodities, why did wage-labour come into being, and so on—then you do not have to look outside the sphere of economic development itself in order to find the explanation.

And then, having established the trend of economic development and the economic causes of it, it can be explained why, on the basis of that development, people grew dissatisfied with some ideas and developed other ones, rebelled against some institutions and set up other ones.

At the same time, the ideas and institutions which are developed on the basis of the economy are not simply a "reflex" or by-product—they are not simply passive consequences, but play an active role in relation to the economy. The economic development of society is the development of men's mastery over nature, to which end they develop their forces of production and enter into corresponding relations of production. Men's ideas and institutions are not irrelevant to this economic development. On the contrary, they play an indispensable role in it.

Thus, for example, from the economic processes of feudalism in Europe arose not only what we now term feudal ideas and institutions but also ideological controversies and institutional rivalries and upheavals which reflected the conflict between nascent capitalism and decaying feudalism; great ideological battles, political upheavals and religious wars took place—and all this played an indispensable part in the development of the feudal economy itself and in the economic change from feudalism to capitalism.

Similarly today, the basis of current ideologies and institutions, and of ideological and institutional conflicts, is economic.

But it is by employing ideologies and institutions, and by struggle in the sphere of ideology and institutions, that we today work out our economic destiny.

Hence in the history of society the economic process is always the basis for explaining the ideological and institutional process. But simultaneously the ideological and institutional process has a necessary function in relation to the economy, and explains how the economic process is actually carried on. For people cannot carry on their basic economic activity—they cannot live in society—without ideas whereby they represent to themselves their state of being and their purposes, and without institutions through which to realise their purposes. Yet how they represent themselves to themselves, and what purposes they set before themselves, must always depend upon their actual material circumstances—their economic activity, their relations of production, and the economic conflicts which thence arise.

What makes the economic process basic in social development is that the direction of the economic process is explicable in terms of economic laws. Once these laws are grasped, the whole of social development, the whole immensely complex interaction, becomes explicable—at least in general outline. But in terms of ideas and institutions alone, it cannot be explained—since ideas and institutions develop on the basis of the economy and have no independent development. "They have no history, no development," Marx and Engels declared in *The German Ideology*; "but men, developing their material production and their material intercourse, alter, along with this their real existence, their thinking and the products of their thinking."

So long, then, as ideas are regarded as being the determining factor in the development of society it is impossible to arrive at any scientific explanation of social development, that is, to explain it in terms of laws of development. For if the changing ideas and motives operating in social life are considered by themselves, as an independent sphere, then it is impossible to discover any universal laws that regulate them. In that case, as the Right Hon. H. A. L. Fisher stated in the

Preface to his *History of Europe*, "there can be only one safe rule for the historian: that he should recognise in the development of human destinies the play of the contingent and the unforeseen". In other words, the very possibility of a scientific treatment of social phenomena, of a science of society, is ruled out. It is only when we turn to the economic basis that we discover the universal law of social development—that people enter into production relations corresponding to their forces of production. Then the apparently fortuitous development of ideology, religion, politics and so on fits into a pattern and finds its explanation.

Marx "was the first to put sociology on a scientific basis," wrote Lenin, in *What the Friends of the People Are*, "by establishing the concept of the economic formation of society as the sum total of relations of production, and by establishing the fact that the development of such formations is a process of natural history."

Lenin went on to point out that in *Capital* Marx not only exhaustively analysed the capitalist economic structure and its laws of development, but also showed how corresponding to its development there arise definite modes of consciousness.

Having in the 1840's arrived at the general conception of historical materialism, Marx proceeded to apply, develop and verify it.

"He took one of the economic formations of society—the system of commodity production—and on the basis of a vast mass of data gave a most detailed analysis of the laws governing the functioning of this formation and its development.

"This analysis is strictly confined to the relations of production between the members of society. Without ever resorting to factors other than relations of production to explain the matter, Marx makes it possible to discern how the commodity organisation of society develops, how it becomes transformed into capitalist economy. . . .

"Such is the 'skeleton' of *Capital*. But the whole point of the matter is that Marx did not content himself with this skeleton . . . that while explaining the structure and development of the given formation of society exclusively in terms of relations of production, he nevertheless everywhere and always went on to trace the superstructure corresponding to these relations of production, and clothed the skeleton in flesh and blood. . . .

"*Capital* . . . exhibited the whole capitalist social formation to the reader as a live thing—with its everyday aspects, with the actual social manifestation of the antagonisms of classes inherent in the relations of production, with the bourgeois political superstructure which preserves the domination of the capitalist class, with the bourgeois ideas of liberty, equality and so forth, with the bourgeois family relations."

Capital demonstrated, by the close scientific study of a particular economic formation, how the production relations develop, and how an entire superstructure of ideas and institutions develops on the basis of the production relations. Lenin therefore concluded that "since the appearance of *Capital* the materialist conception of history is no longer a hypothesis but a scientifically demonstrated proposition".

Historical materialism provides a methodology for historical explanation. Its truth is demonstrated by applying this methodology in concrete cases, and finding that it really does explain.

Historical Materialism versus "Vulgar Marxism"

From what has already been said it should be evident that the explanation of the development of the various elements of the superstructure in the actual history of any people is by no means a simple matter.

One species of oversimplified, mechanistic or "vulgar" explanation is that which seeks to explain the development of ideas and institutions directly from the productive forces. Thus, for example, it has been suggested that the rise of new ideologies in the ancient world was due to the development of new techniques, in employing which people came to change their ideas. Indeed, it is true that people conversant with iron-working do think differently from people who know only stone tools, just as people acquainted with nuclear bombs and electronics do think differently from people acquainted only with bows and arrows and hand-labour. It is therefore suggested also that modern ideas and institutions arise directly from the modern forces of production—and so the present is called "the nuclear age" or "the age of science". But while it is true that there exists a certain correspondence between ideas and institutions on the one hand, and forces of production on the other, it is not true that the former can ever be explained directly from the latter. For employing their forces of production people enter into relations of production, and it is on the basis of the relations of production that they create their ideas and institutions. It is obvious enough, for instance, that today both capitalist and socialist countries employ the same production techniques—yet the course of the ideological development and the character of institutions differ greatly in the two cases, for in the one case there is a basis of capitalist relations of production and in the other case of socialist relations of production.

A more common type of vulgarisation is that which treats the development of the superstructure on its economic basis as an automatic process. But ideas and institutions are not the automatic products of a given economic and class structure, but products of people's conscious activities and struggles. To explain the superstructure, these activities and struggles must be studied concretely, in their actual complex development. Therefore it is certainly not Marxism, just as it is certainly not science, to attempt to conclude from the specification of certain economic conditions what the form of the superstructure arising on that basis is going to be, or to deduce every detailed characteristic of the superstructure from some corresponding feature of the basis. On the contrary, we need to study how the superstructure actually develops in each society and in each epoch, by investigating the facts about that society and that epoch.

Quite a few vulgarisers of Marxism—some calling themselves "Marxists", others serving out absurd travesties of Marxism in order to refute it—have represented Marxism as saying that every idea and institution in society is directly produced by and serves some immediate economic need. Of such vulgarisers Engels reports (in a letter to C. Schmidt, August 5th, 1890) that Marx himself used to say: "All I know is that I am not a Marxist."

In the same letter Engels stressed that "our conception of history is above all a guide to study, not a lever of construction. . . . All history must be studied afresh, the conditions of existence of the different formations of society must be examined in detail, before the attempt is made to deduce from them the political, civil-legal, aesthetic, philosophic, religious, etc., notions corresponding to them".

Engels repeatedly stressed the need to examine concretely in every case the way in which particular ideas and institutions arise and take shape on the basis of given economic development, and the influence which they in turn exert upon the further development of society.

He expressly warned against misunderstandings arising from the manner in which he and Marx had occasionally presented the theory.

"Marx and I are ourselves partly to blame for the fact that younger writers sometimes lay more stress on the economic side than is due to it," he wrote to J. Bloch (September 21st, 1890). "We had to emphasise this main principle in opposition to our adversaries, who denied it, and we had not always the time, the place or the opportunity to allow the other elements involved in the interaction to come into their rights."

"According to the materialist conception of history," he continued, in the same letter, "the *ultimately* determining element in history is the production and reproduction of real life. More than that neither Marx nor I have ever asserted. Hence if someone twists that into saying that the economic element is the *only* determining one, he transforms that proposition into a meaningless, abstract, senseless phrase."

"Political, juridical, philosophical, religious, literary, artistic, etc., developments are based on economic development," Engels further wrote—in a letter to H. Starkenburg, January 25th, 1894. "But all these react upon one another and also upon the economic basis. It is not that the economic condition is the *cause* and *alone active*, while everything else is only a passive effect. There is, rather, interaction on the basis of economic necessity, which *ultimately* always asserts itself."

Engels also emphasised that while, in general, ideas and institutions are products of economic conditions, the exact form which they take in a particular country at a particular time cannot be explained exclusively from the economic conditions of that country at that time. On the contrary, while the influence of economic development always asserts itself, current ideas and institutions must always depend on a variety of factors in a country's life, including the character and traditions of its people, the personalities of its leading men, and, above all, its past history.

Considering, for example, the development of legal ideas, Engels pointed out that while law always reflects existing economic conditions, "the form in which this happens can vary considerably. It is possible, as happened in England, in harmony with the whole national development, to retain in the main the forms of the old feudal laws while giving them a bourgeois content; in fact, directly giving a bourgeois meaning to the old feudal name. But also, as happened in Western continental Europe, Roman law, the first world law of a commodity-producing society . . . can be taken as a foundation. . . . After the great bourgeois revolution, such a classic law code as the French *Code Civil* can be worked out on the basis of this same Roman Law" (*Ludwig Feuerbach*, chap. 4).

Thus in these cases legal ideas and codes of law arose, not as a direct product of economic conditions, but by a process of working upon and adapting the already existing law, which belonged to a past epoch, into forms suitable for the new epoch.

It has been the same, Engels points out, with philosophy. "I consider the ultimate supremacy of economic development established," he wrote in a letter to C. Schmidt, October 27th, 1890. "But it comes to pass within conditions imposed by the particular sphere itself: in philosophy, for instance, through the operation of economic influences (which again generally act only through political etc. disguises) upon the existing philosophic material handed down by predecessors."

The actually existing ideas and institutions of a country, therefore, cannot be explained solely from the economic conditions of that country at a particular time. "Economy creates nothing absolutely new," Engels wrote in the same letter. "But it determines the way in which existing material of thought is altered and further developed."

What is of fundamental importance in the development of ideas and institutions is, then, simply that they do not have an independent development but are created on the basis of the given economy. The problem always remains of explaining the peculiarities of the development of ideas and institutions in each particular country, and what role they play in each particular period of its history. This problem can never be solved by means of general formulas alone, but only in the light of the facts themselves.

In short, when it is a matter, not of the abstract enunciation of general principles, but of the application of these principles in the explanation of particular historical events, then the detailed study of the actual mode of derivation of ideas and institutions on the basis of economic conditions, and of the active role they play in events, cannot be neglected. And Marx himself has provided examples of this application in his historical writings.

In *The Eighteenth Brumaire of Louis Bonaparte,* for example, he shows in detail how particular ideas and institutions, political parties, political conflicts and trends of ideas, arose on the basis of definite economic and class relations in French society in the mid-19th century, and how the ensuing struggles in the realms of politics and ideology influenced the fate of the various classes and of the French economy as a whole.

Such detailed understanding of the political and ideological factors, their basis and influence, is, of course, vitally important in the analysis made of a present situation with a view to mapping out practical policy. We cannot arrive at a policy for the working-class movement in a given situation simply from an analysis, however exact, of the economic position. It is necessary to take into account all the existing political factors, in all their complexity, and also the various trends of ideas, and to understand how these not only reflect but influence the economic situation, in order to arrive at a practical policy. For in given economic circumstances, political action, and also ideological struggle generally, has a decisive effect in influencing the further course of economic development, the fate of the various classes and of the whole economy.

Chapter Six

CLASS IDEAS AND CLASS RULE

The Establishment

On the basis of given relations of production there are always created ideas and institutions adapted to maintain, consolidate and develop that basis. These are ideas which implicitly accept and justify the established property and class relations, and institutions which work to preserve those class relations and to administer, consolidate and develop that form of property. People could not carry on social production without entering into definite relations of production, and those relations of production could not be maintained without the appropriate ideas and institutions.

Thus when a given economic system is established there always crystallises out from the whole process of ideological and institutional activity a complex of ideas and institutions which serves the definite function of preserving the established order. To this may be conveniently applied the newly invented, though ill-defined, term—"the establishment". It is created in controversy and struggle by the class whose interest it is to establish and consolidate the particular economic system.

At the centre of the establishment is the state power and the legal system. The state and the laws serve to defend property and to regulate its use and inheritance. The political and legal system, with the corresponding ideology, become established as guardians of property.

The Romans, for example, to consolidate their slave empire developed first republican institutions to supplant the petty kings of an earlier period, and a republican ideology; and when these institutions and ideas proved unable to hold social antagonisms in check, they developed a centralised military dictatorship.

With the break-up of the Roman Empire and the rise of feudalism in Europe, the forms of government changed. The kingdoms, principalities, dukedoms, etc., which were established all over Europe developed as forms of feudal rule, which served to defend, maintain and consolidate the feudal system. And of central importance in what may be termed the feudal establishment in Europe was the Catholic Church.

The rising bourgeoisie came into conflict with the feudal system and with feudal rule, and as a product of its struggle set up national republics, parliamentary states, constitutional monarchies, which allowed free scope to the development of capitalism, defended the interests of the bourgeoisie, stood guard over their property, and so served to shape and consolidate the basis of capitalist society.

Lastly, the working class in its struggle for socialism has to establish a democratic socialist state, which will have the task of eliminating the remnants of capitalism, guarding socialist property, and directing the work of socialist construction.

Without such means none of these economies could have been consolidated. It is only with the help of a state, of a political and legal system, and of corresponding ideologies, that a system of economy becomes established and is able to develop. The exact form and character of the state—whether it is a monarchy like Britain, or a republic like the U.S.A.—and of the political and legal ideas and institutions, and the various changes which they undergo, depend on a variety of circumstances in the life and tradition of each people. Such features are determined historically by special circumstances of time and place. But they are always subject to the controlling condition that they serve to consolidate and develop a particular economic basis.

Religions, philosophies, literary and artistic movements develop as ramifications of the establishment. No social-economic formation could be kept in being and made to work without them, any more than without politics and laws. And they are no more independent of the economic basis than are politics or law. These types of ideology, and the corresponding institutions, are developed by people on the basis of their given production relations; and in this development there crystallise out religious orthodoxies, philosophical schools, literary and artistic canons, which come to assume a special authority as bulwarks of the social order.

In the heyday of feudalism in Western Europe the Catholic Church possessed enormous authority, and Catholic orthodoxy permeated philosophy, literature and the arts. This orthodoxy was upheld by the temporal power—by the feudal rulers and their states, and by the laws. The cruel zeal with which the Church pursued heretics, and was supported by the rulers, is not explicable simply as religious fanaticism. For why was there such fanaticism? Catholic orthodoxy had become established as an essential part of the social order; and the Church, as a great landowner, together with the other great landowners, sensed the danger of social disruption—and rightly too—lurking behind every heresy.

With the rise of the bourgeoisie, new religious and philosophical ideas came into ascendency. In religion emphasis was placed on the individual conscience and the individual's direct relation with God. Philosophers propounded the sovereignty of science and reason, and from this point of view subjected the old feudal ideas to devastating criticism. They examined anew the foundations of knowledge and tried to show how knowledge could be extended and humanity be set upon the road to progress. In this they effectively served the new bourgeoisie in getting rid of feudalism and consolidating capitalism.

Now, when capitalism is in decay and is being challenged by socialism, the philosophers of the establishment have a very different tale to tell. They say that reason is powerless, that knowledge is an illusion, that material progress is a mistake and that the means whereby men have hoped to achieve it lead them into difficulties and disasters. These new orthodoxies in turn help to defend the dying system and to stave off the challenge of socialism.

In the same way can be traced out how the medieval songs and stories and religious art, for example, helped the feudal system take shape and consolidate itself; and how the modern novel, drama, etc., helped to eliminate feudalism and helped the capitalist system take shape and consolidate itself.

Ruling Class and Ruling Ideas

Since the dissolution of primitive communism, society has been divided into antagonistic classes, into exploiters and exploited, these classes themselves being products of economic development. And corresponding to the economic structure of society at the given stage of development, to the given system of production relations, one or another class has occupied the dominating position in economy and has assumed leadership of society as a whole.

It is always a particular class which plays the leading part in establishing and then in consolidating a given economic system, in which that particular class is dominant, the ruling class. It is accordingly always this class which is primarily responsible for establishing the ideas and institutions to guard the social order. The establishment is a class establishment—developed on the basis of the forms of property and the class relations with which the interests of the ruling class are bound up.

"Upon the different forms of property, upon the social conditions of existence, rises an entire superstructure of distinct and peculiarly formed sentiments, illusions, modes of thought and views of life," wrote Marx, in *The Eighteenth Brumaire* (chap. 3). "The entire class creates and forms them out of its material foundations and out of the corresponding social relations."

The ruling class is able to achieve this because of its ownership of the material means of production and its control, through the state, of material power. "The class which is the ruling material force in society is at the same time its ruling intellectual force," wrote Marx and Engels in *The German Ideology*. For "the class which has the means of material production at its disposal has control at the same time over the means of mental production, so that thereby, generally speaking, the ideas of those who lack the means of mental production are subject to it".

Thus Marx and Engels declared in *The Communist Manifesto:* "The ruling ideas of each age have ever been the ideas of its ruling class."

This ideological domination is, indeed, an essential element of class domination. Class domination cannot continue unless the ruling class can establish ruling institutions according to its own ideas, and by the general acceptance of those ideas secure the general acceptance of its institutions and rule. To maintain its material rule, the ruling class must always maintain its rule over the minds of men. It must bind the intellectual forces of society to itself, and secure the propagation of ideas which, by expressing its dominance, forestall any challenge to its dominance.

The Role of Intellectuals

When we speak of the ideas of the ruling class being the ruling ideas, this does not mean, of course, that all the members of the ruling class participate in forming and propagating those ideas. The consolidation of the economic system, and of the system of class rule, always requires certain individuals to undertake administrative and executive functions; and similarly, certain individuals always come to specialise in an intellectual function.

Every class which plays an active as distinct from a merely passive role in social change always finds its own intellectual representatives. And the ruling class has always its cadres of intellectuals, who no more constitute a separate class than do administrators and officials. It is true that such specialised sections do, from time to time, acquire vested interests of their own. They become adepts at feathering their own nests. This may even, on occasion, as Marx and Engels observed in *The German Ideology*, "develop into a certain opposition and hostility" between them and the chief part of the ruling class. But "in case of a practical collision, in which the class itself is endangered", this always "automatically comes to nothing".

We can occasionally observe this happening today: many intellectuals who habitually speak or write the rudest things about industrialists or financiers rally solidly around them whenever the system itself is endangered.

The intellectuals of the ruling class constitute, so long as that rule remains secure, the dominant intellectual force of society, who elaborate its "sentiments, illusions, modes of thought and views of life". That they are in general not conscious of performing this function does not contradict the fact that this is the function they perform.

"Ideology is a process accomplished by the so-called thinker consciously, indeed, but with a false consciousness," wrote Engels in a letter to Mehring (July 14th, 1893). "The real motives impelling him remain unknown to him. . . . He works with mere thought-material, which he accepts without examination as the product of thought; he does not investigate further for a more remote process independent of thought."

We find this ideological process strikingly exemplified today. Thinkers with the most diverse views—atheists and devout Christians, social democrats and conservatives—are all impelled to express one and the same point of view, namely, that man is ignorant of his fate and at the mercy of events which he cannot control. What is this but the point of view of the ruling capitalist class in the throes of its final crisis? These thinkers come from the most diverse social strata, but they all peddle the same views in the service of the ruling class, poisoning the minds of hearers and readers with the same ideas.

The relation of intellectuals with the class they represent was defined by Marx in writing about the literary and political representatives of the petty bourgeoisie in the 1848 period in France.

It should not be imagined, he wrote, that these ideologists of the shopkeepers "are indeed all shopkeepers or enthusiastic champions of shopkeepers. According to their education and their individual position they may be as far apart as heaven from earth. What makes them representatives of the petty bourgeoisie is that fact that in their minds they do not get beyond the limits which the latter do not get beyond in life, that they are consequently driven, theoretically, to the same problems and solutions to which material interests and social position drive the latter practically. This is, in general, the relationship between the political and literary representatives of a class and the class they represent." (*Eighteenth Brumaire*, chap. 3.)

Thus the intellectuals of the ruling class are not necessarily themselves members of that class, in the sense of being born into it, or of owning property, or of enjoying all its privileges. Sometimes, indeed, far from enjoying such privileges their position is insecure—they are merely hired and fired, like court poets in the past or journalists today. Many leading intellectuals of the feudal nobility came from the peasantry, and many leading intellectuals of the capitalist class have been drawn from the petty bourgeoisie or from the working class. Indeed, as Marx pointed out in *Capital* (vol. III, chap. 36), "the more a ruling class is able to assimilate the most prominent men of a ruled class, the more solid and dangerous is its rule".

This process also works in reverse. When a ruling class is in decay, and another class is rising to challenge it, individuals from its own ranks, including generally some of the most able and intellectually gifted, pass over to serve the rival revolutionary class.

As we have stated, every class which is active in the arena of history finds its own intellectual representatives, who express its social tendencies, its sentiments and views. It is evident, therefore, that in times of profound social change, when all classes are brought into activity, a great creative ferment of ideas takes place. The intellectual life of such periods expresses, not the activity of one class only, but the ferment of activity of all classes.

The class which plays the leading part in shaping the social order has not only to find means to formulate and systematise its own ideas, but secure their acceptance by the whole of society. Here revolutionary intellectuals, revolutionary thought and propaganda, have an important part to play. When the old social order is in decline, the ideas of the ruling class begin to lose their vitality, become incapable of further development, and are more and more rejected by wide sections of people. All the harder do the rulers fight to retain their hold and to use all the means at their disposal to discredit and persecute "dangerous" thoughts. The revolutionary class, on the other hand, in taking the lead of the whole movement against the old social system, has not only to get its own ideas worked out but make them the rallying, mobilising force of the whole movement. It was with this in mind that Marx wrote, in the *Critique of Hegel's Philosophy of Law*: "Theory becomes a material force as soon as it has gripped the masses."

The Transformation of the Superstructure

In those revolutionary periods when the material forces of production come into conflict with the existing relations of production, the entire establishment which guards the existing forms of property begins to be shaken. In such periods, the property relations which had served as forms of development of the material forces of production, turn into their fetters. And in the sphere of social consciousness this fact expresses itself in consciousness of the dominant ideas and institutions as fetters, in other words, as outmoded, oppressive, unjust, false. New, revolutionary, ideas arise.

"When people speak of ideas that revolutionise society," Marx and Engels wrote in *The Communist Manifesto*, "they do but express the fact that, within the old society, the elements of the new one have been created, and that the dissolution of the old ideas keeps even pace with the dissolution of the old conditions of existence."

The class struggle, by which the social transformation is effected, is based on the conflict of economic interests between classes occupying different places in the system of production relations, each class striving for its own economic interest. It is at basis economic. But it is carried on and fought out in the sphere of politics and law, of religion and philosophy, of literature and art. It is carried on and fought out, not only by means of the economic pressure plus coercion and violence exerted by one class against another class, but also by means of a battle of ideas, in which are expressed the tendencies of all classes of society.

"All historical struggles, whether they proceed in the political, religious, philosophical or some other ideological domain, are in fact only the more or less clear expression of the struggle of social classes," wrote Engels in his Preface to the third German edition of Marx's *Eighteenth Brumaire.*

Just as there is a distinction between the production relations and the corresponding forms of social consciousness, so there is a distinction between the material economic interests of the contending classes and their consciousness of their aims and of the issues over which they contend. But when the decisive moment of action arrives, the underlying economic interests and aims are always openly revealed.

"As in private life one differentiates between what a man thinks and says of himself and what he really is and does," wrote Marx in the *Eighteenth Brumaire* (chap. 3), "so in historical struggles one must distinguish still more the phrases and fancies of parties from their real interests, their conception of themselves from their reality. . . . Thus the Tories of England long imagined that they were enthusiastic about Monarchy, the Church, and the beauties of the old English Constitution, until the day of danger wrung from them the confession that they are only enthusiastic about ground rent."

Contradictions and conflicts are always arising in the superstructure of society, in the sphere of social consciousness, just because on the basis of given relations of production men cannot live together in complete harmony. Such contradictions may find temporary solution, only to break out again in new forms. So even the best established ideas and the most conservative institutions undergo changes.

In such contradictions fought out in the superstructure we should distinguish those which only reflect a readjustment to new events on the basis of the same relations of production, and those which reflect the striving of a revolutionary class to change the relations of production.

Of course, the ruling and possessing classes themselves are continually enmeshed in contradictions, which receive expression in ideological and political controversies as a result of which the establishment may be changed, perhaps profoundly, in response to changed circumstances. And it often happens that "revolts" break out against some or other part of the establishment, expressing the discontent of some particular grouping. Such revolts sometimes fizzle out; in other cases they are carried to success, and then yesterday's "rebels" become today's men of the establishment.

Any real challenge to the social system is preceded by and accompanied by such revolts. But there is a difference between revolutionary ideas which express the outlook and aims of a revolutionary class impelled by class interests to attack the property of the rulers, and ideas which would at most make some changes in the superstructure and leave property unmolested.

It is also worth noting, in passing, that just as at feudal courts there were ecclesiastics who rebuked the sins of the rulers and jesters who made jokes about them, so every establishment has its conscience-keepers and its jesters. This phenomenon should never be confused with real opposition.

When, as outcome of the class struggle, the old ruling class is overthrown, then, as Marx put it in the Preface to *Critique of Political Economy*, "with the change of the economic foundation the entire immense superstructure is more or less rapidly transformed".

The upheaval in the economic sphere, in the basic social relations, brings an upheaval also throughout the whole sphere of ideas and institutions. The old is overcome by the new. This means, primarily, that the former revolutionary ideas become developed into the authoritative ideas of a new establishment; and in part new institutions, constituted in accordance with these ideas, replace the old ones, while in part old institutions are reconstituted in accordance with new ideas and to serve new purposes. With this the entire content of social consciousness is eventually changed. With the dissolution of old relations of production, ideas which were formed on that basis become at first outmoded and reactionary, and in the end irrelevant and absurd. Ideological controversies which absorbed attention on the old basis become pointless, and new ones take their place.

But of course this does not mean that nothing remains from the old superstructure—or that development in the superstructure proceeds only by revolutionary negation, and not at all by evolution.

"Men never relinquish what they have won," wrote Marx in a letter to Annenkov (December 28th, 1846). "But this does not mean that they never relinquish the social form in which they have acquired certain productive forces. On the contrary, in order that they may not be deprived of the result attained, and forfeit the fruits of civilisation, they are obliged, from the moment when the form of their intercourse no longer corresponds to the productive forces acquired, to change all their traditional social forms."

When this change is made, the "fruits of civilisation" won in the past are preserved. They are preserved by .the new social forms, whereas they were placed in jeopardy by the decay and decadence of the old social forms. Thus not only the productive forces acquired, but advances achieved in culture, are retained and carried forward in new ways.

Even when something is lost, perhaps for a long time, as a result of revolutions and wars, it is eventually regained. Engels remarked that much of the old Roman law in Europe was eventually utilised in the development of bourgeois law. And why is this? It is because the Roman law contained much that is of value for regulating men's relationships not only in slave society but in any commodity-producing society based on private property.

Similarly, while certain views expressed in Greek art belonged to a slave society and have disappeared, the inspiration of that art has not disappeared and is not likely to do so. That is because Greek art gave expression not only to special aspects of life and human relationships in slave society but to universal aspects of life and human relationships in any society. It is also because Greek art made a permanent contribution to artistic technique. For these reasons, incidentally, Greek art is likely to survive much longer than Roman law, since while Roman law will have nothing but a purely historical interest left in communist society, Greek art will still retain a living interest.

At the present day the whole heritage of culture acquired up to and during the capitalist period is being threatened in the phase of the decadence of capitalism—not only by the well known and degrading tendencies of commercialism, but by physical annihilation. It is being claimed, preserved and carried forward in the fight for socialism.

Institutions, Ideas and Classes

What is the practical conclusion to be drawn from the Marxist theory of the basis and superstructure?

It is that dominant ideas and institutions which are products of a particular economic structure can no more be regarded as sacrosanct and unchangeable than the economic structure itself. They express neither eternal truths nor inviolable forms of human association. They simply express the outlook and interests corresponding to the given economic structure of society. And in society based on exploitation, this outlook and these interests can be none other than the outlook and interests of the dominant exploiting class.

The ancient Greeks, for example, were taught that their laws were instituted by divinely inspired legislators. And so these laws were regarded as sacrosanct. But Marxism shows that in fact these laws were the laws of a slave society, defining the privileges, rights and duties of the citizens of such a society and defending the property of the possessing classes. They were the expression of definite historically constituted class interests.

Similarly, we today are told that the state institutions in Great Britain and the United States have come into being as the realisation of Christian ideals, of Western values, of the conception of individual liberty, and so on. And so these institutions and the ideas with which they are associated are represented as sacrosanct, just as quite different institutions and ideas were represented in the past. But Marxism shows that in fact these institutions are institutions of capitalist society, based on the capitalist economic system, expressing the interests of the ruling capitalist class. The Christian ideals, Western values, conception of individual liberty are in fact capitalist ideals, capitalist values, a capitalist conception of liberty.

Marxism, therefore, by calling attention to the economic, class basis of established institutions and ideas, teaches us to regard no institution and no ideas as "sacred".

"People always were and always will be the stupid victims of deceit and self-deceit in politics," wrote Lenin, "as long as they have not learned to discover the interests of one or another of the classes behind any moral, religious, political and social phrases, declarations and promises. The supporters of reforms and improvements will always be fooled by the defenders of the old, as long as they will not realise that every old institution, however absurd and rotten it may appear, is kept in being by the forces of one or other of the ruling classes. And there is only one way of breaking the resistance of these classes, and that is to find, in the very society which surrounds us, and to enlighten and organise for struggle, the forces which can and, by their social position, must form the power capable of sweeping away the old and of establishing the new." (*Three Sources and Three Component Parts of Marxism.*)

When the classes discontented with the existing social system begin to take up the struggle against it, they immediately find themselves confronted with a whole set of institutions, laws, customs, principles and views which serve to protect the existing system and to suppress opposition to it.

From the very moment when the British workers, for example, began to combine to demand higher wages and shorter hours of work, they found themselves confronted with oppressive laws enacted by oppressive institutions which thwarted their demands. They found themselves confronted with a parliament from which they were excluded, by laws which protected the employers, by views which approved the profit-making of the rich while condemning any combination of the poor.

Similarly, at an earlier stage, the English bourgeoisie had come into conflict with the royalist regime of King Charles I.

Their economic expansion was blocked by royal monopolies and taxes; and when they wanted these removed, they immediately came into conflict with both government and laws, and were denounced by churchmen and scholars for daring to infringe upon "the divine right of kings".

In general, the class which in pursuit of its material, economic interests comes into opposition against the ruling class, is thereby always brought into opposition against the whole establishment. The whole record of class struggles proves that the dominant, established ideas and institutions of any society protect and uphold the economic structure of that society and, therefore, the interests of the ruling class.

Marxism, then, advises us always to look for the class, material, economic interests behind and motivating all declarations and principles, all institutions and policies. It advises us not to respect but to despise ideas and institutions which serve the capitalist class against the working class, and to fight for new ideas and new or transformed institutions which will help organise and inspire the broad alliance of all working people to break the power and overcome the resistance of the capitalists, and build socialist society.

Chapter Seven

SOCIALISM AND COMMUNISM

Social Production and Social Ownership

Socialism means the establishment of new relations of production, a new economic basis for society, namely, the social ownership of the principal means of production.

With such an organisation of production, all exploitation of man by man is finally done away with. The capitalist ownership of factories, mills, mines, transport and other means of production is abolished; the entire system of finance and trade is taken out of capitalist hands; the ownership of land by landlords is abolished. After that, no worker is slaving any more for capitalist profit, no small producer is fleeced by landlords, moneylenders or middlemen. The drive to oppress and exploit other peoples and to force a way into markets is ended. No longer is any productive equipment under-employed because it is not profitable to use it. No longer are any workers unemployed because it is not profitable for the capitalists to buy their labour-power. No longer is good land made waste by greedy exploitation; no longer is food production limited, and stocks hoarded or destroyed, while millions are undernourished. There are no more economic crises; for their root cause—that while social production expands, the capitalist appropriation of the product renders the mass of people incapable of buying back the goods produced—is done away with. No one has a motive for war, or stands to make a profit out of it.

With socialism, production is no longer undertaken for profit, but for the sake of producing what people need. The primary consideration is to raise the standards of the people.

Production relations no longer act as fetters on production, but are adapted to the continuous development of social production in order to satisfy the continuously rising requirements of the whole of society.

Socialism is the organisation of plenty. The means to create plenty for all are already in being, thanks to the development of the social forces of production under capitalism. What remains is to use them.

In socialist production, the entire social product is disposed of by the producers, and is used (a) to replace means of production used up, to build reserves and further to expand production, (b) to carry on and expand social services, (c) to maintain defence forces so long as a socialist country is threatened by hostile capitalist neighbours, and (d) to provide means of consumption to the individual members of society.

It is in its power to increase the total social wealth that socialism proves its superiority over capitalism.

"In every socialist revolution," Lenin wrote in *The Immediate Tasks of the Soviet Government*, "there comes to the forefront the fundamental task of creating a social system superior to capitalism, viz. raising the productivity of labour." This task is soluble, because socialism can not only take over all the technological achievements of capitalism, and then better them; the greatest power of socialism, which makes it a social system superior to capitalism, is the power of people, of social labour released from the fetters which compel it to serve private profit. The drive for higher productivity is not undertaken as an end in itself, or as a task imposed upon people by self-appointed taskmasters. It is undertaken for the sake of enjoying plenty, of making plenty available to every individual. "Everything for the sake of man, for the benefit of man" is the slogan of a socialist party.

The Road to Socialism

Socialism came onto the agenda of history and became established as a result of the concurrence of three causes. First, after the establishment of capitalism the productive forces of modern industry developed rapidly and reached the point where they had only to be brought under social ownership to be capable of producing plenty for all. Second, the working class achieved that degree of organisation and self-education where it was capable of taking command of production for itself. Third, scientific socialist theory was established, defining the socialist task and the necessary means to its fulfilment.

The victory of socialism is and can only be the outcome of class struggles, conditioned by the totality of social antagonisms brought into being by capitalism. Under a working-class leadership guided by scientific socialist theory the majority of the exploited succeeds in winning a political victory over the exploiters and depriving them of state power.

The socialist revolution is not, however, a single act but occupies a whole epoch of many years duration. The epoch in which the advanced capitalist countries develop to the monopoly stage and extend their imperialist conquests over the whole world is also the epoch in which imperialism is increasingly undermined and finally abolished, and in which socialism is established, grows in strength and finally triumphs everywhere.

The socialist revolution began with the October Revolution of 1917. After the second world war, socialist revolution was successful too in parts of Eastern Europe, in China and other parts of Asia and, later, in Cuba, in Latin America. It is always where the class contradictions are sharpest and the economic and political power of capital weakest that the break-through is made. At the same time, the U.S.S.R. proved a strong friend and protector for the newer socialist states: without this protection the people's democracies of Europe would hardly have escaped large-scale imperialist intervention, and certainly not the revolutionary regime of Cuba. From October 1917 those socialists of all lands who were both sincere and scientific regarded the defence of the socialist Soviet Union as amongst their first concerns, because its success was a success for socialism everywhere, and its defeat would have been a disaster for socialism everywhere.

The October Revolution gave a great impetus to anti-imperialist struggle in the colonial empires. From that time, the resistance of colonial peoples against imperialist exploitation grew into strong and organised liberation movements, with ever more clearly formulated anti-imperialist aims. After the second world war the barriers began to crack. Today a large part of the former colonial world has already won political independence. The independence of the rest cannot be long delayed. And the politically liberated peoples can count on the assistance of the economically strong socialist sector of the world in building their economies as something other than raw material bases and spheres of investment for capitalist monopolies.

The economic growth of the socialist countries, which have come together to constitute a world socialist bloc, and the downfall of colonialism, have brought about a decisive change in the balance of world economic and political forces in favour of socialism. The imperialists are hemmed in, and cannot any longer do as they please with the peoples of the world.

"The world is going through an epoch of revolution," said Khrushchov, speaking for the Central Committee at the 1961 Congress of the Communist Party of the Soviet Union. "Socialist revolutions, anti-imperialist national-liberation revolutions, people's democratic revolutions, broad peasant movements, popular struggles to overthrow fascist and other despotic regimes, and general democratic movements against national oppression—all these merge in a single world-wide revolutionary process undermining and breaking up capitalism. . . . Today practically any country, irrespective of its level of development, can enter on the road leading to socialism."

The economically more developed capitalist countries have, as is obvious, been economically ripe for socialism for a long time. The building of socialism in these countries would not face those difficulties of building up industries from scratch which socialist construction has so far had to face whenever it has been undertaken. Socialism is delayed primarily by political causes—by the firmly consolidated economic and political power of the monopolies, by the influence they exert over people's minds by hundreds and hundreds of well-worn channels, and by the existence, itself an effect of economic causes, of an opportunist leadership within the working-class movement which is not merely indifferent but hostile to scientific socialist ideas. However, the revolutionary movement in these countries does not face such discouragements and insuperable difficulties as its enemies like to pretend. It is the monopolies that have to face insuperable difficulties in view of their own economic contradictions, the growing strength of the socialist world and of the colonial liberation movements, and the demands of the people of their own countries. Capitalism is falling behind in competition with socialism, which year by year will increasingly demonstrate not only its technical superiority but its power to raise the people's standards of living. Every day the rationality and practicality of the ideas of scientific socialism for the working-class movement become more evident. It is clear, therefore, that the central fortresses of capitalism are by no means impregnable.

Socialist revolution, occurring at different stages of the development of the world crisis of capitalism and under different local conditions, follows different courses and exhibits different patterns.

The Russian Revolution was accomplished in the midst of war, by the forcible seizure of power by the popularly elected Soviets; this power was preserved only by revolutionary civil war and by beating off armed intervention; socialism was successfully constructed thanks to enormous sacrifices and great revolutionary discipline amidst conditions of hostile capitalist encirclement. Evidently it was these latter circumstances which made possible the inexcusable distortions of socialist policies and the crimes against individuals which took place during a period under the Stalin regime, and which jeopardised the construction of socialism and partly disoriented a whole generation of socialist intellectuals. The European people's democracies were established in the aftermath of war, following the dismantling of former fascist regimes or regimes of fascist occupation. The Chinese People's Republic and other people's republics of Asia were established as a result of revolutionary wars. The revolutionary regime in Cuba was established by a popular armed uprising against a U.S.-backed fascist dictatorship.

The perspectives which socialists set before themselves in the period now opening up are not those of war. A war fought with nuclear weapons does not offer favourable prospects for building socialism—very much the reverse. But with the balance of world forces in favour of socialism and of the national liberation movements, war can be prevented. The socialist aim, which no setbacks or imperialist manoeuvres can blot out, is one of international agreements and measures of disarmament—the peaceful coexistence of socialism and capitalism.

This is not a hopeful perspective for capitalism. It contains the brightest prospects for the democratic transfer of power in capitalist countries to the working people, though local violence provoked by imperialists at the end of their tether is not ruled out.

Already in 1951 the British Communist Party adopted the programme, *The British Road to Socialism*, which proclaimed the possibility of ending capitalist power and inaugurating socialism in Britain by a socialist parliament which would be elected and its legislative measures backed and implemented by the mass action of the majority of the working people. The 1958 edition of the programme stated: "Using our traditional institutions and rights, we can transform parliament into the effective instrument of the people's will, through which the major legislative measures of the change to socialism will be carried. Using the rights already won in the labour movement's historic struggle for democracy, we can change capitalist democracy, dominated by wealth and privilege, into socialist democracy, where only the interests of the people count . . . the working class has the strength, united in struggle for socialism, to overcome all resistance and reach its goal."

The perspective of peaceful coexistence also contains the prospects of a non-capitalist development in the former colonial countries, leading by stages to socialism. "Only active struggle by the working class and all working people, only the unification of all democratic and patriotic forces in a broad national front, can lead the peoples on to that path," said Khrushchov in the speech already quoted. "The peoples who have achieved national independence are entering upon the road of independent development at a time when the forces of imperialism and their ability to affect the course of events are steadily declining, while the forces and influence of socialism are steadily growing. In the circumstances, it will be immeasurably easier for them to solve the problems of economic and social development."

Socialist Planning

Socialist relations of production allow, for the first time, production to be planned. Because the means of production are socially owned, their use is a matter of social decision, and becomes subject to social planning.

With private ownership, production cannot be planned. It is planned within the workshop or, where an industry is sufficiently monopolised, for a whole industry—but not for society generally.

There is often talk of planning under capitalism, but the fact that the means of production are privately owned and the product privately appropriated makes planning impossible. Particular capitalist concerns or groupings plan their production; but each concern plans for its own profit. An overall plan, on the other hand, would require that all branches of production should be planned together as a single whole, the production of each sector being subordinated to the requirements of the general plan rather than to its own greatest immediate profit. And yet, under capitalism, each concern must pursue its own profit, or go under. Any overall plan breaks down. The fact that some industries or public services may be nationalised makes no essential difference here. The fact that railways, or fuel and power, may be nationalised, as in Britain, can be of some advantage to the great private monopolies which make use of their services; but it does not mean that production as a whole can be planned, any more than it could if private ownership were universal.

It is only when society has taken over the whole direction of all the principal branches of production on the basis of social ownership, and adapts production to the systematic improvement of the conditions of the masses of the people, that planning comes effectively into operation over production as a whole.

And then production not only can but must be planned, if it is to go on successfully. Planning is an economic necessity of socialist production. For obviously if there were no plan, and different people in different sectors of production did as they pleased, everything would soon be in confusion.

A socialist plan takes, to begin with, the form of a law promulgated by a socialist government. The word "law" has two senses: there are "laws" enacted by governments, which are thus expressions of the will of men; and there are "objective laws" which regulate real relationships and processes of both nature and society independent of the will of men. The use of the same word with two such different meanings is no doubt due to the historical fact that people originally believed that laws of nature were decrees of God imposed upon his creation just as laws are decreed by governments. Governments, however, are not like God, though they sometimes think they are. When God said "Let there be light", there *was* light—or so we are told. But when a government promulgates a law, what comes of it does not depend only on the intentions of the government but on objective laws regulating the social relations of the people who are supposed to obey the law.

Production is an activity carried on by people in society, and the actual results of what people do by way of productive activity depend on both the objective properties of their means of production and on the interdependencies of their own social relations and social processes. In production people are related to one another and to nature: the results of productive efforts depend on the laws of these relations. Hence any production plan which is capable of being fulfilled must be based on knowledge of those laws, and must take account of them. If you want to produce results, you must know the laws which regulate the production of such results and proceed in conformity to those laws and in no other way.

Thus, for example, no plan to build steel-framed buildings will come off unless there is a supply of steel; there will be no supply of steel unless it is made and transported; it will not be made unless iron and the other ingredients are dug up and processed, and it will not be transported unless oil or coal is obtained, or electric power produced. Again, if you want to produce an abundance of any kind of consumer goods —nylon stockings, say—then you must produce the equipment necessary for making them: no equipment for the artificial fibres industry, no nylon stockings. Similarly, if you provide such equipment in excess of what is required for whatever it is proposed to produce, then some of it will stand idle. And so on. Again, in the fields of finance and distribution, that amount of currency must be provided which is needed for the exchanges of activities and products which are actually going to take place; excess or deficiency will alike cause dislocation.

Suppose, then, that the government of a socialist country enacted a "Five-Year Plan Law" decreeing a vast increase of production, but without taking exactly into account the existing economic resources of the country, its existing sources of raw materials and productive capacity. Would such a law be effective? It certainly would not, and what would happen would not be a vast increase of production but a vast increase of muddle and discontent.

A socialist plan, therefore, must be drawn up on the basis of scientific knowledge of economic laws and of scientifically ascertained economic and technical data. This knowledge must be exact and quantitative. Political slogans and vague economic generalisations incapable of mathematical expression are, by themselves, liable to be worse than useless. This scientific knowledge—the knowledge of objective necessity the appreciation of which adds up to the freedom of socialist planning—relates both to the social-economic relations of human beings and to the properties of the materials and natural forces used in production. In the science of socialist planning there is already coming into being the unity of the natural and social sciences.

From this it follows that much more is required for socialist planning than political slogans and enthusiasm, and that it is not at all a question of arbitrarily setting targets. The fact that means of production are socially owned does not imply that mistakes, and serious mistakes, cannot easily be made in socialist planning. Methods of improvisation and decree, which may be necessary in the immediate aftermath of socialist revolution and are based largely on political expediency, need to be abandoned as quickly as possible.

Does this imply that planning should be in the hands of a commission of experts, a kind of technocracy? Of course, it needs experts; and the more expert they are, and the better they work together as a collective, the more effective will be the planning. But a socialist plan is carried out by people and for people. It is people, with their skill and enthusiasm, who do the work, and it is their requirements which the plan is meant to satisfy. Obviously, people's requirements cannot be dictated to them by experts, nor can they be herded and directed like sheep. Since people are themselves the most important of all the forces of production, a socialist plan fails unless people are mobilised for production; and the productive force of people working for themselves is not mobilised by decision of any commission of experts, but only by decision of those very people. Successful socialist planning must, therefore, combine the use of the most exact scientific knowledge of nature and of economic laws with the most democratic methods of deciding what is to be done and of organising the doing it. There is no contradiction here—except in the minds of such high and mighty experts as regard the majority of working people as "the common herd", invincibly ignorant and incapable of knowing what they want or what is good for them.

Moreover, the initiative of working people in finding their own means of tackling a particular job is a tremendous factor in the development of production—as the Stakhanov movement in Russia, or aspects of the Great Leap in China, sensationally demonstrated. New inventions, new techniques, new ways of working together spring from the democratic co-operation of working people who are their own masters; great talents, both individual and collective, and both mental and manual, come to light. Thus the establishment of democracy in work is itself a revolutionising element in the forces of production. It is the discovery of how to release and use in production the talents of the masses, which is comparable to the discovery of how to use a new source of physical energy—steam power, or nuclear power.

From Socialism to Communism

When socialism is established, how does society continue to develop? Marx showed that after production has been placed on a socialist basis and all exploitation of man by man has disappeared, a further stage of transition begins—the transition to communist society. He regarded socialism as only "the first phase of communist society"—a comparatively brief phase of transition from society based on the exploitation of one class by another to a fully developed classless society.

"Between capitalist and communist society lies the period of the revolutionary transformation of the one into the other," he wrote in *Critique of the Gotha Programme*. And in this period, the period of socialism, there is "communist society, not as it has developed on its own foundations, but, on the contrary, just as it emerges from capitalist society; which is thus in every respect, economically, morally and intellectually, still stamped with the birthmarks of the old society from whose womb it emerges."

In what respects is socialism as it emerges from capitalism still "stamped with the birthmarks of the old society"? In what respects does it reveal its transitional character? And how are these defects to be got over?

"*To each according to his needs*"

The first respect in which socialism reveals its transitional character is in production itself and in the way the social product is distributed. Socialism starts off with the productive forces at the level they have reached under capitalism. Hence while the aim of socialist planning is to satisfy every requirement of every individual, this aim cannot be fully realised for a long time—not until there has been an immense advance of production, far away beyond capitalist production.

Such an advance is certainly practical. The 20-year plan adopted by the Soviet Union in 1961, which is a sober and scientific plan, envisages that in twenty years Soviet industry will produce nearly twice as much as is now produced in the whole of the non-socialist world, and that the production of Soviet agriculture will increase by three and a half times.

Meantime individuals can only receive a share of the social product, not according to the full needs of each, but according to the quantity and quality of the work each has contributed. As production is still restricted, the principle of socialist production is: "From each according to his ability, to each according to his work." But in the higher phase of communism production has been so much enlarged that an entirely different principle operates: "From each according to his ability, to each according to his needs."

In *Critique of the Gotha Programme* Marx regarded the principle of equal pay for equal work—the principle of socialism—as still a hangover of "bourgeois law". This law is only finally abolished in communist society. Then all have an equal right to satisfy their needs.

Of course, the principle of equally satisfying the needs of all implies an inequality in what each receives, since needs are not equal—just as equal pay for equal work implies inequality, since some do more work than others. It is worth noting, therefore, that the idea that the social product should be equally divided amongst all has nothing to do with either socialism or communism. The social product is always unequally divided, first corresponding to unequal work and then corresponding to unequal needs. The equality which communism brings is the equal opportunity for everyone to develop all his capacities as a many-sided individual.

The inequality of needs has a peculiarly obvious application as between men and women—although this obvious fact is often obscured by speaking of the whole human race as "him". Women have special needs, as women; and to give women the same opportunities in life as men, which has never been done to this day, would still never be done by allocating to them the same share as men, or bestowing on them equal pay for equal work. The "equality of women" does not mean that they should have the same as men. It means that they, as women, should have every opportunity to live fully—to have children and enjoy bringing them up, to gain knowledge, to do creative work, and, generally speaking, to enjoy life—without suffering any disadvantage as compared with men.

The Status of Labour

A second respect in which socialism reveals its transitional character is in the status of labour and people's attitude to work.

Under capitalism, the workers sell their labour-power to the capitalists. Labour is therefore a task undertaken for someone else, a burden. It is, in Biblical phrase, "the curse of Adam".

In socialism, labour-power is no longer bought and sold. The producer who receives according to his work is not receiving the price of the labour-power he has sold. He is receiving his share of the social product according to the contribution he has made to social production. And so the more he helps to produce, the more he will receive—which is not the case under capitalism, despite the promises that when productivity increases everyone's real wages will go up: they have never gone up yet except after a hard battle.

However, "incentives" are still required for labour. And these incentives are provided in socialist society precisely by the principle: "To each according to his work." Each knows that the better he works, the more he will get. At the same time, the *social* incentive grows in significance. People work because it is a good thing to do, because of companionship and the desire to contribute to social well-being, because of the social approval it earns. And this social incentive grows in significance as the memories of capitalist conditions fade and as the reward for labour increases; and also as, with technical innovations, work becomes less dull and heavy, more interesting and enjoyable, and the working day shorter.

"Productive labour, instead of being a means to the subjection of men, will become a means to their emancipation, by giving each individual the opportunity to develop and exercise all his faculties, physical and mental, in all directions," wrote Engels in *Anti-Dühring* (part III, chap. 3). "Productive labour will become a pleasure instead of a burden."

Only with the appearance of such a status of labour and such an attitude to it could communist society exist. When each receives no longer according to his work but according to his needs, it is evident that work is no longer done under any kind of compulsion but because people take pleasure in it and it is recognised as an indispensable part of life.

In capitalist conditions, driven by the lash of economic compulsion, working people sacrifice a third or more of their lives working for others. A man's own life begins only when he knocks off work; his working time is not his own, he is robbed of it. Only for a privileged few is reserved the pleasure of creative work, the consciousness that in their working time they are living their own lives as they wish to live, and not being robbed of life. For the mass of the people, their life is as Robert Tressell described it in *The Ragged Trousered Philanthropists:* "When the workers arrived in the morning they wished it was breakfast time. When they started work after breakfast they wished it was dinner time. After dinner they wished it was one o'clock on Saturday. So they went on, day after day, year after year, wishing their time was over and, without realising it, really wishing that they were dead."

In communism, the whole of people's time is their own. The contrast was pointed by William Morris, in his imaginary conversation in *News from Nowhere* with people of a communist society. To the question, "How you get people to work when there is no reward of labour," came the answer: "The reward of labour is life. Is that not enough? . . . Happiness without daily work is impossible." And the question, "As to how you gained this happiness" was answered: "Briefly, by the absence of artificial coercion, and the freedom of every man to do what he can do best, joined to the knowledge of what productions of labour we really want."

Division of Labour and the Individual

A third respect in which socialism reveals its transitional character is in the continued subordination of the individual to the principle of division of labour.

Division of labour is a fundamental feature of the advance of production. It is carried to a very high pitch in modern industry, where co-operative production depends on the division of labour into, and the co-ordination of, a very large number of labour processes, both manual and mental.

But in society based on exploitation, and in capitalist society in particular, "in the division of labour, man is also divided. All other physical and mental faculties are sacrificed to the development of one single activity". And this represents, as Engels went on to insist in *Anti-Dühring* (part III, chap. 3), "a subjection of the producers to the means of production". For "it is not the producer who controls the means of production, but the means of production which control the producer."

Socialism, by instituting social ownership of the means of production, begins to make the worker no longer the servant of the machine, but its master. Associated producers do now control their means of production. Therefore the way is open to overcome the stunting of men's faculties caused under capitalism by the division of labour. But this is a long process. It involves a thorough-going retraining of labour—to educate and train all-round people who, masters of their whole production process, are not individually tied to one particular part of it.

Marx pointed out in *Capital* (vol. I, chap. 15, sect. 9) that while the effect of capitalism is to turn the worker into a detail labourer, nevertheless the development of industrial production demands the opposite. It demands well-educated, all-round workers who can take on new jobs corresponding to new technical developments. "Modern industry, indeed, compels society, under penalty of death, to replace the detail worker of today, crippled by life-long repetition of one and the same operation and thus reduced to a mere fragment of a man, by the fully-developed individual, ready to face any change of production, and to whom the different social functions he performs are but so many modes of giving free scope to his own natural and acquired powers."

As the technique of capitalist production has advanced, so has deadening repetition work of the conveyor-belt type become more prevalent. But the next step of technical advance is automation, where all repetitive drudgery is done by machines, and workers need to be highly skilled and adaptable, able to master and understand the machines they control and not merely to serve them.

The fullest scope of industrial development requires such people, but capitalist exploitation strangles them. For such people can flourish only as the masters of industry and not as wage-slaves. In socialism there begins the process of removing the subordination of the individual to division of labour and creating "all-round" individuals. Such people and only such people are the creators of the great new productive forces of communism. In this way, again, socialism is the first stage of communism: in socialist production is being created the new man of communist society.

This process also implies the ending of the very oldest effect of the division of labour—the separation, amounting to an antithesis, of mental from manual labour, and of town from countryside. The superior status of the mental compared with the manual worker and the exclusion of the one from the privileges of the other, and the superior opportunities of town as compared with country life, which still inevitably persist during the first phase of socialist society, lead to the stunting of individuals. The mental worker becomes divorced from reality, and the manual worker from the full understanding of it; the townsman becomes divorced from the life of nature, and the countryman too much immersed in it. These divisions will be brought to an end as people create communism. Then agriculture will become as highly equipped technically as industry, and the industrial centre not be cut off from the countryside; the level of all workers will be raised to that of men of science, and there will not be any stratum of intellectuals who imagine themselves a cut above the others.

A Single Form of Public Property

The fourth and final respect in which socialism reveals its transitional character is in the continued existence of different forms of property.

The whole tendency of the development of capitalism is to expropriate individual producers, depriving them of ownership of their means of production and converting them into wage-workers, and to drive small traders out of business while capital is more and more concentrated into the hands of a small number of very big concerns. But this is never more than a strong tendency. Monopoly capitalism is never more than a gigantic superstructure imposed on a basis of petty production and petty trading.

Socialism begins with the expropriation of the big capitalist concerns and big landowners, converting their property into public property, the property of the whole people. There remains a mass of small producers and small traders, including exploiters of labour. And these have to be eventually absorbed into the fabric of socialism, by making their property either public or co-operative property, as far as possible securing their consent by making this worth their while as individuals, partly enforcing it by economic pressure and legislative measures.

This problem especially concerns agriculture. In Britain the expropriation of individual producers has been carried through by capitalism in agriculture as well as in industry. Here not only industrial but agricultural production is performed mainly by wage-labour. But Britain is not typical in this respect. In many other countries where capitalism has developed or into which it has penetrated, agriculture has remained predominantly a peasant economy, in which the greater part of production is carried on, not by wage-labour, but by small peasant proprietors.

Under such conditions, could it be proposed not only to expropriate the big capitalists and landlords but also the working peasants? Recognising the necessity of the working class forming an alliance with the working peasantry in the fight against capitalists and landlords, Engels answered this question long ago. In *The Peasant Question in France and Germany* he wrote: "When we are in possession of state power we shall not even think of forcibly expropriating the small peasants. Our task relative to the small peasant consists in effecting a transition from his private enterprise and private possession to co-operation, not forcibly but by dint of example and the proffer of social assistance for this purpose."

For peasant agriculture the task of building socialism involves expropriating the landlords, eliminating the exploitation of wage-labour, and converting small-scale peasant farming into large-scale co-operative farming and individual peasant property into co-operative property. At the same time, while the main branches of farming go over to co-operative methods, it is quite possible for the individual farmers to retain small plots of land for their own family use.

So then there arise, as in the U.S.S.R. and all other socialist countries at the present time, two forms of socialist property: public and co-operative. Both are socialist, because they are both forms through which associated producers hold their means of production in common and dispose of the product, work for themselves and not for exploiters, and receive according to their work. Their essential difference is the difference between a state or public enterprise, which belongs to the whole people, and a co-operative enterprise which belongs to a particular group of people.

This distinction means that while industrial production can be planned in a direct way, since all the means of production are public property the planning of agricultural production must proceed by indirect methods of encouraging a particular volume and direction of co-operative, peasant production by offering suitable economic incentives in the form of prices. This is why socialist planning has encountered greater difficulties in the sphere of agriculture than of industry.

When productivity had developed sufficiently, these different forms of property will fuse into a single form of public property. For when not only does each work according to his ability but receives according to his need, there is no sense left in some claiming exclusive, even though co-operative, ownership of particular means of production and consequently appropriating the product. As they can receive all they need from the common product of the production of all, there is no advantage to them in co-operative ownership, and its retention would simply prove a hindrance to the organisation of social production and distribution.

This perspective, as envisaged in the U.S.S.R. by the Central Committee of the Communist Party, was outlined by Khrushchov at the 1961 Congress. "The still existing remnants of distinctions between classes will be eliminated," he said, "classes will fuse into a classless society of communist working people. . . . Agriculture will ascend to a high level that will make it possible to go over to communist forms of production and distribution. . . . Life itself is steadily bringing the national and co-operative forms of property closer together, and will ultimately lead to the emergence of a single, communist property and a single, communist principle of distribution."

The development of a complete communist society from its first phase of socialism is the consequence, then, of a great increase of social production. It means that, as *The Communist Manifesto* put it, "all production has been concentrated in the hands of a vast association of the whole nation", which plans production in all its branches in accordance with the needs of the people; the whole social product is then at the disposal of the same "vast association", so that it may be distributed according to need. The stunting of human capacities by inequalities of opportunity has been ended. There is possible what Marx, in the *Critique of the Gotha Programme*, called "the all-round development of the individual", and "all the springs of co-operative wealth flow more abundantly".

The transition from socialism to communism does not entail any sharp revolutionary break, any revolutionary change in the relations of production. On the contrary, socialism and communism are phases of one and the same social-economic formation, distinguished as phases simply by the degree of economic development and the completeness of the elimination of all earlier forms of ownership of means of production and of appropriation of the product. The vestiges of the economic and social relations of the old class-divided society of exploitation, in struggle against which people build socialism, gradually disappear; and as they are sloughed off, the higher phase emerges. Unlike the opening phase, which is "still stamped with the birthmarks of the old society", the higher phase of communism, therefore, develops entirely "on its own foundation", that is, on the foundation of social ownership of all the means of production.

Chapter Eight

TOWARDS A HUMAN WAY OF LIFE

Measures of Transition from Socialism to Communism

By what means is the transition from socialism to communism effected in practice? Along with the introduction of ever higher techniques and increase of labour productivity goes the necessity of a series of related social measures.

It is necessary to provide all-round education, with a basis in scientific and technical education, for all members of society, and finally higher education for all. It is necessary to raise the general skill of all working people, to plan incentives accordingly, to level out distinctions and end the bracket of lower-paid unskilled and semi-skilled workers. It is necessary to provide for all ever fuller and more open opportunities for the exercise and development of all their faculties, for culture and knowledge, for contributing to life and understanding and enjoying life. And, in close association with all this, it is necessary progressively to shorten the working day.

Marx pointed out in *Capital* (vol. III, chap. 48) that people must always spend time producing to satisfy their wants. When exploitation of man by man is abolished, he wrote, they can accomplish this task "with the least expenditure of energy and under conditions most favourable to and worthy of their human nature. But it none the less remains a realm of necessity. Beyond it begins that development of human energy which is an end in itself, the true realm of freedom, which, however, can blossom forth only with this realm of necessity as its basis. The shortening of the working day is its basic prerequisite". Shortening of the working day is a fundamental measure in socialist production, and a condition without which the all-round development of people's physical and mental abilities cannot be achieved. This all-round development is, as Marx declared, "an end in itself". It is not sought in order to increase production. On the contrary, the technical advance of production is sought in order that this development shall be achieved.

Along with all these measures go such measures as providing full maintenance for all citizens who are not able-bodied, rent-free housing, free travel and holidays, and generally the accumulation and use of public funds to provide first all kinds of services and then consumer goods to all members of society.

None of this is utopia. Every one of the measures mentioned here is either actually being put into operation or else being realistically planned today in the U.S.S.R.

The State in the Transition to Communism

The legislation and execution of all the measures for the transition to communism is done by the socialist state.

The socialist state is the instrument by means of which the working people undertake the management of social production in the interests of the whole of society. The state, as the representative of the whole people, controls the whole publicly-owned sector of socialist production. In this capacity it also exerts an ever increasing influence over economic development in its entirety, since all sectors of economy are dependent on the state sector. Thus, directly or indirectly, the state directs the whole development of socialist economy.

It is an organ of the whole working people. Hence it is from the start a state of an entirely new type, not the instrument of rule of a minority exploiting class, but the instrument of rule of the working masses.

"Our aim," wrote Lenin in 1917, in *Immediate Tasks of the Soviet Government*, "is to draw the whole of the poor into the practical work of administration . . . to ensure that every toiler shall perform state duties. The more resolutely we stand for ruthlessly firm government, the more varied must be the forms and methods of control from below, in order to weed out bureaucracy." And in *Can the Bolsheviks Retain State Power?*

he declared: "For the administration of the state in this spirit, we can immediately set up a state apparatus of about ten million, if not twenty million people—an apparatus unknown in any capitalist country."

At the same time, the state is essentially a means of coercion. In the socialist revolution state power is exerted to destroy the resistance of the dispossessed exploiters, to protect socialist property and the personal property of citizens from infringement by either individuals or groups inside the country and from foreign enemies, and to ensure that all the necessary measures for the construction of socialism are carried out. Such power requires a concentration of authority and material means in the hands of the workers' government and its executive forces. This is true for so long as conditions of class struggle remain within a socialist country and the building of socialism is resisted by the dispossessed exploiting classes and a dissident petty bourgeoisie. The socialist state first takes shape, and must always do so, as "the dictatorship of the proletariat".

This situation changes as the economic foundations of socialism are consolidated and all exploitation of man by man is abolished. Class struggles within the country then become a thing of the past. Of course, discontent and protest on the part of individuals is likely to continue; and so long as they have grounds for discontent, their protest is not anti-social.

"It would be wrong," said Khrushchov, reporting for the Central Committee at the 1961 Congress of the C.P.S.U., "to think that there is a wall between a state of the dictatorship of the proletariat and the state of the whole people. From the moment of its inception, the dictatorship of the proletariat contains features of universal socialist democracy. As socialism develops, these features become accentuated, and following its complete victory they become determinant. The state develops from an instrument of class domination into an organ expressing the will of the whole people."

How is this change from "dictatorship of the proletariat" to "state of the whole people" effected? By strengthening the elective basis of all organs of central and local government, and extending their real powers; by enlarging the activities of mass organisations such as the trade unions, the co-operatives and cultural and educational societies, and extending public control over the activities of all government bodies; by drawing more and more people—not in hundreds or thousands but, as Lenin said, in millions—into work of day to day administration; by the practice of nation-wide discussion of the most important plans and laws; and by reducing the number of state officials and regularly renewing the composition of government bodies, so making government less of a full-time career or profession.

All this means that the role of state power as an instrument of coercion becomes less.

"The interference of the state power in social relations becomes superfluous in one sphere after another," wrote Engels in *Socialism, Utopian and Scientific* (chap. 3), "and then ceases of itself. The government of persons is replaced by the administration of things and the direction of the processes of production. The state is not abolished, it withers away". And in *The Origin of the Family etc.* (chap. 9) he concluded: "The society that will organise production on the basis of a free and equal association of the producers will put the whole machinery of state where it will then belong: into the museum of antiquities, by the side of the spinning-wheel and the bronze axe." There will then exist economic organs of society, and cultural organs, but not state organs.

This process of "the withering away of the state" is sure to be very prolonged, and cannot be complete until the attitude of all members of society towards work and other social obligations is such that social obligations are fulfilled without any external coercion. Moreover, it could not in any case be complete anywhere so long as socialism was not established everywhere, because for all that time affairs of defence would require state attention.

The Role of the Communist Party

Besides the state, as the public power of socialist society to enforce and direct the carrying out of the will of the people, there is also necessary the party. The socialist state comes into being from the conquest of power by the working people, led by the working class. The working-class party, without whose leadership the working class cannot win power, is then the leading force which guides the state and the people in building socialism and advancing to communism.

So long as class struggle in any form continues; and beyond that, so long as the consequences of the old class divisions and division of labour remain in any shape or form; so long will there be a distinction between the vanguard and the masses. A necessary feature of the existence of classes is the conditioning of the material and mental activities of these classes by the place they occupy in social production. From this there invariably results the separating out of a conscious minority of the class, who become actively conscious of the long-term class interests and aims, and lead the whole class. The majority, on the other hand, carry on their lives in accordance with existing conditions, and become actively conscious of long-term social aims and enter into struggle for them only under the leadership of the minority. This is bound to be the case until not only do class distinctions disappear but all individuals are living and developing their capacities as members of society with equal status and opportunities. At that point the distinction between vanguard and masses will vanish, and the party, along with the state, will cease to exist.

The party in socialist society is not an organisation which "dictates". It is not an organ of power. As Sidney and Beatrice Webb put it long ago in their *Soviet Communism* (chap. 5), it exists to fulfil "the vocation of leadership". Without the exercise of such a vocation by a party equipped with social science, it is impossible to rally millions and lead them along the road to communism.

Lenin, in *What is to be done?*, described the party as not only the vanguard but "the tribune of the people". This, too, remains its function in socialist society. From the very nature of the state, as a special organ of administration and coercion, no state is immune from tendencies to bureaucracy, arbitrariness and even tyranny. It is for the party to represent and uphold the interests of the people in ensuring that the socialist state does fulfil their requirements and that the people do take charge of it. How else should this be done? No democracy can function simply by agreement of the people, spontaneously and without a party to represent them and act as their voice.

The experience of the U.S.S.R. has demonstrated how real is the danger of state organs of coercion getting out of hand. This only became possible because the party itself was to some extent prevented from functioning—its democratic machinery was impaired and its members were intimidated; indeed, that was where intimidation by the Stalin regime was chiefly directed. Later, it was the action of the party which put matters to rights.

The Socialist Establishment

The socialist state and the party are the centre of what, in the terminology of a previous chapter, may be called the socialist establishment. But this establishment is so different from anything that existed previously that the use of the same word becomes doubtful.

The Communist Party came into existence and took shape in the struggle against capitalism, and the form of the socialist state wherever it is established is determined by the character of the preceding struggles and of the organisations and institutions that took part in them. In this the socialist establishment is just like any other—institutions, parties and ideas born of the struggle against the old system become the formative elements of the new establishment.

The difference begins in this, that the capitalist organisations and ideas, and the capitalist state, are products of the development of the capitalist method of exploitation and serve the purpose of upholding the exploitation of man by man; whereas socialist organisations and ideas, and the socialist state, are products of the struggle against exploitation and serve the purpose of bringing all exploitation of man by man to an end and consolidating a socialist society.

The object of the one is to impose a system of exploitation, but to do this under a disguise—not openly, but in the name of liberty, free enterprise, the rights of the individual, law and order, religion. The object of the other is to further the complete emancipation of the whole of society from every form of exploitation and oppression, and not under any cover but in the name of human emancipation.

The development of the structure and functions of the socialist state and party and all socialist institutions, and likewise of the political, philosophical, legal, literary and artistic ideas of socialism, is undertaken with a conscious purpose of securing people's emancipation from all oppressive and limiting conditions and enabling them to live in brotherhood, producing and satisfying all their needs and developing all their capacities. Institutions and ideas all take shape in a conscious struggle to overcome whatever served the function of upholding the old methods of exploitation, and to develop whatever is useful to help build the new society without exploitation and to enrich its material and cultural life.

This difference leads to a second one. In society based on exploitation, the whole establishment serves to impose this exploitation and to justify it and make people accept it. There are propagated the biased and deceptive ideas of a minority, which are imposed on the majority; and the institutions are imposed institutions. It is quite otherwise in socialist society. There the ideas proper to the establishment teach people how to combine in association to satisfy their material and cultural needs, and the institutions serve the same purpose. Institutions and ideas are not imposed on the people, but are of the people and serve their deepest interests.

Hence instead of the institutions of society being run by a privileged few, as they are in capitalist society even when everyone has the vote, the aim is to draw wider and wider masses of people into running them. And instead of ideas being elaborated by an intellectual élite together with a corps of hired hacks (and it is sometimes difficult to make this distinction), the aim is to have wider and wider popular debate and discussion about all ideas.

Of course, all this is easier said than done. Old ways die hard. And just because socialist ideas are at first the ideas of a minority, and socialist institutions have the task of enforcing the requirements of the new society against resistance from the remnants of the old, it is not surprising if tendencies exist towards a few authoritative persons keeping a tight hold on institutions and towards authoritarianism and dogmatism in ideas, suspicious of democratic ways and democratic discussion. However, if such tendencies should grow instead of being put down, it is to the detriment of the development of socialism. Naturally, the institutions and ideas of socialist society become enlivened and enriched as a result of the ever wider participation of people in shaping them, and become ossified and impoverished in the contrary case.

Thirdly, in capitalist and other societies based on exploitation the established institutions do not take shape to enable people to realise their common interests, but to serve the interests of the ruling exploiting class; and the established ideas likewise serve the interests of the exploiting class and cannot advance mankind's understanding of the real conditions of life except in so far as such understanding may be useful to the exploiters—apart from that, established ideas disguise reality. There is nothing to gain for socialism, on the other hand, from ideas which in any way disguise, distort or falsify things—even if a few individuals may temporarily insinuate themselves into niches where they have a vested interest in such ideas. On the contrary, the truer, the clearer and the more profound is people's understanding of nature and society, the better will their ideas serve their social purpose. Socialist ideas are developed in the search for such understanding and in the fight against whatever contradicts it. Similarly, the object of socialist institutions is to enable people to co-operate together to satisfy their needs, and they are developed by such co-operation and by removing whatever hampers it.

Consequently, the development of the ideas and institutions of socialist society is effected in the process of people's advancing their understanding of the real conditions of life and organising themselves to secure their common interests. Whatever does not satisfy these conditions gets altered, as socialism grows into communism—not as a result of any conflict of contradictory interests, but as a result of the assertion of the community of interests.

This means that the basis for ideas about society and nature is scientific; that the basis for the development of culture and the arts is the exploration and expression of people's real relations with one another and with nature; that the basis for institutions is that they enable people to satisfy their needs; and apart from that, every kind of authority is set aside.

With the complete achievement of communism, therefore, anything resembling "an establishment" comes to an end.

Man's Mastery of Nature

Where is socialist and communist development leading?

The economic development of communist society, proceeding on the basis of man's complete mastery of his own social organisation, is first and foremost a gigantic development of man's mastery of nature. It is the mastery of nature, achieved by intelligent work, that distinguishes the human way of life from that of the lower animals. "The animal merely uses external nature, and brings about changes in it simply by his presence," wrote Engels in *The Part Played by Labour in the Transition from Ape to Man*. "Man makes it serve his ends, masters it. This is the final, essential distinction between man and other animals, and it is labour that brings about this distinction."

The opposition of man and nature, which is born as soon as human society is born, has always contained an element of antagonism, in the sense that uncontrolled natural forces threaten human existence and frustrate the realisation of human purposes. Thus in primitive society natural forces assume the proportions of menacing enemies, which have to be fought, cajoled or tricked. Natural catastrophes periodically destroy what man has made. In so far as natural forces are not understood and are not controlled, they are antagonistic to man and, even when their action is beneficent, they always contain an element of threat and danger.

In the course of the development of production, men have increasingly mastered natural forces. Increasing mastery of nature is, indeed, the essential content of material progress.

In mastering natural forces men learn their laws of operation and so make use of those laws for human purposes. Man does not master natural forces by somehow weakening them, or changing their properties and laws to suit his designs, but by learning to know them and use them, to turn them from enemies into servants.

But men's mastery of natural forces has been offset by their own subjection to the means of production which they have created in mastering them, and to their own products. They are subject to their own means of production in the sense that the cultivator is himself dominated by the soil, and the machine-minder by the machine. And when products are produced as commodities, the producers are subject to their own products, in the sense that they do not produce what they want in order to enjoy it but are utterly dependent on whatever happens to their own products in the market, where the products themselves seem to take control over the fate of the producers. And in this common subjection, man has been subject to and exploited by man.

In communist society, however, every obstacle is removed which their own social organisation offers to the furthest development of men's freedom. People now go forward without hindrance to know and control the forces of nature, to use them as servants, to remake nature, co-operating with nature to make the world a human world since humanity is nature's highest product.

In communist society the social control by associated producers over the use of their means of production and the disposal and enjoyment of their social product is at length made absolute, unqualified, unlimited. Each individual is free from the straitjacket hitherto placed on his all-round development by the social division of labour, and is free from the restriction to his satisfying his needs hitherto imposed by the necessity of paying for the means of satisfaction. In communist society, people in association, acting through the economic planning organs of society, can plan production in a complete and direct way—by simply reckoning up their productive forces and their needs, and then disposing of the productive forces in such a way as to produce the needs.

As William Morris made his communist people say in *News from Nowhere:* "The wares we make are made because they are needed; men make for their neighbours' use as if they were making for themselves, not for a market of which they know nothing, and over which they have no control. We have now found out the things we want, and we have time and resources enough to consider our pleasure in making them."

The End of Alienation and Estrangement

With communism, then, there disappears the last vestige of the domination of man by his own means of production and his own products. Henceforward man is fully the master of his own social organisation and increasingly the lord of nature. With this, as Marx said, the prehistory of mankind ends and human history begins.

Indeed, what most profoundly distinguishes man from other animals is man's consciousness of his own aims and his conscious use of the laws of the objective world in pursuit of his aims. Hitherto men have mastered natural forces in the process of production, but have not been masters of their own social organisation. They have produced, but not been masters of their own means of production and their own products. In producing, they have created social forces and set in motion economic laws which have ruled human destinies as an alien power. That was not human history, but only the history of man in the making.

In his earliest philosophical work, the *Economic-Philosophic Manuscripts of 1844*, Marx wrote of the human condition of "alienation" and "estrangement". This conception was actually the fountainhead of the ideas of communism.

As men emerge from the condition of primitive communism they begin to cut themselves free from the navel string which ties them to nature. In primitive communism the individual is so dependent on and so submerged in the group that he has hardly any individuality, and the group is tied to and dependent on its natural habitat and the means of life it offers. Once people proceed from primitive food-gathering to food-producing, and begin as associated individuals with division of labour to interfere drastically with their natural environment, private property and exploitation begin. And with them come what Marx called alienation and estrangement.

Alienation means that what belongs to a man passes out of his possession, and may be used against him. People alienate the products of their labour; and when they are exploited, their very labour becomes alienated because, as we have seen, it is taken from them and used by others. More, with private property and class divisions, people's social creations pass out of their own control; independent of their will, they set up social relations and create institutions and organisations which they cannot control and to the action of which they become subject.

In this condition, people become estranged from one another. Of course, people desire things and it is good to possess the use of things; but now attachment to things contradicts attachment to people, and people treat one another as things to be owned and used. The possession of things becomes the great and necessary object of life, and in pursuing this object people become estranged and treat one another as means to be used to help gain possession of things.

It is easy to recognise that this condition has not been eased but has rather been worsened with the development of class-divided society. The hatefulness and inhumanity of capitalism is due to the fact that men's alienation of their own powers and products and estrangement from one another is carried to the highest pitch under capitalist conditions. Throughout the ages, artists and writers, visionaries and reformers, have been aware of this, and have portrayed its effects and struggled against them, without fully understanding their causes. Communism begins with this understanding. And the great and humane aim of communism is to end forever the human condition of alienation and estrangement.

It is then that, as Marx expressed it in his earliest writings, "the human essence" will achieve its realisation. What does this mean? It does not mean some wonderful transfiguration of man made perfect. What is essential to the human animal, differentiating him from others, is purposive co-operation to produce the means of life. Communism simply means that this is done, with knowledge of nature and without hindrance from man's own social organisation. Communism means that people like us, with our hands and brains, sense organs and physical needs, co-operate to produce what we want and to allow to each the opportunities to benefit from the common stock of all.

What is there in this contrary to "human nature"? The idea of communism is based on scientific understanding of human nature and of the laws of man's social development. It has long been fashionable to sneer at communism as the idea of a "millennium". This sneer was answered long ago by Robert Owen, in an *Address to the Inhabitants of New Lanark*: "What ideas individuals may attach to the Millennium I know not; but I know that society may be formed so as to exist without crime, without poverty, with health greatly improved, with little, if any, misery, and with happiness increased a hundredfold."

The Future of Communist Society

The transition from capitalism to socialism is, as we now know, a prolonged and uneven process, some nations achieving socialism while others still remain capitalist or even, in some respects, pre-capitalist. It follows from this that, on a world scale, the transition from socialism to communism will also be a prolonged and uneven process, since some nations will advance to communism while others lag behind and may even still remain in the capitalist stage.

What will happen after communism? This is a natural enough question, but one which we cannot possibly answer at present, or can answer only in the vaguest terms.

In general, it may be said that there is no reason whatever to believe that the same fundamental laws of social development which have always operated will not continue to operate. For these are laws of the human condition itself.

It remains true that in carrying on production people enter into relations of production which must correspond to the character of their productive forces.

It remains true that people's consciousness is determined by their social being.

It remains true that as production develops so must new social tasks develop with it.

But instead of asserting their sway through class conflicts, crises and catastrophes, and by the frustration of men's intentions, the laws of social development will be more and more consciously utilised by associated humanity, just like the laws of nature, in the interests of society as a whole, to realise men's intentions. Associated on the basis of a common interest, men will be in full control of their own social course. They will be able to direct it by the compass of their knowledge of their own needs and of the real conditions of their social existence.

All that we can know in advance about communist society follows from what we already know about previous society, and about capitalist and socialist society in particular. Thus we know that certain features of capitalist and socialist society, which we have analysed, will have to be eliminated, and we can work out in a general way how that can be done and what sort of society will exist afterwards. Whatever goes beyond that we have no means of predicting.

When a world exists so completely different from our present world, how are we to say what the people who live in it will decide to do? Of course, we cannot say. And if we did say anything, they would take no notice of us; for what they do will be based on their own requirements, and not on ours.

At most we can venture to assert two propositions.

(1) In communist society, property has reached its highest stage of development. Private property has ceased to exist. It is simply the case that people in association make use of all the resources of nature, including their own human resources, to satisfy all their needs. These resources belong to no one in particular, the products of associated labour belong to the

whole of society, and means of consumption are distributed among the members of society according to their needs, as their own personal property for purposes of personal use. Property as we now generally understand it—as the ownership and control of means of production and products by particular individuals, groups and organisations—has, in fact, ceased to exist. That is what is meant by the highest stage of development of property.

If, then, this is what has happened to property, it will never again be the case that people will feel the necessity of changing property relations and instituting any higher form of property.

(2) At the same time, society need not stand still. There may well take place new developments of the forces of production, derived from new discoveries of science. What these will be we cannot tell—if we knew of discoveries beforehand, they would not be discoveries. Today we tend to be very impressed by the potentiality of the physical sciences, making available new sources of energy and possibilities not only of transforming the earth's surface but of travelling to the moon or other planets. It is possible that discoveries of the biological sciences may prove even more revolutionary, enabling us to control the growth of living organisms and to prolong greatly the span of human life. In any case, with new discoveries new horizons open up, new needs are felt, and old habits, ways of life, ideas and institutions are felt as a hindrance and have to be changed. For example, if the average duration of human life were greatly prolonged it is obvious that all kinds of social readjustments would become necessary to satisfy the needs of such longer life.

Hence the contradiction between the old and the new—between old forms of association into which men enter in carrying on production and new forces of production—hitherto expressed as a contradiction between existing relations of production and new forces of production, which has always been the mainspring of human progress, will continue to operate—but in new ways. It will not take the form of a conflict between existing forms of property and the new requirements of social development, but will take other forms.

And changes will not be effected without prevision as a result of conflicts, but by deliberation and discussion.

At this point it is necessary to rein in the argument and bring ourselves back to present realities. When all mankind is free from exploitation, people will live without want, in security and happiness, and will be fully capable of taking care of the future. We need not further concern ourselves about their future problems, but rather about our own problems. For the future of mankind depends on how we solve the present contradictions of society.

Conclusions

What conclusions can we draw from the materialist conception of man and his social development?

(1) The epoch in which we live is the one in which mankind is finally taking the decisive step to the achievement of truly human conditions of existence. Historical materialism lights up the wonderful perspectives which lie before the present generation.

Hitherto, since the first phase of primitive communism, society has always been based on the exploitation of the masses of working people. The wealth of the few has contrasted with the poverty of the many. The great advances of material production, which have created that wealth, have been achieved only at the expense of increased exploitation of the producers. The overwhelming majority have been denied the enjoyment of the culture the creation of which was made possible by their labour. There has been continual war of class against class and of people against people.

From such conditions of social existence mankind is emerging to create a new order of society in which exploitation of man by man is abolished, and in which the development of society no longer takes place through conflicts and upheavals but is consciously regulated in accordance with a rational plan.

All this has become necessary because the new forces of social production prove incompatible with private ownership of the means of production and private appropriation of the product.

They can be fully utilised and developed only on the basis of social ownership and social appropriation.

Modern science and technique make it possible for the first time in history for everyone to enjoy a high and rising standard of life, and for everyone to enjoy leisure, education and culture. To realise this possibility, society must take over control of the whole of production and plan it for the satisfaction of the needs of the whole of society.

That means that everyone will be able to enjoy without question the basic material necessities of life—good housing, food and the maintenance of health. Monotonous and arduous work will be abolished by high technique, and all will be free to work creatively. Work will cease to be a burden and become one of life's necessities, a matter of pride and pleasure. Rest and leisure, education and a cultured life, will be enjoyed by all. All will be able to raise their qualifications and develop their various abilities. Such are the truly human conditions of life which it is the goal of socialism to establish.

(2) Socialism can be established only through the action of the revolutionary class in modern society, the working class, in its struggle with the capitalist class.

Socialism cannot possibly be achieved by any gradual transition based on class-collaboration, since by its very conditions of existence the capitalist class is bound to resist to the end the introduction of socialism, which would deprive it of its property and profits. On the contrary, it can be achieved only by the struggle of the working class to emancipate itself from capitalist exploitation. By emancipating itself, the working class will thereby emancipate society at large from all exploitation.

To achieve socialism the working class must unite, and lead all the working people to struggle to end capitalist rule and establish a new democratic state, based on the rule of the working class in alliance with all the working people.

(3) To defeat capitalism and build socialism the working class must have its own political party, the Communist Party, equipped with scientific socialist theory and able to apply it.

Through the experience of mass struggles the workers begin

to be conscious of the antagonism of their interests with those of the employers, of the need to unite and organise. But this consciousness can become socialist consciousness only with the aid of scientific theory. Only with the benefit of socialist theory can the working class see the need not only to fight for better wages but to end the wages system, and realise how to carry this fight through to victory. Thus what is necessary for the waging of the struggle for socialism is above all the union of scientific socialism with the mass working-class movement.

(4) Today the scientific theory of Marxism-Leninism is tried and tested and has proved its truth in practice. Guided and inspired by it, socialism has been built in the Soviet Union and the shape of the future communist society is becoming clear. New socialist people are at work, more proud and free than any who have trod the earth before. Millions more are advancing to socialism. A new world has come into existence whose growth the forces of the old are utterly powerless to prevent.

Completely different is the world of capitalism, dying on its feet, torn by insoluble crisis and conflict. Here the ruling monopolies try to solve their problems and increase their profits by cutting at the people's standards, by deceiving the people and undermining their liberties, and by piling up armaments. They pin their hopes for the future—or rather, for delaying the future—on the hydrogen bomb. Their final accomplishment is the means of mass destruction.

Our final conclusion, then, is clear. All over the world the common people can and must unite to preserve peace. We must strive for co-operation with the countries which are already building socialism and guard their achievements. We must work for the ending of capitalism and establishment of socialism in our own country.

READING LIST

The following are the principal writings by Marx, Engels and Lenin available in English setting forth the theory of historical materialism. However, everything they ever wrote has relevance to this theory and contains an application of it. Works marked with an asterisk are the best for beginners.

MARX AND ENGELS

*The Communist Manifesto**
The German Ideology
Correspondence

MARX

Capital, volumes I, II and III
*Critique of Political Economy, Preface**
*Critique of the Gotha Programme**
The 18th Brumaire of Louis Bonaparte
Economic-Philosophic Manuscripts of 1844

ENGELS

*Socialism, Utopian and Scientific**
*Speech at the Graveside of Karl Marx**
*Ludwig Feuerbach**
*The Origin of the Family, Private Property and the State**
*The Part Played by Labour in the Transition from Ape to Man**
Anti-Dühring

LENIN

What the Friends of the People are and how they Fight the Social-Democrats
Materialism and Empirio-Criticism
*Karl Marx**
*The State and Revolution**
*Imperialism**

VOLUME III

THEORY OF KNOWLEDGE

FOREWORD

THE theory of knowledge[1] is concerned with questions about ideas—their source, the way they reflect reality, the way they are tested and developed, their role in social life. These questions have always formed an important part of philosophy.

In bourgeois philosophy the theory of knowledge has come to occupy the first place, on the grounds that before any philosophical conclusions can be drawn about anything whatever we must first make certain of what we really do know and the foundations on which we know it. But bourgeois philosophers have generally approached the subject in the most abstract possible way. Taking nothing else for granted than the bare existence of the individual human mind, they have asked how knowledge could be born and grow up in it. But since human individuals, and still less their minds, do not exist in a void, this kind of inquiry was bound to raise unanswerable questions and to remain comparatively sterile.

Marxism, on the other hand, considers that we ought to study the subject more concretely, and to ask how ideas actually arise, develop and are tested in the concrete conditions of real human life, in the material life of society. This volume is about how human consciousness actually arises and develops. It tries to trace this process step by step from its beginnings in the simple conditioned reflex, which is the basic way in which an animal organism enters into active relationship with the external world, up to the development of human knowledge and human freedom.

1 Those who consider Greek a more philosophical language than English call it *epistemology*, or sometimes *gnosiology*.

Part One

THE NATURE AND ORIGIN OF THE MIND

Chapter One

MIND AND BODY

Matter and Mind

IT is very commonly believed that however closely the mind may be connected with its body it is nevertheless distinct and separable from the body. According to this belief, the mind "animates" the body and makes use of the organs of the body both to receive impressions of the external world and to act on the external world; but its existence does not depend on that of the body. Moreover, while in some of its activities the mind makes use of the body, in other of its activities it does not. For instance, the mind makes use of the body in its sensuous activities, but in its "purer" intellectual or spiritual activities it does not.

This is in essence a very ancient conception. Thus some primitive peoples think of the soul as being a very fine vapour —this is what the word "spirit" originally meant—which resides in the body but which can come out of it and lead an independent existence. For example, the soul journeys out of the body during sleep, issuing forth from the mouth. Again, the wrong soul can sometimes get into the wrong body—as in "possession": a lunatic or an epileptic is said to suffer from an evil spirit having got into his body. And as part of this primitive conception of the soul there arises the conception of the survival of the soul after death and also of the pre-existence of the soul before birth.

Idealist philosophical theories about the mind are, in the last analysis, only refinements and rationalisations of such superstitions.

Amongst such refinements and rationalisations is the doctrine that mind and body are two distinct substances—

spiritual substance and material substance. Material substance, or body, is extended, has weight, moves about in space. Spiritual substance, or mind, thinks, knows, feels, desires. This view is still very widely held. It is believed that such properties as thinking, feeling and so on are so absolutely different from the properties of matter, that however closely our thinking and feeling may be bound up with the state of our bodies, they belong to an immaterial substance, the mind, which is distinct from the body.

Idealist philosophers, who consider that the mind is separable from the body, maintain that thoughts, feelings and so on are in no sense products of any material process. If we think and feel and act intelligently, for example, such behaviour is not to be explained from the conditions of our material existence but from the independent functioning of our minds. Admittedly, the mind makes use of the bodily organs; but intelligent behaviour stems from the fact that the body is animated, informed and controlled by an immaterial principle or a spiritual being, the mind.

But such idealist theories, widespread as they are, have long been offset by opposing materialist views. According to materialism, so far from mind being separable from body, all mental functions depend on their appropriate bodily organs and cannot be exercised without them. All people's conscious and intelligent activities can be traced back to material causes, so that far from such activities being exclusive products of mind, mind itself is a product—the highest product—of matter.

Modern materialism, which is equipped with the results of scientific investigations into the forms of organic life and with the conception of evolution, is able to give a decisive answer to the idealist conception of the mind. Mind is a product of the evolutionary development of life. Living bodies which have reached a certain level of development of the nervous system, such as we find in animals, can and do develop forms of consciousness; and in the course of evolution this consciousness eventually reaches the stage of thought, the activity of the human brain. The mental functions, from the lowest to the highest, are functions of the body, functions of matter. Mind is a product of matter at a high level of the organisation of matter.

Once this is admitted, there is an end to the conception of the mind or soul as separable from the body and capable of leaving it and surviving it. A mind without a body is an absurdity. Mind does not exist in abstraction from body.

To say that mind does not exist in abstraction from body is not, however, to say that mental processes do not exist or that the mind of man is a myth. Of course, mind, consciousness, thought, will, feeling, sensation and so on are *real*. Materialism does not deny the reality of mind. What materialism does deny is that a thing called "the mind" exists separate from the body. The mind is not a thing, or a substance, distinct from the body.

This point can be illustrated by any example when we ordinarily speak about "the mind". Philosophers and theologians have imagined that the mind has an existence of its own, and qualities and activities of its own, distinct from the body. But nothing of the sort is ever implied in practical life when we talk about the mind.

Suppose, for example, that you are asked, "What's in your mind?" This means quite simply, "What are you thinking about?" In other words, it is a variant of the question, "What are you doing?" It does not in the least imply that there exists a thing called your mind, distinct from your body.

Similarly, if you are told, "You have a first-rate mind", or "You have a dirty mind", or "You ought to improve your mind", all these remarks are understood as referring to certain things which you normally do. And if you die, or if you are hit on the head or in some other way suffer a disturbance of the brain, then these remarks about your mind no longer apply. For the activities to which they refer can then no longer be performed, since the means of performing them have been destroyed.

A man is endowed with mind, then, in so far as he thinks, feels, desires and so on. But all these activities are activities, functions, of the man, of a material being, an organised body, dependent on appropriate bodily organs. Given a body with the appropriate organisation and the appropriate conditions of life, these activities arise and develop. Destroy the body or its organs, and these activities are destroyed with it. All the mental functions and activities, which are said to be products of mind as distinct from matter, are functions or activities of a living material organism. The mind is a product of material organisation.

Consciousness and the Nervous System

Not every body is capable of thinking and feeling, but only organic, living bodies. And not every living body manifests those activities which are associated with the development of mind. The appearance of mind is in fact bound up with the evolution of the central nervous system in animals.

When living bodies evolved the nervous system, and when from the central nervous system there developed the brain, then the elementary functions of mind, centring on sensation, came into being. And with the further development of the brain—of the cerebral cortex and its higher centres, which we find in man—there came into being the higher functions of mind, the functions of thought. The brain is the organ of thought. Thinking is a function performed by the brain.

Few people nowadays would deny these well-established facts. Nevertheless beliefs are widely held which contradict them. Such, for example, is the belief in personal survival after death. Those who hold this belief usually suppose that in our future conscious existence after death many things will become much clearer to us than they are now. In other words, they believe that our minds cannot attain their full development until after we are dead. They believe that so far from the brain being the organ of thought, our thought will reach perfection only when we have no brain left to think with.

Lenin maintained that in order to arrive at "an analysis and explanation" of mental processes, in order to understand their nature and origin, it was necessary to "set about making a direct study of the material substratum of mental phenomena —the nervous processes". (*What the Friends of the People Are,* etc., Part I.) The foundations of this study have been laid by modern physiology, in which the work of the Russian physiologist Ivan Pavlov was especially significant.

Organism and Environment

Before Pavlov, the nervous system was generally regarded as fulfilling the primary function of co-ordinating the action of the different parts of the organism; Sir Charles Sherrington called this "the integrative action of the central nervous system". Pavlov insisted, however, on the need to investigate "a second immense part of the physiology of the nervous system". For he regarded it as "a system which primarily establishes the relation, not between the individual parts of the organism, with which we have been mainly concerned hitherto, but between the organism and its surroundings."

The primary function of the central nervous system is not simply to regulate the functioning of the different parts of the organism in relation to one another, but to regulate the functioning of the organism as a whole in relation to its surroundings.

Through the functioning of its nervous system, the animal in the course of its activity builds up most complicated relations with its environment, thanks to which it is able to live in its environment, to obtain its requirements and to react to definite conditions in a definite way. Thus the animal relates itself to its surroundings in such a way that it is actively aware of its surroundings, reacts appropriately to events, and in turn acts back upon them. To do all this, the animal uses its sense organs and its limbs, and the organ controlling the whole process is the brain.

The simplest sort of reflex, whereby a stimulus affecting the sense organs evokes a muscular response, constitutes a relation or connection between the animal and its environment. Such and such a stimulus evokes such and such a response—this describes an active relationship of the animal with its surroundings. Pavlov showed that the active relationship of the animal with its surroundings begins from certain fixed and constant connections between the animal and the external world, which he called *unconditioned reflexes*, and develops through the building up of temporary and variable connections, which he called *conditioned reflexes*.

In order to study the development of reflexes, Pavlov used the very familiar fact that animals discharge saliva from the salivary glands in their mouths as a preparation for eating food. Thus a dog presented with food discharges a certain amount of saliva. This is a simple, unconditioned reflex. Present the dog with food, and saliva forms in its mouth. Pavlov then found that if a bell was rung whenever a dog was presented with food, then, after a time, the sound of the bell would itself be sufficient to cause the dog to salivate, even though the food had not yet been presented. This he called a conditioned reflex. For as a result of definite conditions, that is to say, the repeated association of the bell with food, the dog had become conditioned to react to the bell—whereas it never had to be conditioned to react to the food. In other words, the dog had learned to associate the bell with food, and had come to expect food on hearing the bell and so to get ready for the food even before it was actually presented.

Whereas unconditioned reflexes are a part of the heredity of the animal, developed in the course of the evolution of the species, conditioned reflexes are brought into being in the course of the life of the individual—and, having been brought into being, can also be changed or destroyed. Thus if after a time food is no longer presented when the bell rings, then the dog will cease to react to the bell; or it can be taught to react not to any bell but only to a bell of a particular pitch; and so on.

The mechanism of reflexes is found in the brain, in the connections which exist between the sensory and motor centres of the brain. The sensory centres are distinct from the motor centres, the function of the former being to receive messages and of the latter to send messages out. They are connected in such a way that when a message comes in from the sense organs to the sensory centres, it travels across to the motor centres, which then dispatch a message to the muscles, glands, etc.—so that to a given stimulus an appropriate response is made.

An unconditioned reflex is based, then, on a fixed and constant connection which exists between the sensory and motor centres of the brain. And conditioned reflexes are based on temporary, variable and conditioned connections which are formed between the sensory and motor centres in the course of the animal's life.

Such connections between sensory and motor centres within the animal's brain constitute connections between the animal and the external world. For the function of the connections inside the animal's brain is to connect the animal with what lies outside—that is, with its surroundings.

Thus the unconditioned food-saliva connection within the dog's brain connects the dog with its surroundings in such a way that when food is presented the dog gets ready to eat and digest it. And the conditioned bell-saliva connection within the dog's brain connects the dog with its surroundings in such a way that when a bell sounds, which the dog has learned to associate with food, then, once again, the dog gets ready to eat.

An animal lives only by means of its connections with its surroundings, that is, by its external connections which are established through the internal connections within its own brain. Pavlov showed that these connections of the animal with its surroundings are formed through the development of conditioned connections from unconditioned connections, that is, by the development of conditioned reflexes from unconditioned reflexes.

To sum up. An unconditioned connection is a relatively constant, inherited connection between an animal and its environment. If, for instance, something suddenly passes in front of the eye, the eyelids blink: this is an unconditioned connection, which serves to protect the eye. Quite irrespective of the varying conditions which it encounters, the animal relates itself to the surrounding world through such reflexes. It is born with such reflexes, which were formed in the course of the evolution of the species.

A conditioned connection, on the other hand, is a temporary and very variable connection between the animal and its environment, which is acquired by it in the course of its individual life, and which can likewise disappear. A dog, for instance, will go to a certain place for its dinner. This is a connection which it has acquired in the course of its life: it has become conditioned to seek its dinner in that place, in other words, it has learned to seek its dinner there. And if conditions change, then such conditioned connections can be changed correspondingly. The dog can learn to look for its dinner somewhere else.

Pavlov showed that the nervous system of the higher animals has the function of acquiring and establishing temporary and variable connections between the animal and its surroundings, whereby the animal adjusts its reactions to the varying conditions of its environment, and also, by means of its own action on its environment, adjusts its environment to the requirements of the animal.

This function is performed in the brain, and consequently Pavlov called the brain "the organ of the most complicated relations of the animal to the external world".

Activity and Consciousness. Sensations

Pavlov insisted that mental activity is the same as higher nervous activity, and that the different aspects of mental life must be explained by data obtained from the investigation of higher nervous activity. "The dualism which regards the soul and the body as quite separate things is still too firmly ingrained in us," he wrote. "For the scientist, such differentiation is impossible."

Mental activity is an activity of the brain. And if the brain is the organ of the most complicated relations of the animal to the external world, then we must regard mental activity as a part of the activity whereby the animal relates itself to the external world. Its basis is the formation of conditioned reflexes.

Mental life begins when things begin to take on a meaning for the animal, and this happens when the animal, as a result of the formation of conditioned reflexes, begins to learn to connect one thing with another. Something has a meaning for an animal when the animal has learned to connect its presence with something else. For example, a dog learns to connect a particular stimulation of its sense of smell with the presence of some particular food, or of another dog, or of its master, etc., An animal is constantly receiving an enormous number of stimuli through its external and internal sense organs, and it learns to connect the various stimuli with various things. Thus the various stimuli become not simply stimuli to which a fixed response is automatically called forth, but they constitute for the animal a system of signals of the external world and of its own relations to the external world, to which a whole variety of responses are made.

Thus the animal becomes actively aware of things. To be aware of things is essentially an active state, and not a passive state. To be aware of things is not simply to be affected by them, but to respond to them.

Awareness means first of all that the animal, by the use of its sense organs, discriminates certain features of its environment from the total environment, and responds to them. For example, it picks out its food by smell, touch and sight, and eats it.

And awareness means, secondly, that the animal attaches a meaning to various features of its environment, in the sense that it connects them with other things. For example, certain things become for the animal signals of the presence of food, or of the approach of something dangerous, and so on, and the animal responds accordingly.

Thus the active awareness of things which is engendered by the formation of conditioned reflexes means that the animal learns to connect the stimuli which it actually receives with other things by which it is not at the time directly affected. And so it is able to form expectations and to learn by experience.

In this way the formation of conditioned reflexes gives rise to the difference between the subjective and the objective. This difference, which has been the subject of much speculation and mystification by philosophers, has a natural explanation. For the difference between the subjective and the objective begins to arise as soon as animals begin to be aware of things.

It is simply the difference between the totality of actually existing material conditions and the aspects of them of which the animal is aware and the meaning it attaches to them.

Hence the subjective as opposed to the objective, the mental as opposed to the physical, awareness as opposed to that which it is awareness of—all these differences arise as a result of the development of the higher nervous activity of animals through the building up by conditioned reflexes of ever more complicated relations of the animal with the external world.

The subjective is different from the objective, because (*a*) the animal is aware only of some parts or aspects and not of the whole of its surroundings, and (*b*) the meaning it attaches to things may be wrong—that is to say, things may become connected together subjectively in different ways from those in which they are connected together objectively, in actual fact.

And the objective is prior to the subjective, because (*a*) the existence of things is a condition for awareness of them whereas awareness of things is not a condition for their existence, and (*b*) things existed long before any awareness of them arose or could have arisen on the part of living organisms.

It is, then, in the activity of the nervous system—the activity of building complicated and variable relations with the external world—that *consciousness* arises. When, through the formation of conditioned reflexes, the stimulations which an animal receives begin to function for it as signals, and it learns to recognise such signals and to regulate its behaviour in accordance with them, then a new quality comes into existence in the nervous process of the animal, namely, consciousness.

Consciousness is not a mysterious "something" which comes into being parallel to, side by side with, the material life process of the brain. It is rather the new quality which distinguishes that life process. The brain process becomes a conscious process as a result of the brain's functioning as "the organ of the most complicated relations of the animal to the external world". Consciousness is the peculiar quality of the relationship of the animal to the external world effected by the life process of the brain. This relationship becomes one in which the animal is aware of its surroundings through the stimulations of the various centres of its brain and the connections established in the brain. In so far as an animal lives in such relationship with its surroundings, it is conscious and its existence is conscious existence.

The elementary form of consciousness amongst animals is sensory consciousness, or sensation. This arises when, through the formation of conditioned reflexes, various stimulations of its sense organs acquire a meaning and become signals for the animal. For an external observer, these stimulations are simply modifications of the sense organs to which the animal responds in definite ways. But the life of the animal has then become a sensuously conscious life. Its brain process, or rather, a part of its brain process, has become a conscious process in which stimulations of the sense organs become sensations.

Development of the Higher Mental Activity of Man

The higher mental activity of man, speech and thought, is not separated by any unbridgeable gap from the sensory consciousness which man possesses in common with other animals. On the contrary, it arises from the evolutionary development of the structure and functions of the human brain, as the organ of the connections of the animal to the external world.

"When the developing animal world reached the stage of man," Pavlov wrote, "an extremely important addition was made to the mechanism of the higher nervous activity." This addition consisted of the development of speech—and thought processes, ideas, are inseparable from speech. It is known that speech has its material basis in certain centres of the human brain, the evolution and workings of which constituted that "addition to the mechanism of the higher nervous activity" of which Pavlov wrote and which is peculiar to man. If this part of the brain is injured or destroyed, not only is the ability to speak impaired or lost but so is the ability to think.

Speech develops as a means of communication between individuals in society, without which their social life and so the survival of the species would be impossible. The use of speech, the ability to speak and to understand what is said, is rooted in man's sensory activity, which he has in common with other animals. It has evidently developed as an addition to that sensory activity engendered by the new unique conditions of the human mode of social life and based on the enlargement of the structure and functions of the human brain.

Many animals have evolved means of communicating with other members of their species about situations of which they are aware through their sensations. Thus birds have a warning call to alert other birds to danger. In some cases quite complicated communications occur. Thus a bee returning to the hive performs a dance in response to which other bees fly off in an indicated direction where the first bee has found nectar. By speech the human being can likewise communicate to others particular facts of which he is aware through his sensations. But speech enables us to do far more than this. For it consists not just of cries or gestures, but the combination of words.

Through its sensations an animal recognises objects and their sensible characters, and so responds to the different situations which confront it. In building up conditioned connections with things through sensations, the animal is already learning to react to and so distinguish what is common to different things, that is to say, to recognise the same kind of thing and the same properties of things on different occasions. In human speech there are words, in the first place, for the different kinds of objects and the different properties of objects which we recognise through our sensations. And so, by combining these words, we can speak at will about different kinds of objects, attribute different properties to them, and so communicate not merely information about particular sensible facts of which we are immediately aware and which call for an immediate response, but about the kinds of things which surround us and the properties they have, about how they can be changed, about not only what is immediately and sensibly present but about the past, and future, and the far distant in space, and about not only what is actual but what is possible or imaginable.

Speech performs an abstracting and generalising function in relation to what we are aware of through sensation, and so makes possible the communication of plans and ideas, and the whole higher activity of thought. To have ideas is to have words and the use of speech. And this affords us much wider connections with the world about us and far different relations with each other than those possible to animals without speech. Human beings communicating by speech are placing themselves in a new and more complex relationship with the surrounding world and with each other compared with other animals, which are limited to the connections they build up through sensation alone. The human brain is the organ of this relationship; and the abstracting, generalising, planning and thinking activity of the human brain is the activity of developing this relationship.

Evidently, without the sensation which people have in common with other animals there can be no speech and no thought, since these develop from man's sensory activity. At the same time, the development of human sensation is also modified by speech. Our sensory awareness is conditioned and directed by our ideas. Thus we do not merely have sensations of sight, sound, touch, etc., to which we respond, but these sensations are integrated into perceptions of objects of which we have ideas and know the names. This is shown, for example, by the fact that in children the naming of things is an indispensable part of the education of their senses; or again, by the fact that people who through some brain injury have forgotten the names of things become confused in their reactions to those things.

We may conclude, then, that not only our sensations but our thoughts and ideas as well, all the higher intellectual and spiritual activities of man, take their origin from the material processes of the human organism, depend on a bodily organ of which they are the functions, and grow out of the interactions of the human organism with its environment, natural and social, mediated by the higher nervous activity of the brain.

Chapter Two

MIND AS A PRODUCT AND REFLECTION OF MATTER

Mental Processes are Processes of the Brain, Relating the Organism to its Surroundings

WE shall in this chapter try briefly to summarise the main conclusions about the relations of matter and mind which have been reached by Marxism and are confirmed by every scientific investigation, contrasting them with the views held by idealism.

Mental functions are functions of highly developed matter, namely, of the brain. Mental processes are brain processes, processes of a material, bodily organ.

The essential feature of mental processes is that in and through them the animal continually builds up most complicated and variable relations with its surroundings. When we perceive things we are relating ourselves to external objects through the perceptual activity of the brain. And when we think of things, we are relating ourselves to external objects through the thought activity of the brain.

Believing that consciousness belongs to a mind which exists in separation from matter, idealism generally relies upon the method of introspection in order to give an account of our consciousness. This is the method of looking inside one's own consciousness, so to speak, and trying to analyse what is found there.

The outstanding example of the use of the introspective method in modern psychology is psycho-analysis. Psycho-analysis has evolved a special technique of controlled introspection, applied by the co-operation of a patient and a psycho-analyst. By inducing the patient to report on whatever comes into his mind, to relate his dreams, and so on, the psycho-analyst claims to discover beneath consciousness a whole realm of the unconscious. And so there has been developed a very elaborate theory of the different parts of the mind and of their relations and functions—of the conscious and the unconscious, the ego, the id and the super-ego. This is but an extension of the method used by all idealist philosophers and psychologists when they try to analyse the constituent parts of the human mind, classifying them, relating them and trying to trace their development, all the time treating consciousness as though it were a world on its own, divorced from the external material world.

Adopting such a method, many idealist philosophers have come to the conclusion that the perceptions and ideas which constitute the content of consciousness are a special kind of objects which have a mental existence distinct from the material existence of objects outside our consciousness.

For such idealist philosophers, what we are aware of in our conscious life is not material objects at all. We know only our ideas of things, and not the "things in themselves". Thus the English philosopher John Locke wrote in his *Essay on the Human Understanding:* "The mind, in all its thoughts and reasonings, hath no other immediate object but its own ideas, which it alone does or can contemplate."

Hence idealists conclude that only God knows what are the properties of "things in themselves", for they consider our sensations and ideas to be a kind of wall inside our consciousness, cutting it off from the external world. Some go a step further, and conclude that there is no reason to believe that external, material things exist at all: nothing exists except our minds and the sensations and ideas in our minds. "If there were external bodies," wrote George Berkeley in his *Principles of Human Knowledge,* "it is impossible we should ever come to know it; and if there were not, we might have the very same reasons to think there were as we have now."

But there is another method of studying our consciousness, namely, the method of science, which studies living, conscious organisms in their active relationship with their surroundings. This method does not treat consciousness as a special object of introspective contemplation. And so it does not study consciousness as though it were something existing in abstraction from the life process of living conscious organisms, but, on the contrary, it studies their conscious activity. As Marx and Engels briefly expressed it in *The German Ideology:* "Consciousness is always conscious existence."

As we have said, the essence of conscious activity is to build up complicated and variable active relations between the conscious organism and its surroundings, and this function is performed by the brain. Consequently the processes of consciousness are processes whereby we relate ourselves to the external world. Far from standing in the way of our apprehension of external things, our sensations and ideas are the means whereby we apprehend them.

"Sensation is the direct connection between consciousness and the external world", wrote Lenin. "The sophism of idealist philosophy consists in the fact that it regards sensation as being not the connection between consciousness and the external world, but as a fence, a wall, separating consciousness from the external world." (*Materialism and Empirio-Criticism*, chapter 1.)

Adopting the scientific approach to the study of consciousness, Marxism therefore denies the idealist theory that when we perceive, feel or think there are *two separate processes* going on—the material process of the brain and the mental process of consciousness. *Only one* process is involved, namely, the material process of the brain. Mental processes are simply one aspect of the processes of the functioning of the brain as the organ of most complicated relations to the external world.

And so Marx wrote that thinking is "the life process of the human brain." (*Capital*, Preface to 2nd edition.)

Consciousness is a Product of the Development of Matter

(2) According to idealism, such phenomena as perceptions, feelings and thoughts could not be produced by the workings

of any material system. Idealism holds that the peculiar quality of consciousness, which distinguishes mental processes, cannot be explained as arising from any possible combination of material conditions, but is a quality absolutely incompatible with all qualities of material systems. Such a quality, idealism concludes, can belong only to something non-material, namely, the mind.

But all the known facts point to the conclusion that consciousness is a product of the development of matter, namely, of living bodies with a central nervous system, and that perceptions, feelings and thoughts are, in fact, the highest products of matter.

"If the question is raised: what, then, are thought and consciousness and whence they came," wrote Engels in *Anti-Dühring*, Part I, chapter 3, "it becomes apparent that they are products of the human brain, and that man himself is a product of nature, which has been developed in and along with his environment."

"The material, sensuously perceptible world to which we belong is the only reality", Engels further wrote in *Ludwig Feuerbach*, chapter 2. "Our consciousness and thinking, however suprasensuous they may seem, are the products of a material, bodily organ, the brain. Matter is not a product of mind, but mind itself is merely the highest product of nature."

When animals develop a nervous system and begin actively to relate themselves to their environment by conditioned connections, then the nervous process becomes a conscious process, a process of sensation and, in man, of thinking. Hence sensations and thoughts are the peculiar products of the nervous process.

Sensation, wrote Lenin in *Materialism and Empirio-Criticism*, chapter 1, is "one of the properties of matter in motion".

"Matter acting on our sense-organs produces sensation", he continued. "Sensation depends on the brain, nerves, retina, etc., i.e., on matter organised in a definite way. . . . Sensation, thought, consciousness are the supreme product of matter organised in a particular way."

Consciousness is Reflection of the Material World

(3) Many idealists, who believe that the mind exists in separation from the body and that perceptions and thoughts cannot be products of any material process, say that perceptions and thoughts are creations of the mind which occupy our consciousness independently of the existence of external, material things.

But Marxism maintains that perceptions and thoughts are nothing but reflections of material things. The processes of consciousness are processes reflecting external, material reality, and nothing can come to birth in consciousness except as a reflection of the material world.

Marx wrote, in the Preface to the 2nd edition of *Capital*, that "the ideal is nothing else than the material world reflected by the human mind and translated into forms of thought."

He considered that in the process of thinking, and in consciousness in general, there is produced a reflection of different parts or aspects of the material world in one particular material process, namely, the life process of the brain. In our consciousness, different parts or aspects of the material world are translated into forms of consciousness—perceptions and thoughts. They are reproduced in the life activity of the brain, in forms appropriate to that activity.

Thus, for example, the properties of various bodies absorbing and reflecting light are, in the sensory activity of the brain, reproduced in the form of sensations of colour. Again, the relations and common features of things are, in the thinking activity of the brain, reproduced in the form of concepts.

What exactly do we mean by "reflection", when we say that consciousness is a reflection of material reality? There are four features of the process of reflection to which we may specially draw attention

Material Reality is Primary and its Mental Reflection is Secondary or Derivative

(*a*) The process of reflection involves a relationship between two separate material processes, such that features of the first process are reproduced in corresponding features of the second process. The first process is primary, and its reflection in the second is secondary or derivative. For the first process develops in complete independence of the second, whereas the reproduction of features of the first process by reflection in the second could not occur unless those features were first there to be reproduced or reflected.

This fundamental feature of any process of reflection is illustrated by reflection in a mirror—although, as we shall see, the active reflection of external reality in consciousness differs in important respects from the passive reflection which takes place in a mirror.

Thus when objects are reflected in a mirror, those objects which are set before the mirror do not depend on being reflected in the mirror for either their existence or their characteristics; but, on the other hand, the reflection in the mirror depends on what is set before the mirror, and nothing is reflected in the mirror which does not reproduce in some way the characteristics of what is set before the mirror. Hence the object is primary, and its reflection secondary or derivative.

Similarly, the existence of material objects does not depend on our being conscious of them; but, on the other hand, there is nothing in our consciousness which does not reproduce in some way or other something which exists in the material world.

There are many characteristics of things which are not reproduced in our sensations; but we have no sensation which does not correspond, in some way or other, to some definite characteristic of things. There are many relations of things and common features of things which are not reproduced in our concepts; but we can form no concept in our minds which does not reproduce, in some way or other, even if in fantastic ways (as in a distorting mirror), some features or some relationship of things.

Of course, many concepts give an appearance of having no basis in the reflection of material reality, just because, once formed, concepts can be freely combined in all sorts of fantastic ways. For example, everyone knows that no real animal is reflected in the concept of a mermaid, but that this concept is formed by combining ideas of real animals, namely, of women and fishes. Similarly, materialists can consistently argue that no real object corresponds to the concept of God as a trinity of persons with infinite power and infinite knowledge, but that the several concepts of persons, power, knowledge and infinity have all been formed as reflections of material reality.

When we say, therefore, that material reality is reflected in consciousness, we mean that features of material reality are reproduced in consciousness, and that material reality is primary and its reproduction in consciousness secondary or derivative.

"Our consciousness is only an image of the external world," wrote Lenin, in *Materialism and Empirio-Criticism*, chapter 1, "and it is obvious that an image cannot exist without the thing imaged, and that the latter exists independently of that which images it."

Material Reality is Reflected in Consciousness in Forms Determined by the Activity of the Brain

(*b*) What exists in one form in the primary process is reproduced in another form in the secondary process of reflection. What exists independently in one form is, so to speak, translated into another form in the process of reflection. The process of reflection is therefore a process of translation or transformation from one form into another. And the form of the reflection depends, of course, on the nature of the process of reflection.

When we say, therefore, that material reality is reflected in consciousness, we mean that features of material processes are reproduced—in another material process, namely, in the life process of the brain—in special forms, namely, in the forms of perceptions and thoughts.

These forms are created in the operation of the processes of the brain. Material reality is thus reproduced or reflected in consciousness in forms created by and adapted to the practical requirements of living, conscious organisms.

Our sensations, for example, are the reflections in the conscious process of our brains of features of material things. Those features are not, however, themselves sensations but are reflected in sensations, and our sensations are the form in which we are perceptually conscious of them and so are able to react to them.

Thus when we see colours, for instance, we are not seeing things which exist only in our minds—as some philosophers have asserted—but are seeing things which exist independently, outside our minds, the properties of which are reflected in our sensations of colour. Properties which exist in real things as properties of the absorption and reflection of light are reflected in our perceptual consciousness in the form of sensations of colour.

Thus Lenin, in the chapter already quoted, wrote: "If colour is a sensation only depending on the retina (as natural science compels you to admit), then light rays, falling upon the retina, produce the sensation of colour. This means that outside us, independently of us and of our minds, there exists a movement of matter . . . which, acting upon the retina, produces in man the sensation of a particular colour. This is precisely how natural science regards it. It explains the sensations of various colours by the various lengths of light-waves existing outside the human retina, outside man and independently of him."

Thought, again, produces a more abstract, more general reflection of reality than perception. In what form is reality reflected in our thoughts? It is reflected in the form of propositions. Thought issues in propositions in which, for example, a subject is combined with a predicate. The material world does not exist in the form of a combination of subjects and predicates. This combination is a product of speech, of the thinking activity of the brain, and through it reality is reflected in thought. This is how the material world is "translated into forms of thought."

Consider, for example, any object—a red pencil, say. When we think about such an object we express our conclusions about it in propositions, such as, "This pencil is red". This proposition is divided into a subject and predicate, which are combined in the proposition. But the object is not so divided in concrete reality. A red pencil does not divide into two parts —a subject, the pencil, and a predicate, red. Nevertheless, it is obvious that when we say, "This pencil is red", the proposition does reflect the objective reality of the pencil, which is thus correctly "translated into forms of thought".

The Reflection of Material Reality in Consciousness Takes Place through the Active Relationship of the Living Organism and its Surroundings

(*c*) Reflection is always a product of the relationship and interaction of the process in which the reflection occurs and the primary process which is reflected. Its source is the primary process.

Thus the life process of the brain reproduces or reflects in its products—perceptions and thoughts—the surrounding material reality, which is the source of all perceptions and thoughts. And this reflection takes place in, and is the result of, the interaction of the conscious organism with its environment. This interaction is regulated by the brain, as the organ of the most complicated relations of the animal to its environment. The brain is continually active in the process of reflection, continually producing the reflection of external objects in consciousness.

It follows, therefore, that the way in which the material world is reflected in consciousness is governed by the active relationship between the living conscious organism and its surroundings, by the circumstances of the animal, by its internal state as well as by its external relations.

When we take this into account, it becomes obvious that in the process of reflection of external reality in our consciousness, the objects reflected can become considerably altered in the reflection. For the reflection is not at all like a direct mirror-image of the object, but is the product of a complex process of interaction in which the brain is continually active.

This accounts for the well known fact that our perceptions of objects are very often misleading; they may misrepresent objects, or even (as in certain illusions and hallucinations) lead us to suppose that objects are present which are not really there at all.

Many philosophers have opposed the materialist view that

consciousness reflects external reality. And one of the arguments they have advanced for opposing this view is based simply on the character of our perceptions.

"Take a penny," they say. "You believe that the material penny has a definite shape and size, and that this material object is reflected in your perceptions when you look at it. Very well. If you look at this penny from a distance it looks small, while if you hold it close to your eye it looks big; if you hold it one way it looks circular, while if you hold it another way it looks elliptical. In fact, your perceptions of it change in all sorts of ways, while the material object, of which your perceptions are alleged to be the images in your mind, does not change at all. How, then, can perceptions be said to reflect external reality, since they change while the latter does not?"

This question, which is so confidently posed as an unanswerable argument against the theory of reflection, can be very easily answered. The philosoohers who argue in such a way have simply forgotten that reflection is an active process, conditioned by the actual relations between the organism and its surroundings.

Thus if we look at the same thing from different distances or from different angles, then of course it will be differently reflected in our perceptions—its size or shape will differ. Again, if we see a thing through different mediums, of course it will look different—as when a straight stick held in the water looks bent. Again, the reflection will necessarily be altered by the actual state of our sense organs—press the corner of your eye, and you will see two of everything; make one hand hot and the other cold, and plunge them both into a bowl of water, and the water will feel colder to one hand than to the other. Lastly, since perceiving is an activity of the brain, it is not surprising that, objects having been once reflected in that activity, the brain can reproduce reflections of those objects under certain circumstances even when they are not there—as in dreams, illusions of all kinds and hallucinations.

Still more in the processes of thought can we misrepresent to ourselves the properties of things, ascribe to them properties which they do not possess, and think of things which do not exist at all. By means of thought we often correct illusions occurring in perception. But we also often produce new and greater illusions.

The Reflection of Reality in Consciousness is an Active Factor in Directing the Practice of Changing Reality

(*d*) The fact that reflection in consciousness is the product of life activity, of the activity of the organism in relation to its surroundings, means that the consciousness of man, both his perceptions and his thoughts, is continually conditioned by his experience and his social activity. What men perceive and what they think does not arise by a direct process of the reproduction of external reality in perception and thought, but is conditioned by their experience, manner of life and social relations.

Thus it is well known that differences in people's experience and manner of life determine differences in what they perceive in things. The perceptions of a skilled engineer examining a complex machine, for example, are not the same as those of a man not familiar with such machines, although their sense organs may be affected in precisely similar ways. The perceptions of a farmer looking at a country scene are not the same as those of a townsman, and an artist perceives the same scene in still other ways.

Still greater are the differences which arise between men's concepts and thoughts about things on the basis of differences in class, experience and upbringing.

In the human being, moreover, ideas about things also exert an influence back on perceptions. The fact that we do not merely perceive things but form ideas of them influences perception. This was exemplified, indeed, in the examples just cited. If a skilled engineer perceives more in a machine than other men do, this is because he has more ideas about it than they. Again, while artists may perceive more in things than inartistic people, different artists also perceive things differently according to their ideas of them. This is shown, for example, in the very different ways in which painters of different outlook portray human beings.

The reflection of our surroundings and of our connections with our surroundings in our consciousness is a very active factor in determining our activity of changing our surroundings. The fact that consciousness is reflection does not mean that consciousness is not an active factor in life. Consciousness is in the first place a product of life activity, in the second place it is a product which plays a major part in directing that very activity of which it is a product. In consciousness, life has produced the means of directing life towards definite ends.

Indeed, we can say that that is why consciousness was bound to be produced in the course of the evolution of living organisms.

Conscious existence is life activity governed by the reflection of external conditions in the brain. This reflection is, in the first place, a product of the active relationships of the conscious organism to its surroundings; and, in turn, it actively conditions the further development of those relationships through the practice of men in changing their surroundings. Man's consciousness is a product of his practice which plays the part of directing his practice.

Finally, in considering this active role of consciousness we should bear in mind that the reflection of the material world in consciousness does not take the form only of perceptions and thoughts. In his active, conscious existence man also feels emotions.

According to many idealists, emotions well up out of man's inner spiritual being. But for materialism, emotions, too, are modes of the reflection of material reality in the consciousness of man. They reflect the active relationship of man to his environment. And being active, being affected by things in his activity, and taking a definite attitude towards things and possible changes in things, man feels emotions about things and is impelled in his activity by emotions. In his conscious existence man is not only aware of things in perception and thought, but also feels his active relationship to things emotionally.

Emotional consciousness is, then, a necessary part of life. A man relates himself to surrounding reality by perceiving it and forming ideas about it, but this relationship needs to be completed by the emotions he feels about it. Similarly, emotions need to be guided and directed by perceptions and ideas.

Matter and its Reflection

To conclude.

There is no consciousness apart from a living brain. The source of all consciousness, of everything that enters into consciousness, is the material world. In consciousness there occurs the reflection of the material world in the life process of the brain, and this reflection is what constitutes the content of consciousness.

There are not, therefore, two separate and distinct spheres of existence, material and spiritual. There are not two worlds, the material and the spiritual worlds. But there exists only the material world, only material processes.

"The antithesis of matter and mind has absolute significance only within the bounds of a very limited field," Lenin wrote in *Materialism and Empirio-Criticism*, chapter 3, "exclusively within the bounds of the fundamental problem of what is to be regarded as primary and what as secondary. Beyond these bounds the relative character of this antithesis is indubitable."

In the course of material development there arises the reflection of material processes in one particular material process, the life process of the brain. And when we distinguish material and spiritual, matter and mind, what we are distinguishing is simply material being, movement in space and time, from its reflection in the life process of the brain.

The process which gives rise to the reflection and the process in which the reflection occurs are both material processes. But the reflection is not material but mental—that is to say, not material but a reflection of matter.

Chapter Three

SOCIAL LABOUR AND SOCIAL THINKING

The Human Brain and What We Do with It

THE human brain, which alone is capable of producing general ideas, conceptual consciousness, thinking, is the product of a long evolution of the forms of life. It is the culmination of a process of evolution in the size and structure of the brain. In particular, the cerebral cortex is far larger in man than in other animals, and a large part of the cortex has come to be specially concerned with controlling the hands and the organs of speech.

It is true that we are only at the beginning of scientific knowledge of how the brain works. But enough is known to assert confidently that the brain is the organ of thought, that thinking is done by the brain, and that the evolution of a certain size and structure of the brain was necessary as a condition of our being able to think with it.

The biological evolution of the brain into an organ capable of thinking took place in the pre-human stage of the evolution of man, in that stage during which ape-like animals were evolving into men. The decisive step in man's evolution was probably taken when an erect posture was adopted by these animals. For this set free the hand, with which the whole of man's productive activity has been accomplished. With the use of the hand went the physical development of the hand into the human hand, and with that, the development of the brain which controls the hand into the human brain.

The first men already had the same kinds of brains as we have, just as they had the same kinds of hands, feet, eyes, noses, teeth, stomachs and so on. Our organs, including our brains, are no different from theirs, although in the meantime we have learned to do many things which they did not do.

Thus once biological evolution had produced the human brain and hands, man started a new kind of evolution of his own. The evolution of man is not biological. What man evolves is his social organisation, his techniques, his culture and his knowledge, his conscious mastery over himself and external nature.

Hence in relation to the brain, what has developed since man first came into existence is not his brain but the use he has made of it—his development of the capacities contained in it. Man has developed his material activities, his perceptions and his thoughts; and through doing this has continually revolutionised his own conditions of life and increased his capacities and powers.

From Perceptions to Ideas

Thinking arises only out of sense-perception and must be preceded by it. To think about the world we must first perceive the world. We can form no concept that is not based on and prompted by perception. And in general, no ideas at all are formed without the perceptions which are the necessary material on which the activity of thinking has to work.

A man isolated from childhood in a confined space, for instance, might have as good a brain as anyone else, but he would have very little to think about, and his ideas and the range of his ideas would be very limited. Similarly, the range of ideas of primitive peoples is limited as compared with civilised men, though their brains are in no way inferior.

It is as our perceptions increase with increased activity and social contacts that our ideas develop.

Thinking, then, grows out of perception. And this development takes place only in and through the active relationship to the external world which men establish for themselves in the course of their practical social activity. Perception itself is not just a passive receiving of impressions from external objects. The development of sensation into perception is the product of the development of active relationships to the external world. And the more varied and complex is the active relationship of the organism to its surroundings, the more varied and complex will be the content of the perception of those surroundings.

"The real intellectual wealth of the individual depends entirely on the wealth of his real connections," wrote Marx and Engels (*The German Ideology*, Part 1, section 2.).

Human perception is much wider in scope than that of any other animal. And this is because man has wider activities and interests, and in developing these activities and interests has effected a corresponding development of his senses. It is because man has developed his activities and his perceptions that he has been able to think and to develop his ideas—and this has then reacted back again on the further development of his activities and of his perceptions.

"The eagle sees much further than man, but the human eye sees considerably more in things than does the eye of the eagle," wrote Engels. "The dog has a far keener sense of smell than man, but it does not distinguish a hundredth part of the odours that for man are definite features of different things. And the sense of touch, which the ape hardly possesses in its crudest initial form, has been developed side by side with the development of the human hand itself, through the medium of labour." (*The Party Played by Labour in the Transition from Ape to Man*).

The basis for this heightened perception and wider range of perception in man was established by our early ancestors, when they first began to stand erect, to look around them, and to use their hands, not to swing among the branches of trees and grab food, but to fashion tools and implements.

As man's activity developed, so there developed the wealth of his connections with the world around him. Man achieved a heightened perception and wider scope of perceptions, and then speech, which marks the transition from concrete sense-perceptions to abstract, general ideas. The interaction in the course of man's activity of his ideas with his sensations led to the still greater development of his perceptions, and so again to the further development of ideas.

The capacity of the human brain to perceive and then to think is realised and developed in human activity.

Labour

Man lives in society, and acts together with his fellow men. His whole mode of life is social. Therefore just as it is in his social activity that he enlarges his perceptions, so it is in his social activity that, starting from these perceptions, he begins to form ideas, to think and to develop his ideas.

The basis of man's social activity is labour. It is in and through labour that man first of all enlarges his perceptions and first of all begins to use his brain to think—to form ideas and to communicate them, to develop thought and language.

In labour, then, is to be found the source and origin of thought and language.

"Labour . . . is the primary basic condition of all human existence," wrote Engels in his essay on *The Part Played by Labour in the Transition from Ape to Man*, "and this to such an extent that, in a sense, we have to say that labour created man himself."

In the evolution of man, Engels pointed out, the first decisive step was taken when an erect posture was adopted. This set free the hand. And when men began to fashion tools and implements with their hands for use in changing external objects and producing the means of life, that was the real beginning of men and of human society.

"The first premise of all human history is, of course, the existence of living human individuals," wrote Marx and Engels. "Thus the first fact to be established is the physical organisation of these individuals and their consequent relation to the rest of nature." But having established that fact, it is necessary to establish what they do—their activity, their mode of life. "Men . . . begin to distinguish themselves from animals as soon as they begin to produce their means of subsistence, a step which is conditioned by their physical organisation. By producing their means of subsistence men are indirectly producing their actual material life". (*The German Ideology*, Part I, chapter 1.)

It is in producing their means of subsistence and so indirectly producing their actual material life that men, conditioned by their physical organisation, begin to act as men, to develop social organisation and "make their own history", and in so doing to form ideas, to think and to speak.

Distinctive Features of Human Labour

What are the distinctive features of human labour, as compared with the ways in which other animals secure the means of life?

(1) First, men fashion tools and implements, changing natural objects so as to use their properties to bring about desired ends.

"An instrument of labour," wrote Marx (*Capital*, Volume I, chapter 7, section 1), "is a thing, or a complex of things, which the labourer interposes between himself and the subject of his labour, and which serves as the conductor of his activity. He makes use of the mechanical, physical and chemical properties of some substances in order to make other substances subservient to his aims."

The animal, on the other hand, collects and rearranges objects to hand, but does not transform them and use their properties and the natural forces contained in them for producing his means of life and affecting large-scale transformation of his surroundings in accordance with his own needs.

"The tool implies specific human activity, the transforming reaction of man on nature, production," wrote Engels. "Animals in the narrower sense also have tools, but only as limbs of their bodies: the ant, the bee, the beaver. Animals also produce, but their productive effort on surrounding nature in relation to the latter amounts to nothing at all. Man alone has succeeded in impressing his stamp on nature, not only by shifting the plant and animal world from one place to another, but also by so altering the aspect and climate of his dwelling place, and even the plants and animals themselves, that the consequences of his activity can disappear only with the general extinction of the terrestrial globe." (*Dialectics of Nature*, Introduction.)

"Animals change external nature by their activities just as man does, if not to the same extent", Engels further wrote. "... But if animals exert a lasting effect on their environment, it happens unintentionally, and, as far as the animals are concerned, it is an accident. The further men become removed from the animals, however, the more their effect on nature assumes the character of a premeditated, planned action, directed towards definite ends known in advance. . . .

"In short the animal merely *uses* external nature, and brings about changes in it simply by its presence; man by his changes makes it serve his ends, *masters* it." (*The Part Played by Labour in the Transition from Ape to Man.*)

By his labour, then, man masters nature, fashioning tools and using them so as to make nature serve his ends. "In the labour process," wrote Marx, "man's activity, with the help of the instruments of labour, effects an alteration, designed from the commencement, in the material worked upon." (*Capital*, Volume I, chapter 7, section 1.) And it is in thus mastering and changing nature that man changes himself, develops his own human attributes.

(2) The second distinctive feature of human labour follows from the first, and lies in its conscious and co-operative character.

In making tools and using them, in compelling natural objects and natural forces to serve his ends, man is conscious of his ends, has an idea of the result he intends to bring about. And men work co-operatively, according to a conscious design and plan, to bring about the ends they intend to achieve.

While such social creatures as bees, for example, build elaborate structures, they do so in an automatic way, by instinct. Human builders, on the other hand, work according to a conscious plan.

"We presuppose labour in a form which stamps it as exclusively human," wrote Marx. "A spider conducts operations that resemble those of a weaver, and a bee puts to shame many an architect in the construction of her cells. But what distinguishes the worst of architects from the best of bees is this, that the architect raises his structure in imagination before he erects it in reality. At the end of every labour process we get a result that already existed in the imagination of the labourer at its commencement." (*Capital*, Volume I, chapter 7, section 1.)

Labour, Speech and Thought

These distinctive features of labour—that labour is the use of tools and implements to effect changes of external objects by human beings co-operating to realise results which they consciously set before themselves—explain why labour necessarily gives rise to speech and thought, and cannot develop without the aids of speech and thought.

"The mastery over nature, which begins with the development of the hand, with labour, widened man's horizon at every new advance. He was continually discovering new, hitherto unknown properties of natural objects." (*The Part Played by Labour, etc.*)

In these words, Engels points out that labour, even of the most primitive kind, as in the fashioning and use of hunting and fishing implements, makes men perceive things with a new interest, enlarges their perceptions, "widens their horizon", makes them aware through their practical activity and from their perceptions of ever more properties of natural objects. And indeed, from these first beginnings, it has always been through their advancing mastery over nature that succeeding generations of men have come to know more and more of the properties of natural objects: each stage of advance has meant enlarged perceptions, new discoveries, wider horizons.

"On the other hand," Engels continues, "the development of labour necessarily helped to bring the members of society closer together by multiplying cases of mutual support and joint activity, and by making clear the advantage of this joint activity to each individual. In short, men in the making arrived at the point where *they had something to say* to one another."

This something which they "had to say to one another" concerned, in the first place, the properties of those objects which can be used by man, and the ends to be achieved and the results to be aimed at by human co-operation. And this is precisely something which can *only* be "said", which can only be expressed by *articulate speech*, and not by calls and gestures such as are employed by the animals.

"The little that even the most highly developed animals need to communicate to one another can be communicated even without the aid of articulate speech," Engels pointed out.

Animals signal to one another the presence of particular objects—as in the gestures made by bees, the so-called dances by which they indicate the presence of a source of honey in a particular direction; they arouse one another to particular actions—as in the call of the leader of a pack. But that is all. If their mode of life were such that they needed to communicate with one another about the different properties of things, about how these were to be used, and about the ends they aimed to achieve by different forms of co-operative activity, then such gestures and calls would no longer avail them. For they would then need to communicate not the particular but the general. Animals have no such need. But men do have such a need immediately they embark upon even the most elementary forms of social labour. They then have something they need to *say* to one another, as Engels pointed out. And so they develop the means to say it.

"The need led to the creation of its organ," Engels continues. "The undeveloped larynx of the ape was slowly but surely transformed by means of gradually increased modulation, and the organs of the mouth gradually learned to pronounce one articulate letter after another. Comparison with animals proves that this explanation of the origin of language from and in the process of labour is the only correct one."

Men needed to communicate with one another about the properties of objects and the practical use to be made of those properties. And Engels here describes how they developed the use of the larynx and the mouth in order to articulate words and sentences by which to effect this communication.

Ideas

Speech marks the advance from sensation to ideas.

Language has words for the properties and relations of objects which we have come to recognise through our senses in the course of practical life. And so while we *perceive* only what is actually confronting us, according to the impression it makes on our sense organs, we can *speak* and *think* of the objects we perceive not merely in their given relations, with their given properties, but in different relations and with changed properties. Hence we can speak and think of what we can do with objects of different kinds, and how we can change their properties for various purposes.

In this resides the power of thought. We can think of what is to be done with things, of changes which we intend to bring about, and can work out the means to achieve those changes. In thinking we work out experiments in our heads, as it were—representing what must be done, what must happen, in order that some changed state of affairs shall be realised. The conclusions of the experiment in thought are then checked by the results of practice. This is the very essence of the process of thinking, as it arises out of the process of labour.

We should here note that ideas are not the same as images. The idea or concept of, for example, a colour or shape is not the same as the image of a colour or of a shape which we can form in the imagination. The older empiricist philosophers (especially Berkeley and Hume) used to confound ideas and images; but, on the contrary, they should be carefully distinguished. Images are only a continuation of sensation; but ideas mark the development of speech, representing an abstraction from reality and permitting the forming of generalisations.

No doubt the higher animals as well as man can form in their minds sensuous images of objects. For instance, a fox can no doubt picture to itself the process of finding, hunting, killing and eating a rabbit, and then proceed to turn this image into reality. It can, and does, show considerable cunning and foresight in carrying out its purpose. But a man who uses even the simplest instrument of production employs methods which no other animal could employ. To make and use even the simplest instruments of production, he must not only have pictured things to himself but have formed ideas of the properties of things which can be put to use in realising the ends he desires.

Thus we can see in what way thought is a higher form of consciousness than sense-perception. Sense-perception reproduces things as they immediately appear through their action on our sense organs. When we form ideas, on the other hand, we can think of things in their essential character apart from their particular existence and mode of appearance; and so we can represent to ourselves in thought what transformations things undergo in different circumstances, how they interact, their various potentialities, interconnections and laws of change and motion.

It is evident, therefore, what a tremendous leap was made in the development of consciousness when ideas were formed. This leap to human consciousness was simply the ideal side of the leap from the animal to the human mode of life, made when men began to design and use tools.

Just as man no longer merely collects, rearranges and uses natural objects, as animals do, but masters nature, so in his ideas he does not merely register the appearances of things, as in perception, but traces their interconnections and causes.

Chapter Four

THOUGHT, LANGUAGE AND LOGIC

Language and Thought

THE power belonging to ideas, of representing things not merely in their immediate existence as presented to the senses but of representing properties and relations in abstraction from particular things—this power is a product of speech. The development of thinking and the power of thought are inseparable from and dependent on the development and power of speech.

Speech arises, as we have said, in the social activity of man, as a product and instrument, in the first place, of social labour. From the very beginning it serves as a medium of human social communication. Speech, therefore, obviously could not develop as the personal or private possession of individuals, each of whom uses it for his own purposes without relation to other individuals. On the contrary, it arises because, from the beginnings of human social activity, men need to communicate general ideas and conclusions to one another—and so they evolve the means of doing this.

Speech, therefore, arises through the formation of a *language* common to a social group. Those people know and understand a language who can use it for communicating with one another. A common territory, a common economic activity and tradition go with a common language—and this is why a common language forms part of the very definition of peoples and nations.

A language is characterised by vocabulary and syntax—that is, by a stock of words the constant reference of which has become fixed in the common use of a social group, and by rules governing the way the words are combined together for purposes of communication.

It is when men begin to use tools for social production that they also begin to speak and to evolve a language, and thereby to form ideas about the surrounding world. It was "from and in the process of labour" that language originated. And this origin explains the essential, elementary features of language as an instrument for communication and exchange of thoughts.

But language which thus originates in man's productive activity serves the whole of the human social intercourse and activity that develops along with and on the basis of production. In everything that people do together they make use of language; and all their thoughts, plans and aspirations, all their ideas about the world and about one another, come to birth only because they have language in which to express and communicate them.

Can there be Thought without Language?

The study of the nature—the material basis, the functions and the laws of development—of thought and language leads to the conclusion that the formation of ideas and the exchange of ideas are impossible without language, and that ideas only take shape and develop through the means of language.

Ideas are formed and take shape only through words and the combination of words. It is by means of words and the combination of words in sentences that reality is reproduced in thoughts. Thoughts only become definite thoughts in so far as they are, as Stalin expressed it in his *Concerning Marxism in Linguistics*, "registered and fixed in words and in words combined into sentences". Ideas without language are as non-existent as spirits without bodies.

Does this mean that to think is the same thing as to utter words, and that the process of thinking is a process of "talking to oneself"? No. For in the first place, it is possible to utter words and sentences without meaning anything by them. And in the second place, once one has learned the uses of language many processes of thought can be performed without actually uttering, either aloud or "to oneself", all the words and sentences whose use would be needed for the full enunciation of the thoughts involved.

It is well known, for example, that with people who have often discussed some subject together a few words are enough for them mutually to understand some very complex point, which it would take many words for them to explain to an outsider. This is because they have been through their explanations together earlier, and these few words recall all those explanations.

It is very much the same with thought processes in an individual brain. One can come to conclusions without the intervention of elaborate processes of inner verbalisation. But at the same time, a man deceives himself if he supposes that he has ideas of things for which he lacks words, or that he has thoughts which he is unable to express in language.

Of course, this does not mean that there is no distinction between an idea and some particular word or phrase. It means that ideas only exist as embodied in particular words or phrases, which are used to express ideas. Ideas have no separate disembodied existence apart from their expression.

For example, the English word "red" and the French word "rouge" both express the same idea of a colour. So the idea cannot be identified with either word. But the idea of colour no more exists apart from words in which it is expressed, than colour exists apart from particular coloured objects. What makes the two words expressive of the same idea is that they have the same significance in the respective languages—that is, the two words play similar parts in elaborating through language connections between man and the external world. The thinking activity of the brain consists in nothing but such elaboration of connections with the external world; and this is done not prior to language, nor apart from language, but precisely and only by means of language.

Language Conventions and What They Express

A feature of language is its apparently arbitrary or conventional character. A particular sound is used for a particular purpose in a language—but some other sound would have done equally well and is, perhaps, used for that very same purpose in some other language.

The discovery that words are in this way arbitrary or conventional signs was an important discovery in science, obvious as it may seem. For it used often to be believed—and some people still believe it today—that a particular word is in some mysterious way "the right word" for a particular thing, and that words are connected with things by some internal tie, and not merely by the conventions of language.

The ancient conception of a secret tie between words and things was bound up with magic and religion. Thus it was thought that each man had a name which was peculiarly his own and that no other name for him could fit. His "real name" was then often kept a secret, for it was believed that if his enemies knew it, then they could curse his name and so do him an injury. Similarly, the names of gods were believed to be among the essential properties of the gods. And similarly with other words, besides proper names. Thus there was an old proverb (quoted by C. K. Ogden and I. A. Richards, in *The Meaning of Meaning*) which stated, "The Divine is rightly so called": this expressed the idea that there was something peculiarly divine about the word "divine".

But not only is the vocabulary of a language conventional, its rules of grammar and syntax are conventional too. For different languages employ different rules. Thus the rules of the Chinese language, for example, are entirely different from those of any European language; the rules of English are different from those of Latin or Slavonic languages; and the rules of what we are pleased to call "primitive" languages are again different from them all. Nevertheless, the same propositions can be stated in all these languages, and any one can be translated into any other. This shows that not only vocabulary but grammar is a conventional feature of languages.

The particular sounds which constitute the words in a given language, and the particular rules of its grammar, are, then, conventional. They are conventional in the sense that these particular sounds and rules come to be used by a particular people for historical reasons, whereas the same thoughts could equally well be expressed by different sounds and different rules, such as are employed by the historically evolved languages of other peoples. But they are not, of course, conventional in the sense that they were ever resolved upon and fixed by some linguistic decision of the people concerned. In general, linguistic conventions are formed by an unconscious process in the lives of peoples. Only at a late stage are they recorded in dictionaries and grammars and do people begin consciously and deliberately to record and fix the conventions of their language.

But while both vocabulary and grammar are in the above sense conventional, nevertheless what words a language possesses, in the sense of the objects denoted by its vocabulary, is not conventional, but is determined by the objective conditions and requirements of life of the people using the language.

For example, whatever sounds are used for the purpose, a language must have words for all the things, properties, relations, etc., which are of practical importance in the life of the people. In general, the higher the stage of development of production the greater is necessarily the basic word stock of language.

Similarly, the relations and connections among things and people which are expressed by combining words into sentences according to the rules of grammar and syntax are not conventional either, but are determined by what has to be reflected in sentences.

For example, whatever the grammar of a language is, it must have conventions for expressing the action of one thing on another, the connection between a thing and its different or changing properties, and so on. Different languages employ different conventions for expressing propositions, but those conventions must all satisfy the same requirements arising from what has to be expressed, which is common to all languages.

Hence while people fix the conventions of their language, both as regards its word stock and its grammar, those conventions express objective requirements common to every language, and must always satisfy those same requirements.

Language and Logic

Whatever thoughts we think, and whatever language they are expressed in, they must satisfy the basic requirements of the reflection of reality in thought. These requirements give rise to laws of thought, to principles of logic. For thoughts are reflections of the real world, and in the process of reflection, as Marx said, the material world is translated into forms of thought. This process of reflection and translation has its own laws—the laws of thought, the principles of logic.

The laws of thought involve, in the first place, the logical principles for constructing significant propositions.

There are, for example, simple propositions and compound propositions. The construction of simple propositions involves such logical operations as affirmation, negation, relation and so on; and compound propositions are constructed by combining simple propositions through such logical operations as we express by words like "and", "or", "if . . . then", and so on. Thus, "This is red", "This is not red", "This is getting red", "This is redder than that", are all simple propositions. And "This is red and that is green", "Either this is red or I am colour blind", and "If this is red then it will soon be green", are compound propositions. The construction of all such propositions involves definite logical principles governing the construction of significant propositions.

The laws of thought involve, in the second place, the logical principles for determining which propositions logically follow from other propositions and which are logically inconsistent with them. These are the principles which we use in argument and reasoning.

For example, "If all A is B, and all B is C, then all A is C". This is a general logical principle, which tells us that the third proposition logically follows from the first two. This particular principle was originally formulated by Aristotle, who called it "the first figure of the syllogism".

Such a principle, of course, contains no guarantee as to the truth of propositions: it is concerned with their logical relations with one another, not with their truth. Thus it tells us that if we have discovered that the first two propositions are true, then we need no further investigations to assure ourselves of the truth of the third, for it follows from the first two. But if the first two propositions are in fact untrue, then, though the third proposition follows from them, it may be true or it may be false. Logic by itself tells us nothing about the truth of propositions, which can be discovered and verified only by empirical investigation.

Another example of a logical principle is the principle of non-contradiction—which would be better called "the principle of consistency". This states that a proposition must not be combined with its negation. The negation of "A is B" is "A is not B", and if you say "A is B and A is not B", the two parts of what you say cancel each other out so that you have said nothing (just as in mathematics plus and minus cancel each other). In that case what you say is inconsistent or self-contradictory.

It is worth noting that ever since the logical principle of non-contradiction was first formulated by Aristotle it has led to a lot of confusion in the discussion of logic. Thus the scholastic philosophers formulated it as a law governing the way in which "attributes" belong to "subjects". This alleged law said that the same attribute cannot both belong and not belong to the same subject; and it was coupled with a second law, called "the law of excluded middle", which said that an attribute must either belong or not belong to a subject. This was then taken to mean that you can always decide definitely which is true: "A is B" or "A is not B". One must be true and the other false.

But it is not difficult to see that such a decision cannot always be made, so that this is not a correct formulation of a law of logic. For since things exist only in interconnection and motion, a thing can very well manifest some characteristic only in certain respects and relations and not in others—so that you cannot definitely decide whether it has or has not that attribute. And it is equally evident that if a thing is in process of change, it may be impossible either truly to affirm or to deny that it has some fixed characteristic.

Many crude and inaccurate formulations of logical principles have been written down by philosophers with a metaphysical rather than a dialectical approach. Dialectics shows us how to correct such mistakes. But dialectics does not thereby go against or change the principles of logic. The aim of the dialectical method is to enable us logically and consistently to express the real interconnections and motion of things.

For example, is a certain man "bald" or "not bald"? According to the scholastic or metaphysical philosophers, with their inaccurate formulation of logical principles, a definite decision must always be made. Yet while in some cases it may be possible to decide, in many other cases no such definite decision is possible. Are we then, in such cases, driven to accept an inconsistency: "He is bald and he is not bald"? Not at all. Such cases can be consistently described by means of a qualification: "He is partly bald" or "He is going bald".

People with a metaphysical approach try to express changing things in fixed categories, and try to express the relations of things in categories suited only to considering things in separation. As a result, they are often landed in inconsistency. Just as when a motor car splutters we know there is something wrong with the engine, so when a person contradicts himself we know there is something wrong with his ideas. Dialectics enables us to order our ideas so as to keep clear of logical contradictions and to be absolutely consistent. Hence dialectics always respects the logical principle of non-contradiction or consistency, although metaphysics often leads to its violation.

Logical principles are laws of thought, not laws of reality; they are not the laws of material processes, but the laws of the reflection of material processes. And because they are requirements of the reflection of reality in thought, arising from the very nature of the form of the reflection as it has developed in the course of human practice, the laws of logic require to be satisfied in the working out and expression of views. If our thoughts violate the laws of logic, then they become incoherent and self-contradictory.

This accounts for what is sometimes called the "normative" character of the laws of logic, and for their character of "logical" as opposed to "natural" necessity. Our thoughts need not be logical, but unless they are they cannot satisfy the requirements of the reflection of reality: this is why the laws of logic constitute a "norm" for thought. And the laws of logic arise from the very nature of thought, quite independent of the particular object of thought: this is why the laws of logic have a self-evident and axiomatic character, as distinct from the laws of nature, which have to be discovered through an empirical investigation of external reality.

So whatever the views which are being worked out in society, they are all subordinate to the same laws of thought, to the same principles of logic. Just as the same language is used to express different views, so do different views employ the same laws of thought, the same logic.

New views do not, therefore, give rise to a new logic, any more than they give rise to a new language. On the contrary, the principles of logic are inherent in the very process of thought and of its expression in language, and are not altered with alterations of views.

Some people, of course, ignore logic in the working out of their views. So much the worse for their views. This does not mean that they have evolved a different logic, but rather that they fail to be logical.

No discussion, no controversy or argument, no development of thought whatever would be possible, if the laws of thought changed and were different for different people. Anyone who thinks that the laws of thought change, that different epochs have a different logic, thereby denies the very possibility of thought as a reflection of objective reality. Logic arises from the universal requirements of the reflection of reality in thought, and not from the particular interests which particular processes of thought may serve from time to time.

Hence if, for example, a socialist is arguing with a defender of capitalism, they both appeal to and try to base their arguments on the same principles of logic, just as they both speak the same language. Just as "two plus two equals four" for the accountant of a capitalist or of a socialist enterprise, so "if all A is B, then some A is B" for a defender of socialism or of capitalism. Similarly, anyone who has read accounts of the labours of Christian missionaries among primitive peoples will realise that both parties to the argument appeal to the same laws of logic, though it must be confessed that the primitive people are often more logical than the missionaries.

What is here said about logic does not, however, apply to the philosophical views expounded by those who have written books about logic. Those philosophical views, often labelled "Logic", are, of course, the views of particular classes and of particular epochs.

Thus we conclude that language develops as the means of expressing and communicating thoughts by people in society, arising from and developed in the course of their productive activity and all their other social activity; and that the thoughts of men, expressed in language, are subordinate to logic, to the laws of thought as reflection of material reality. At the same time, the social views which are expressed in language and worked out with the aid of logic develop on the basis of men's economic relations, of the activities and interests of social classes.

Part Two

THE DEVELOPMENT OF IDEAS

Chapter Five

ABSTRACT IDEAS

The Formation of Abstract Ideas

WHILE thought and ideas, like language, originate from labour, men likewise develop their thinking and their ideas in the course of the whole of their social activity.

Writing of the development of ideas or of human consciousness—for the peculiarity of human consciousness is that man is conscious of things not only through perceptions but also through ideas—Marx and Engels showed that man's consciousness arises and develops "only from the need, the necessity, of intercourse with other men. . . . Consciousness is therefore from the very beginning a social product, and remains so as long as men exist at all." (*The German Ideology*, Part I, chapter 1.)

Ideas are not the products of a pure intellectual process, nor are they mere automatic responses to stimuli reaching us from external objects. They are produced by human brains in the course of human social activity. They reflect the connections of men with one another and with the external world, the real conditions of men's existence.

Marx and Engels went on to point out that "consciousness is at first merely consciousness concerning the immediate sensuous environment and consciousness of the limited connections with other persons and things. . . . This beginning", they added, "is as animal as social life itself at this stage. It is mere herd consciousness".

The first and most elementary ideas are ideas directly derived from immediate practical intercourse with other people and surrounding objects. They are formed by giving names to the common features of things recognisable in perception. From the start, as Marx has stressed, "the production of ideas" arises from "the material activity and material intercourse of men". And out of this activity and material intercourse at its most elementary level is already formed a complex of elementary ideas of external objects, of the self and of other people—of the kinds and properties of objects and their various connections with and uses for people.

In such ideas are more or less directly reflected the salient features of objects and human activities as we are immediately aware of them in perception. Such ideas constitute the basic, elementary equipment of human thought and communication. They are expressed in words denoting familiar objects, and properties and relations of objects, and everyday activities.

We all possess a rich equipment of such ideas. Our possession of them represents a considerable social achievement, but we take them quite for granted, use them all the time, and every child learns them at an early age. Such are our ideas of the things about us with which our normal affairs are concerned, such as men and women, tables, chairs, motor cars, trees, flowers, dogs, cats, etc., etc.; of sensible properties of things, such as red, blue, hard, soft, big, small, and so on; and of actions and relations, such as running, walking, falling, above, below, etc., etc. Our own equipment of elementary ideas is obviously far greater than that of primitive man, precisely because we do many more things and concern ourselves with many more objects and relations. Nevertheless, the consciousness represented by such elementary ideas remains, as Marx and Engels put it, "consciousness concerning the immediate sensuous environment and consciousness of the limited connections with other persons and things".

The feature of such elementary ideas is that they have a concrete, sensuous content, because to them correspond objects directly perceptible to the senses. The development of social intercourse, however, leads to the formation of ideas to which no directly perceptible object corresponds.

Can we form ideas to which no directly perceptible object corresponds? Yes, of course we can, and we do. For example, men are directly perceptible objects, and their properties of being tall, short, thin, fat, and so on, are directly perceptible properties. But we also think of men in terms other than these, although nothing directly evident to the senses corresponds to what we think about them. If I see a very fat man and say "He's a bloated capitalist", his perceptible fatness corresponds to the word "bloated", but no corresponding property corresponds to the word "capitalist". Nevertheless, the ideas of "capitalist" and "capitalism" are well thought-out, well established ideas. We are, in fact, continually employing in ordinary speech, and still more in theoretical work, an enormous range of such ideas. For example, all kinds of social and political ideas, moral and legal ideas, scientific ideas, aesthetic ideas and philosophical ideas are of this kind.

To understand how such ideas arise, and their function in the processes of thought in which the world is reflected in terms of ideas, we should remember that ideas are always embodied in words. To have an idea is to have the use of certain words, and different kinds of ideas correspond to different uses of words. If, then, one says that "The fat man is running", one is using words in such a way as to refer to the perceptible motion (running) of a perceptible object (a fat man). It is quite easy to explain what one means. One needs only point to a fat man, and to someone running, and say: "I mean that a man like that is doing that." If, on the other hand, one says "The capitalist exploits the workers", one is still referring to certain familiar sensible objects (men), but one is at the same time making a generalisation about them which refers to a relationship between them which is not open to immediate observation but which requires a very elaborate definition in terms of other relationships. One cannot explain what one means by "capitalist" and "exploitation" in the same way as one can explain what one means by "fat" and "running". A complicated explanation of another kind is required—the sort of explanation which Marx required many pages of *Capital* to elaborate. The idea of "capitalist exploitation" is derived by generalisation, not from the direct comparison of a number of perceptible objects, but from reflection upon very complicated processes and relationships in which such objects are involved.

Our ideas, then, are not confined to the reflection of the common features of external objects presented to the senses. Ideas are always formed according to the needs of social intercourse. And with the development of production and the consequent development of production relations, and of social relations and social activity generally, ideas are developed beyond the stage of consciousness of the common features of objects perceived through the senses. Men form general concepts and views about the world and their own social life. Such ideas become formed and embodied in words and uses of words as a product of men's active relationship to external nature and to one another, and serve the development of social intercourse based on those relationships. But no directly perceptible objects correspond to them.

It is to such ideas that the term "abstract" is commonly applied.

The Sources of Abstract Ideas

All abstract ideas, without exception, have their source through experience in the objective material world, in men's practical relations with things and with one another. For it is definite experiences of men, derived from their intercourse with one another and with nature, which lead them to form abstract ideas. These ideas serve the continuance and development of that intercourse. And they reflect definite relations objectively existing between things, between men, and between men and things, which are translated in the minds of men into terms of ideas.

One important source of the development of abstract ideas is the development of social relationships between people. Thus, for example, the primitive gentile organisation of society—with its complicated rules about who can marry whom, who belongs to what gens, and, in general, who can do what—gives rise to a whole set of ideas about social relationships, which are at once the products of those social relationships and their regulators. Later, ideas of social status, chieftainship and so on arise. And later, with the development of property, ideas connected with property relations.

For example, when certain people have taken possession of the land, then there are formed ideas of landownership and of corresponding duties, rights and privileges. Such ideas of ownership are abstract ideas, to which corresponds no object immediately perceptible to the senses. Thus the idea of a ploughed field, say, is the idea of a reality presented to our senses; but the idea of the ownership of that field is an abstract idea to which no directly perceptible object corresponds. Similarly, the produce of that field is a concrete, perceptible reality—we can eat it, for example; but the right of the landowner to take possession of that product is not perceptible. But these abstract ideas are the ideal reflection of something real and objective—the production relations established at a definite stage of the evolution of social production.

Other abstract ideas are formed as a consequence of the development of men's productive and other activities concerned with external nature. For example, this is the source of such ideas as those of cause and effect, and, again, of all ideas concerned with counting and measuring, such as those of number, space and time.

One very important influence in the development of men's ideas is their relative ignorance and helplessness in the midst of their social activities. This starts off the development of all kinds of mystical and illusory abstract ideas.

At a very early stage of society people begin to think about the underlying causes which operate in the various processes with which they are familiar and on which they depend for their livelihood. Thus, for example, people see the crops growing or the animals multiplying, and they are aware of what they themselves have to do to promote these processes. But they do not see and are not aware of the underlying causes which operate in these processes, nor have they any but most inadequate means of controlling them. And so they begin to form the concepts of unseen powers. Most primitive peoples have the concept of a secret power residing in men, animals and things, which they regard as something not perceptible to the senses which nevertheless penetrates and controls all sensible things. Thus certain Red Indian tribes called this power *wakanda*, and one of their elders, trying to explain the idea to a visiting anthropologist, told him: "No man has ever seen *wakanda*." From this type of abstract idea—this idea of unseen powers—develop the abstract ideas of religion and theology.

Division of Mental from Material Labour

Abstract ideas are formed, as we can see from these few examples, as a consequence of the process of social development. And Marx and Engels connected the development of abstract ideas with the fundamental social process of division of labour.

The formation of all abstract ideas—of whatever type, and whatever the particular source of the ideas—presupposes a certain development of men's productive powers and social relations. It therefore presupposes a certain division of labour. This division of labour begins to separate the single productive group or "herd" into distinct individuals—distinct not merely as different members of the species but as persons with distinct social functions and positions, with individuality. This gives rise to the activities, relations and experiences from which the formation of abstract ideas arises. And it likewise brings to an end the stage of "herd" consciousness, and permits the development of individual thought.

With the formation of abstract ideas, a division of mental from material labour appears. It marks a definite beginning of mental as distinct from material labour. And with this, there begin to appear wise men, elders and leaders of various kinds who are the specialists in ideas and who expound and develop them. This specialisation in ideas develops as an indispensable feature of social life; for without ideas, division of labour and the various consequent productive processes and social relations cannot be maintained or developed. And so Marx and Engels observed in *The German Ideology:* "Division of labour only becomes truly such from the moment when a division of mental and material labour appears."

In general, the formation of abstract ideas corresponds to

new social needs arising. At the same time, the development of ideas becomes a special form of social activity, a special department of the division of labour. And the ensuing separation of mental from material labour then leads to further consequences.

Once an abstract idea is formed and embodied in words, then the possibility arises that these words will be taken to refer to special kinds of objects which exist apart from the objects of the material world which are reflected in sense-perceptions. And this possibility is the more apt to be realised, the more the handling of abstract ideas becomes a special social activity separated from material labour.

It is obvious that this takes place with concepts of unseen powers, supernatural beings, and so on. The people who employ these ideas consider that certain mysterious beings and powers, whose existence is separate from and independent of the existence of perceptible, material things, correspond to the ideas. And the witch doctors, priests or theologians who specialise in such ideas work out the most elaborate doctrines in terms of them.

But similar illusions can grow up around all abstract ideas. Abstract ideas are such that no directly perceptible object corresponds to them. But they do relate to perceptible objects. To explain such an idea, to say what the word in which it is embodied means, it is necessary to refer to definite perceptible objects and processes and their relationships which are reflected in the idea. On the other hand, it is possible to forget about the concrete reality which is reflected in ideas, and to manipulate ideas as though they dealt with some separate realm of abstractions revealed to the intellect but independent of the perceptible world of experience and practice.

"The approach of the mind to a particular thing, the taking of a cast of it," wrote Lenin, in his *Philosophical Notebooks*, "is not a simple, direct act, a lifeless mirror reflection, but a complex, twofold, zig-zag act, which harbours the possibility that the fantasy may entirely fly away from reality. What is more, it harbours the possibility that the abstract idea may be transformed, imperceptibly and unwittingly, into fantasy—and in the long run, into God. For even the simplest generalisation and the most elementary general idea is a fragment of fantasy."

This "flying away" of the abstract idea from reality is the more apt to take place, the more mental labour is divorced from material labour, the more theoretical activity is divorced from practical activity.

With the development of abstract ideas, then, thinking is no longer tied down to the features of things and the connections of persons and things of which we are immediately aware in practice through the senses. And just because thinking becomes the special province of mental as distinct from material labour, all the more does it cut loose from the practice and the experiences of ordinary working life. It becomes free to elaborate all manner of general concepts and general views about the world and about society. What we think becomes distinct from what we experience or perceive.

"From this moment onwards," wrote Marx and Engels, in *The German Ideology*, "consciousness can really flatter itself that it is something other than consciousness of existing practice, that it is really conceiving something without conceiving something real [i.e., something directly perceptible to the senses—M.C.]. From now on, consciousness is in a position to emancipate itself from the world and to proceed to the formation of 'pure' theory, theology, philosophy, ethics, etc."

Learning How to Think

A condition for the development of abstract ideas is the separation of mental from material labour. And it contains within itself contradictory potentialities. On the one hand, it permits the acquisition of profounder knowledge of the real connections of things and of the conditions of human existence than is contained in immediate perceptual consciousness. On the other hand, it permits the growth of all kinds of fantasies and illusions.

Consequently the whole process of the intellectual development of society presents contradictory aspects. On the one hand, there has been the undoubted growth of genuine knowledge, in other words, of true ideas, whose correspondence with reality has been verified, concerning nature, society and the relations of men with nature. On the other hand, there has been the growth and elaboration of illusory ideas. As society has developed, so men have developed in their minds illusions about themselves and the world they inhabit. Each epoch has added to the sum total of human knowledge. And at the same time, each epoch has produced its characteristic illusions, which circumscribed, penetrated and coloured the entire intellectual production of that epoch.

It is here, then, that we find the root of the opposition and struggle of materialist and idealist tendencies which has run right through the whole development of thought.

The opposition of materialist and idealist tendencies is a fundamental opposition, arising from the very nature of thought itself, once it has developed to the level of abstract ideas. It arises with the separation of mental from material labour. When mental labour first begins to "emancipate itself from the world" as a theoretical activity, and to "become something other than existing practice", then there immediately arise the two alternative paths of theory—to strive to understand things in their own connections and to explain what happens in the material world from the material world itself, which is materialism; or to launch out into the realm of pure thought and represent the material, sensuous world as dependent on thought and the product of thought, which is idealism. In other words, to regard being as prior to thinking, or thinking as prior to being.

Understood in this light, the struggle of the materialist tendency in thought against the idealist tendency is understood as a struggle, carried forward through ages of human history from primitive times up to the present day and into the future, to learn to think truthfully and correctly, in a way that truthfully reflects the real conditions of human existence and helps human progress. It is the struggle for knowledge and enlightenment against ignorance and superstition.

Chapter Six

IDEOLOGY

The Formation of Ideologies

IN the course of the development of society abstract ideas are used for the elaboration of more or less systematic theories, doctrines or views about things. General views and ways of thinking, systems of abstract ideas, become established as characteristic of the outlook of a whole society, or of a section of society.

And considerable differences exist between the views entertained in different societies and in different stages of social development. Each possesses its typical social views of politics, morality, law, property, religion, philosophy—and these views penetrate social thinking on all particular topics, and mould and influence the development of ideas of all individuals.

With the development of private property and the state, for example, ideas about legal and political "rights" are always formed. But in different stages of the development of property, the views which are held about rights—the theories which are entertained about them, the systematic doctrines about rights—vary considerably. In slave society, slaves were thought to have no rights whatever. In feudal society, everyone was thought to have rights, but the character of his rights depended on his actual position in the feudal order, so that the rights of a serf were not equal to those of a lord. With the rise of capitalism, the theory of "human rights" began to be formed—the view that every man, simply as a human being, possesses certain "inalienable human rights" which are the same for all men—and there has been a great deal of argument as to the exact definition of these rights and from what they may be deduced.

Again, from the very beginnings of social production people have formed ideas about the causal processes in nature. But in different stages of society the views about causality in nature have varied considerably. The most primitive theory is the theory of animism, which thinks of everything as though it were alive and conscious. Later on, animism is given up, and everything is thought to be directed by its specific form or principle, which determines its nature, its place in the hierarchy of being and its peculiar ways of acting on other things and reacting to them. This view of causality was elaborated in great detail during the Middle Ages. Then again there has developed the mechanistic view of causality which was characteristic of the beginnings of modern natural science, according to which the motions of all bodies are governed by a single set of natural laws and everything that happens is determined by the external interactions of bodies taking place in accordance with these laws.

Such more or less systematic views, which are historically evolved by definite social groups in definite stages of social development, and which vary according to their social origin, are called *ideologies*. And the development of such views is called *ideological development*.

The Material Basis of Ideological Development

Ideology is essentially a social rather than an individual product. In dealing with the development of ideology, we are dealing with the social development of ideas. We are not so much concerned with how ideas are formed and elaborated in the mind of the individual, as with how broad currents of ideas are formed as characteristic of a whole phase of social development.

Of course, individuals contribute as individuals, according to their capacities and circumstances, to the formation of ideologies. On the other hand, the ideologies prevailing or rising in society always constitute the background and condition for the development of the opinions and views of every individual in society. Individuals, in their own opinions and views, are always influenced by the ideologies, express them, are their mouthpieces.

In the course of social development there is change and development of ideology. One ideology supplants another. And in the same society, different and rival ideologies interact and clash with one another. But ideology has no independent development. There is no "history of thought", independent of the development of the material conditions of social life.

An ideology is always the ideology of definite people, living in definite conditions, depending for their life on a definite mode of production, with definite social relations, doing definite things with definite desires and aims. And their ideology is not formed independently of the process of their material life.

"We set out from real, active men," wrote Marx and Engels, "and on the basis of their real life process we demonstrate the development of the ideological reflexes and echoes of this life process. The phantoms formed in the human brain are also, necessarily, sublimates of their material life process, which is empirically verifiable and bound to material premises. Morality, religion, metaphysics, all the rest of ideology, and their corresponding forms of consciousness, thus no longer retain the semblance of independence. They have no history, no development; but men, developing their material production and their material intercourse, alter, along with this their real existence, their thinking and the products of their thinking." (*The German Ideology*, Part I, chapter I.)

It is the development of production, and the consequent development of production relations and of the social intercourse based on them, which give rise to the conditions for the formation of abstract ideas and to the social need for the ideological development of such ideas. Ideologies develop not as a consequence of the inner working of men's minds going on independently of the material life of society but as a consequence of the development of the material life of society, which conditions the products of intellectual production.

In class-divided society, therefore, ideologies take on a class character. Different views are developed on the basis of the different places occupied by different classes in social production, their different relationships to the means of production, their different roles in the social organisation of labour, their different ways of obtaining their share of the social wealth, their different material interests. The different ideologies are thus developed in the service of different class interests.

The Ideological Reflection of Reality

Ideological development is, then, governed by the material development of society—by the development of production, of the relations of production, and of classes and the class struggle.

Hence the causes impelling ideological development in one or another direction are always to be found, in the last analysis, not within the sphere of ideological development itself but in the sphere of the conditions of material life. To explain, for example, why the bourgeois idea of human rights supplanted the feudal idea of rights, it is necessary to consider the changes taking place in the mode of production of material life—for these changes gave rise to a contradiction between the feudal idea of rights and the actual rights the recognition of which was necessary to carry on the bourgeois mode of production, and necessitated a change in the idea of rights to correspond with reality. Similarly, in the sphere of ideas about nature, these same changes in the mode of production imparted a new direction to the development of ideas about nature. And in general, feudal ideology was supplanted by bourgeois ideology because, in the material life of society, feudal social relations were being supplanted by bourgeois social relations.

But at the same time, ideological development, as a development of abstract thinking, has its own special characteristics, its own internal laws. Its direction is determined by the development of the material life of society, and every ideology is developed on the basis of definite material social relationships and activities in the service of definite material interests. But it remains none the less true that ideology must always satisfy certain intellectual requirements, and that these requirements are continually posed and met in the course of ideological development.

Ideologies are developed to serve definite class interests. They are intellectual instruments, intellectual weapons, made and forged by definite classes corresponding to the material position and requirements of those classes. But just because they are intellectual instruments and intellectual weapons, to be serviceable they must satisfy intellectual requirements. They must obey the rules of working with ideas, just as, for example, material instruments and material weapons must obey the rules of working with, say, metals.

From what do these internal, intellectual requirements of ideological development arise? They arise from the fact that ideology is a reflection of the real, material world in the form of abstract ideas. Every ideology is an attempt made by people to understand and give an account of the real world in which they live, or of some aspect of it and of their own lives, so that it may be of service to them in the definite conditions in which they live. Therefore they must always strive to develop their ideology as a coherent system of ideas which squares with the facts so far as they have experienced and ascertained them. This poses intellectual requirements to be satisfied by ideologies, and to satisfy them is a law which is continually at work influencing the development of ideologies.

Ideologies must be made to satisfy, in the first place, the general requirements of the reflection of reality in ideas, that is to say, the laws of logic. In the second place, they must satisfy the particular requirements of the reflection of a particular part of reality, that is to say, they must be made to square with the facts so far as people have experienced and ascertained them.

Ideologies, therefore, are developed on the basis of the given structure of society to serve the interests of one or another class, and in this ideological development the effort is always being made to render the views developed self-consistent and logical, and to make them cover and give some consistent account of the principal facts which emerge in the experience of society at the given stage of development.

This gives rise to continual contradictions in the development of ideologies. For on the one hand, the views developed by the representatives of various classes prove logically inconsistent and inconsistent with plain facts; and on the other hand, facts and the requirements of logic lead to conclusions which do not accord with views tenaciously held. Such contradictions give rise to a continual process of the elaboration of ideologies, as the ideologists endeavour to find ways and means of resolving them.

The Criticism of Ideologies

No matter what field of ideas is in question, the development of ideas expresses the effort to argue them out, make them consistent, present them logically, and adapt them to the facts of experience. And this effort plays a major part in the detailed elaboration of ideologies. Indeed, the more concretely we study the development of particular ideologies—that is to say, the more we study their development in detail, rather than confining attention to their most general features—the more is it necessary to take into account the intellectual aspect of ideological development. For the effort to square up ideas with obtrusive facts, and to eliminate contradictions and present a consistent, argued case, influences very greatly the real development of ideas. And in the course of this development, it inevitably happens that the expression of economic relations and class interests in the given field of ideas becomes less obvious, less direct, more obscure and roundabout.

Thus Engels wrote, for instance, of the development of legal ideology:

"Law must not only correspond to the general economic condition and be its expression, but must also be an *internally coherent* expression which does not, owing to inner contradictions, reduce itself to nought. And in order to achieve this, the faithful reflection of economic conditions suffers increasingly. . . . Thus to a great extent the course of the 'development of law' only consists, first, in the attempt to do away with the contradictions arising from the direct translation of economic relations into legal principles and to establish a harmonious system of law, and then in the repeated breaches made in this system by the influence and pressure of further economic development, which involves it in further contradictions." (*Letter* to C. Schmidt, October 27, 1890.)

The same process takes place in all ideological spheres—in philosophy, theology, moral ideas, ideas about nature, and so on.

Ideologies are always peculiarly vulnerable and open to criticism on the score of self-contradiction and of failure to reckon with experienced facts. Those who, as intellectual representatives of a given class, espouse a general point of view in ideology, are always being driven for this reason to elaborate their ideology, which leads them to the creation of often very complicated and far-fetched ideological structures. Then again, as Engels observed, the structures become unsuitable for the service of the given interests in new conditions, and the process begins anew. This shows itself in philosophy, for instance, in the multiplication of "systems" of philosophy.

If this process of criticism goes on in the development of the ideology of a particular class, it takes a different and sharper form when, on the basis of new factors in the material life of society, new and rival views begin to be formed, expressing the interests of different classes. Such new views do not emerge until the development of material life gives birth to them. But once they emerge, then they attack from the new point of view the manifold inconsistencies of the already established views. They make use of logic and appeal to facts as powerful intellectual weapons with which to discredit and demolish the old views.

Historians of ideas have most often erred by attempting to understand ideological development exclusively in terms of the posing and satisfaction of intellectual requirements. As Marx and Engels pointed out, that cannot be done, since one cannot say why new views should arise at particular times, or why the views should be of one rather than another type, without looking for the reasons in the material life of society. But it is also impossible to trace the development of ideologies without taking the intellectual requirements into account. And

Marxism certainly never says that we should attempt to do so.

This is the opposite error into which some schools of sociologists have fallen—namely, those who embrace the doctrine of "economic determinism", which regards economic activity as the sole agency determining the whole of social development in all its aspects. Failing to recognise that in ideology there takes place a process of the reflection of the real world in men's ideas, they regard ideology exclusively as a development of various ideas expressing and serving various material, economic interests. This leads them to one or other of two conclusions. On the one hand, they conclude that since all ideas are merely practical instruments serving various material interests, no ideas, including their own, can lay any claim correctly to reflect reality—so that every ideology, including their own, is as illusory as every other in all respects. On the other hand, they are led to make an exception of themselves and of their own ideas, representing themselves as special people who, by some intellectual miracle, have transcended every class point of view and can look down on the rest of mankind from an ivory tower of complete and absolute "objectivity". In either case, they are clearly involved in self-contradiction.

However, there is always and always has been a basis for the criticism of ideologies in terms of reason and experience—that is to say, for their critical comparison with reality. And this comparison has been continually carried out in the course of ideological development itself. It has not been carried out by people who have managed to detach themselves from social life, for such people do not exist; but it has been carried out in the course of the long development of human practice—of production, of science and of the class struggle.

Thus in the development of ideologies there does take place a development of the truthful and coherent reflection of the real world in men's ideas. For the continuous process of reckoning with facts and striving for consistency—despite all the intellectual dishonesty, special pleading, invention, fantasy, sophism and inconsistency which accompanies it at every stage—does continuously yield positive results. And these results are continuously verified, consolidated, criticised and carried forward through the developing practice of mankind.

Truth and Illusion in Ideologies

All ideas are a reflection of objective material reality, which is their ultimate source. But while, as we have just seen, there is a development in ideology of the truthful reflection of reality in ideas, this takes place amid a development of all kinds of illusions, of distorted, fantastic reflection of reality.

The opposition and interpenetration of truth and illusion in ideological development expresses the fact that the reflection of reality in ideas is effected in different ways, through different processes, by different routes.

One way in which our ideas about things are formed and elaborated is in the process of our practical interaction with things, founded on and tested in practical experience, and further developed by scientific investigation of real processes, of the real properties of things, their motions and interconnections. In so far as ideas about things are formed in this way, the ideas and conclusions about them embodied in ideologies are more or less truthful—that is to say, they more or less correctly reflect reality and correspond with it.

But this is not the only way in which ideas are formed. They are also formed in a more indirect and roundabout way. And ideas formed in a more indirect and roundabout way are profoundly influential in the formation of ideologies.

This roundabout process which enters into the formation of ideologies involves three main steps. First, abstract ideas are formed on the basis of various social relationships and experiences of people. Second, those abstract ideas are separated from the actual experiences and relationships from which they were derived. Third, both particular conclusions and general ideas about all kinds of things are then worked out with the aid of those abstract ideas.

For example, when society divides into classes and a ruling class is formed, then, on the basis of definite social relations and social experiences and activities, there is formed the idea of the relationship between ruler and ruled and of the power and prerogatives of the ruler. From that, the next step is to separate this abstract idea from the actual experiences and relationships from which it was originally derived, to consider it as expressing a general truth about the universe, and to go on to form the idea of God, the ruler of the universe. The third and last step is to proceed to interpret existing social relations as decreed by God, and to interpret nature as the creation of God.

When ideas about things are formed and worked out in this way, it means that we are approaching things with certain more or less fixed preconceptions about them already in our minds. Indeed, such preconceptions are often so fixed in our minds as a result of education and habit, that we never dream of questioning them, but take them as axioms, as natural and obvious ways of thinking. And then we form our general views and particular conclusions about things not primarily as a result of critical investigation and practical verification of conclusions but independent of practice, uncritically, without investigation.

When ideas about things are formed in this way, then they generally cease to be truthful and become more or less illusory. They do not correctly reflect and correspond with reality, but, on the contrary, they give an incorrect, illusory, fantastic or distorted picture of reality.

Illusions, however, are always founded in reality. They are not pure inventions of the mind, but they arise, as we have just seen, by a process of forming ideas from one source, and then extrapolating them (i.e., extending them beyond the sphere in which they were originally established) and using them as preconceptions applied in many different contexts, replacing the critical formation and verification of ideas through actual practice and experience.

Every illusion has its source in reality. It reflects definite conditions of material life, arises from definite social relations, experiences and activities. That is why many illusions are so persistent. It is not simply a question of the indoctrination of individuals with certain illusory ideas, but it is a question of existing social relations continually generating certain illusions, and of these illusions serving definite material interests.

Illusions take two main forms.

In the first place, there arise illusions about real things—misconceptions of real processes and relations familiar in experience and practice. Such, for example, is the illusion that certain social relations and institutions follow from human nature, or were decreed by Reason.

In the second place, illusions develop into sheer mythology and fantasy, the invention of imaginary things. Thus people not only misconceive nature and society, both of which really exist, but they also form ideas of heaven and hell, of the spiritual world, and so on, which have no existence; they invent all kinds of imaginary beings, such as gods, fairies and devils.

In this connection, we should note that illusion cannot be simply equated with error. Of course, illusion is error; but it is a special kind of error.

Suppose, for example, that someone says that thirteen squared equals 166. This is a simple error, an error in calculation (since the right answer is 169). But suppose, on the other hand, he says that thirteen is an unlucky number. This is not like an error in calculation, which can be made by people possessing on the whole correct ideas about numbers. It expresses an illusion, namely, the illusion that numbers are lucky or unlucky. Such an error does not arise simply from a mistake in operating with numbers, but it arises from applying to numbers preconceived ideas about luck which, though they have a definite source in experience and practice, are wrongly and uncritically applied to numbers.

Similarly, if someone says that the British Constitution was introduced into Parliament by Oliver Cromwell, this is an erroneous statement, arising from an insufficient study of British constitutional history. But suppose he says that the British Constitution is an expression of the unique genius of the Anglo-Saxon race, or is God's gift to the British people. These statements, though also erroneous, are not simply errors in history. They arise from applying to social affairs preconceived ideas about racial genius or God.

Thus illusions constitute a special kind of error, arising

from a quite definite mode of misconceiving things in terms of preconceived ideas.

Scientific and Illusory Ideology

Both processes of the formation of abstract ideas—that is to say, both the process of forming more or less truthful ideas critically through practical experience and interaction with things, and the process of forming more or less illusory ideas as preconceptions applied in the formation of views—enter into the formation of actual ideologies. At the same time, one or other of these processes may dominate in the constitution of particular ideologies, so that they are predominantly scientific in the one case or predominantly illusory and unscientific in the other case.

All ideology in class-divided society is developed by the intellectual representatives of definite classes, and corresponds to the actual position and serves the requirements of definite classes in their class struggle. This being so, we can see how inevitably the two processes interact and interpenetrate in the formation of class ideologies.

On the one hand, in so far as the interests of a class do demand a true apprehension of reality based on critical investigation of some kind, its ideology does contain a scientific element. For example, the class interests of the capitalist class certainly do require that considerable work should be done on discovering the real laws governing various natural processes, and such discoveries do play their part in bourgeois ideology. The same interests also require that certain social investigations should be carried on, and from this source again a certain scientific element does enter into bourgeois ideology.

On the other hand, in so far as the interests of a class and the place it occupies in social production give rise to certain preconceptions and illusions which serve the class in its struggle, its ideology is illusory. And so, for example, if we consider bourgeois ideology, there are many elements in it which merely embody the illusions of the bourgeois class and the views peculiar to bourgeois society.

Bourgeois ideology, indeed, is formed by the development

of both processes. And this gives rise to contradictions in its development, since the products of the two processes continually come into contradiction and the resolution of such contradictions has to be sought in the development of ideology. The same has been true of the ideologies of other classes, though the scientific element is far stronger in bourgeois ideology, so that the contradictions have become sharper.

Thus, in the development of bourgeois philosophy, for example, there has been a continual effort to reconcile scientific discoveries with bourgeois preconceptions. The most obvious way in which this contradiction has expressed itself in bourgeois philosophy is in the contradiction between the materialist picture of the world afforded by scientific discoveries and the religious views which form an essential part of the ideological preconceptions. Philosophers have continually sought ways and means of resolving this contradiction; they keep resolving it to their own satisfaction, and as often as they resolve it, it crops up again.

Again, in bourgeois science, discoveries are always being interpreted—with the help of philosophers—in terms of the bourgeois preconceptions. We can see this happening today, for example, in the development of physics, where the discoveries of quantum physics are interpreted as meaning that events are unpredictable and their real nature unknowable. This is simply an application in physical science of bourgeois ideological preconceptions generated by the general crisis of capitalism. On the other hand, certain preconceptions, at least in their old forms, have had to be given up and replaced by others, because of their contradiction with advancing knowledge of nature. This has happened, for example, with religious doctrines, which have often been modified in the course of the struggle to reconcile religion with science—as when the theologians eventually ditched both Adam and Eve as a concession to the theory of evolution.

Considering such examples, we can see that the opposition and interpenetration of scientific and illusory elements in ideology cannot be conceived so simply, as if ideas about one thing were scientific while ideas about some other thing were illusory. The fact is rather that scientific and illusory elements oppose each other and interpenetrate in the ideas formed about one and the same thing.

Thus bourgeois ideology, for example, is a contradictory compound of truthful and illusory elements, with the latter always persisting and maintaining themselves. It might be said that the scientific element is stronger in the bourgeois views about natural processes, while the illusory element is stronger in the bourgeois views about social processes. But both elements enter into all parts and all fields of bourgeois ideology, and the illusory element is the most characteristic feature of the ideology. What stamps bourgeois ideology as peculiarly bourgeois is the character of its illusions.

The same may be said of other ideologies of the past. At the same time, we may consistently claim, and do claim, that Socialist or Marxist ideology is primarily a scientific ideology, and in this respect distinguishes itself from every other ideology without exception. This is because the struggle to end capitalism and, with it, all exploitation of man by man, which this ideology serves, does demand above all a true apprehension of reality and opposes itself to all the illusions of societies based on exploitation.

Chapter Seven

IDEOLOGICAL ILLUSIONS

Ideological Reflection of Production Relations

IN this chapter we shall consider the development of ideological preconceptions or illusions, and will then turn, in the next two chapters, to the development of scientific ideas.

There are five main, characteristic features of the development of ideological illusions in class-divided society, which can be traced in every ideology up to and including bourgeois ideology.

(1) The first feature of ideological illusions is that they always arise as reflections of particular, historically constituted relations of production. Their source is the production relations of society.

In the development of ideological illusions, it seems as if abstract ideas, general theories, were being spun out of people's heads—developed and controlled, to all appearances, simply by the thinking process itself. Yet how did such ideas come into people's heads? What is their source? Unless we are to believe that ideas are formed spontaneously in the mind, or that we are born already equipped with "innate ideas", then we must suppose that a source in objective reality outside the mind can be found for all our ideas, including the most abstract and illusory—a source from which they are derived and of which they are the reflection.

Consciousness is never anything but a reflection of material existence. First there is matter, objective being, and then, secondarily, there is consciousness, the reflection of matter. The mind has no inner sources of its own, from which ideas can be derived. Every idea, every element of ideology, is derived from and reflects some objective reality, some real aspect of the material world.

The source of the illusions in ideology is always the real economic structure of society. As men live, so do they think. Corresponding to the relations they enter into in producing the means of life, they produce social ideas and social theories.

Thus, for example, it is the real relations of landowners and serfs established in the feudal model of production that are reflected in the feudal ideas of landownership, and in feudal ideology in general. Similarly, it is the capitalist relationships which are reflected in capitalist ideology. And it was the far simpler relationships within the tribe, the solidarity of the individual with the tribe, which were reflected in the "primitive" ideology of primitive communism.

Thus as society develops, the ideas which reflect the property relations of society become elaborated in the form of systems and theories concerning politics, social rights and obligations, law, and so on. All such ideology has its source in the social relations of production, and constitutes, in the last analysis, nothing but an ideological reflection of those relations.

The same is true of moral ideas. If we have ideas of absolute standards of good and bad, right and wrong, virtue and vice, these ideas are reflections not of any objective property of persons or actions but of the social relations into which people have entered and within which their personal activity takes place. No wonder, therefore, that moral judgements change with fundamental changes in social relations; and that there is only one objective standard for saying that one morality is higher than another, namely, that it reflects and serves a higher social system.

And the same is true of the ideology of the supernatural, of religious ideology. The supernatural world which men conjure up for themselves in their ideas is never, in the last analysis, anything other than a reflection of the real world of society, of the social relations within which men live their earthly lives. The world of the supernatural always serves as the guardian of the basic fabric of society. The tribal religion stands guard over the tribe and protects tribal relations, just as the ideas of Christianity today have been so adapted that heaven seems to stand guard over the bourgeois order of society. The supernatural world which guards and justifies the social order is created in the image of that social order.

These are examples of the way in which various forms of ideological illusions are developed in terms of abstract ideas whose source lies in the development of social relations, more precisely, of the relations of production. The objective reality which is reflected in such ideas is never anything else than the existing complex of social relations which spring from the production of the material means of life.

The Spontaneous Character of Ideological Illusion

(2) The second feature of ideological illusions is that, although their source lies in the complex of real social relations, they are neither consciously derived from that source nor are they put forward as an analysis of existing social relations.

The ideas which people employ may reflect their social relations, but their ideological illusions are not created by their *consciously* reflecting on their own social relations and working out for themselves, in a scientific manner, an accurate and systematic account of the social structure which they find in existence.

The ideas of political economy, for example, as set forth in such a book as Marx's *Capital*, are derived from a conscious, methodical investigation of actually existing relations of production. For that reason they are not illusory but scientific in character. Ideological illusion, on the other hand, arises as an unconscious, unintended reflection of an existing social structure, expressed in general ideas about the world. It has an unconscious, spontaneous character. That is why, if we want to discover the most essential features of some illusory ideology, we shall not discover them in the reasoned forms in which men have presented their ideas, but rather in the unreasoned assumptions, the preconceptions which they take for granted, which underly their reasoning.

For example, in the ideology of the medieval Catholic Church, the whole world, heaven and earth, was regarded as a hierarchy in which the lower members were necessarily subordinate to the higher. In the production of this ideology there was no intention of giving an account of the feudal order; the conscious intention was to give an account of the necessary order of the whole world, and this was consciously worked out as a logical system. But yet the ideology was in fact a reflection of the existing feudal social relations, which were thus reproduced in men's ideas by a spontaneous, unintended, unconscious process. The general ideas employed were a reflection of actual social relations, but they were not consciously produced as such a reflection, but arose unconsciously and spontaneously in men's minds. These ideas then became fixed as preconceptions which were used for the purpose of interpreting and working out the theory of everything which people were interested in, whether in nature or society or the imaginary realm of heaven.

The spontaneous, unconscious character of the ideological reflection of relations of production is due to the spontaneous, unconscious character of those relations of production themselves.

Men's relations of production, wrote Marx, are "indispensable and independent of their will". This is the key to understanding the nature of the illusory ideological reflection of those relations in abstract ideas about the world and society. The given relations of production are not deliberately instituted, but they are at the same time, at the given stage of social development, indispensable. And because people never decided to institute them but at the same time cannot get on without them, they are not conscious of them as transitory social relations which have been instituted at a definite time, in definite circumstances, to answer definite but only temporary historical needs of society. Rather do they appear as part of the necessary order of things. The characteristic features of men's social relations and relationships with nature, which are in fact the historically determined result of a definite mode of production, are reflected in abstract ideas in the form of preconceptions and illusions about the nature of man and society, as ideas about God and divine providence, about right and justice, about the eternal and necessary characteristics of all being, the ultimate nature of reality, and so on.

The Illusion of Pure Thought

(3) The third feature of ideological illusions is that, just because their spontaneous character precludes people's being aware of their true source, they seem to themselves to have produced them by a free process of thought, but a pure and unfettered operation of the mind.

"Ideology[1] is a process accomplished by the so-called thinker consciously, indeed, but with a false consciousness," wrote Engels in a letter to Mehring, July 14, 1893. "The real motives impelling him remain unknown to him, otherwise it would not be an ideological process at all. Hence he imagines false or apparent motives. Because it is a process of thought, he derives both its form and its content from pure thought, either his own or that of his predecessors. He works with mere thought material which he accepts without examination as the product of thought, and he does not investigate further for a more remote process independent of thought."

And again, Engels wrote that ideology—the working out of ideological illusions—is "occupation with thoughts as with independent entities, developing independently and subject only to their own laws. That the material life conditions of the persons inside whose heads this thought process goes on in the last resort determine the course of this process, remains of necessity unknown to those persons, for otherwise there would be an end of all ideology." (*Ludwig Feuerbach*, chapter 4.)

[1] Marx and Engels often used the term "ideology" to refer exclusively to the process of ideological illusion, thus employing it in a restricted sense. When the term is used in this restricted sense, scientific modes of thought are by definition excluded from the ideological process. But the term "ideology" is more often used in a wider sense, so that one may speak, for example, of "scientific socialist ideology", and characterise Marxism as such an ideology. In this book I have employed the term throughout in the wider sense, so that the word "ideology" is used to denote the typical outlook or theory of a period or of a class, in which both illusory and truthful or scientific elements may enter, and which, with the rise of the revolutionary working class movement and of socialism, becomes primarily scientific and dispenses with the illusory modes of thought of previous ideologies.

Ideological Inversion

(4) The fourth feature of ideological illusions is that a process of inversion takes place in them, by which real social relations are represented as the realisation of abstract ideas.

In the process of ideological illusion, products of abstract thought are treated as though they were independent of the material social relations which they in fact reflect. And so it follows that reality is turned upside down in this process. The source of abstract ideas is taken to be the mind, rather than the material reality of social relations. And so the ultimate ground for the existence of those relations themselves is conceived as being the abstractions of the mind.

According to this inverted way of looking at things, men create their social relationships in obedience to their abstract ideas, and not the other way round.

Take, for example, abstract conceptions of right and justice, which constitute an important part of all ideology. Abstract right and justice are represented as independent of actual social relationships, and those relationships are represented as reflecting and realising—perhaps imperfectly—an abstract right and justice. According to this topsy-turvy way of looking at things, the abstract ideas of right and justice seem to determine the real relationships of men, whereas in fact it is the real relationships of men that determine their ideas of right and justice. And similarly, the social system seems to be justified by how far it corresponds to abstract ideas of right and justice, whereas in fact ideas of right and justice are justified by how far they serve the material progress of society.

"Economic, political and other reflections are just like those in the human eye," wrote Engels. "They pass through a condensing lens and therefore appear upside down, standing on their heads. Only the nervous system which would put them on their feet again for representation is lacking. . . . This inversion . . . forms what we call ideological conception." (*Letter* to C. Schmidt, October 27, 1890.)

And Marx and Engels further wrote:

"If in all ideology men and their circumstances appear upside down as in a camera obscura, this phenomenon arises just as much from their historical life process as the inversion of objects on the retina does from their physical life process." (*The German Ideology*, Part I, chapter 1.)

As a result of this ideological inversion, it follows that in every epoch people have shared the illusion that their institutions and public activities are the expression of their abstract ideas—of their religion, philosophy, political principles, and so on. Thus the slave owners of ancient Rome thought of themselves as actuated by republican principles, just as modern capitalists thought of themselves (and still try to get others to think of them) as actuated by democratic principles. The wars of the Middle Ages were fought avowedly for religious principles, just as the wars of today are fought avowedly for national or political principles.

According to this way of looking at things, wrote Marx, "each principle has had its own century in which to manifest itself. The principle of authority, for example, had the eleventh century, just as the principle of individualism had the eighteenth century . . . it was the century that belonged to the principle, and not the principle to the century. In other words, it was the principle that made the history, and not the history that made the principle." (*The Poverty of Philosophy*, chapter 2, section 1, 5th observation.)

Every epoch, then, produces its characteristic illusions, which are expressed in its dominant ideology—illusions as to the real grounds and motive forces of its institutions and activities.

"For instance," wrote Marx and Engels, ". . . an epoch imagines itself to be actuated by purely political or religious motives, although religion and politics are only forms of its true motives. . . ." It is this which constitutes "the illusion of that epoch". In this illusion, "the idea, the conception of these conditioned men about their real practice is transformed into the sole determining active force which controls and determines their practice." (*The German Ideology*, Part I, chapter 1.)

In ideological illusion, the products of the mind are represented as the dominating, compelling influence in human affairs. And so it also happens that these products of the mind, which are mere distorted fantasms of real conditions of existence, come to be endowed in men's imaginations with a real existence of their own. In this way are created what Marx called "the mist-enveloped regions of the religious world. In that world the productions of the human brain appear as independent beings endowed with life, and entering into relation both with one another and the human race." (*Capital*, Volume I, chapter 1, section 4.)

And so, while men imagine their whole social life and institutions to be based on and motivated by their ideology, at the same time this ideology conjures up a fantastic world of powers and forces superior to and independent of both man and nature, to which men feel themselves subject, on which their destinies seem to depend and whose aid they seek to enlist for their enterprises.

The "religious world", as Marx said in *Capital* (Volume I, chapter 1, section 4), is never anything "but the reflection of the real world".

In the most primitive social organisations men are relatively helpless in the face of natural forces; they are banded together to get a living, and would be doomed to destruction without this elementary social cohesion and co-operation. This fact is reflected in their minds in the illusions of magic. Men seem to possess a special power and virtue as members of their tribe or clan, and this virtue takes the form, in their imagination, of a special magical force. All sorts of procedures are invented for exerting it—and later, with division of labour, it comes to be regarded as the possession and concern of certain individuals only, and not of the whole people. At the same time, natural objects and natural forces are assumed to be animated, and are later personified; so that the whole intercourse of man with man, and of man with nature, is represented as depending on the activity of unseen, mysterious powers.

The development and ramification of religious ideas has kept pace with and reflected the development of men's social life.

"The primitive religious notions, which in the main are common to each group of kindred peoples," wrote Engels, "develop, after the separation of the group, in a manner peculiar to each people, according to the living conditions falling to their lot." (*Ludwig Feuerbach*, chapter 4.)

As with all ideology, religion is not created anew in each new phase of social development. On the contrary, every ideology in its development makes use of traditional materials which are taken over from previous ideology, and incorporates in itself materials borrowed from other ideologies. It is the same in religion; and so, for example, we can still recognise even in the religious doctrines and practices of Protestant Christianity today elements which have been carried over from primitive tribal magic, overlaid and transformed as they may be with new meanings.

"Religion, once formed," Engels continued, "always contains traditional material, just as in all ideological domains tradition is a great conservative force. But the transformations which this material undergoes spring from class relations—that is to say, out of the economic relations of the persons who execute these transformations."

This characteristic of all ideological illusion—that, because it is occupation with thoughts as with independent entities, it continually develops ideas out of the material of other ideas—effectively disguises the fact that every ideology, and every element of ideology, is but a reflection of material social existence, and makes it appear as though it were really what it purports to be, an independent march of ideas.

The nature of ideology is never obvious on the surface, but comes to light only as a result of Marx's profound scientific discovery, that "the mode of production of material life conditions the social, political and intellectual life process in general." (*Critique of Political Economy*, Preface.)

So long as men are not the masters of their own social organisation, so long are their real social relations reflected in ideological inversions which, far from rendering their real social relations intelligible, mystify them and conceal their real character, together with the real springs and laws of human social action, behind a veil of religious, political, legal, artistic and philosophical illusions.

Ideology and Class Interest

(5) The fifth feature of ideological illusions is that, in society divided into classes, they constitute a class-motivated system of deception, a mode of disguising the real social relations in the interests of a definite class.

Illusion always reflects the real social relations in such a way as to disguise them.

For example, the religious ideology of the Middle Ages, with its conception of a heavenly hierarchy which reflected the feudal order, meant that the exploitation of the serf by the lord was disguised as a subordination of the serf to his natural superiors under the rule of God. And similarly, the naked fact that the feudal lord appropriated the produce of the serf's labour was disguised by the abstract feudal ideas of ownership, dues, rights and obligations.

Once again, the naked fact that the capitalist appropriates the values produced by the workers' unpaid labour is disguised by the abstract capitalist ideas of ownership, contract and equality of rights. This disguise is completed by capitalist forms of religion. That is why, though bourgeois ideology has often taken non-religious or anti-religious forms, it always leaves a loophole for religion and continually comes back to it, while in periods of crisis, when the system is seriously endangered, religious ideology is always brought to the fore and takes the offensive.

"For a society based upon the production of commodities," wrote Marx, "in which the producers in general enter into social relations with one another by treating their products as commodities and values, whereby they reduce their individual private labour to the standard of homogeneous human labour —for such a society, Christianity, with its cultus of abstract man, more especially in its bourgeois developments, Protestantism, Deism, etc., is the most fitting form of religion." (*Capital*, Volume I, chapter 1, section 4.)

The whole of bourgeois ideology, from its religion to its political economy, disguises the fact of capitalist exploitation.

The disguise and deception inherent in all ideological

illusion is always socially motivated. In other words, it serves definite social ends, definite social interests.

In primitive societies, before the birth of classes, it serves to strengthen and consolidate the bonds of solidarity between members of the tribe, on which their survival depends. And in conditions when people are almost totally ignorant of the natural forces which environ them, magical ideas make them feel that nevertheless they can control these forces. Primitive ideology is thus motivated by the self-preservation of the whole tribe, by the interest of the whole people to preserve their social organisation and to feel strong and secure in it.

When society splits into antagonistic classes, and when, consequently, history becomes the history of class struggles, then class interest becomes the main motivation of ideology. Every ideology becomes the ideology of a class, expressing, in however roundabout a way, the conditions of existence of a definite class and serving that class in its struggle against other classes. The dominant ideology in any period is that of the ruling class. And when this ideology is challenged, that is but the expression of the fact that the existing state of class relations is being challenged by another class.

The disguise and deception of class ideology, motivated as it is by class interest, is not to be interpreted, however, as primarily a deliberate, conscious deception.

To suppose that the thinking representatives of a class deliberately invent misleading ideas with the conscious purpose of disguising from the people what they know to be the real character of the social relations is to suppose that these thinkers do in fact know what is the real character of the social relations. But the very essence of ideological illusion is that it is a false consciousness of social relations. The mystifying ideological conception of these relations takes the place of a correct, scientific conception. This false consciousness arises, as we have seen, not by a deliberate process but rather by a spontaneous, unconscious process. It is not deliberate falsehood but—illusion. If this is deception, it is also self-deception.

Those who would interpret ideological illusions as mere deliberate deceptions, therefore, mistake the very nature of what Marx and Engels called "false consciousness". For they suppose that the class whose interests are served by the ideology possesses in fact a true consciousness of the basis of its existence—which is just what no exploiting class possesses or ever can possess. The explanation of ideologies as products of well-laid plans to deceive the people in the interests of a class is an absurd vulgarisation of Marxism. That is not how ideologies arise.

Of course, spokesmen and ideologists of ruling classes do constantly engage in conscious, deliberate deception of the people. But behind the system of deliberate deception lies always a system of self-deception.

As a case in point we may take the example of Plato, who was a representative of extreme ideological reaction in ancient Greece. In his *Republic* he advocated that, to keep the people down, the rulers should propagate what he called "a noble lie": although they knew very well it was not true, they should proclaim that rulers and ruled were men of two different kinds, the rulers being "golden" men and the rest being men of mere "brass and iron". At the same time, Plato maintained that aristocracy was the best system of society and that any departure from it meant anarchy and degeneration. This, however, he undoubtedly believed. It was one of the illusions of his class, and constituted the very basis of his outlook. From the point of view of the aristocratic slave-owners' ideology, which Plato expounded and which he did much to shape, it was quite in order to tell the people lies, and such lies were "noble".

Such has been the situation with all ruling class ideologies. Genuine false consciousness becomes involved in deliberate deception, so that the two become closely intertwined and even, at times, indistinguishable. This is especially the case in capitalist society, in which all things, including ideas, are bought and sold. Those who have ideas to sell come to regard them as commodities to be exchanged for cash, not as truths to be believed.

The class-motivated character of particular ideologies has long been recognised. When a new class is rising to power, and consequently posing a new ideology against that of the old ruling class, it generally recognises that the old ideology expresses the interests of its political opponents. It attacks this ideology, therefore, as a system of falsehoods motivated by class interest. It advances its own ideology, on the other hand, as a system of truth, corresponding to the profounder needs of the whole of society.

"Each new class which puts itself in the place of the one ruling before it," wrote Marx and Engels, "is compelled, merely in order to carry through its aim, to represent its interest as the common interest of all the members of society, put in an ideal form; it will give its ideas the form of universality, and represent them as the only rational, universally valid ones. The class making a revolution appears from the very start, merely because it is opposed to a *class*, not as a class, but as the representative of the whole of society." (*The German Ideology*, Part I, chapter 1.)

A newly formed ideology, therefore, generally starts with a profound impulse to development, as a universal system of ideas opening up new horizons, corresponding to deeply felt social needs, as if it were based not on the interests of a class but on the aspirations of a whole people. In the course of time, however, as the new ruling and exploiting class becomes entangled in its own contradictions, its ideology loses its revolutionary *élan* and becomes conservative; it begins to decay and disintegrate; until finally it stands revealed in its turn as a system of class-motivated deceptions, while its exponents degenerate from original thinkers into mere hired propagandists of the ruling class.

Chapter Eight

SCIENCE

The Ideas of the Production Process

ALONG with the development of the illusory, inverted reflection in consciousness of the relations of production goes the development of men's true ideas of the material objects which environ them and with which they are concerned in the process of production, of the production process itself and of their own activities and social relations.

For the development of production, and of the social intercourse which arises from production, demands and gives rise to the working out of true ideas about things and their interconnections and motions, and about various human activities and relations. Unless people do evolve such true ideas, they cannot successfully carry on production or manage their social affairs. And the more various and powerful their forces of production, and the more various and complex their social activities, the more do they need to find out about nature and about themselves in order to bring their various projects to a successful conclusion.

In the development of ideology, as Marx and Engels pointed out, "consciousness can really flatter itself that it is something other than consciousness of existing practice". But at the same time as consciousness thus abstracts itself from existing practice, the consciousness of existing practice also develops as practice develops. That very development of production, of division of labour, and of relations of production, which leads to illusory flights of inverted ideology, also leads to a growth of men's true ideas about their real conditions of life.

Such true ideas do not arise of themselves. They have to be laboriously formed, worked out and tested in practice. They represent so many *discoveries* made by people in the course of their social practice.

The first source of people's discoveries is the practice of social production.

We have already seen that it is a characteristic of the social process of production that in it men have an idea of what they aim to produce. There is and can be no production, in the human sense, not even the most primitive kinds of food-gathering and hunting, without this consciousness. And so in producing, men are also necessarily forming their ideas of the objects with which they come into relation, of the materials they use and the techniques which they employ, and making discoveries about the properties of those objects and materials and about what can be done with them.

"The elementary factors of the labour process," wrote Marx (*Capital*, Volume I, chapter 7, section 1), "are (1) the personal activity of man, i.e., work itself; (2) the subject of work; and (3) its instruments." And none of these factors can be set in motion without corresponding ideas and discoveries. With development of production and division of labour, the forms of work become more varied, its subject extends and its instruments are improved. And this means that men's ideas are correspondingly enlarged and that they make new discoveries.

Primitive man, for example, who expressed his social relations and relationships with nature in a magical ideology, had already very precise and accurate ideas of the different species of animals which he hunted, and of their various habits and properties—as is shown, among other things, by the records he made of his knowledge in cave paintings. With the development of agriculture and handicrafts new discoveries were made and men's ideas of natural objects and their properties, and of the principles involved in the various production processes, were greatly enlarged. And now, in modern capitalist society, the very same institutes and universities which churn out all manner of bourgeois religious, political and philosophical illusions, are the repositories of a vast and growing store of accurate and systematic knowledge of nature and of the principles by the application of which man advances his mastery of nature.

All this is the fruit of thousands of years of human endeavour and, in particular, of the mighty advances in production achieved in the capitalist era.

Thus if men's illusions have their ultimate source in the relations of production, men also continually make discoveries which arise in the last analysis from the production process itself. In these discoveries there is a development of abstract ideas which reflect various features and properties of things and of the production process without ideological preconception, inversion or disguise.

Such ideas of nature and of technological processes constitute, in fact, an important aspect of the productive forces themselves. The forces of production include people, with their production experience and skill. People's production experience and skill is recorded, generalised and systematised in their ideas; and, equipped with these ideas, they utilise the instruments of production and also improve them. Further, the growth of knowledge of the production process, of its subjects and instruments, of the principles of technology and of nature generally, is not only an essential condition for the continuance of production at a given level; under suitable conditions it contributes to new advances of production, and so may become one of the factors making eventually necessary revolutionary changes in the relations of production to bring them into correspondence with new forces of production.

The Rise of Natural Sciences

The natural sciences spring from the ideas, or the knowledge, accumulated in the production process.

"From the very beginning," Engels wrote in *Dialectics of Nature*, "the origin and development of the sciences has been determined by production."

Throughout antiquity, he observed, scientific investigation proper remained restricted to astronomy, mathematics and mechanics. For "astronomy . . . if only on account of the seasons, was absolutely indispensable for pastoral and agricultural peoples. Astronomy can only develop with the aid of mathematics. Hence this also had to be tackled. Further, at a certain stage of agriculture and in certain regions (raising of water for irrigation in Egypt), and especially with the origin of towns, big building operations and the development of handicrafts—mechanics. This was soon needed also for navigation and war. Moreover, it requires the aid of mathematics and so promotes the latter's development." Later, with the great new developments of the forces of production which led to and then took place within the capitalist system, new sciences arose one after the other—physics, chemistry, the biological sciences, geology. "If . . . the sciences suddenly arose anew with undreamed-of force, developing at a miraculous rate, once again we owe this miracle to—production."

If the development of the sciences is determined by production, this also accounts for the uneven rate in history of the development of the sciences and for the often one-sided character of that development. The varying character of production and of the emphasis placed on different production processes accounts for it. Thus chemistry, for example, was never far developed until modern times, though mechanics and certain parts of the biological sciences had a considerable development. Again, the agricultural sciences are relatively neglected under modern monopoly capitalism, while all the sciences connected with war production are energetically fostered.

Sciences as Specialised Undertakings Distinct from Production

Sciences are essentially specialised undertakings, with their own specialist techniques and theories. The rise of sciences occurs when, as a product of division of labour, there begins a special investigation of the properties of various natural objects and natural processes, distinct from production itself; and when, consequently, there also occurs a special elaboration, a generalisation and systematisation, of ideas in connection with such investigation.

Only under such conditions may we speak of sciences. Thus we would hardly allow the title of "science" to the knowledge possessed by primitive tribes, extensive and accurate as it is, of the various kinds of animals and plants, or of the properties of various materials, or of the succession of the seasons. Such knowledge is raised to the level of science only when these things are made the subjects of special investigation distinct from actual production—in the first place from hunting, making tools, gardening and the like; and when, consequently, what is discovered about them is generalised and systematised as a special body of knowledge.

We may distinguish three outstanding characteristics of sciences, which progressively distinguish scientific theory from the knowledge of natural objects and processes inherent in the production process itself and constituting the producers' own consciousness of their work, its subjects and instruments.

(1) Sciences engage in *systematic description and classification* of natural objects and processes. Such, for example, is the charting of the heavenly bodies and their apparent movements undertaken by the pioneers of astronomical science, like the ancient Egyptians; or the "natural histories" compiled by early students of living nature, like Aristotle, whose zoological works comprised a systematic description and classification of most known (as well as some imaginary) kinds of animals, with attempts at formulating laws correlating the various properties of different animals.

(2) Basing themselves on such description and classification of natural objects and their motions, sciences proceed by abstraction to formulate the *principles and laws* manifested in and governing the observed properties and motions of natural objects. By such abstraction, for example, are derived such concepts as mass, momentum, etc., in mechanics; or the concepts of number and geometrical form in mathematics.

(3) Utilising such concepts, the sciences proceed by the formulation of *hypotheses*. Such hypotheses seek to *explain* the observed properties, interconnections and motions of the things investigated, and so to *predict* their further properties, interconnections and motions; they seek to provide a systematic theory of the phenomena, and to enable men to understand and make use of them.

Consequently, while science has its roots in production, and is applied in production, at the same time it is developed as a

G

specialised activity distinct from production.

It follows that those who develop it are frequently unaware of, and may even deny, its connection with production. So far as their own consciousness of their activities is concerned, they may be carrying out their investigations out of curiosity, sheerly for the sake of knowledge, from love of mankind and the desire to enlighten people, because they enjoy it, because they are paid to do it, because they wish to become famous, or because they wish to do opponents a bad turn by proving them wrong. Many different subjective motives may and do operate in scientific work, and, of course, these motives may and do influence the character and outcome of the work.

Further, once science is put on the track of certain discoveries, these often lead of themselves to others, and the process of following up conclusions and generalising and systematising the resulting ideas proceeds with a logic of its own, independent of particular practical problems connected with production.

For this reason important scientific problems are often elucidated in advance of practical needs and even long before any practical application is possible. For example, scientific conclusions about the existence of electromagnetic waves were reached well in advance of any practical application in radio techniques. Atomic fission was discovered many years before any practical application of the release of atomic energy was attempted. Thus scientific advance tends to acquire a momentum of its own independent of practical application. What is more, even when that application becomes technically possible, it is often delayed on account of political and economic circumstances.

Sciences, as the theory of production, are thus from the outset distinct from the practice of production, both in their organisation and in the personal activity and consciousness of their practitioners. At the same time, the character of the sciences and their level do always depend on those of production, their problems arise in the last analysis from production, and their results are fed back into production. The development of sciences is always dependent on the development of production, and in turn sustains and pushes forward production. The distinction of science from production is not a disconnection, but a very close connection. And in the event that this underlying connection ever becomes severed, the sciences themselves always begin to stagnate and then to decay. In general, the times when a new impetus is given to science are times when new techniques of production are being developed. Those who then pioneer the new paths in science are usually closely associated in their practical interests with the new productive processes. Then follows a process of the scientific elaboration and development of the new ideas and discoveries. But this process cannot be long sustained if it fails to achieve technical application and lacks the stimulus of problems arising from that application.

Science and Classes

What has been said shows that the rise of sciences is a product of division of labour. Sciences are developed as a product of mental as distinct from physical labour—as a special field of theoretical activity separated from the labour of production. It follows from this that the development of the sciences is closely bound up with that of classes. At different times different classes have taken a hand in the development of the sciences and have, in consequence, influenced that development to suit their class requirements, and imposed on the sciences certain features of their class ideology.

From the division of labour arose private property and exploiting classes, and so the division between the mass of producers, wholly engaged in productive toil, and the privileged and leisured minority who took over the general management and direction of society. The development of sciences, as a branch of mental labour, was dependent upon the existence of such a minority, freed from the physical labour of production and able to undertake such mental labour.

Thus the class which, in any particular period, has taken over the general management and direction of society, and therefore of the state, religion and so on, also takes charge of the sciences and exercises a controlling influence over their development.

Sciences develop essentially as part of the means which are required for the general direction and management of social affairs, as well as of particular undertakings. Hence the sciences develop as means or instruments in the hands of various classes, serving their requirements in the way of (*a*) carrying on and expanding production, and (*b*) managing and controlling social affairs generally. These classes promote and foster the development of sciences in so far as their interests require that they find things out, as distinct from merely remaining in ignorance or inventing false theories.

Thus the expansion of science, and also the limits to that expansion, are governed by the interests arising from the conditions of existence of particular classes from time to time.

In slave society and in feudal society, for example, the conditions of existence of the ruling classes, which were bound up with the existence of a comparatively low level of development of both agriculture and industry, dictated only a most limited interest in the development of sciences. But once the bourgeoisie arose, its interests demanded an enormous extension of scientific work, connected primarily with the development of manufactures and industries, but also, in the conditions of its revolutionary struggle, with man and his social relations. Modern science is the creation of the bourgeoisie, one of the most typical products of bourgeois society, the means for understanding and controlling the processes of nature and society created under the conditions of the development of capitalism.

Class Ideology in Science

The fact that a particular class takes the leading part in the general development of science also places definite conditions and limits upon the development of the ideas of science.

On the basis of the material conditions of existence of a class, preconceptions are formed which determine the character of the class ideology. These preconceptions are used and applied, in one way or another, by the intellectual representatives of the class in every sphere of their ideological activity. And so they are used and applied in scientific work, penetrate into and impose themselves upon the theory of the sciences, and in that way influence and colour the entire development of the sciences in each particular period.

In slave society, for example, the idea was developed, and it was more fully worked out in feudal society, that everything which existed constituted a hierarchy, stretching down from God, through the grades of inferior spiritual beings, to the grades of men, animals, plants and minerals. Everything existed for a purpose, corresponding to its place in the system, and this was what determined its essential properties as well as its movements and changes. This type of conception dominated the sciences. Every theory concerning man or nature had to be formulated in terms of it and made to fit in with it.

For example, it was considered that the heavens beyond the circle of the moon were of a superior nature, belonged to a superior grade of being, to the earth beneath. Hence the heavenly movements (which were supposed to be necessarily circular, because such movements were supposed to be the most perfect) were considered to be movements obeying different laws from earthly ones. Earthly bodies naturally tended to fall towards the centre, which accounted for gravitation as observed on the earth; but this did not apply in the heavens. Such ideas were expressed in the Ptolemaic conception of the base earth at the centre of the universe, with the sun and stars circling beyond it. Copernicus, putting the sun at the centre and making the earth one of the planets, effected a decisive break with this type of conception, and paved the way for the Newtonian conception of universal gravitation and the laws of motion, which subsumed the movements of all the bodies in the universe under one universal scheme of mechanical causality.

Bourgeois ideology in general and bourgeois science in particular attacked and in the end largely got rid of the old, traditional conceptions. This attack arose from and developed on the basis of the growth of the bourgeois social relations. What took the place of the old conceptions were new and typically bourgeois conceptions—conceptions of the basic qualitative identity of all material beings, and of mechanical causality. At the same time, apart from its most radical representatives, the bourgeoisie by no means threw over the conceptions of God and of spirit. But in place of the single graded hierarchy of being, from the basest sort of material being at the bottom to the highest sort of spiritual being (or God) at the top, there was introduced the division of the universe into two totally different spheres—material being subject to fixed, deterministic laws on the one hand, and God and the spiritual world on the other hand.

In one way or another such bourgeois conceptions have entered into the whole theoretical fabric of modern science, as slave and feudal conceptions did into that of ancient and medieval science. But there is this difference—that whereas the old conceptions were hostile to the exploration of nature by experimental methods, the new conceptions were favourable to it and demanded it.

Discovery and Preconception

Because of this class ideological influence in scientific theory, a distinction is always arising in the development of the sciences between the discoveries which science makes and the preconceptions which science takes over and uses.

A discovery is made when, as a result of investigations, something becomes known about the kinds of things which exist, their properties, interconnections and laws. But discoveries must always be expressed in propositions formulated with the aid of definite concepts, and such propositions are always made to form part of a general theory. Considering, therefore, the sum total of the ideas and theories of the sciences at any time, we find that, in one aspect, they consist of the formulation of actual discoveries, and in another aspect, they consist of the general preconceptions in terms of which the discoveries are formulated and knitted together into a general theory.

This distinction between discovery and preconception, which is always present in science, often gives rise to a contradiction between discovery and preconception. And this contradiction is continually at work in the development of the sciences.

This contradiction is in essence a contradiction between content and form in science—a contradiction between the actual content of the discoveries of science and the theoretical forms in which they are expressed and generalised. It can work out in either of two ways, a positive way or a negative way. Positively, new discoveries help to shatter old preconceptions and to lead to new ways of understanding things. Negatively, the retention of old preconceptions hinders the advance to new discoveries.

For example, at the dawn of modern natural science the old preconceptions were hindering the advance to new discoveries—as when the notion that heavenly motions were completely different from earthly ones hindered the advance of astronomy and mechanics. And then the new discoveries in astronomy and mechanics helped to shatter the old conceptions and to lead the way to a new outlook.

Again, in modern bourgeois natural science a contradiction has arisen between the discoveries of science and the traditional, bourgeois mechanistic-metaphysical method of interpreting them.

Thus Engels pointed out that the cumulative effect of the discoveries of modern natural science is to show "that in the last resort nature works dialectically and not metaphysically. . . . But the naturalists who have learned to think dialectically are few and far between, and this conflict of the results of discovery with preconceived modes of thinking explains the endless confusion now reigning in theoretical natural science." (*Socialism, Utopian and Scientific*, chapter 3.)

On the one hand, this contradiction leads to "endless confusion" in science, which holds up the advance of science. In biology, for example, extremely rigid mechanistic ideas about living processes were imposed and, when these created difficulties, recourse was had to mystical ideas about life forces, resulting in a sterile controversy between "mechanism" and "vitalism". Again, when modern discoveries in physics upset the traditional scheme of mechanistic causality, it was claimed that the whole idea of causality had broken down and that "no picture" could be given of fundamental physical processes. On the other hand, the accumulation of discoveries has led to new ways of thinking, to the supplanting of bourgeois ideology by dialectical materialism. Thus Lenin concluded from his examination of new developments in physics: "Modern physics in in travail, it is giving birth to dialectical materialism." (*Materialism and Empirio-Criticism*, chapter 5, section 8.)

Social Science

So far we have discussed only the natural sciences. But there is also social science.

The development of natural sciences, which carry out investigations into the properties and laws of natural phenomena, has ultimately been determined by production. That of social science, on the other hand, which carries out investigations into the properties and laws of social phenomena, has been determined by the class struggle. Social science has its roots in the experience of various classes gained in the course of their class struggle.

Sciences always arise from some need. It is, in the last analysis, the needs of production which call forth natural sciences, and their investigations are carried out on behalf of whatever class is directing production. In turn, the needs of the general management and control of social affairs call forth social science. And its investigations are carried out on behalf of whatever class is either actually managing and controlling social affairs or is struggling to secure such management and control.

The investigation of social phenomena has had considerable development during slave, feudal and capitalist society. The most painstaking investigations have been made into the various different forms of society and of government, and into the social laws which any government must take cognisance of, as well as the investigations of historians, which have established the sequence of public events in the history of various communities.

But up to the emergence of the modern working class, these

investigations have been carried out by representatives of exploiting classes. And so it has been primarily the lessons and conclusions about man and society drawn by the exploiting classes which have been incorporated into social science. This has given social science a character profoundly different from natural science. As developed by representatives of exploiting classes, social science—which deals with men's relations and interactions with one another—has been completely separated from natural science—which deals with external nature and man's action on nature. And it has proved impossible to establish the basis of a trustworthy science of society in the way that the same classes have been able to do in the case of external nature.

There are four principal features of social science which have fundamentally distinguished it from natural science.

(1) Class interests inhibit certain investigations and discoveries in social science, in a way they do not in natural science. The fact that social science has been developed by exploiting classes as an aid to their class struggles sets impassable limits on the possibilities of discovery by social science—so long as it remains in the hands of those classes.

It is true, of course, that various discoveries about nature have been resisted for a time by representatives of the ruling classes, for their own ideological reasons. And in this respect the path of the natural sciences has sometimes been anything but smooth. Such was the case, for example, with Galileo, or more recently Darwin, or more recently still Michurin. But invariably, in the end, the facts themselves compel recognition, the discoveries are assimilated and used, and the ideologies adapt themselves to the new discoveries. But in the social field, on the other hand, resistance is much stronger. An exploiting class will not recognise facts and laws about society if this would fatally prejudice its class interests. It will not recognise facts which would expose the real nature of its own system of exploitation, and laws which would make clear the inevitable downfall of that system.

(2) While exploiting classes have developed the natural sciences as instruments of men's collective mastery over

nature, they have not developed social science correspondingly as an instrument of men's collective mastery over their own social organisation. The exploiting classes have developed social sciences only as an instrument to help them secure and maintain their own class rule. Many investigations about society have been undertaken, from which theoretical and practical conclusions have been drawn. But in contrast to the investigations and conclusions of the natural sciences, these have never enabled people to secure such control over the results of their actions that they could direct and plan their co-operative efforts to the realisation of definite ends.

Exploiting classes have been interested in developing instruments of production which have been the means for people's establishing and increasing their mastery over nature. And so, under the patronage of these classes, the natural sciences have more and more helped to realise man's mastery over nature. But at the same time, the development of private property and exploitation has made people subject to effects of their own social relations which lie beyond their conscious social control. And this must be so for as long as exploitation continues to exist. Hence the very same historical process which creates for the exploiting classes the possibility of developing a natural science which helps to realise man's mastery over nature, withholds from them the possibility of developing a social science which helps to realise man's mastery over his own social organisation.

(3) While exploiting classes have been able to develop further and further the scientific investigation not only of the surface phenomena of nature but of the underlying causes and laws of these phenomena, their social science is never able to penetrate to the basic causes and laws of the movement of society.

The basic causes and laws of the movement of society lie in the sphere of the production relations, of the property and class relations. But it is impossible to carry through to the end a scientific investigation in this sphere without finally exposing the truth about the basis of the privileged position of the exploiting classes, and the contradictory and transitory nature of the system of exploitation, which these classes are vitally concerned to hide and disguise. Hence even when, during a progressive phase, the social science of an exploiting class begins to make a more profound analysis of the economic basis of society (as with the British bourgeoisie in the initial phase of industrial capitalism), the class soon falls back from its own achievement, and its social investigations revert to a superficial descriptive level, replete with misleading ideas. The sociologists of exploiting classes can in the end never rightly classify, analyse and explain the phenomena investigated, and constantly introduce illusory motives and false explanations into their accounts of society.

(4) In the hands of the exploiting classes, social science has remained far more profoundly under the influence of class ideology than the natural sciences. In the natural sciences, class ideological preconceptions have often hindered but in the end not prevented the sciences from discovering many of the objective laws and essential interconnections of the phenomena they were investigating. In social science, on the other hand, the general theory of society has been primarily determined by class ideological preconceptions.

Because class interests prohibit certain investigations and discoveries; because the classes in charge of social science cannot develop it as a means towards man's mastery over his own social organisation and so submit its conclusions to the test of social practice; because social science draws back from investigating the basic causes and laws of the movement of society—it follows that the general conceptions of society employed in social science are not derived from scientific investigation but have the character of false consciousness, of class ideological illusion. Consequently, the investigations and conclusions of social science have tended, in the hands of representatives of exploiting classes, to develop primarily as a mere elaboration of class ideological preconceptions—as a classifying and interpreting of social facts in such a way as to reinforce a given class's illusions about society, and to provide arguments to support its political policies.

For all these reasons, therefore, social science in the hands of representatives of exploiting classes has not attained, and never could attain, the same scientific status as the natural sciences. And it has constantly tended to degenerate into mere ruling class apologetics.

The Social Functions of Science

We shall sum up this chapter with some conclusions about the nature of science and the part it plays in social life, in economic and cultural development. Then in the next chapter we shall consider some of the general features of the historical development of science, and the part it is destined to play in the future, in the construction of socialist society.

The distinction between scientific and illusory modes of consciousness is dependent on the different methods of forming ideas about things—on the one hand, forming ideas on the basis of practical interaction with things, developing them by systematic investigation and testing them continually in practice; on the other hand, proceeding from ideological preconceptions.

These two modes of consciousness are not mutually exclusive. They are opposites, but they interpenetrate. They are opposite tendencies at work in the total development of social consciousness, which interpenetrate at every stage, and which together determine the actual formation of the ideas entertained about nature and society, and about particular aspects of nature and society. And this in turn gives rise to continual contradictions in such ideas. As we have seen, the scientific mode of consciousness has gradually become the predominant influence in the formation of ideas about nature, while the illusory mode of consciousness has remained the predominant influence in the formation of ideas about society.

Scientific investigation and discovery is bound up with social practice, with the practice of production and with the practice of the class struggle. In the last analysis, it always arises from and is governed by the requirements of practice. And meeting the requirements of practice, it makes an essential contribution to practice.

Scientific investigation and discovery plays an indispensable part in the development of the forces of production; and the higher the development of the forces of production the greater and the more necessary is the part played by science in their development. For example, science played no part in the forces of production in the Stone Age. It began to play a part in the development of agriculture, metalworking, public works. It plays a major part in the modern forces of production, since modern technology would be impossible without science; more than that, it plays a leading part, since scientific research pioneers the way of technological development and leads directly to great revolutions in technology.

Contributing thus to the development of forces of production, science becomes a revolutionising force in society. For it is a principal factor in those advances of the forces of production which bring them into conflict with existing relations of production and thus render necessary a change in the whole economic structure of society. This is evident today in the development of physical science, for example. Thus atomic energy production is one of the factors which make the replacement of capitalism by socialism urgently necessary, in order that such production may be fruitfully developed in the service of society.

At the same time, science plays a part in class struggle. The natural sciences play such a part indirectly and as a secondary function, social science directly and as a primary function.

The primary social function of natural science is to assist production. From this follows its secondary function in the class struggle. Definite advances in science and technology serve the interests of definite classes, either in their struggle for power or in the consolidation of their régime when they are in power. Thus, for example, the early advances of modern science and technology served the rising bourgeoisie in two ways—first, by enabling them to increase their wealth and so strengthen their social position; second, ideologically by helping their struggle against the feudal ideology. And when the bourgeoisie was established in power, science and technology were powerful aids in consolidating the capitalist régime. Today they still serve the régime of monopoly capitalism. At the same time, they are also pressed into the service of the working class and the cause of socialism, and developed in that service—in the countries where socialism is being built, as a mainspring in socialist construction; and everywhere as part of the essential equipment of socialist ideology.

Various kinds of social investigation, on the other hand, serve the class struggle directly, and the requirements of class struggle provide the principal motivation of such investigations. And in the case of exploiting classes, this, as we have seen, accounts for the fact that class ideological illusions play a far greater part in social than in natural science. The comparative study of different forms of society and of government, the description and classification of various forms of social activity, the investigation of the best way of carrying out various forms of economic activity—these have been essential occupations of the various ruling and exploiting classes, which have served them in planning and directing their activities both in gaining power and consolidating it, and in developing their class views in the ideological struggle with other classes. In the class struggle of the working class, in the struggle for socialism, social science is for the first time developed as an essential means for finding out how to transform society; and in this it for the first time begins to attain a scientific status equivalent to that of the natural sciences.

The chief and most essential social function of science is, then, to be found in the part it plays in the development of social practice. By carrying on scientific investigations to find things out and to reach general conclusions on the basis of what they have found out, people are able to expand and develop their productive forces, and regulate their social intercourse, their individual and social activities, corresponding to the level of their productive forces and the consequent character of their production relations. Thus the development of science is an essential means to the perfection of human life, serving to increase men's mastery over nature, their social wealth, the scope and power of their activities, their ability to manage their affairs and satisfy their requirements.

This bears on the question, formerly raised amongst

Marxists, whether science develops as part of the class ideology conditioned by the economic relations of society. Is it correct to contrast "bourgeois science" and "socialist science" as rival ideologies serving rival classes and social systems?

On the one hand, since class ideological preconceptions do enter into science, it is clear that in actual practice the theories current in particular fields of science do include views which arise and develop as part of a class ideology. Such preconceptions arise precisely as products of a given basis of property and class relations, serve the consolidation and development of those relations, and disappear when that economic basis disappears. We cannot understand the history of science, or its specific character and contradictions at any particular stage, without taking into account the fact that it *is* developed by definite classes, whose class preconceptions play an active part in its development, and whose economic interests may further its development in one direction and inhibit it in another. In this sense it is quite correct to contrast "bourgeois science" and "socialist science", since the development of scientific work is differently conditioned in bourgeois and socialist societies.

On the other hand, the *content* of the discoveries of science is not determined by class interests or an economic basis. Those discoveries are directly connected with the needs of production and of social intercourse consequent on production, reflect objective facts and laws, serve society generally and remain valid for any economic basis. A discovery is a discovery, whoever makes it.

To take a concrete example, that of quantum physics as it has been developed in bourgeois society today. The discoveries concerning the laws of motion of matter on the sub-atomic level reflect those laws of motion, embody the results of experiments, and so are in no way determined by the ideological preconceptions of particular classes conditioned by economic relations and economic interests. This is why scientists from capitalist and socialist countries can meet in a scientific conference on common ground, compare their results and assist one another in furthering the advance of science—

so far, at least, as the security regulations of their governments allow. But the theory that events happen without causes, which has been built around these discoveries and which no experiment can confirm, is a characteristic product of bourgeois ideology. Hence in its essential discoveries quantum physics has not developed as a class ideology, but certain temporary features of its general theory have been influenced by class ideology.

So, does science develop as a class ideology? The economic and class relations of society do condition the development of science, and the ideological preconceptions of definite classes do enter into science and influence its development. They influence its development either positively or negatively, assisting scientific discovery or hindering it—just as, in general, the economic basis of property and class relations may be favourable or unfavourable to the further development of science. But the discoveries of science and the advance of scientific theory do not reflect the preconceptions and interests of any classes but directly reflect the processes of the objective world—and this is secured by the progressive application of scientific methods, which are fact-finding methods and not methods for spinning out theories to suit the interests of any particular people.

Moreover, it is evident that science itself plays a very important part in the ideological development of society.

Scientifically formed concepts, scientific discoveries, enter into ideologies, and science is a strong and growing influence in the formation of ideologies—which thus, in some of their features, become scientific rather than illusory. The higher the development of science the greater the part it must play in general ideological development.

For example, the conception of the evolution of species through natural selection, the conception of the cell as the unit through which life develops, the conception of the atom, the conception of the earth as part of the solar system within the island universe of the milky way, are all scientifically formed conceptions which have become part of the accepted view of nature in bourgeois society, and so part of the current bourgeois ideology. In general, bourgeois ideology not only penetrates science by imposing preconceptions on it but is also itself penetrated by science, at the same time often seeking to "interpret" and explain away scientific discoveries.

But above all, science plays a part as a weapon of criticism in the development of ideology. New concepts and discoveries of science conflict with existing ideology, and shake its preconceptions and the conclusions derived from them. So when new classes are rising to challenge the sway of the old ruling classes, and new ideas are being opposed to the old ideas, scientific investigation and the conclusions derived from it become a revolutionary weapon of criticism.

Above all, therefore, science plays a progressive and liberating part in social development. Its discoveries enhance men's collective power to satisfy their requirements, and serve as means of enlightenment, dispelling the clouds of error and superstition, and furnishing men with knowledge of nature and of themselves.

Particular classes, and particular nations led by particular classes, have made their contributions to the development of the sciences, temporarily stamping upon them their own peculiar characteristics and limitations, and often, having advanced so far in scientific discovery, drawing back, confusing the theory of science with their own illusions and perverting its uses. But whatever the limitations and setbacks, what has been achieved by one class or nation is taken over and carried on by another. Hence in the history of science there has developed, and is developing, a heritage of human knowledge and power. This is the common heritage of mankind, destined to be used for the emancipation of all the people.

Chapter Nine

SCIENCE AND SOCIALISM

Achievements of Bourgeois Science

PRIOR to modern capitalist times, the sciences developed mainly at the most elementary, descriptive and classificatory level. The discoveries of science, considerable as they were in certain fields, were piecemeal in character, being concerned with the properties of particular objects and with particular laws and conceptions, not yet penetrating to the more general and fundamental laws or affording any reliable general picture of the interconnections in nature. Since scientific work was mainly confined to description and classification, the abstractions and generalisations of the sciences, which constitute the two other major aspects of scientific work, were of necessity mainly speculations and guesses. And the general theory of nature was developed as a part of philosophy and theology, and embodied all the philosophical and theological illusions of the times.

It was a feature of science in this stage that it made use of some extremely primitive conceptions about nature. The alchemists, for instance, accumulated a considerable store of knowledge about chemical substances and their combinations, but their chemical theory was extremely primitive, in the literal sense that it made use of ideas taken over from primitive times. Such, for example, was their idea that chemical substances were living beings made up of matter and spirit, and also possessing sexual attributes. Again, there was a considerable development of astronomical observation in slave and feudal society, but the cosmological theories about the layout of the universe remained under the influence of primitive ideas.

Engels, in a letter to C. Schmidt, October 27, 1890, pointed out that there has existed "a prehistoric stock of what we should today call bunk", which has been drawn on (it is still sometimes drawn on, by the way) for the purposes of men's general conception of nature.

"These various false conceptions of nature," he wrote, "... have for the most part only a negative economic basis; the low economic development of the prehistoric period is supplemented and partially conditioned and even caused by the false conceptions of nature. And even though economic necessity was the main driving force of the progressing knowledge of nature and becomes ever more so, it would surely be pedantic to try to find economic causes for all this primitive nonsense. The history of science is the history of the gradual clearing away of this nonsense or of its replacement by fresh but always less absurd nonsense."

The position was, therefore, that the ideology of the ruling classes imposed a certain philosophical and theological character upon the general theory of the sciences. And at the same time, the relatively low level of economic development brought it about that many primitive and nonsensical conceptions found their place in the theories about particular things. These factors could not but hinder the development of the sciences. They acted as powerful negative factors which had to be swept away before the modern development of science, and of production, could become possible.

Modern natural science arose in the period when the power of the feudal nobility was being broken and the modern European bourgeois nations were being formed. "Natural science developed in the midst of the general revolution and was itself thoroughly revolutionary", wrote Engels in *Dialectics of Nature*. And the same class forces which were carrying through the revolution carried through the development of sciences. Science appeared as a great force of enlightenment, breaking through past ignorance and superstition. It challenged the old authorities with knowledge based on observation and experiment. The men who laid the foundations of modern natural science were of a very different type from the clerks and monkish scholars of the feudal order. They were intensely interested in the development of industry and trade, in new techniques, in travel and discovery. In their hands the discoveries of science became instruments for improving the conditions of human life.

The rise of new sciences was consequent upon a new development of industry.

"Following the crusades, industry developed enormously and brought to light a quantity of new mechanical (weaving, clockmaking, milling), chemical (dyeing, metallurgy, alcohol), and physical (lenses) facts, and this not only gave enormous material for observation, but also itself provided quite other means for experimenting than previously existed, and allowed the construction of new instruments; it can be said that really systematic experimental science had now become possible for the first time." (Engels, *Dialectics of Nature.*)

In the modern development of natural science which was thus initiated, the abstractions and hypotheses of the sciences ceased to be mere speculations and guesses, and began to be established as verified scientific truths. Scientific theory began to replace the former coupling of primitive bunk with philosophical and theological speculation. And what made this possible for those now engaged in scientific work was the new equipment which they possessed for accurate observation and controlled experiment, and the fact that scientific theories began to be tested not only by scientific observations and experiments but in the practice of social production. The new successes of natural science were dependent, therefore, on advancing technology in social production and the social utilisation of science as a force of production.

From this starting point, modern bourgeois natural science has gone on to score great achievements.

(1) There has been achieved the successive development of separate branches of natural science—the evolution of the different sciences one from another, and their differentiation one from another. In this process, the successes scored in one field have created the possibility of beginning the scientific investigation of new fields. The whole process has unfolded out

of the development of the productive forces of capitalist society, which at one and the same time have presented new problems for science to tackle and provided the technical means for tackling them.

(2) In all the successive fields of science there have been major achievements of analysis—the analysis of the phenomena of nature into their parts or elements, the demonstration of the properties, interconnections and laws of motion of the parts, and so of the laws of motion of the whole. And at the same time as this analysis of nature has been carried out there has been carried out a process of generalisation, demonstrating how the most diverse properties and motions of things are all the consequences of the operation of very general, universally applicable laws.

(3) A third major achievement of modern natural science has been the discovery of the laws of change and development in nature.

In the initial period of modern natural science the view prevailed that, despite ceaseless changes and interactions, nature in its main features always remained exactly the same. "The planets and their satellites, once set in motion by the mysterious 'first impulse', circled on and on in their predestined ellipses for all eternity. . . . The stars remained for ever fixed and immovable in their places. . . . The earth had persisted without alteration. . . . The five continents of the present day had always existed. . . . The species of plants and animals had been established once and for all when they came into existence. . . . All change, all development in nature was denied." (Engels, *Dialectics of Nature*, Introduction.) But the successive discoveries of the sciences—in astronomy and cosmogony, in physics, in chemistry, in geology and in the biological sciences—shattered this whole picture of the fixity of nature. It was demonstrated that nature in all its parts changes and develops. And this conclusion emerged not as a general speculation—such as had been put forward, for instance, in ancient Greek philosophy—but as a result of detailed investigations, of the analysis of the various processes of nature and the discovery of their laws and interconnections.

(4) Finally, from the discoveries of the natural sciences there has gradually emerged a knowledge of nature which is at once general and detailed—general, in the sense that it embraces the main processes which take place in nature and their interconnections; and detailed, in the sense that it embraces particular laws and interconnections of things. And this knowledge to an increasing degree has enabled the sciences to give an account of natural processes entirely based on and tested in the investigation of those processes themselves.

"We have arrived at the point", wrote Engels, "where we can demonstrate as a whole the interconnection between the processes in nature not only in particular spheres but also in the interconnection of these particular spheres themselves, and so can present in an approximately systematic form a comprehensive view of the interconnection in nature by means of the facts provided by empirical natural science itself." (*Ludwig Feuerbach*, chapter 2.)

As a result, scientific knowledge of nature gradually supplants philosophical speculation about nature. The account which is given both of particular processes and of their general interconnection is based on and tested in detailed investigations, and not arrived at by philosophical deductions or imaginative guesses.

Formerly, as Engels observed, a "comprehensive view" of nature could be arrived at "only by putting in place of the real but as yet unknown interconnections ideal and imaginary ones, filling out the missing facts by figments of the mind and bridging the actual gaps merely in imagination". But once scientific investigations have supplied the missing facts, such a procedure becomes "not only superfluous, but a step backwards" (*Ludwig Feuerbach*, chapter 2).

Of course, many gaps remain; and though they keep on being filled, gaps will always remain. Indeed, the filling in of one gap often reveals new and hitherto unsuspected ones. Yet even by the latter part of the last century science had discovered enough to discredit the old type of philosophical-theological account of nature. It has become clear that missing knowledge must always be supplied by pushing on with scientific investigation and not by any other means.

Limitations of Bourgeois Science

The sciences, by assisting in the development of industry and trade, have played an indispensable part in making possible the establishment and development of the capitalist mode of production. But the establishment of the capitalist mode of production has then set limits upon the further development of the sciences.

The great achievement of capitalism is to have transformed small-scale individual production into large-scale social production, which is able to harness natural forces and make use of modern mechanical instruments of production. The growth of social production—above all in industry, since agriculture remained relatively backward—brought about, and was assisted by, an unprecedented growth of the sciences. In field after field discoveries were made, new sciences were established and developed rapidly, nature gave up her secrets to man and the principles were established for correctly understanding the laws and interconnections of natural processes.

But social production was directed to definite capitalist ends. It was capital which exercised the controlling and directing function in social production. The co-operation in labour, which is the essential feature of social production, was not brought about by the labourers themselves but by the capital which employed and exploited them. It was "not their own act but the act of the capital which brings and keeps them together. . . . The directing motive, the end and aim of capitalist production is to extract the greatest possible amount of surplus value, and consequently to exploit labour-power to the greatest possible extent." (Marx, *Capital*, Volume I, chapter 13.)

Marx regarded science as a distinct but necessary part of the production process in modern society. Social labour, he observed (*Capital*, Volume III, chapter 5, section 5), includes labour of two kinds. First there is the scientific side, involving the scientific mastery of materials and processes, issuing in inventions and discoveries which improve the existing instruments of production and create new ones. This he termed "universal labour". And secondly, there is co-operative labour itself, the co-operation of workers in utilising the instruments of production.

In capitalist production these two kinds of labour are separated, and both compelled to serve capital. Co-operative labour is the source of surplus value, and the labourer is simply "a hand" to work under the direction of the capitalist, or his managers, for the profit of the capitalist. Advances in production technique are made and applied not because they lighten labour or help to satisfy human needs but because and in so far only as they yield an increased profit. And therefore science, the theory of production, does not develop as an adjunct and instrument of social labour but as an adjunct and instrument of capital which exploits labour-power and directs production towards capitalist profit.

"The labourer is brought face to face with the intellectual potencies of the material process of production, as the property of another, and as a ruling power", wrote Marx. "Modern industry . . . makes science a productive force distinct from labour and presses it into the service of capital." (*Capital*, Volume I, chapter 14, section 5.)

At first science could advance with giant strides within the limits of the capitalist relations. For capital needed to penetrate the secrets of the natural processes which it used in its drive for profit, and, realising the vital importance of science, was also willing to encourage research along lines for which no immediate practical application was in sight. Scientists felt themselves free and unfettered; it seemed to them that they were conducting their researches for the sake of humanity, or for knowledge for its own sake, and that society was ready to honour and reward them for their discoveries and to put their discoveries, where circumstances permitted, to practical use. Nevertheless, the reality of this bourgeois freedom of science was that science was working all the time for capital, which relied on its discoveries, inventions and theories to effect those improvements in production which would swell capitalist profit.

With the development of capital to its modern, monopoly stage, however, the direct and open subjugation of science to monopoly capital has gradually come about. This has been aided by the very advance of science itself, which has entailed a great increase in costs and so rendered the sciences almost completely dependent on financing by the monopolies, directly or through the state. Not only the researches, inventions and discoveries of scientists have been pressed into the service of capital, but scientists personally. They have lost their former independent status, and been turned into employees and agents of the monopolies—or of the state, which is itself subjugated to the monopolies. And their work is correspondingly regimented. The effect of this is to disorganise scientific work, which can proceed only in directions which the monopolies will pay for; to pervert it, principally and increasingly for military ends, with the growing evils of secrecy and "security", police and military supervision, "loyalty" tests and tests of ideological orthodoxy; and finally to make science appear not as a source of strength and hope to humanity but as a menace.

The subjection of science to capital, and latterly to monopoly capital, is equally reflected in the theory of science. From the viewpoint of the capitalist class, science, necessary as it is, has always harboured a dangerous ideological trend. This is because of the materialist tendency of its conclusions, which begin to explain everything in men's experience from the material world alone. The bourgeoisie early began to realise that scientific materialism can be socially subversive, if it begins to submit the foundations of society and of ruling class privilege to scientific criticism and to show how, armed with science, the people can achieve their emancipation. Hence for a long time philosophical theories have been woven around science, seeking to explain away its radical materialist tendency, and above all seeking to impose limits upon its possible development and application.

Thus it has been laid down that science can only deal with certain aspects of the forces of nature, but not with the underlying and controlling spiritual forces in the world; that, indeed, it cannot penetrate to the real forces at work in nature, but can only deal with some of their effects; that, finally, it can only record and correlate the sensations which are produced in our minds, while the real world outside remains unknowable and mysterious. Such views about science and in science, which have become extremely widespread in the capitalist world today, were already being developed as long ago as the seventeenth century (for example, by Malebranche, *Dialogues on Metaphysics and Religion*, 1688).

So we find eminent scientists proclaiming that science is compatible with almost any kind of "faith"—except faith in humanity; that the real world is unknowable; that the aim of progress based on scientific knowledge is illusory. At the same time, the advance of scientific discovery cannot be halted. Great new discoveries continue to be made, based on the new techniques developed in modern society. But scientists themselves become all the more acutely aware of the restrictions imposed upon them in practice by monopoly interests and in theory by anti-scientific ideas. Many begin to seek the way out, some in a kind of anarchic and frustrated individualism, others in joining the working-class struggle for a new social order in which science will have unrestricted development in serving the interests of all members of society.

Science for the People

In capitalism, the direction of social production is a function of capital, whose aim is capitalist profit. In socialism, on the other hand, the direction of social production becomes a function of social labour itself, the aim of which is satisfaction of the material and cultural requirements of society. The task of developing the theory of production must always be in the same hands as the direction of its practice. In capitalism science is separated from labour and pressed into the service of capital which exploits labour. But in socialism, science becomes united with labour. Socialist science is the scientific department of social labour—in other words, that department which carries out the research, invention and theoretical work necessary continuously to expand and perfect socialist production, and to satisfy the constantly rising material and cultural requirements of socialist society.

Removed from the control of the monopolies and turned into a public concern, the all-round development of science becomes a subject of planning under socialism. This does not mean, of course, that the discoveries to be made over a period are planned in advance, since no one can know what is going to be discovered until the discovery is made. It means that the allocation of the resources and the direction for research in all fields are planned. Such planning entails the combination of short-term and long-term considerations. At one and the same time science concentrates on the solution of immediate practical problems, and undertakes fundamental researches dictated by the requirements of theoretical advance and aspiring to results far beyond current practice.

A new type of scientist emerges, recruited from the ranks of the working people. And science, from being the preserve of a single social group associated with the exploiters, eventually becomes the common possession and concern of all. This can only set free immense new forces for scientific work and for the utilisation of its results, and lead to an immense acceleration and expansion of science.

At the same time, ideological preconceptions are finally thrown off. The theory of science is developed in line with its discoveries, on the basis of socialist practice, as a guide to further discovery and practical application, with free discussion and criticism.

At an early stage, before the development of the separate sciences, science was scarcely distinguished from philosophy. One feature of the history of philosophy and of science is the separating of the sciences from philosophy. As sciences branch off from philosophy, general ideas about nature are established on the basis of the scientific investigation of nature. Yet, as we have seen, philosophical ideas continue to penetrate the sciences, influencing particularly the more abstract parts of scientific theory. The emancipation of science from philosophical preconceptions is only completed with the development of science under socialism. For then philosophy ceases to exist in its old form as a theory of the world independent of science and imposing its views on science, but develops as a summation of the principles inherent in scientific thought itself—the principles of logic and dialectics—and therefore as a theoretical instrument and guide in scientific work.

Commenting on the relations of science and philosophy, Engels wrote in *Dialectics of Nature:*

"Natural scientists believe that they free themselves from philosophy by ignoring or abusing it. They cannot, however, make any headway without thought, and for thought they need thought determinations. They take these categories unreflectingly from the common consciousness of so-called educated persons. . . . Hence they are no less in bondage to philosophy, and those who abuse philosophy most are slaves to precisely the worst vulgarised relics of the worst philosophies. . . . Natural scientists allow philosophy to prolong a pseudo-existence by making shift with the dregs of the old metaphysics. Only when natural and historical science has adopted dialectics will all the philosophical rubbish . . . be superfluous, disappearing in positive science."

In socialism alone, moreover, can there be realised completely the true disinterestedness essential to the fullest development of science.

The process of scientific investigation demands that conclusions shall be drawn on the basis of thorough investigation alone, without consideration for what this or that interest would like to be the case, or this or that school of thought believes. And it demands that every conclusion shall be subject to criticism on the basis of further investigation.

This necessary characteristic of scientific work was repeatedly stressed by Marx. Thus, for example, in contrasting Ricardo's scientific approach in political economy to that of Malthus, he wrote in his *Theories of Surplus Value* of "Ricardo's disinterestedness" and "scientific honesty", of "Ricardo's scientific impartiality", which "comes out just as inconsiderately against the bourgeoisie as in other cases he comes out against the proletariat and the aristocracy". Malthus, on the other hand, committed a "sin against science" by adapting his conclusions to the interests of ruling class apologetics. "The contemptible Malthus draws . . . only those conclusions which are acceptable and useful to the aristocracy as against the bourgeoisie and to both as against the proletariat." He sought to "accommodate science to a point of view not derived from science itself . . . but borrowed from outside, from extrinsic interests foreign to science".

In society based on exploitation barriers cannot but arise against disinterested inquiry. Investigations are started, but the point comes when stronger and stronger social pressures operate to persuade many scientists to trim their conclusions to various ideological and political requirements of the ruling class, or even to bring the investigations to a premature end. Only when exploitation of man by man is abolished, and inquiry is consciously directed to the end of making life more abundant for everyone, are all the barriers to disinterested inquiry thrown down. For then the very interest which promotes inquiry—that is to say, the common interest in obtaining reliable knowledge as a means to life—demands that nothing shall stand in the way of prosecuting inquiries to the end.

Of course, the old habit of demanding that investigations shall prove what some particular group wishes to be proved, and of objecting to any questioning of certain conclusions, is one which dies hard. The development of socialism, on the other hand, demands that science shall be truly disinterested, and shall carry on its inquiries without consideration for what any particular person or persons have asserted or wish to be believed. This was vigorously asserted by Stalin. "It is generally recognised that no science can develop and flourish without a battle of opinions, without freedom of criticism." (*Concerning Marxism in Linguistics.*) "Science is called science just because it does not recognise fetishes, just because it does not fear to raise its hand against the obsolete and antiquated, and because it lends an attentive ear to the voice of experience, of practice." (*Speech at First All-Union Conference of Stakhanovites.*)

In general, socialism sets science free from all the limitations and restrictions hitherto imposed on its development. Just as the socialist ownership of the means of production removes the fetters imposed on the development of production by private ownership and appropriation, and renders possible the unrestricted development of production to satisfy people's needs, so does it remove the fetters imposed on the development of the sciences. The methods of scientific investigation are no different under socialism from capitalism; for these methods, gradually perfected during the successive stages of economic development, are not the product of any particular system. The point is that the economic, political and ideological factors hindering their universal application are removed.

From socialism, wrote Engels in *Dialectics of Nature*, "will date a new epoch in history, in which mankind itself, and with mankind all branches of its activity, and especially natural science, will experience an advance that will put everything preceding it in the deepest shade".

The Science of Society

Bourgeois science could penetrate deeply into the laws of natural processes because the bourgeoisie needed such knowledge for the sake of its profits. The capitalists do not want fairy stories about electricity, for example, but knowledge of its real laws (although their ideology still impels them to believe not a few fairy stories). But as regards the laws of social development, the capitalists, though they can use masses of superficial data about society, can never recognise them. For to do so would lead straight to the conclusion of the fall of themselves and their whole system.

Whatever the achievements of the natural sciences in capitalist society, the greatest limitation which that society places on the development of the sciences consists of the divorce of natural from social science. There is no unified science. Instead there are natural sciences, with no science of society, and so no scientific knowledge of how to develop and apply the sciences in the service of mankind.

The placing of social science on a firm basis, the discovery of the fundamental laws of development of society, only begins with the beginning of the struggle for socialism, and continues only in association with that struggle and then with the actual building of socialist society. The science of society develops as the scientific theory guiding the working-class struggle for socialism. It arises and develops as the theoretical basis for the social conceptions of the working class.

Bourgeois social science reached its highest development in the work of the British investigators Adam Smith and David Ricardo, whose inquiry into the laws of the production and distribution of the means of subsistence in human society laid the foundations for the science of political economy, the science of the economic basis of society. These investigations were undertaken to serve the needs of management of nascent capitalist economy. But the conditions of development of capitalist rule and capitalist exploitation inhibited any further scientific advance by bourgeois investigators. They could not go on, as Marx did, to uncover, by the discovery of surplus value, the secret of capitalist exploitation.

Subsequent bourgeois economics, and bourgeois social science generally, has busied itself with the accumulation of a vast array of facts and correlations of facts. It has also accumulated a considerable amount of practical knowledge about how to operate the capitalist system. But it has sedulously avoided investigation into the real relations of production on which those facts are based and from which alone they can be understood, substituting superficial or false explanations.

What Marx said of "vulgar" bourgeois economics can be said of bourgeois social science generally. It "deals with appearances only . . . seeks plausible explanations of the most obtrusive phenomena for bourgeois daily use, but for the rest confines itself to systematising in a pedantic way, and proclaiming for everlasting truths, the trite ideas held by the self-complacent bourgeoisie with regard to their own world, to them the best of all possible worlds." (*Capital*, Vol. I, ch. 1, section 4 (footnote)). And with such science, "it was no longer a question whether this theorem or that was true, but whether it was useful to capital or harmful, expedient or inexpedient, politically dangerous or not. In place of disinterested inquirers, there were hired prize-fighters; in place of genuine scientific research, the bad conscience and the evil intent of apologetics." (*Capital*, Preface to 2nd edition.)

So while there are bourgeois investigations establishing numerous facts and a few isolated and superficial laws of social science, there is, and can be, no bourgeois science of society embracing the fundamental laws, but only the Marxist, socialist science of society. Marx's discoveries about the fundamental laws of social development were possible only because he took up a standpoint against capitalist society, and recognised the revolutionary role of the working class and the necessity of the replacement of capitalism by socialism. By these discoveries, he established the basis of social science as Galileo and Newton of physical science, or Schwann and Darwin of biological science.

The End of the Old Ideology

Because the socialist movement develops scientific conceptions of society, of social relations and the laws of social development, it follows that it opposes and begins to destroy ideological illusions.

The socialist movement opposes scientific ideas to the ideological preconceptions of the exploiting classes. In other words, in the struggle for socialism scientific ideas are pitted against old illusions. The aim of society without exploitation carries with it the struggle to end ideological illusions of all kinds and to supplant them by science—in other words, to develop a universal scientific ideology.

Instead of developing a false consciousness, the struggle for socialism requires the endeavour to conceive things as they are and not in fantastic connections. Instead of employing illusory ideas to disguise real social relations and real social motives to serve the exploitation of one class by another, it requires true ideas to serve the ending of all exploitation and the satisfaction of the needs of the whole of society.

In the struggle under capitalism, the working-class party must continually fight to eradicate the influence of capitalist ideology in its own ranks and among the working people, to base its whole policy, mass work and propaganda on scientific theory and to educate the whole movement in this theory. Unlike the views of the exploiting classes, the view of society of the working class, which serves the working-class struggle, does not, and cannot, arise and develop spontaneously as a class ideology, but arises and develops as a science.

And when the working class has conquered power and is leading in the building of socialist society, then the task is posed of finally eradicating all the hangovers of the old ideology from all departments of social life. From ideological misconception, society as a whole must advance to a scientific outlook.

This advance is possible and necessary because the ideologies of the old society based on exploitation, with their false consciousness and mystification, lose their basis when socialism comes into being.

In socialism, property in the means of production is public or co-operative property, and production is consciously regulated and planned. For what sort of ideas, then, does socialist economy provide the basis? Precisely for scientific ideas, developing through the extension of scientific understanding of man and his conditions of life. Such ideas alone can serve the consolidation and development of the socialist economic basis. For this end cannot be served by ideas which mystify and delude people. Its success requires knowledge of the laws of nature and society, and a social consciousness informed by such knowledge.

In so far, therefore, as other modes of consciousness persist in socialist society, they are merely hangovers from the old conditions, injurious to the consolidation and development of the socialist system. They must therefore be actively combated, and eventually must give way and disappear before the new scientific socialist consciousness.

The illusions which last longest are those of religion—these being also the oldest. For so long as numbers of people remain comparatively poor and ignorant, some basis remains for religious illusions. Moreover, a religious form can be given also to socialist strivings; and in this respect religion can, under certain conditions, play even a subsidiary positive role in the building of socialism, as we see in the case of the reformed churches in socialist countries.

"The religious reflex of the real world can, in any case, only finally vanish," wrote Marx, "when the practical relations of everyday life offer to man none but perfectly intelligible and reasonable relations with regard to his fellow men and nature.

"The life process of society, which is based on the process of material production, does not strip off its mystical veil until it is treated as production by freely associated men, and is consciously regulated by them in accordance with a settled plan." (*Capital*, Volume I, chapter 1, section 4.)

When the life process of society is indeed carried on by freely associated men in accordance with a settled plan, and when in consequence men are involved in none but perfectly intelligible and reasonable relations with their fellow men and nature, then, naturally enough, there is no basis left for any illusions about the conditions of human life, for any mystification, and human consciousness finally sheds such mystification and illusions.

Scientific Foundations of Communist Consciousness

The new communist consciousness, which is achieved as a universal mode of consciousness in communist society, is the consciousness of new communist people—of working people who have never known exploitation and who are masters of their country, who live by co-operation and are free of the selfish individualism of the private property owner. The conscious existence of such people requires no ideological illusions. On the contrary, it requires a clear, unclouded consciousness, constantly enriched and developed as a result of free inquiry, discussion and criticism.

This presupposes knowledge of society and its laws, and of how to utilise those laws in the interests of society; and knowledge of nature and of how to make it serve man—both constituting parts of a single developing whole of scientific knowledge.

In communist society, natural and social science are no longer divorced. "Only if science starts from nature is it real science", wrote Marx. ". . . History itself is a real part of natural history, of the development of nature into man. Later natural science will include the science of man in the same way as the science of man will include natural science. There will be only one science." (*Economic-Philosophical Manuscripts.*)

In this "one science", Marx observed, "man" or society, becomes "the object of material consciousness"; that is to say, the conception of man and society loses its former illusory ideological character, and is as scientifically based as the conception of nature. And similarly, "the higher needs of 'man as man' become real needs"; that is to say, in place of illusory ideas concerning "the higher needs of man", which in fact express the ideology of exploiting classes who stifle the satisfaction of the real needs of the masses, the conception of man's needs is based on his real needs. These real needs which develop on the basis of the material life of society include far more than elementary physical needs, since from this basis arise the needs of culture, knowledge and fellowship.

The essential feature of "man as man", of man as distinct from the animal, is the creation and satisfaction of his own needs through the social mastery of nature. In society based on exploitation, the mass of people are producing for the benefit of others, not for themselves; only their minimum physical or animal needs are satisfied; hence they are denied a properly human existence, and, as a compensation, their "higher needs" are represented as belonging to some spiritual life, divorced from material life. In communist society, when exploitation of man by man is abolished, the whole of men's requirements, material and spiritual, can be understood as arising from their co-operative mastery of nature, and as being satisfied on the basis of the continuous expansion and perfection of social production.

As a result of the development of socialism, therefore, it eventually comes about that science plays the determining part in forming people's whole outlook. People will then have made themselves free to build up knowledge and control of all the aspects of their lives, for the sake of welfare and happiness and of realising the fullness of life.

Part Three

TRUTH AND FREEDOM

Chapter Ten

TRUTH

Absolute and Partial Truth

WE have seen that in the development of our ideas all kinds of illusions arise, but also truth. What, then, is truth? It is correspondence between ideas and objective reality.

Such correspondence between our ideas and reality is only gradually established, and then the correspondence is often no more than partial and incomplete. For an idea may not in all respects correspond to its object but may correspond only partially; and there may be much in the object which is not reproduced in the idea at all, so that the idea and its correspondence to the object are incomplete. In such cases, we should not say that our idea was false, but yet it would not be absolutely—completely and in all respects—true. Truth, therefore, is not a property which an idea, or a proposition, either possesses or does not possess; it may belong to an idea to a certain degree, within certain limits, in certain respects.

Of course, there can be no doubt that some propositions are indeed absolutely true: they are quite well enough established for us to be able confidently to assert this.

This applies, for example, to many statements of particular facts. These facts were the case, and consequently the propositions which state them are true, absolutely true, and always will be true without modification. William the Conqueror did in fact invade England in the year 1066: therefore the proposition asserting that fact is an absolute truth.

And certain general statements, too, are absolutely true. Lenin instanced two of them in *Materialism and Empirio-*

Criticism—people cannot live without eating, and platonic love alone will not beget babies. These general statements correspond to facts, and their correspondence is absolute. And there are plenty more such general statements whose title to absolute truth need never be questioned.

But most of the statements which we make cannot be said in this way to be absolutely true. For we do not in general confine our statements to "truisms" and to the bald assertion of well-established facts. Most of the statements we make, whether statements of particular facts or of general conclusions, may be true enough for certain purposes but yet not be absolutely true, in the sense of an absolute correspondence between statement and reality. On the contrary, they require to be corrected, improved upon, restated in the light of new experience and new knowledge. But they are not for that reason untrue: they are partial, relative, approximate truths.

This characteristic of truth—that it is for the most part partial and not absolute, approximate and not exact, provisional and not final—is very well known to science. The laws which science establishes certainly reflect objective processes; they correspond to the real motion and interconnection of things in the external world. Yet science has established few laws which can claim to be absolute truths.

For example, the laws of classical mechanics, which formulate the principles of the mechanical interactions of bodies and are continually and confidently employed in all kinds of engineering projects, are now known not to correspond to the movement of matter on a sub-atomic scale. In other words, they are not absolute truths. But we do not for that reason hold that classical mechanics is now shown to be false. Quantum mechanics provides a better approximation than classical mechanics, because its laws not only correspond to the movement of matter on a sub-atomic scale but also include the laws of classical mechanics as limiting cases; but even so, no scientist would claim that quantum mechanics either was an absolute truth.

In general, science has no interest in absolute truth. Indeed, if once any proposition is asserted as an absolute truth, there is an end of all further inquiry: if absolute truth is attained, then there is no room for further investigation. The claim to establish absolute truth is therefore actually antithetical to science, since such a claim must prevent us from carrying on further investigation, from advancing our knowledge, from proceeding from less approximate to more approximate truth, in other words, from pursuing science.

"Really scientific works therefore as a rule avoid such dogmatic and moral expressions as error and truth," wrote Engels, "while these expressions meet us everywhere in works . . . in which empty phrasemongering attempts to impose on us as the sovereign result of sovereign thought." (*Anti-Dühring*, Part I, chapter 9.)

Truth and Error

If we recognise that, outside a very limited field of statements of undoubted fact, the truth of every statement is partial, approximate and provisional only, then it follows that we must always be prepared to correct and modify our statements in the light of new experience.

But more than that. When new experiences arise, calling for the correction and modification of certain statements, then to persist in still asserting them in their old, unmodified form means that they turn from truth into falsehood in the new conditions.

For example, the laws of classical mechanics are still as true as ever they were for most engineering purposes, and no one proposes to dispense with them and reject them as false. Nevertheless, since experience has shown that they do not hold without modification for all known movements of matter, it follows that to assert the Newtonian laws as applying without qualification to all matter in motion would be to assert an untruth.

An approximate and partial truth, which is true enough within certain limits, can become, therefore, an untruth if it is applied beyond those limits.

Again, Marx and Engels stated that when socialist society was established, then the state would eventually wither away.

This was and is true—but not without qualification. Marx and Engels could not state the qualification, because they lacked the necessary experience. But the experience of building socialism in one country, the Soviet Union, has shown that so long as socialist and capitalist countries continue to coexist the state must remain in being in socialist countries; only when socialism is established on a world scale can the state finally wither away. It follows that to assert now, without qualification, that when socialism is established the state will wither away is to assert something false. Indeed, it would be to assert something not merely false but definitely harmful in relation to existing socialist countries: for such an assertion would lead to a lack of concern for strengthening the socialist state, therefore to a possible weakening of the socialist state and to the capitalists' taking advantage of this weakening to intervene and overthrow the socialist system.

This shows that, as Engels pointed out in *Anti-Dühring*, "truth and error, like all concepts which are expressed in polar opposites, have absolute validity only in an extremely limited field . . . As soon as we apply the antithesis between truth and error outside that narrow field . . . both poles of the antithesis change into their opposites, truth becomes error and error truth."

Just as truths are for the most part only approximate and contain the possibility of being converted into untruths, so are many errors found to be not absolute falsehoods but to contain a germ of truth.

Whatever people say is said in terms of the experiences and ideas available to them. It follows that while they may be led to make quite erroneous statements, nevertheless it can happen that erroneous statements reflect, though erroneously, something which is actually the case.

For instance, the Puritans in the English Revolution said they were the elect of God. But even this contained a germ of truth—namely, that they were in fact the rising progressive social force which was bound to overthrow the decaying forces of the old society. Their ideas about being "the elect of God" were certainly erroneous; but this was their way of expressing something which was undoubtedly the case.

Similarly many erroneous views in science and philosophy, which have had to be, not modified, but rejected as errors, concealed a certain truth which received in them an erroneous, distorted expression.

In general, errors which are simply plain, downright errors and nothing else—errors which contain no element of truth at all—are less important and are more easily disposed of than errors which have a certain basis in fact. The former can be refuted by pointing to facts which contradict them, or can be exposed as simple nonsense. The latter are apt to be far more influential, and therefore far more dangerous. And to refute such errors, it is necessary not simply to reject them and sweep them aside but to show how the truth is distorted in them and to re-state that truth free of distortion.

This illustrates what Lenin meant when he wrote in his *Philosophical Notebooks:*

"Philosophical idealism is only nonsense from the standpoint of crude, simple, metaphysical materialism. On the other hand, from the standpoint of dialectical materialism, philosophical idealism is a one-sided, exaggerated . . . development . . . of one of the features, sides, facets of knowledge into an absolute, divorced from matter, from nature, apotheosised. Idealism is clericalism. True. But philosophical idealism is . . . a road to clericalism through one of the shades of the infinitely complex knowledge . . . of man. . . . It is not groundless; it is a sterile flower undoubtedly, but it is a sterile flower that grows on the living tree of . . . human knowledge."

We should recognise, then, that certain erroneous views, including idealist views, could represent, in their time, a contribution to truth—since they were, perhaps, the only ways in which certain truths could first begin to come to expression. But that does not mean that we need have the slightest use for such erroneous views, once their erroneousness can be detected. Idealists made a contribution to philosophy, for example: but that does not imply that we should have the slightest use for idealist philosophy today, in our present conditions, when such truth as was expressed by idealism can be expressed much better without it, and when the essential distortion and falsehood contained in idealism can be fully exposed.

The Relativity of Truth

We have seen, then, that most truth is approximate, partial and incomplete, and that error is to be found in truth, and truth in error. Hence on any subject we generally possess a measure of truth, but not the absolute truth. The measure of truth about anything which we can achieve at any particular time, and how—in what terms and how adequately—we express it, depends on the means which are available at that time for discovering and expressing truth.

Truth is always relative to the particular means whereby we have arrived at it. We can only express the truth about things in terms of our own experience of them and of the operations whereby we have come to know about them.

But at the same time, this truth does relate to the objective, material world and constitutes an ever more adequate reflection of the real properties and laws of motion of objective things and processes.

Therefore while the form of expression of truth and the limits of its approximation to objective reality depend on us, its content, what it is about, the objective reality to which it corresponds, does not depend on us.

In this sense there is an element of both relativity and absoluteness, of subjectivity and objectivity, in every truth. Truth is relative inasmuch as it is expressed in terms depending on the particular circumstances, experience and means of arriving at truth of the people who formulate it. It is absolute inasmuch as what is expressed or reproduced in these terms is objective reality, existing independently of men's knowledge of it.

If the side of relativity only is stressed, then there results subjective idealism and relativism, for which truth relates exclusively to our own observations and operations, not to the objective world, the nature of which is said to be unknowable and inexpressible. Sir Arthur Eddington, for example, noting that our knowledge of the atom was mainly derived from observations of pointer readings and flashes on screens—since these were the indications afforded by the apparatus used to explore the atomic world—concluded that we in fact knew nothing about atoms existing in the objective world but only about the "pointer readings and similar indications." (*The Nature of the Physical World*, chapter 12.)

If, on the other hand, only the other side is stressed, the side of absoluteness or objectivity, then what results is dogmatism. Thus earlier physicists, for example, confident that their physical theories did reflect objective material reality, stated that the world consisted of nothing but little, hard particles like microscopic billiard balls, and that no other kind of material reality existed.

Clearly, it is necessary to take into account, both that truth is reflection of objective reality, and that this reflection is at the same time conditioned and limited by the particular circumstances under which it was created.

"For dialectical materialism," wrote Lenin, "there is no impassable boundary between relative and absolute truth. . . . The materialist dialectics of Marx and Engels certainly does contain relativism, but is not reducible to relativism, that is, it recognises the relativity of all our knowledge, not in the sense of the denial of objective truth, but in the sense of the historically conditioned nature of the limits of the approximation of our knowledge of this truth." (*Materialism and Empirio-Criticism*, chapter 2.)

Asking "Does objective truth exist?" Lenin pointed out that two questions must be distinguished and not confounded together:

"(1) Is there such a thing as objective truth, that is, can human ideas have a content that does not depend on a subject, that does not depend either on a human being or on humanity?

"(2) If so, can human ideas, which give expression to objective truth, express it all at one time, as a whole, unconditionally, absolutely, or only approximately, relatively?"

The answer to these questions is clear.

(1) Human ideas can, and do, have a content that does not depend either on particular people or on humanity generally,

since these ideas reproduce objective reality existing independently of any person's idea of it.

(2) These ideas do not reproduce objective reality in its entirety and with complete faithfulness, but only approximately, and relatively to the way in which people have been able to discover and express truth.

Since truth consists in the correspondence of ideas with objective reality, it is evident that we have always to reckon with both sides of the relationship—the subject as well as the object. On the one hand is objective reality, which depends in no way on the ideas which we may form about it. On the other hand, ideas are formed in the process of human activity and are therefore conditioned by the nature of the activity out of which they are produced. How, in what form, with what approximation, reality is expressed in our ideas depends on us and our activity—that is, on the subjective factor. But that which is expressed in our ideas, their content, what they are about, does not depend on any subjective factor, but constitutes as Lenin expressed it in the same chapter, an "objectively existing measure or model existing independently of humanity to which our relative knowledge approximates".

Relative and Absolute Truth: Causality, Space and Time

As an example of how absolute truth is expressed through relative truth, we can consider the conceptions of causality, and of space and time.

Our ideas about causality in nature are produced as a result of our experiences in dealing with natural objects. We learn from experience that we ourselves can produce changes in nature in a regulated way, and on this basis we formulate ideas of causal connections and causal law. Thus the way in which we come to recognise causality, and the ideas of causal connections which we express from time to time, are subjectively conditioned. With the development of production and of social relations and social activities, the conception of causality has been modified and changed—animism, final causes, mechanical interaction and dialectical interaction being so many stages in the development of the idea of causality.

But while our ideas about causality arise from our experience and depend upon the character of that experience, the existence of causality in nature is an objective fact, altogether independent of ourselves and our experience. It is because we, as subjects, experience our own power to cause changes in external objects, and similarly experience the compelling power of those objects upon ourselves, that we first arrive at the idea of causality; and that idea is elaborated and developed in relation to the development of social life. But the reality which corresponds to this idea, and which is reproduced with a greater or lesser degree of adequacy in our ideas of causal connections, is an objective reality, independent of ourselves, independent of any relationship between subject and object.

Idealism stresses only the subjective side of the idea of causality. Idealist philosophers have maintained that causality was invented simply to bring a rational order into our experience and that it is then erroneously attributed to the external world independent of experience. But in opposition to idealism, "the recognition of objective law in nature and the recognition that this law is reflected with approximate fidelity in the mind of man is materialism". (Lenin, *Materialism and Empirio-Criticism,* chapter 3.)

It is the same with our conceptions of space and time. Starting with our perceptions of the passage of time and of the spatial characteristics and relations of objects, and with the discovery of methods of expressing the spatial and temporal properties and relations of things by means of measurements, our general conceptions of space and time have been gradually developed and elaborated. The conception of space and time is always relative to human experience, but space and time do not depend on human experience. On the contrary, "the basic forms of all being are space and time" (Engels, *Anti-Dühring,* Part I, chapter 5), and human conceptions of space and time are always approximate reflections of real spatial and temporal relations.

"Recognising the existence of objective reality, i.e., matter in motion, independently of our mind, materialism must also inevitably recognise the objective reality of space and time," wrote Lenin. "... The mutability of human conceptions of space and time no more refutes the objective reality of space and time than the mutability of scientific knowledge of the structure and forms of matter in motion refutes the objective reality of the external world. . . . It is one thing, how, with the help of various sense-organs, man perceives space, and how, in the course of a long historical development, abstract ideas of space are derived from these perceptions; it is an entirely different thing whether there is an objective reality independent of mankind which corresponds to these perceptions and conceptions of mankind. . . . Our experience and our perceptions adapt themselves more and more to objective space and time, and reflect them ever more correctly and profoundly." (*Materialism and Empirio-Criticism*, chapter 3.)

The Progress of Truth

How far is the human mind capable of attaining to and establishing truth?

Complete, full, absolute truth—the whole truth and nothing but the truth about everything—is something we can never attain. But it is something towards which we are always approximating.

We advance towards full, comprehensive truth, embracing not only particular facts but general laws and interconnections, by means of a series of particular, provisional and approximate truths. The truth which can be formulated by any individual, or by mankind at any particular time, is always approximate, incomplete and subject to correction. But individuals learn from each other, both from each other's achievements and from each other's mistakes; and the same applies to the succeeding generations of society. Therefore the sum of incomplete, particular, provisional and approximate truths is always approaching nearer to but never reaching the goal of complete comprehensive, final and absolute truth.

The world which is reproduced in our ideas and statements really exists. They are true in proportion as they correspond to it and reproduce it correctly. We test this truth in experience, in practice. The correspondence is never complete, exact, absolute. But it continually approaches yet is always infinitely distant from that absolute limit as truth and knowledge continually advance, as men perfect their instruments of production and their means of acquiring knowledge.

Thus Engels wrote (*Anti-Dühring*, Part I, chapter 3):

"The perception that all the phenomena of nature are systematically interconnected drives science on to prove this systematic interconnection throughout, both in general and in detail. But an adequate, exhaustive, scientific statement of this interconnection, the formulation in thought of an exact picture of the world-system in which we live, is impossible for us and will always remain impossible.

"If at any time in the evolution of mankind such a final, conclusive system of the interconnections within the world—physical as well as mental and historical—were brought to completion, this would mean that human knowledge had reached its limit. . . . Mankind therefore finds itself faced with a contradiction: on the one hand, it has to gain an exhaustive knowledge of the world system in all its interrelations; and on the other hand, because of the nature both of man and of the world system, this task can never be completely fulfilled. But this contradiction lies not only in the nature of the two factors—the world and man—it is also the main lever of all intellectual advance, and finds its solution continuously, day by day, in the endless progressive evolution of humanity. . . .

"Each mental image of the world system is and remains in actual fact limited, objectively through the historical stage, and subjectively through the physical and mental constitution of its maker."

Nevertheless, through the endless progressive evolution of such limited mental images of the objective world, mankind continually attains more complete truth, more comprehensive knowledge.

"Is human thought sovereign?" Engels asked, meaning thereby: can we achieve the complete truth about everything, can we achieve comprehensive and fully certified knowledge?

"Before we can answer yes or no we must inquire: what is

human thought? Is it the thought of the individual man? No. But it exists only as the individual thought of many billions of past, present and future men. . . . In other words, the sovereignty of thought is realised in a series of extremely unsovereignly-thinking human beings; the knowledge which has an unconditional claim to truth is realised in a series of relative errors; neither the one nor the other can be fully realised except through an endless eternity of human existence.

"Here again we find the same contradiction as we found above, namely, between the character of human thought, necessarily conceived as absolute, and its reality in individual human beings with their extremely limited thought. This is a contradiction which can only be solved in the infinite progression, or what is for us, at least from a practical standpoint, the endless succession, of generations of mankind. In this sense human thought is just as much sovereign as not sovereign, and its capacity for knowledge just as much unlimited as limited. It is sovereign and unlimited in its disposition, its vocation, its possibilities and its historical purpose; it is not sovereign and it is limited in its individual expression and in its realisation at each particular moment." (Engels, *Anti-Dühring*, Part I, chapter 9.)

The materialist theory of truth shows us how to avoid dogmatism, which lays down general principles, however arrived at, as unalterable and final truths—refusing to examine their foundations and refusing to alter and correct them, or if need be reject them altogether, in the light of new experience and new circumstances.

And at the same time it shows us how to avoid the narrow empiricism which confines itself to collecting and co-ordinating facts, is not interested in discovering the underlying laws of motion and interconnection manifested in those facts, and is sceptical about all bold generalisations and theories. Like dogmatism, empiricism cannot see beyond the limited experience of the present moment.

These attitudes, common enough in philosophy and the sciences, confront us also in the working-class movement. In the working-class movement dogmatism consists in learning certain formulas by rote and thinking that every new problem can be solved by simple repetition of these formulas. As a result of this, people fail to assimilate the lessons of experience and prove unable boldly to advance new policies to meet a new situation. Empiricism, on the other hand, consists in being engrossed in petty, day-to-day "practical" problems, attending only to these and regarding all other questions as unimportant, as the concern of "intellectuals" and not of practical workers. As a result of this, too, people fail to assimilate the lessons of experience and prove unable boldly to advance new policies. Thus both dogmatism and empiricism lead to the same result, and are capable of doing great harm to the working-class movement, preventing it from finding the right road leading towards the achievement of socialism.

Marxism is both critical and revolutionary.

It is critical because it is against dogmas, insists on continual testing and re-testing of all ideas and all policies in the crucible of revolutionary practice—recognising that truth changes, that what is true enough today may become false tomorrow unless it is corrected and developed into new truth.

But simply to be critical is not enough. A merely critical attitude is negative and can lead to paralysis of action.

Marxism is also revolutionary. It is revolutionary because it does not only criticise, it goes forward to replace the old by the new. It is firm in its standpoint, certain of the truth and justice of its cause, confident in the correctness of its principles as the basis for the future advance, and verifies its revolutionary ideas in revolutionary practice.

Chapter Eleven

THE ROOTS OF KNOWLEDGE

What is Knowledge?

IN achieving true ideas about things we also win and extend knowledge about them. What, then, is knowledge?

Unless we make our ideas correspond with reality, we certainly do not possess knowledge. To win knowledge is to replace ignorance or untrue ideas by true ideas. Hence the growth of knowledge is to be found in the growth of true ideas within the totality of ideas, some of which are true while others are not.

But simply to equate knowledge with truth is not to define knowledge. For the question arises: How do we *know* that our true ideas are true? Simply to state or believe something true is not to know it.

For example, some astronomers say there is life on Mars. Perhaps there is, in which case what they say is true. But they do not yet *know* there is life on Mars, for they have not yet gathered sufficient evidence. The question will be settled when space-ships make a thorough survey of Mars. On the other hand, when astronomers say that Mars is a planet they are expressing knowledge of the matter; for in this case what they say is based on reliable methods of investigation.

Again, the ancient Greek philosophers said that bodies were composed of atoms. We today know that this is true—but they did not. It was simply a lucky guess on their part. How do we know that bodies are composed of atoms? It is because while they merely speculated and made lucky guesses about the nature of matter, we have systematically investigated it, have based our ideas on such investigation, and so have tested and proved the truth of those particular ideas. On the other hand, there remain many things about which we know no more than the ancient Greeks—we are merely speculating about such things, just as they were; and just as with them, it remains to be found out how near the truth are our speculations.

We gain knowledge, then, only in so far as we develop our ideas in such a way that their correspondence with reality is proved and tested. Only then can we lay claim to knowledge.

The development of knowledge is therefore the development of a special quality within the total development of our ideas, theories and views about things. Many ideas, theories and views about things have been worked out, often in the most systematic and logical way, but they have been merely speculative even if true, and have mostly been quite illusory. But in the course of the development of ideas there also occurs a development of knowledge, which is the development of ideas which not only correspond with reality but whose correspondence is proved and tested.

Our knowledge, then, is the sum of our conceptions, views and propositions which have been established and tested as correct reflections, so far as they go, of objective reality.

The Social Character of Knowledge

Knowledge is essentially a social product. It is built up socially, as a product of the social activity of men.

Some philosophers give both themselves and their readers a lot of trouble by trying to trace the growth of knowledge in the mind of the isolated individual and to find its roots in individual experience. In trying to do this, they set themselves an insoluble problem, since knowledge is not, and cannot be, built up in that way. An individual acting alone, cut off from contact with other people and relying only on himself, could acquire scarcely any knowledge at all—and that only of particular facts. Hence some of these philosophers were only following their own premises through to the logical conclusion when they announced that a man can know nothing except his own momentary existence, and certainly not the existence of the material world and of other people—though they were less logical in publishing this conclusion, since on their own showing they had no reason to believe that there existed anyone capable of reading it.

Of course, knowledge is built up by individuals—just as everything man creates is created by individuals; but it is built up by individuals acting in co-operation, depending on one another, communicating their experiences and their ideas. Many individuals in society can do what none of them individually could possibly do—and one of these things is to build up human knowledge. Every individual acquires a great deal of knowledge from his own experience; but he would not do so apart from his association with others, and if he did not learn from others what they had already learned. The very means for forming and expressing ideas, namely, language, without which no ideas would be possible, is a social product and exists only as the common possession of a society. Some individuals make especially great contributions to building up new knowledge, while many make no contribution at all; yet the former would not have made their contribution if they had not been members of a particular society, if they were not in communication with their fellows, if they had not learned what their society had to teach, if they had not had at their disposal the numerous material and intellectual means for acquiring knowledge which their society had produced.

It is, then, only in society that knowledge is acquired and built up, and its roots lie in the social activities of man. It is built up by the interchange of experiences and ideas between members of society in the course of their various forms of social activity, and it is sifted and tested in the same process.

As a result, the sum of social knowledge—that is, of knowledge stored and available to society—is always greater than the knowledge possessed by individuals. Many people and many generations build up far more knowledge than any individual can possibly acquire. This knowledge is stored by society, being distributed in the first place amongst the many memories of many people, and secondly, being permanently recorded in writing—so that in this respect books and records of various kinds serve as a physical repository of the knowledge acquired in society. For instance, no one knows all the telephone numbers in London, but this knowledge is socially available and constantly made use of through the telephone directory. Again, no one knows everything discovered by the sciences, but the totality of this knowledge is socially available, and the organisation exists (though it could be greatly improved) for making use of it. So there exists in society an accumulation of social knowledge, to which individuals contribute and which individuals can draw upon.

Social Practice and Social Knowledge

All human association arises and develops from man's basic association in production. The development of knowledge, therefore, which is a product of human association, depends in the last analysis upon the development of social production. Men first began to form ideas in the process of production. And the development of thought and of knowledge, beginning in men's productive activity, can at no point be dissociated from it.

In the course of history knowledge has been won and consolidated step by step. And it is as men have striven to develop their forces of production, and to reconstitute their production relations corresponding to the development of their forces of production, that they have been impelled to strive for new knowledge and to overcome both the ignorance and false ideas which impeded their material progress.

The sum total of knowledge, and its character, at any stage of social development is always dependent on and relative to the stage of development of production. For what men have been able to find out about nature and society always depends on their practical intercourse with nature and with one another, relates to the practical problems set by that intercourse, and is tested in the practical solution of those problems. On this basis they work out the categories of thought, modes of inference and methods of investigation by means of which the edifice of knowledge is built.

But while the development of knowledge depends in the last analysis on the development of production, it does not depend on production alone, but its development is mediated by the various forms of social activity and relationship which arise from production. The build-up of knowledge, dependent on material productive activity, is also dependent, in class society, on classes and the class struggle. The task of preserving and enlarging the body of knowledge has in the main devolved upon the representatives of definite classes. And it has been largely as a result of the activity and struggle—economic, political, scientific and artistic—of different classes in different periods that new knowledge, both of nature and of society, has been won.

Theory and Practice in the Build-up of Knowledge

In general, the acquisition of knowledge in society is something which arises out of the sum total of the practical activities of the members of society, their intercourse with external nature and with one another. Apart from such practical activities, such active relationships, we could not acquire knowledge of anything, for there would be no basis on which to derive ideas which corresponded with objective reality or to test that correspondence.

Hence Lenin wrote: "The standpoint of life, of practice, should be first and fundamental in the theory of knowledge." (*Materialism and Empirio-Criticism*, chapter 2.)

What exactly do we mean by "practice" or "practical activity"?

(1) First of all, practice consists of movements of the organs of the human body which cause changes in the surrounding world.

(2) But not simply any such movement, any such act, counts as practice or as practical activity. For instance, we would not count various simple reflex actions as examples of practice. Nor would we give the title of practical activity to the actions of a sleepwalker. Practical activity is essentially human conscious activity; that is to say, it is done deliberately, with (*a*) an idea of the end result, or aim, to be achieved, and (*b*) some consciousness of the conditions of the action and of the properties of the subject of the action and of the means through

which the aim can be achieved.

(3) Thirdly, practice is social. There is, of course, individual practice—that is, the practical activities carried out by an individual on his own—and also social practice, activities which can be carried out only by a number of individuals acting in association. But no conscious practical activity would develop apart from man's social life and the conditioning of individuals by their society.

In society, people develop many means to their practical activity. Speech, by which we communicate with one another, is one of them. Hence a large and important part is played in our practical activity by speech, for this is certainly an important means of bringing things about.

The above three points define what we mean by "practice".

Knowledge, then, arises out of practice because it arises out of the development of ideas corresponding to the various conditions, subjects and means of our practical activities. Practice demands such ideas, and they are developed in accordance with the development of practice. Knowledge is acquired just in so far as practice creates the demand for true ideas about various things, and provides the means and opportunities for working them out and testing them.

At all times it has been social practice which has impelled people to develop and perfect their knowledge—the requirements of the development of material productive activity, and no less the requirements of the different classes, who have experienced the necessity of acquiring ever deeper knowledge about various aspects of nature and society in order to carry forward their own practical interests.

Thus as men have improved their instruments of production, their production technique, their practical ability to master nature, so has their knowledge of nature advanced. For changes in production set problems for knowledge and at the same time provide the means for tackling them. New fields of knowledge are thus opened up, and new and far-reaching conclusions reached. These in turn contribute to further technical advance and are tested, and also further developed, in their application in practice.

The capitalist class, in undertaking the development of modern industry, gave a profound impulse to the deepening of natural knowledge, particularly of physical and chemical processes. The working class in turn, in undertaking and leading the building of socialism, requires and creates the conditions for far more comprehensive natural knowledge.

Similarly, as men have striven to improve their well-being and have succeeded in establishing new and higher social relations in place of old and outmoded ones, so has their knowledge of themselves and of society advanced.

The knowledge of the laws of social change embodied in scientific socialism could be achieved only when, with the development of the working class, the struggle for socialism became a practical question. In general, in each historical epoch the extent of knowledge of society and its laws has always corresponded to the practical social tasks of the epoch. Thus capitalism, by the development of the world market and then the division of the world among imperialist powers, stimulated studies in world history and in societies at various stages of their development, which resulted in a tremendous enlargement of social and historical research. Going beyond this, the struggle for socialism laid the basis for truly scientific knowledge of society, penetrating to the basic social relationships and laws of social development.

On the other hand, people do not and cannot acquire knowledge of things about which their practice has not yet given them the need or opportunity of finding out anything. For example, while people still lived in small local communes and used very primitive instruments of production they did not and could not develop any knowledge of geography, or mathematics, or astronomy, or mechanics. They knew very little, though they had all sorts of ideas about things of which they knew little. Before capitalism and the emergence of the working class people did not and could not acquire much knowledge about the laws of development of society. They had all sorts of ideas about such things, including ideas of socialism, but very little knowledge.

Knowledge, which arises out of practice, is tested in practice.

For the correspondence of our ideas about the conditions, subjects and means of practical activity with the objective reality independent of our ideas is tested, and can in the last resort only be tested, by the results of the activity which is guided by those ideas.

Every act is done with certain expectations, which are based on the ideas which guide the act. The only final test of the correspondence of ideas with reality lies in the fulfilment or non-fulfilment of the expectations based on ideas.

If, on the other hand, we have ideas which are in no way related to expectations of the results of practice, and which therefore cannot be tested by reference to the fulfilment or non-fulfilment of expectations, then there is no way of ever deciding the correspondence or non-correspondence of such ideas with reality—in other words, they can form no part of knowledge, but are merely illusory or speculative.

So Marx wrote: "The question whether objective truth can be attributed to human thinking is not a question of theory but is a practical question. In practice man must prove the truth, i.e., the reality and power, the 'this-sidedness' of his thinking. The dispute over the reality or non-reality [that is, the correspondence or non-correspondence with reality—M.C.] of thinking which is isolated from practice is a purely scholastic question." (*Theses on Feuerbach*, II.)

We gain knowledge, then, by working out ideas arising out of problems of practice, and we test our knowledge step by step, in other words, establish it as knowledge, by reference to the fulfilment or non-fulfilment of our expectations in practice.

Hence knowledge in its development continually passes through a cycle of three phases:

(1) Social practice, the development of production and of social relationships, setting problems for theoretical solution.

(2) The elaboration of theories arising from those problems, based on the available experiences, and the logical working out of those theories.

(3) The application of those theories in social practice, testing, verifying and correcting them in the process of putting them to use.

This is a never-ending process. For whatever may be our knowledge, new demands of practice lead to new extensions of knowledge. Moreover, existing knowledge must always be brought into conformity with the lessons and demands of practice. Hence as new knowledge is won, old theories are reformulated, existing knowledge is both corrected and deepened.

Sense-Perception, the Beginning of All Knowledge

In this whole process of acquiring and building knowledge, on what do we have to rely in obtaining information about things, and in carrying out the test of the fulfilment or non-fulfilment of expectations? We have to rely on our senses.

Separating knowledge from practice, many philosophers have also maintained that knowledge is built up by a process of "pure thought". The senses, they say, are unreliable, and cannot be a source of knowledge, to gain which we should ignore the data of sense and rely on the intellect alone.

Yet human knowledge, capable as it is of indefinite expansion, is always the work of the human brain. The brain is the organ of the most complicated relations of man with the external world, and in elaborating these relationships we are dependent, in the first place, on the information received through the senses as a result of our interaction with the things outside us. The beginning of all our knowledge, then, can be nothing else than the sense perceptions we acquire in the course of life activity. Knowledge can be built on no other basis than the information gained through the exercise of our senses, through sense perceptions which have their source in the objective material world.

This materialist point of view in the theory of knowledge was embodied in Lenin's well-known definition of matter, as "the objective reality which is given to man by his sensations, and which is reflected by our sensations while existing independently of them". (*Materialism and Empirio-Criticism*, chapter 2.) This emphasises that the material world is the world accessible to the senses. What we know about the material world is derived from the exercise of our senses. Any supposed knowledge which goes beyond that is not knowledge but fantasy, and any supposed objective reality inaccessible to the senses is not real but imaginary.

It may be objected that these are dogmatic statements. But there is no dogma here. On the contrary, once we get away from this fundamental materialist position we get away from all verifiable knowledge and into the realms of pure speculation. Once we allow ourselves to start inventing "realities" which cannot in any way be detected by the instrumentality of the senses, we are away into the clouds. We are faced with the sort of questions the later scholastics used to ask: "How many angels can stand on the point of a needle?" There is no possible way of detecting them, and so of checking the answer to the question. That is why we can be sure that such questions and such speculations have nothing whatever to do with knowledge, and are simply ways of bamboozling people.

Indeed, to say we gain knowledge only through the exercise of the senses in the course of practical activity is no more a dogma than to say we cannot live without eating. To promise people "supersensible" or "transcendent" knowledge is like promising them the means of eternal life while offering them nothing to eat—and the promises are often made by the same learned and pious people. The materialist theory of knowledge is a defence and weapon against such deceptions.

Hence we should steadily reject all "principles" and dogmas which claim to be known independent of experience, independent of the exercise of the senses, whether by some inner light or by virtue of some authority. We should not trust those who seek to impose their views because they claim to possess some special intellectual gift, or to have been initiated into some mystery, or to be empowered with some special authority. We should be sceptical, and accept nothing from anyone which cannot be explained and justified in terms of practice and sense experience. For we cannot know of the existence or properties of anything except in so far as its existence and properties are capable of being detected, in some way, directly or indirectly, by our senses.

The Reliability of the Senses

But can we trust our senses? How do we know that our senses do not always deceive us, as they sometimes do in hallucinations and dreams? More generally, how do we know that anything at all exists corresponding to our perceptions?

To answer these questions we must remember that we acquire and build up our perceptions of objects only in the course of practical activity. The information which we gain through the senses does not just come to us. We get it in practical life, by conscious, practical interaction with the objects outside us.

A new-born baby, for example, starts with a mass of confused impressions of itself and the outside world. It begins to use its senses and to get information about the objects which surround it when it begins to reach out for those objects, to see what it can do with them, to investigate them, to experiment with and test them in all sorts of ways.

Just as each member of the human race starts getting information about the world in that way, so that is the way in which all knowledge about the world is acquired and built up. Our first confused impressions of an unfamiliar thing are certainly not reliable and provide little if any information about it. We use our senses to obtain information about it by investigating it. And we continually test the reliability of our perceptions of it in the course of our practical dealings with it.

Apart from such practical dealings with things outside us, we have no way of telling whether our perceptions agree with objects or, indeed, whether any object at all corresponds to them. But when we act on our perceptions, and when we turn things to our own use according to the qualities we perceive in them, then we test whether or not, and how far, our perceptions agree with reality outside ourselves.

A philosopher sitting alone in his study and trying to conjure up knowledge from the inner resources of his own mind may make great difficulty about this. He wonders whether his study, his books, the chair he is sitting on, and his own body sitting on it, really exist, or whether they are some kind of dream or illusion in his mind. But outside his study, outside the academic discussions of philosophers, there is no difficulty.

"Human action had solved the difficulty long before human ingenuity invented it", wrote Engels. "The proof of the pudding is in the eating. From the moment we turn to our own use these objects according to the qualities we perceive in them, we put to an infallible test the correctness or otherwise of our sense perceptions. If these perceptions have been wrong, then our estimate of the use to which an object can be turned must also be wrong, and our attempt must fail. But if we succeed in accomplishing our aim, if we find that the object does agree with our idea of it, and does answer the purpose we intended for it, then that is positive proof that our perceptions of it and of its qualities, so far, agree with reality outside ourselves. . . . So long as we take care to train and use our senses properly, and to keep our action within the limits prescribed by perceptions properly made and properly used, so long we shall find that the result of our action proves the conformity of our perceptions with the objective nature of the things perceived." (*Socialism, Utopian and Scientific*, Introduction.)

The material world exists, and we are part of it. We learn about the bodies outside us and about the state of our own bodies by our senses. So naturally we have no other way of finding out about the world—that is, of gaining knowledge—than through the exercise of our senses. Nor can our senses be so constituted as always or even usually to deceive us. If they were, we would not be able to live at all.

"The products of the human brain," wrote Engels, "being in the last analysis also products of nature, do not contradict the rest of nature but are in correspondence with it." (*Anti-Dühring*, Part I, chapter 3.) Our senses are necessarily so constituted as to provide us with perceptions which agree with reality outside ourselves. These perceptions, which are the beginning of all our knowledge, are gained in the course of practical activity, and their agreement with reality is brought about and tested in practical activity.

So all our knowledge—that is to say, the sum of our conceptions which are established and tested as correct reflections so far as they go, of objective reality—is established on the basis of the perceptions we gain in our practical activity, and is likewise tested in the same activity.

The Expansion, Incompleteness and Criticism of Knowledge

Some philosophers have believed that the goal of knowledge is to attain a complete, rounded-off system, encompassing knowledge of everything that exists to be known. And a few have believed that they themselves had actually attained such a goal—as was alleged of the late Master of Balliol, Professor B. Jowett:

> Here I stand, my name is Jowett,
> There's no knowledge but I know it.
> I am Master of this College,
> And what I don't know isn't knowledge.

Yet neither as a whole nor in any of its various departments can human knowledge ever be finished, finalised and rounded-off. Knowledge is always growing and developing. Indeed, this is obvious when we consider that our knowledge all arises from and is tested in practice, and is derived from the sense perceptions we gain in practical activity. We shall never have done everything that can be done, or have examined every aspect of everything that ever existed, exists or will exist. There will always be more to do, more to find out in doing it, and therefore more to know.

So knowledge is always expanding, or, at least, capable of expansion; and therefore always incomplete. And there are two aspects of this expansion and incompleteness of knowledge.

The first aspect is a quantitative one. New knowledge is always being added to old knowledge, so that we come to know more. And this expansion takes place in two dimensions, so to speak—in breadth and depth of knowledge. We get to know about new things which we did not know about before; and we get to know more about the things concerning which we already knew something. In this way we can always know more, but never know all.

For example, in modern physics we have got to know about "fundamental particles" the existence of which was not previously known; and in getting to know about them, we have also increased or deepened our knowledge about atoms and their structure, concerning which something was already known. But because we have in this way increased the breadth and depth of our physical knowledge, we cannot conclude that we have completed our physical knowledge. On the contrary, all we should conclude is that while we have more physical knowledge than our predecessors, our successors, starting where we leave off, will have more still.

The second aspect is a qualitative one. When we get to know more, the addition of this more to what we already knew does not leave what we already knew unaffected. On the contrary, knowledge of new things and more knowledge of old things throws a new light, so to speak, on what we already knew. As a result, we can find new implications and new significance in what we had already established; and at the same time we find that, in the light of the new knowledge, certain implications drawn from the old were wrong, and it must be reconsidered and reformulated in various ways.

For example, new discoveries in physics which were summed up in quantum mechanics cast a new light on the older discoveries in physics which were summed up in classical mechanics. As a result, the old knowledge had to be reconsidered and reformulated in various ways, and it became clear that some of the conclusions drawn from it were wrong. Again, when in the practice of building socialism in one country, the Soviet Union, new knowledge was gained about the nature and functions of the socialist state, it became necessary to reconsider and reformulate some of the propositions about the socialist state previously put forward by Marxism, and it became clear that some of the conclusions drawn from it were wrong.

None of this means that old knowledge turns out to have been illusory and so not to have been real knowledge at all. All it means is that the incompleteness of old knowledge leads to the necessity of its being critically reformulated in the light of new knowledge. And the same will apply, of course, to the new knowledge itself, when it in turn becomes old knowledge.

Knowledge grows through a process of not only adding to but also perfecting and correcting the already existing body of knowledge. In no field is knowledge ever perfect, final and complete. Consequently, whatever knowledge has been established must be accepted only as a point of departure for further advances of knowledge—just as whatever has been achieved in practice should not be regarded as a final achievement but only as a point of departure for further gains. This means that we must also be prepared to recognise that all knowledge is always limited, incomplete, defective, and so requires not only supplementation but also criticism in order to carry it forward and advance to new conquests.

Chapter Twelve

THE GROWTH OF KNOWLEDGE

From Ignorance to Knowledge

THE acquisition of knowledge, and the build-up of knowledge, is by its very nature always a process of the passage from ignorance to knowledge, from not knowing things to knowing them. Whether we consider our knowledge in general, or our knowledge of some particular thing, it is always the case that first we knew nothing and then gradually acquired knowledge.

Hence in his Encyclopaedia article on *Karl Marx* Lenin wrote that the theory of knowledge must study "the transition from *non*-knowledge to knowledge". "We must not regard our knowledge as ready made", he wrote, ". . . but must determine how knowledge emerges from ignorance, how incomplete, inexact knowledge becomes more complete and more exact." (*Materialism and Empirio-Criticism*, chapter 2.)

Many philosophers, on the other hand, have taken it for granted that knowledge can only be derived from previous knowledge. Therefore they have supposed that there must be fundamental certainties, from which all knowledge is derived. This leads them to two opposite but equally misleading conclusions. On the one hand, they invent various principles which they say are certain, and then claim that they know and have proved all the propositions deduced from these principles. On the other hand, they deny a great part of our real knowledge, because it cannot be so deduced. Thus, for example, philosophers have deduced all manner of conclusions about God and the ultimate nature of reality from first principles; and on the other hand, they have rejected the whole of our knowledge about the material world on the grounds that it cannot be justified by anything they are prepared to accept as absolutely certain and self-evident.

Yet the real starting point of knowledge is not knowledge but ignorance, and not certainty but uncertainty. We always build up knowledge from a previous state of lack of knowledge. Hence to try to build up systems of knowledge from self-evident premises is to misunderstand the whole problem of building knowledge, and must always be in vain.

How, then, is knowledge built up from ignorance? This is done, and can only be done, through our sensuous interaction with things. It is done by human brains, which, as we have repeatedly said, are the organs of the most complicated relations between man and the external world. By the perceptual awareness of things which results from entering into various active relations with them, we come to know them where previously we did not know them. And the more various the relations with things into which we enter, the more do we consequently get to know about them. Hence knowledge is the product of our consciously entering into active relations with things. The transition from lack of knowledge to knowledge is wrought by human activity passing from lack of relation with things to relation with things.

For instance, we did not know the source of the Nile; we got to know it by going there. We did not know the composition of atoms; we got to know it by performing experiments. We did not know the distances of the stars; we got to know by devising methods of measuring them. We did not know the laws of development of human society; we got to know by consciously striving to utilise them for bringing about a new stage of social development.

Perceptions and Judgments

The first requisite for the build-up of knowledge is obtaining perceptions—that is, making observations arising out of various relationships with things. First we had no observations relative to some thing or process, then we obtained such observations; this is the first step. Without performing it, there can only be ignorance, not knowledge—either blank ignorance or else, as often happens, ignorance camouflaged by illusory or speculative theories about things.

Secondly, having entered into relationship with things and obtained observations about them, we must go on to formulate judgments or propositions about them and their properties and relations. We must employ the laws of thought—that is, the logical laws for the reflection of objective reality in terms of ideas—in order to express in ideas, in judgments or propositions, the results of observations.

The build-up of knowledge always involves the passage from sensations to ideas. All the higher animals have sensations, and in their sensations possess definite, concrete information about things, which they learn to make more reliable and which they use in their life activity. But only in man is this information provided by the senses converted into knowledge, in the sense of being expressed in ideas and propositions.

Here we understand the term "knowledge" in the definite sense of *human* knowledge. The sense in which, for example, a dog knows the way home is different from the sense in which a man knows the way, for in the latter case it is expressible in ideas and propositions which can be communicated. Ideas and propositions are communicated, shared and discussed by people in their social life, and it is this expression of information in ideas and propositions which constitutes the essential feature of human knowledge. People acquire and possess knowledge just in so far as they pass from the sensations which are particular to each individual and which they possess in common with all animals, to the ideas, judgments, propositions which are socially communicated and are peculiar to man.

Perception by itself, then, is only the condition of knowledge, but not as yet its realisation. The knowledge of things possessed by man is achieved by passing from sensations to judgments founded on sensations.

Thus knowledge is always being built up by a continual cycle of qualitatively distinct activities which together make up the whole process of knowing—entering into active relationships with things; obtaining from this relationship perceptions and observations; formulating judgments out of the observations; utilising these judgments to direct the further active relationships with things, leading to further observations, further judgments, and so on without end.

From Superficial to More Profound Judgments

Sense perception reproduces things as they immediately appear through their action on our sense organs. The senses give only particular pieces of information about particular things conditioned by the particular circumstances under which we are perceiving them.

By expressing the information obtained from perception in propositions people arrive at judgments expressing conclusions from the comparison and putting together of many particular data of perception. "The first step in the process of knowledge," wrote Mao Tse-tung in his essay *On Practice*, in which he summed up the essentials of the materialist theory of knowledge, "is contact with the things of the external world; this belongs to the stage of perception. The second step is a synthesis of the data of perception by making a rearrangement or reconstruction; this belongs to the stage of conception, judgment and inference."

For example, from many perceptions of many members of society we reach such conclusions (all of which represent elementary items of social knowledge) as "dogs bark", "cows give milk", "water turns into ice in cold weather", and so on. Such judgments are, as Mao expressed it, "a synthesis of the data of perception".

To form such judgments about things depends not on a single observation by a single person but on several or many observations by several or many people. And the more various the observations, the more various the circumstances in which and the angles from which they are made, and the more various the changes and relationships of the object which they cover, the more comprehensively and faithfully can the judgment reflect the objective properties, relations and forms of motion of the object.

Observation is itself an activity, since we must consciously bring ourselves into relation with something if we are to observe it, and must bring ourselves into more varied relation —noting various different aspects of the thing, its various changes, and so on—if we are to observe it more fully. But observation itself passes from what may be called passive observation to active observation, and it is the latter which is of primary importance for building up fuller knowledge of things.

Observation in itself does not change that which is observed. In this sense, it is passive. A bird-watcher, for example, obtains knowledge about birds, but he does not interfere with them in any way in making his observations; on the contrary, in this case he must be very careful not to do so. Active observation arises when we ourselves, by our activity, take a part in bringing about various changes in things, and observe the results of the relationships or changes which we ourselves have effected under our own control.

One of the most important methods of active observation of things is, for example, to measure them. The process of measurement, whatever it may be we are measuring, involves bringing one thing into relationship with another thing and noting the results. Other methods of active observation are, for example, to break something down into its parts or elements and then to reconstitute it again, or to effect changes in its properties through the agency of other things. In general, by elaborating methods of active observation suitable to the different things we want to know about and what we want to know about them, we obtain many significant observations, leading us to conclusions about their properties, relations, motions, laws of motion, causes and effects, composition, and so on.

Having acquired, through both passive and active observations and their translation into judgments, a certain body of knowledge expressed in judgments, we can then make use of this knowledge in order to obtain more knowledge. For it will suggest new fields of exploration and methods for establishing new relationships with things. Knowledge already built up is utilised for the direction of more activity and the obtaining out of it of more observations. By this means, the knowledge already built up is further tested and corrected, and the whole build-up of knowledge is continued.

The process of passing from observation to judgment, and then from more active and comprehensive observation to more comprehensive judgment, brings about, in the first place, a correction of immediate conclusions based on insufficient observation.

Ordinary experience already teaches us that there is a difference between the first appearance of things in sense-perception and their reality. For it often happens that things turn out to be different from what they at first appear to be, and this is shown in practice by the non-realisation of expectations based on first appearances. In the process of building up knowledge we are always passing from conclusions which express only the apparent properties, relations and motions of things to conclusions which approximate more fully to things as they really are.

For example, when we perceive the sun it looks a relatively small body—and for a long time people concluded that it was in fact quite small. But we have come to know that the sun is in fact very big. Again, the sun looks as if it goes round the earth—and for a long time people concluded that it did in fact go round the earth. But we have come to know that it is the earth which really goes round the sun.

In the second place, in the process of forming more comprehensive judgments about things we pass from fragmentary knowledge of particular things, with their particular properties, relations and motions, to more connected knowledge of their laws of existence, change and interconnections.

The first knowledge which is based on the first observations of things is knowledge of a number of facts about those things, but not of the laws of their existence and the interconnections between them which manifest themselves in and determine those facts. At the same time, therefore, as we correct the conclusions based on the first appearance of things and form judgments about their real properties, relations and motions which give rise to the appearances, we also form judgments about the general laws and interconnections which are manifested in the particular properties, motions and relations of things first evident to observation.

For example, having established the main facts about the solar system—that the planets, of which the earth is one, go round the sun—we also establish the laws which are manifested in the system and by the operation of which it exists and remains in being.

Again, knowing from common experience that water turns into ice when it grows cold enough, we go on to establish—as a result of the synthesis of, and inferences drawn from, many special observations—the reasons for this phenomenon, namely, that it is due to a rearrangement of the molecules caused by changes in their motion when the temperature is lowered.

Thus in the process of passing from observation to judgment we also succeed in passing from superficial to more profound judgments—from judgments which simply state what we have observed to judgments which go further, and draw conclusions about the composition and internal organisation of things, about their causes and effects, interactions, interconnections and motions, and laws of interconnection and motion.

This is a qualitative change in the content of judgments; a passing from judgments of superficial content to judgments of a more profound content; from judgments in terms of elementary ideas to which correspond objects directly perceptible to the senses, to judgments in terms of abstract ideas, which state the causes, reasons, explanations, effects and laws of the things we observe.

From Superficial to Deeper Knowledge

We can conclude that knowledge in general is realised only by passing from perception to judgment, and that then the process of developing the knowledge expressed in judgments, of extending and deepening it, passes through two qualitatively distinct stages—first, the superficial and fragmentary knowledge of things directly derived from perceptions of them; and second, knowledge of their essential properties, interconnections and laws.

In the first stage, our judgments express merely what Mao Tse-tung called "the separate aspects of things, the external relations between such things". In the second stage, we arrive at judgments which, as he expressed it, "no longer represent the appearances of things, their separate aspects, or their external relations, but embrace their essence, their totality and their internal relations".

The passage from the first stage to the second stage involves, in the first place, active observation. Without active observation, the data on which to found more profound and comprehensive judgments will be lacking, and any judgments which may be made can only be speculative or illusory.

In the second place, however, it involves a process of thought arising from observation—a process of the sifting and comparison of observations, of generalisation and formation of abstract ideas, of reasoning and drawing conclusions from such generalisation and abstraction. Having reached conclusions, they must be again checked with active observation, in order to ensure that they accord with it and that the abstract generalisations reached by thought do express the concrete facts given in perception. The passage from the first stage to the second stage therefore involves a passage from judgments which directly express the data of perception, to judgments which are derived from the data of perception through a process of abstraction and generalisation.

The passage from the judgment that the sun is hot to the judgment that its surface temperature is about 6,000 degrees Centigrade represents, for example, such a passage of knowledge from the first to the second stage. The judgment that the sun is hot directly expresses one way in which the sun affects our senses. But the judgment about its temperature involves, first, that we have formed the abstract idea of temperature, and second, that with the aid of this idea we have reached conclusions about the sun's temperature by an elaborate process of active observation and reasoning based on it. As a result we pass from a judgment which merely expresses certain observations about the sun, to one which expresses its internal state.

Again, suppose that we are considering the state organisation of a given country, of Great Britain, let us say. The first observations which may be made concern particular facts—such as that the capital is London, that laws are made by people sitting in two Houses of Parliament, that these laws are signed by the Queen and enforced by policemen, and so on. Many inquiries into the character of British parliamentary democracy never get further than formulating the judgments summarising such observations, which means that they go no further than the first stage of knowledge. If, however, inquiry is carried further, if the state is considered in its historical development on the basis of the whole development of the economic structure of society, and if reasoned conclusions are drawn from this inquiry, then we will arrive at the judgment that the British parliamentary state is the organ of rule of the British capitalist class. This is to advance knowledge of the state to the second stage, which embraces not merely a number of observed facts about it but its essential nature.

In his work on the theory of knowledge (*On Practice*), Mao Tse-tung wrote that in the first stage knowledge is confined to "the separate aspects of things, the appearances, the external relations of things", whereas in the second stage it "takes a big stride forward to embrace the wholeness, the essence and internal relations of things, discloses the internal contradictions of the surrounding world, and is therefore capable of grasping the development of the surrounding world in its totality, in the internal relations between all its aspects".

Many philosophers (those belonging to the so-called "empiricist" and "positivist" schools) have denied that knowledge develops through two such stages. According to them, first we obtain various "sense data", and then we compare and relate these data in order to formulate judgments or propositions summarising the observations. And for them, that is the whole process of knowledge. Hence, for them, knowledge is entirely confined to "the separate aspects of things, the appearances, the external relations of things", and it is an illusion to suppose that there can be any more profound knowledge of things—of their reality as opposed to their appearance to us, of their essential properties, interconnections and laws.

In opposition to this empiricist or positivist type of philosophy, Marxism traces the growth of knowledge from a lower to a higher stage. First of all, in obtaining information through the senses we pass from sensations to judgments; and then, in the development of our knowledge expressed in ideas and judgments, we pass from superficial knowledge of the appearances and external relations of things to deeper knowledge of their essential characteristics and internal relations.

Appearance and Reality

In passing from elementary to abstract ideas, from superficial to more profound judgments, the passage is made from the appearance of things to their reality. In considering knowledge, a distinction must always be made between appearance and reality—between the particular phenomena which are immediately evident to observation and the hidden processes, interconnections and laws which are manifested in the appearances and underlie the observed facts. The task of knowing things is always to advance from appearance to reality, so as to get to know more about the real movement and interconnections of things manifested in their particular existence and mode of appearance.

Thus Marx stressed that the task of science is always to proceed from the immediate knowledge of appearances to the discovery of the reality, the internal connections and laws underlying the appearances, and so finally to reach a comprehensive understanding of the appearances.

Inquiry, he wrote, "has to appropriate the material in detail, to analyse its different forms of development, to trace out their inner connections. Only after this work is done can the actual movement be adequately described. If this is done successfully . . . the life of the subject matter is ideally reflected as in a mirror." (*Capital*, Preface to second edition.)

So Marx stressed that knowledge of the real character and laws of any subject-matter must always be derived from a detailed analysis of all the relevant facts, and must in turn serve to explain them—to demonstrate their inner connections and actual movement.

His own work in the social sciences provides examples of this point. Thus in *Capital* Marx pointed out that whereas the "vulgar economists" dealt only with the surface appearances of capitalist economy, scientific political economy seeks to uncover the real relations of production underlying the appearances, and on that basis explain the appearances. If the underlying processes had been evident on the surface to superficial observation, there would have been no need for further profound inquiry. But the reality is never evident on the surface, and can be discovered only by painstaking scientific analysis.

"The way of thinking of the vulgar economists", wrote Marx, "derives from the fact that it is always only the immediate form in which relationships appear which is reflected in the brain, and not their inner connections. If the latter were the case, moreover, what would be the need for a science at all?" And explaining his own method of scientific analysis of capitalist economy, he pointed out that at the end of it, "we have arrived at the forms of appearance which serve as the starting point for the vulgar: ground rent coming from the earth, profit (interest) from capital, and wages from labour. But from our point of view the thing is now seen differently. The apparent movement is explained." (Letters to Engels, June 27, 1867, and April 30, 1868.)

It is clear from this, incidentally, that the positivist philosophy, which confines knowledge entirely to dealing with surface appearances, was completely in accord with the procedures of the "vulgar economists" whom Marx criticised, and their procedures were completely in accord with it. This philosophy, indeed, is the most suitable philosophy for the apologists of capitalism, whose whole outlook depends on their never looking below the surface of social life.

As a vivid example of the importance of judging things, not from superficial appearances but from the point of view of their inner relationships and connections, we could take the case of wages. If we judge only from external appearances, then wages are simply payment for work. A man works so many hours and is paid so much per hour. In that case, we could perceive no difference between wages in, say, capitalist society and in socialist society. Whether he works in a capitalist or a socialist factory, a man works so many hours and gets paid so much. What is the difference? The difference is that the external form of wages expresses different social relations. In capitalist society, wages are the price of the worker's labour-power, which he has sold to the capitalist. In socialist society, wages are no longer the price of labour-power, since the factories belong to the working people, who do not sell their labour-power to themselves. Wages now express the allocation to the worker of a definite share of the values he has produced according to the work he has contributed. So while in capitalist society the workers can maintain or raise their wages only by fighting the capitalist class and threatening to strike, in socialist society they continually raise their standards by increasing production. In other words, the laws which determine wages are totally different in socialist from capitalist society. But why they are different can only be understood when we go behind the appearances of things and seek to discover the inner relationships and connections which determine the appearances.

Revolutionary Theory and Revolutionary Practice

To pass from superficial to profound judgment about things, and from their appearance to their reality, is, as we have said, to pass from one stage of knowing things to another. Such a qualitative change in knowledge is also as a rule a revolutionary change. It is revolutionary because it brings about a revolutionary change in what we can do.

When practice is guided only by what we have learned concerning the external appearance of things, then it lacks the power of knowingly bringing about profound changes in those things, or of utilising them extensively for far-reaching purposes. On the contrary, when we know things only by their appearances we generally have in practice to wait on what happens, to adapt ourselves to things—often badly and suffering surprises, set-backs and misfortunes—rather than mastering them and adapting them to purposes of our own.

But when we begin to grasp the reality which determines the appearances, then we can deal with things more effectively, bring about profound changes in them and utilise them for our own purposes.

For example, up to modern times people had only superficial knowledge of chemical processes, and so there could be little effectively planned use of these processes in production. But modern chemistry enables us to break substances down and bring them into being again from their constituents, so that many materials can be made by synthetic methods, with properties to suit our own requirements. We can split atoms, break down one element into others and utilise the energy produced in the process, and even create new man-made elements, such as plutonium.

Again, the utopian socialists and the old working-class movement could not effectively change society. But Marxist theory, which penetrates to the reality of social processes, has enabled the working-class movement thoroughly to transform society in some countries and to begin to build socialism.

Whether we consider knowledge of nature or of society, whenever knowledge has been raised to knowledge of reality and not only of appearance, then this has been a revolutionary development, a revolution in what people can do.

Such profound advances in knowledge—whether they have been consciously linked with practice or not by those who played the major theoretical part in effecting them—are always in the last analysis the products of revolutionary strivings in social practice. It is when people strive to do something new so as to increase their powers and improve their conditions, that they experience the necessity of deepening their knowledge. There can be no revolutionary practice without knowledge, for without knowledge it lacks direction and cannot attain its goal. A leap forward in knowledge is a condition for the realisation of a revolution in practice.

And it is impossible to raise the level of knowledge apart

from or in advance of the corresponding practice, just as practice gropes in the dark without the necessary knowledge. Apart from the appropriate practice no genuine knowledge is possible, but only guesswork and speculation. All genuine knowledge arises out of practice, and in turn is tested in practice—though this does not mean that the theoretical deductions from a discovery may not advance beyond the carrying into effect of all its potential practical consequences. There is no other way to discover the laws of the real world than the way of entering into practical relations with real objects and processes, striving to master and change them, forming concepts on the basis of the experiences gained, and then testing the theoretical conclusions once more in living practice.

Things in Themselves

It follows from this analysis of the growth of knowledge that, in all its stages, it is the growth of the faithful reflection in human consciousness of the objective world.

Many philosophers have maintained that our knowledge is limited to the appearances of things in our own minds, and that "things in themselves", things as they really are "in themselves" and independently of how they appear to us, must be unknowable. According to such philosophers there is an impassable gulf between the data of sense given in our consciousness on the one hand and the things existing independently of our consciousness, things in themselves, on the other hand. And many not only deny that we can know things in themselves but also that such things exist at all.

And yet already in judgments directly based on perception we are gaining knowledge of things in themselves—not in the first place complete or profound knowledge but knowledge at least of various separate aspects and external relations of things. We gain this knowledge precisely by means of the data of sense. And when by further investigations and reasoning we reach conclusions about the relations of things, their properties, the processes into which they enter and their laws of motion, then we are gaining deeper knowledge of the very same things, existing independently of our consciousness of them, which before we knew only superficially.

There is, then, no gulf between things in themselves and their appearances or "phenomena". We know things precisely by means of their appearances to us, and the more we study the appearances the more we can find out about the things. Nor is there any gulf between the appearances of things and their reality, since the appearance is a manifestation of the reality, and we do not know the reality separately from the appearance but only through it. "If you know all the qualities of a thing, you know the thing itself", wrote Engels in the Introduction to *Socialism, Utopian and Scientific*. We know about the real properties and relations of things by practice and study. By finding out what we can do with things, and by studying the various appearances of their various aspects under many conditions, we gain more and more knowledge of the things themselves.

Hence all our knowledge is knowledge of real things which certainly exist independently of their appearances to us. "The materialist affirms the existence and knowability of things in themselves", wrote Lenin, in *Materialism and Empirio-Criticism*, chapter 2. First we know things superficially through perception, and then more deeply and comprehensively by thought operating with the data of perception. There is, and can be, no difference between the things known to us and things in themselves. The only difference is between what is known and what is not yet known, and between what is known only superficially in certain of its aspects and what is known more thoroughly.

Overcoming the Limits of Knowledge

Are there, then, limits to human knowledge?

At any particular stage in the development of humanity knowledge comes up against limits set by the necessarily limited character of the experience available and of the existing means of obtaining knowledge.

But humanity advances by overcoming such limits. New experience throws down the limits of old experience; new

M

techniques, new means of obtaining knowledge throw down the limits of old techniques and old means of obtaining knowledge.

New limits then once again appear. But there is no more reason to suppose these new limits absolute and final than there was to suppose the old ones absolute and final. At every stage there are people who think that the limit has been reached and who look no further. But there are always, sooner or later, other people who throw down those limits and boldly advance beyond them to new limits.

Therefore knowledge is always limited, and advances by overcoming existing limits.

For example, it was impossible for people in feudal society to know anything about socialist society and its laws, to formulate the truth about socialism and the transition from socialism to communism. This became possible only with the development of capitalist society; only then did the means become available for forming a scientific conception of socialism. Similarly it is impossible for us today to know how a fully communist society, after it is established, will further develop; but in due course people will be able to ascertain the truth about this further development and its laws.

Again, it was impossible to gain knowledge of the atom and its structure before the invention of modern techniques of electronics. Today with these techniques we have passed what were once thought to be the limits of all possible physical knowledge. These techniques themselves involve, however, their own limits to physical knowledge—so that now some physicists assert the impossibility of ever knowing anything more about sub-atomic processes than is allowed for in contemporary quantum theory. But it would be both dogmatic and short-sighted to assert that these limits are any more absolute than were the once insurmountable limits of other techniques in the past. "While yesterday the profundity of this knowledge did not go beyond the atom, and today does not go beyond the electron," wrote Lenin, ". . . dialectical materialism insists on the temporary, relative, approximate character of all these *milestones* in the knowledge of nature gained by the progressing science of man. The electron is as *inexhaustible* as the atom, nature is infinite. . . ." (*Materialism and Empirio-Criticism*, chapter 5.)

At every stage and in all circumstances knowledge is incomplete and provisional, conditioned and limited by the historical circumstances under which it was acquired, including the means and methods used for gaining it and the historically conditioned assumptions and categories used in the formulation of ideas and conclusions.

But this development of knowledge, every stage of which has such a conditioned character, is a development of knowledge of the real material world, the discovery of interconnections and laws of motion of real material processes, including human society and human consciousness. It is a progressive development, in which the bounds of knowledge are stage by stage enlarged, in which the agreement of ideas and theories with objective reality is stage by stage increased, and in which stage by stage what was provisional and hypothetical gives place to what is assured and verified.

The progress of knowledge always comes up against barriers which arise from the limitations of existing knowledge and existing practice. But while the progress of knowledge always faces barriers to further advance, knowledge progresses by finding how to get over them.

Chapter Thirteen

NECESSITY AND FREEDOM

Necessity and Accident

WHEN knowledge advances to the stage of knowledge of the laws of motion and interconnection which determine the appearances of things, then we begin to understand the aspect of *necessity* which belongs to phenomena of both nature and society.

We call that necessary which from the nature of the case could not be otherwise. When the real processes which determine the mode of existence of a thing are such that it is bound to manifest certain characteristics and not others, and to develop in a certain way and not in another, then those characteristics and that development are understood as necessary.

In general, in so far as we gain knowledge of the inner connections and laws of development of things, we are able to state not merely what the facts are but to explain them, to understand the reasons for them, to comprehend their necessity.

In the field of natural science, for example, the discoveries of Newton concerning the principles of mechanics revealed the necessity of many phenomena of nature. Thus among other things Newton's principles demonstrated the necessity of certain features of the solar system of which the earth is a part. It is a fact, for instance, that the planets move round the sun in elliptical orbits. This fact was established by Kepler. But the necessity of Kepler's law of planetary motion was demonstrated by Newton, whose analysis of the mechanics of the solar system showed that from the very nature of the forces operating in such a system the planets were bound to move in elliptical orbits, and not in circles or any other kind of orbit. Thus the general character of the solar system is not accidental—it is a necessary consequence of the nature of such a system, of its inner connection and laws of development.

Again, to take an example from social life, it is a fact that in Britain the police always intervene in industrial disputes on the side of the employers. From the point of view of superficial observation, this is merely a fact. But yet it is not accidental. For once we have grasped the nature of the contemporary British State as a capitalist state, then we can understand that if the police help the employers this is no accident but a necessary consequence of the capitalist régime.

If, however, we come to understand the necessity of certain aspects of things, and of certain types of events, this does not mean that everything is understood as necessary, that there is no place left in the world for *accident.* On the contrary, particular events always have a chance or accidental character. The recognition of necessity in things is inseparable from the recognition at the same time of accident.

For example, the police in a capitalist state necessarily serve the capitalist class. But they do not necessarily wear blue uniforms. On the contrary, they could serve the capitalists just as well in uniforms of some other colour; and so the fact that the British police wear blue uniforms is an accident—it is due to accidental circumstances.

Similarly, while it is a necessary feature of the solar system that the earth moves round the sun in an elliptical orbit, it is not a necessary feature that the earth is the exact size it is: its exact size is due to accidental circumstances.

From the point of view of superficial observation, everything appears accidental. We are simply confronted with observed facts and external connections between them. As we have not yet grasped the laws of change and interconnection which govern and manifest themselves in the things we are observing, every fact we observe is apprehended simply as a fact which could quite well have been otherwise. "Every fact could be the case or not be the case, and everything else remain the same" (L. Wittgenstein, *Tractatus Logico-Philosophicus*, 1.21): such is the conclusion of a superficial way of viewing things.

But profounder investigation reveals that "where on the surface accident holds sway, there actually it is always governed by inner, hidden laws and it is only a matter of discovering these laws". (Engels, *Ludwig Feuerbach*, chapter 4.)

Their discovery does not, however, eliminate the conception of the accidental. Rather does it reveal that the necessary features of things manifest themselves through a series of accidents, and that the accidental, on the other hand, is always governed by the necessary.

Thus it is a historical necessity that in the development of society capitalism should be superseded by socialism. Exactly when and how this revolution takes place involves a series of accidental circumstances, but the development of these circumstances is, in turn, governed by historical necessity.

Similarly in nature, the development of matter necessarily follows a certain path, though exactly when and how in a particular material system the different stages of development are realised, or whether in particular cases they are realised at all, depends upon accidental circumstances.

So, dealing with the inter-relation of accident and necessity in nature, Engels wrote that the solar system "was produced in a natural way by transformations of motion which are by nature inherent in moving matter, and the conditions of which therefore also must be reproduced by matter, even if only after millions and millions of years and more or less by chance but with the necessity that is also inherent in chance". And he understood the emergence of consciousness, as the highest form of motion of matter, in the same way. "It is the nature of matter to advance to the evolution of thinking beings; hence, too, this always necessarily occurs wherever the conditions for it (not necessarily identical at all places and times) are present." (*Dialectics of Nature.*)

Engels therefore concluded that "what is maintained to be necessary is composed of sheer accidents, and the so-called accidental is the form behind which necessity hides itself".

If the necessary is that which from the nature of the case

could not be otherwise, the accidental is that which could be otherwise. Both aspects are always present in everything. In general, it is certain overall characteristics of events, and the overall character of their outcome, which are necessary. On the other hand, the details, the particular features of individual events, and the consequent detailed, particular features of their outcome, are not necessary but accidental. It is in this sense that "what is necessary is composed of accidents". It is precisely in the accidental details that the inherently necessary manifests itself, and, accidental in themselves, they are at the same time shaped and governed by what is necessary.

Necessity, Accident and Causality

The discovery of necessity in nature and society is bound up with the discovery of causes and of the laws governing the relationship of causes and effects. What is necessary is necessary because of the operation of causes. If there were things which came into being without any causes, if there were events which took place absolutely at random and without regulation by causal laws, then there could be no necessity discoverable in such things and events.

So if a certain characteristic is a necessary characteristic of certain events, and if a certain result is their necessary outcome, this is consequent upon the nature of the causal processes which operate in these events. To get to understand the necessity inherent in events is to reach a profound knowledge of the causal processes operating in them.

For example, if capitalism will necessarily be superseded by socialism, this is because the causes of the transition from capitalism to socialism are generated within the capitalist system. If we profoundly know the nature of capitalism, then we know that such causes are present and cannot but be present and continue to operate in such a system.

At the same time, the knowledge of causes also enables us to understand the accidental features of things.

The causes of socialism, for example, come into being and operate within capitalism, and so the outcome of socialism is known to be necessary. But the particular features of these causes are accidental. There is no necessity about them. Thus it is necessary that the working class should increase in numbers and organisation as capitalism develops; this is bound to happen, and is one of the causes why capitalism will give rise to socialism. But while the continued development of capitalism necessarily implies that there will be more workers and that they will organise and eventually overthrow the system, it does not necessarily imply that, say, Mr. Jones and Mr. Smith will join an organisation and play a prominent part as leaders of the movement. There are bound to be leaders, but whether a particular child of particular parents will become a leader depends on many accidental factors. Such accidental factors, however, are, in the aggregate and in the long run, bound to have the result that leaders will arise.

Thus the operation of causality brings it about that there is both necessity and accident in the world, and that the necessary manifests itself through the accidental.

It follows that it is wrong to assert, as has often been asserted, that when a cause has been assigned for anything, then that thing has thereby been shown to be necessary. It is equally wrong to define the accidental as that which happens without a cause. All events have causes, necessary events and accidents alike. Merely to trace something back to its remote causes is not to prove its necessity, for accident is at work right throughout the chain of events. If something is necessary, this is not a consequence of particular causes but of general laws.

The inter-relation of accident and necessity in events is grasped, then, as a consequence of the advance of knowledge from the external to the internal connections of things, from appearance to reality, from superficial observation and correlation of facts to investigation of the real dialectic of development. Then we see that necessary consequences of the real interconnections of things manifest themselves through a series of accidental circumstances, and that accidental events are conditioned and governed by an internal necessity and contribute to bringing about a necessary outcome.

Necessity and Freedom in Human Practice

We have considered the inter-relation of necessity and accident and how both arise from the universal operation of causality in nature and society. Now we shall consider the bearing of these conclusions on practical life.

When we carry out practical activities, do we possess any freedom in what we are doing or is it all necessarily determined independently of our will? This is the question we must now answer. And as it is sometimes thought that necessity and accident are incompatible opposites, such that where the one is present the other must be absent, so the same thing is often thought about necessity and freedom. It is thought that where necessity is present there can be no freedom and that, on the other hand, if we do act freely then we must somehow have escaped from necessity.

If this idea were correct, then human freedom would be an illusion. All men's activities, like everything else in the world, are in all respects governed by causal laws. The operations of causality give rise to necessary characteristics of events and determine their necessary outcome; and this applies as much to human actions as to anything else, so that men can never make themselves independent of necessity in nature and society. But it is wrong to oppose freedom and necessity as incompatibles. On the contrary, necessity gives rise to freedom and is its precondition.

The operation of natural and social laws and the necessities consequent on this are independent of our will and of our consciousness. Hence whatever we may think or desire or decide, our actions are always determined in accordance with the laws of nature in general and of our own nature in particular, and conform, in their carrying out and in their consequences, to the dictates of necessity.

Man is himself a part of nature, and "the necessity of nature is primary, and human will and mind secondary. The latter must necessarily and inevitably adapt themselves to the former". (Lenin, *Materialism and Empirio-Criticism*, chapter 3, section 6.)

What characterises human practice, however, and distinguishes it from animal behaviour, is that men in the course of their social practice gain knowledge of necessity, in the first place of necessity in nature, and so learn to act on that knowledge and to use it to produce intended aims, to realise their own purposes.

This begins with the production process itself, in which man "sets in motion the natural forces of his body in order to appropriate nature's productions in a form adapted to his own wants", and so "realises a purpose of his own". (Marx, *Capital*, Volume I, chapter 7, section 1.)

Consequently men are not, like the animals, constrained to follow a predetermined pattern of behaviour. They do not, like the animals, simply adapt themselves to their environment, but also by their own volition adapt their environment to themselves. They *make themselves free* to seek and realise ends which they themselves have conceived and willed. And in so doing they also change themselves, change their own nature.

But the mastery over nature, which distinguishes man from the animals, does not imply the least independence of man from natural law and natural necessity. On the contrary, what it depends on is not the abrogation of natural laws and natural necessity but knowledge and conscious utilisation of them. Similarly, when men learn also to control and plan their own social life in order to satisfy their material and cultural requirements, this again does not imply that they have achieved independence of the objective laws of society, of social necessity. On the contrary, what it depends on is not the abrogation of objective social laws but knowledge and conscious utilisation of these laws—not the ending of necessity in society but its recognition, and the direction of social activity in accordance with that recognition of necessity.

Men are therefore never, in any respect, in any of their activities, independent of natural or social laws and of their necessary consequences. It follows that in so far as they lack knowledge of these laws and of their consequences, they are constrained and unfree. These laws with their necessary consequences then assert themselves as an alien power, with unexpected or destructive effects, frustrating human purposes.

But in so far as men gain knowledge of these laws and knowledge of their necessary consequences, they can learn to utilise them for their own purposes.

Freedom does not consist in cutting loose from the operations of causality but in understanding them. It does not depend on getting rid of necessity but on getting knowledge of it.

There is, therefore, no incompatibility between the existence of necessity and of human freedom. On the contrary, as we have stated, necessity gives rise to freedom, namely, when men gain knowledge of necessity and so can recognise it and make their decisions in the light of real understanding of what they are doing.

What is more, as we have also stated, so far from being in opposition to human freedom, the existence of necessity is its precondition.

What would happen if there were no causal laws in nature and society, if there were no objective necessity regulating the course of events? In that case, anything could happen. We could not decide upon or carry out even the simplest actions, for we could never know what to do in order to secure the results we intended. We would not possess even the freedom to make a cup of tea, for example, for we would never know whether the water would boil or, when we poured it into the teapot, what the resulting brew would turn out like. Still less could we carry out any more complex social activities, for everything would be in chaos. In fact, we could not exist at all.

It is only because things *are* subject to laws, because objective necessity *does* exist in nature and society, that we are able to decide upon definite actions and to carry them out. This is the condition for human freedom. And that freedom is realised in proportion as we extend our knowledge and, consequently, our ability to make decisions on the basis of knowledge and so to carry them into effect.

Further, when we do know the laws governing things, then we can carry out activities in relation to them which we could not carry out without such knowledge. For example, people often dreamed about flying, but until recently considered that the laws of nature prevented them from being able to fly.

When, however, we discovered the laws governing flying, then we were able to construct the means of flight. In many such cases, knowledge of the laws which have given rise to certain limitations on our action enables us in practice to transcend those limitations.

Knowledge as the Means to Human Freedom

But are not our own actions determined by various causes and are they not therefore subject to an overriding necessity? How, then, can we be free?

It is true that we ourselves are the products of definite conditions, would have been different had those conditions been different, and act according to the necessity of our own circumstances and our own nature. But this does not in the least contradict the possibility of our being free agents.

Whatever we do, there was some cause of our doing it. If this cause was an external force of some kind, acting on us in such a way as to make us do something without the intervention of any act of will on our part, then certainly in such a case we are constrained and not free. For example, if someone in a crowd pushes me in such a way that I push someone else, then in this case I am not a free agent. The question of freedom only comes in when we do things of our own volition—that is to say, when the cause of what we do is our own act of will. But how is our own will determined? If it is determined by various external forces operating on and moulding our will so as to effect purposes which are not our own, then we still lack freedom. In that case we may have the illusion of acting freely, but it is only an illusion. But lastly, if our will is determined by our knowledge of the circumstances of our action and of what must be done to realise a purpose which we have made our own, then in that case we not only feel free but really are free.

Such a quality of free operation is not inherent in the will but comes into being. And its coming into being and the extent of its development follow in turn from definite causes which come into operation in social life.

As a result of the operation of the laws of our own development, as a result of the necessities of our own nature, we gain knowledge of external things and of our own nature and requirements, and then we act on the basis of such knowledge. In proportion as this takes place, what we do follows from our own conscious decisions based on knowledge of our own requirements and of how to realise them. And so we are free. What other sort of freedom do we expect or can we desire?

This, incidentally, is a point which was, in its essentials, made clear long ago by the great materialist philosopher Spinoza, when he pointed out that human actions, like all other things, are determined by prior causes; and that men are free not when their actions take place without causes but when their actions are determined by their knowledge of their own requirements and of how to realise them.

"Freedom does not consist in the dream of independence of natural laws," wrote Engels, "but in the knowledge of these laws, and in the possibility this gives of systematically making them work towards definite ends. This holds good in relation both to the laws of external nature and to those which govern the bodily and mental life of men themselves—two classes of laws which we can separate from each other at most only in thought and not in reality. Freedom of the will therefore means nothing but the capacity to make decisions with real knowledge of the subject. . . . Freedom therefore consists of the control over ourselves and over external nature which is founded on the knowledge of natural necessity." (*Anti-Dühring*, Part I, chapter 11.)

Human knowledge, then, is an essential means to human freedom. If knowledge depends on practice, the growth of knowledge has also a transforming effect on practice. Practice based on knowledge is another thing from practice not based on knowledge. For in so far as we know the properties and laws of things, we can in practice master them—make them subject to us, instead of our being subject to them. The growth of knowledge, a product of man's striving to master nature and to organise his own social life, contributes step by step to the realisation of that mastery and to the building of higher forms of social organisation, to the realisation of the possibility of a full and free life for all.

Freedom and Accident

We have already considered the linkage in nature and society of necessity and accident, and have seen that necessity realises itself through a series of accidents. To act freely on the basis of knowledge further means, then, that we, as conscious agents, must exercise practical control over these accidents, so as to eliminate the accidental or chance element in the determination of the results of our activity and make those results fully conform with our own intentions. In other words, the exercise of our freedom of action means that, in carrying out activities directed to a definite end, we, on the basis of our knowledge of the laws of the subject of our action, exercise such control over the subject that the operations of chance are eliminated in the determination of the result.

Thus while the realisation of freedom of human action does not in any sense mean getting rid of necessity, it does, in a certain sense, mean getting rid of accident, or eliminating chance.

In carrying out an undertaking we should not, as everyone knows, leave to chance anything which affects the success of the undertaking. If we do, then the success of the undertaking is jeopardised. If it succeeds, that is due to luck and not to judgment; circumstances have brought about success for us, and it was not we who by our own deliberate actions achieved success for ourselves. But circumstances cannot generally be relied on to be so favourable.

Those organising street-corner meetings, for example, sometimes forget to arrange for anyone to bring the platform along. They leave it to chance, and so occasionally find themselves without a platform. Sometimes they may even be without a speaker for the same reason. Naturally enough, anyone who organises anything has the job of taking all the factors affecting the success of the undertaking into account and leaving none of them to chance.

The elementary characteristics of free action, namely, knowledge of necessity and elimination of chance, are exemplified in the labour process, the fundamental process of human activity.

In the labour process man by his work, using the instruments of labour, operates on the subject of the work to effect a designed alteration in it. To do this he has to know and reckon with the necessary characteristics of the subject of work, and he has also to eliminate the effects of chance on the subject of work.

The more large-scale and ambitious grow the undertakings of human labour, the more does man succeed in eliminating the factor of chance in his undertakings.

This is a very important consideration in any engineering work. To build a bridge, for instance, the engineers base their plans on their knowledge of the essential nature of the location and of the materials employed, and on a reckoning with the various chance factors to which the structure may be subjected. An example of failure to reckon with chance was afforded, not many years ago, by the sea defences on the east coast of England. Those who were responsible for these defences had omitted to reckon with the chance that an exceptionally high tide might coincide with an exceptionally strong east wind. When this chance coincidence took place, the sea burst through the defences. But if sea defences, or any other engineering works, are properly planned, then such chances are reckoned with and their effects eliminated.

The Elements of Conscious Control

By considering such examples we can draw some further conclusions about the inter-relation of necessity, accident and human freedom.

To say that freedom entails the elimination of chances does not mean, of course, that by the exercise of freedom we somehow contrive to do away with the linkage of accident and necessity. The operation of accident or chance, and its linkage with necessity, is an objective fact, a universal feature of events in both nature and society, which we have to reckon with and to which we have to adapt our actions. It exists independently of ourselves and we can by no means do away with or alter it. What we have to do to realise freedom of action is, through knowledge of necessity, to bring a whole process, including the chances inherent in it, under our control and so direct it to an end decided by ourselves. So eliminating chance means controlling it, so as to direct its operation and to render the outcome no longer accidental. This is done by means of (*a*) exercising a direct control over chance factors and (*b*) exercising foresight and taking precautions to cope with them in so far as they remain outside direct control. This is why a socialist economic plan, for example, must always include the building up of "reserves".

One aspect of foresight in relation to chance is expressed in the saying, "Heads I win, tails you lose". If such a situation can be brought into being, then I have ensured that I win. If the outcome depends on the accident of the spin of a coin, then it is decided independently of man's volition and not by man's volition. But if it is arranged that whatever chances, some suitable precaution has been contrived to bring about the desired outcome, then it is man's volition that decides the outcome. If people are making bets, this is called cheating; but we do not consider it cheating in relation to nature.

Another aspect of eliminating chance is illustrated by spinning a coin in which we have been careful to introduce a bias.

We have seen that necessity realises itself through a series of accidents, and also that accidental events are governed by an internal necessity. When this point is grasped in a practical way, and when we are equipped with knowledge of the laws of the subject of our activities, then we are in a position to reckon with and control the accidental factors inherent in the subject, so that we ourselves direct them to a necessary outcome in accordance with our intentions.

This further requires that our knowledge should be not only knowledge of the inevitable but also of the probable. In relation to a given process, for instance, we must know not only what effect universally follows from what cause, so that by bringing the cause into being we can ensure the corresponding effect; but we must also know the probabilities of various causes coming into operation and of various effects following. This enables us to judge how to act in order to control the whole process, including its accidental features.

Judgments of probability express our expectation of the occurrence of accidents. According to some theories, probability is purely subjective, in the sense that a judgment of probability is an expression of nothing but our own subjective uncertainty or lack of knowledge. But on the contrary, the idea of probability reflects an objective reality—or rather, one aspect of objective reality—namely, the operation of accidental causes in a whole sequence of events or in an aggregate of instances. This is just as much an objective reality as the operation of a single cause on a single occasion, which is not a subject of probability.

In proportion as we know the probabilities inherent in events and can arrive at correct judgments of probability, we are able the better to reckon with *all* the factors operating in the course of a whole process, including the accidental factors, and so to direct the whole process towards a definite end.

To sum up.

Freedom is control over ourselves and over external nature which is founded on knowledge of necessity. Such knowledge also requires that we know what chance factors enter into the process with which we are concerned, and the probabilities characterising their operation, so that we can (*a*) control the operation of chance and (*b*) take precautions to meet its operation in so far as we do not control it, as a result of which the whole process is directed to a desired end.

"Chance is only the one pole of a relation whose other pole is called 'necessity'", wrote Engels. ". . . The more a social activity, a series of social processes, becomes too powerful for men's conscious control and grows above their heads, and the more it appears a matter of pure chance, then all the more surely within this chance the laws peculiar to it and inherent in it assert themselves as if by natural necessity." (*The Origin of the Family*, etc., chapter 9.)

When events in which we are concerned thus take place

without our conscious control over them, then the outcome is determined by a natural necessity realised through a series of accidents. But in proportion as we do achieve a conscious control over events, it is we ourselves who consciously determine their course, by acting on our knowledge of the laws of such events and of the factors influencing the outcome.

Chapter Fourteen

THE REALISATION OF FREEDOM

The Winning of Freedom

MOST of the theoretical difficulties people run into when thinking of the problem of freedom result from thinking that freedom is an innate quality of the will. But freedom is not an innate quality of the will, nor is it any sort of gift or endowment which God or nature has bestowed upon man. It is something which is *won*—and which is won gradually, bit by bit, created and realised in the course of ages of human social activity.

J. J. Rousseau began his book on *The Social Contract* with the famous words, "Man is born free". But man is not born free. On the contrary, man is born with no freedom whatever, but is born as a creature determined by circumstances independent of his will. But thanks to his social life and the laws of its development, he gradually develops in social practice those capacities which make him *become* free. This he does in struggle with external nature, in social and class struggle, and also in individual struggle. He creates for himself and wins for himself such freedom as he possesses, and so he can never possess more than he has created and won for himself.

Freedom is not an innate quality, nor is it an "all or none" affair. Metaphysicians argue that either we are free or else we are not free. This is to forget that we may be free in some respects but not in others, and that we may be more or less free.

In the argument between voluntarism, which says that the will is not determined, and determinism, which says that the will *is* determined, Marxism takes the determinist side, since every act of will has a cause. But the important question is not that of whether our actions are determined—since there is no doubt that they are determined—but of how and by what they are determined—by external causes or by our own knowledge of our needs and of how to satisfy them. When the question is put like this, then it is evident that freedom is a matter of degree. We make ourselves free only in so far as we bring it about that our own conscious decision based on knowledge is the thing which determines what we do and achieve. But such freedom can seldom if ever be absolute. The *more* it is our own decision based on knowledge which determines our actions and their outcome, and the *less* they are decided for us by other factors, the *greater* is the *degree of freedom of action* which we have achieved.

Freedom of the Individual and Freedom in Society

Freedom is something which is realised by the individual. It is not mankind in general, or society, that is free, but individuals who are free.

But in the first place, the individual realises freedom only through society. The means to freedom is knowledge, and this is social. The freedom of the individual depends on the acquirements of the society to which he belongs, on the education and assistance which society has afforded him, and also on the extent to which, in society, he can co-operate with others and get them to co-operate with him.

In the second place, therefore, the individual attains to that degree of freedom which has been attained by and is permitted to him by the society to which he belongs. The scope of his freedom is dependent on the acquirements of his society, but it is also dependent on how far society will permit him to share it and make use of those acquirements. The potential scope of his freedom is as great as the existing social knowledge and the means discovered to utilise it. At the same time, his actual enjoyment of this potential freedom may be denied to him by limitations placed by society on his own acquirements and his own actions.

The freedom of individuals, then, depends upon the positive acquirements of society and the opportunities society affords to individuals to utilise those acquirements. This being so, individuals struggle together—both with one another and against one another—for a higher degree of freedom. And they thereby raise the degree of freedom possessed by all individuals and realised by them in society.

It follows, then, that an individual develops as a free agent in the course of his life, corresponding to the education, incentives and opportunities afforded him by society. And similarly, men in society have developed human freedom in the course of social evolution. Mankind gradually advances on the road of greater freedom of action. This freedom of action is, indeed, a measure or criterion of social progress.

The Struggle for Freedom

In primitive societies, people's freedom is restricted mainly by their lack of mastery over nature. They are very much at the mercy of external nature, and the savage's existence is to a very great extent determined for him by external conditions, as is the case with animals.

As civilisation has developed, so has people's mastery over nature developed. Hence their freedom in this respect has become less and less restricted, more and more enlarged. But a new restriction has come into operation. In civilised societies hitherto, people's freedom has been restricted by social circumstances, and in particular by the oppression of one class by another. Hence as the freedom associated with the mastery over nature has increased, so has it been offset by class oppression. This means that people have been exploited and coerced, and at the same time have been denied the opportunity of utilising for their own interests the knowledge and power which exist in society.

If people are to be free, then neither in their economic activities nor in any other of their activities should they be constrained to work or to act or to think contrary to their own interests, to the detriment of their own essential requirements, by external pressure and for the benefit of others. And they should not be denied the opportunity of utilising all society offers for the satisfaction of their requirements. Such conditions are a negation of people's freedom. Their prevalence hitherto has been due to the division of society into exploiting and exploited classes.

Metaphysical philosophers have carefully separated the question of the so-called freedom of the will from the question of economic and political freedom, and this separation has helped them to mislead people about both. But in fact these are not separate questions but two aspects of the one question of men's struggle for freedom. In a society in which one class exploits another, the main part of the struggle for freedom is the struggle to throw off the existing forms of exploitation and oppression. And it is in this struggle that men act freely, make themselves free and enlarge the frontiers of human freedom. A passive slave is simply a slave, but a slave in revolt is acting as a free man even though he still wears his chains. Such people are pioneers of human freedom.

It follows that, in class society, freedom and the winning of freedom has always a class background to it. And the concept of freedom has therefore a class significance. In the first place, the freedom which has been won and realised at any stage, and also the lack of freedom, is always the freedom or lack of freedom of definite classes. In the second place, the freedom or lack of freedom of one class differs in concrete ways from the freedom or lack of freedom of another class; and consequently different classes also have different ideas of what constitutes freedom.

Human freedom has been constantly advanced by the class struggle, and various classes, striving to realise their own aims and to make themselves free to pursue those aims, have advanced the freedom of people generally from one stage to another. Each stage is realised as a result of struggle against the restrictions on freedom placed by a definite system of class rule, and in turn produces its own restrictions on freedom.

Thus, for example, feudal rule and serfdom were ended as a result of the struggle led by the bourgeoisie against feudal restrictions. This was a step forward in men's freedom. It brought with it new forms of exploitation and oppression, but it also brought new advances, the winning of broader political rights and liberties, new and more powerful organisation, advances in knowledge and culture. At the same time, it has meant in practice different things for the two main classes of capitalist society. The capitalist class is concerned to maintain its rule and increase its profits. The working class, on the other hand, is confronted with the task of getting rid of capitalist rule and capitalist exploitation, and of using the freedom which it has already won in order to advance to a higher order of freedom.

Similarly, restrictions of freedom are experienced differently by the different classes. Every system of exploitation imposes definite forms of coercion and oppression on the exploited; and the working class today, for example, experiences this. At the same time, each ruling class, which seems to itself to have realised its own freedom by exploiting others, finds in practice that its freedom is largely illusory. The bourgeoisie, for example, find themselves enslaved by the laws of their own system, and must go on accumulating capital, competing with one another and fighting with one another to the end.

To a poor family today, debating whether to exercise their free will in paying the rent or buying some food, it often seems that a rich capitalist is far freer than they are. They do not realise the extent to which the unfortunate man is the slave of his own business, suffering high blood pressure and perpetual worry and frustration. If they did, simple humanity might prompt them to set him free from these cares, and do themselves a bit of good too, by taking over his business from him and allowing him the freedom of honest work. Members of various exploiting classes have often believed that riches and power would give them complete freedom. But even their own philosophers have sadly but truly pointed out to them that riches and power enslave their possessors at the same time as they are engaged in enslaving others.

From Lack of Freedom to Freedom

The struggle for freedom means in essence people's struggle

to be able to satisfy their own requirements, material and cultural, for which is needed knowledge of those requirements and of how to satisfy them, and the power to effect that satisfaction.

When in socialist society people, having already greatly expanded their mastery over nature, bring their own social organisation under their own conscious control by virtue of the social ownership of the means of production, then a decisive step forward is realised in human freedom. In socialist society, when there is no exploitation of man by man and when the means of production are common property and are utilised for the purpose of satisfying the requirements of every individual, people begin less to struggle for freedom then to enjoy it and learn how to go forward to exercise it to the full. And when in communist society people finally do away with all traces of the subordination of people to their own means of production and products, then people will have attained to the highest degree of freedom we can envisage. Then, as Engels put it, "for the first time man, in a certain sense, is finally marked off from the rest of the animal kingdom, and emerges from mere animal conditions of existence into really human ones. . . . It is the ascent of man from the kingdom of necessity to the kingdom of freedom". (*Socialism, Utopian and Scientific*, chapter 3.)

We can say that people started off from mere animal conditions of existence, but began to create conditions of freedom when they first began social production—that is to say, when they began to use tools and implements to change things, in accordance with the objective laws of nature, with conscious intent to satisfy their own requirements.

In producing, people have entered into relations of production, and in the course of ages of struggle to satisfy their own ever-growing requirements they have continually advanced their knowledge and consequently their control over their own affairs and over external nature. This struggle has advanced through a series of stages, in each of which people have changed their relations of production to correspond with the development of their forces of production, and in each of which different classes have enlarged their own sphere of free activity only at the cost of new forms of domination of one class over another and of new forms of subjection to the objective laws of their own social organisation. At length the class struggle has reached that stage in which the struggle of the exploited class for its own emancipation will finally emancipate society at large from all exploitation and oppression, and so will bring about conditions in which men's own social organisation comes under their own conscious, social control and becomes the result of their own free action. Then, too, the labour process, by which men began their journey to freedom but which became a process of enslavement, will become the conscious means by which they achieve the satisfaction of all their needs; and by limiting the hours of labour each will be able freely to develop and enjoy the exercise of all his capacities.

In this way, by a process which is entirely law governed, which is determined at every point by the operation of objective laws, people gradually emerge from a condition of complete lack of freedom, when what they do and achieve is determined not by their own conscious decision but by their circumstances, and gradually win freedom, attaining at length a condition in which individually and collectively they can consciously decide their own fate on the basis of knowledge of their own needs and of conscious control over the conditions for their satisfaction.

Morality

The stages of the evolution of freedom are closely connected with the evolution of morality, or ethics. The development of morals is, in fact, one side or aspect of the development of freedom, and the various stages of the development of moral ideas are so many stages of the evolution of human freedom.

Many moral philosophers have observed that morality is an expression of freedom and that the moral life has meaning only in so far as people are acting freely. And of course, if all our actions were merely the determined consequences of external causes, then there would be no sense in calling them right or wrong, or in saying that we had a duty to do one thing rather than another, since in that case we could not help what we did. In this, these philosophers were evidently right. What they did not observe is that freedom is something which develops socially on the basis of the activities of definite classes, and that the same is true of morals.

Human morality is not an expression of some eternal moral law decreed by heaven and somehow revealed to mankind; nor is it, as Kant imagined, the expression of a "categorical imperative" inherent in the human will; but it is a natural product of men's social organisation. Since men live in society, they necessarily evolve a moral code to regulate their mutual relations and activities in society. This assumes in relation to individuals the appearance of an externally imposed and morally binding force, because of its character of a social regulator of conduct. It assumes the peculiar character of a "moral" force: we do not have to act rightly, but we "ought" to do so.

Morality consists of certain standards and principles of conduct, and says that certain things ought to be done and other things ought not to be done, irrespective of whether individuals want to do them or not, or actually do them or not. The whole sense of moral terms, like "good", "bad", "ought", and so on, is contained in the assertion of standards which do not depend on the particular desires, impulses and actions of individuals. And such standards come to be conceived, and necessarily come to be conceived, precisely because of the social necessity of regulating individual conduct.

Of course, it is one thing to conceive and recognise such standards and another thing to operate them. Generally speaking, every society evolves various forms of sanctions to teach and persuade people to do what they ought, ranging from mild praise or blame to systems of reward and punishment—the latter, however, being mostly reserved for actions directly involving security of life or property. But in societies containing class antagonisms, and where people profit at others' expense and compete with one another, a large part of morality invariably assumes the form of something which is preached to others but which one tries to evade oneself.

Morality is inseparable from hypocrisy. Finally, when moral standards are not merely often evaded but are placed in doubt and ignored altogether, and when the various moral sanctions vacillate and weaken, that is one sign that the social system concerned is breaking up and changing.

The whole of social intercourse is conditioned by and based on the production relations of society. And so morality, as a regulator of social intercourse, is in every society the product of definite production relations. It reflects them and changes with them, and each class in society evolves its own moral ideas corresponding to its peculiar class position.

"Men consciously or unconsciously derive their moral ideas in the last resort from the practical relations on which their class position is based," wrote Engels, "from the economic relations in which they carry on production and exchange. . . . All former moral theories are the product, in the last analysis, of the economic stage which society had reached at the particular epoch." (*Anti-Dühring*, Part I, chapter 9.)

This being so, it is natural that moral ideas should in many ways differ as between different social systems and different classes. At the same time, we should expect to find, as we do find, that there is always something, and often a great deal, in common between them. For the different social systems and classes represent "different stages of the same historical development and have therefore a common historical background, and for that reason alone they necessarily have much in common. Even more. In similar or approximately similar stages of economic development moral theories must of necessity be more or less in agreement". For example, "from the moment when private property in movable objects developed, in all societies in which this property existed there must be this moral law in common: Thou shalt not steal". (Engels, *Anti-Dühring*, Part I, chapter 9.)

The ethics of any social group is the expression of the concrete nature of their freedom and their aspirations for freedom—which has its basis in the place they occupy in social production and their relationship to the means of production. In so far as such a group may remain under the influence and sway of some other group, they may accept the moral ideas of that other group—often to their own detriment and to the advantage of the other, since it serves to keep them in subjection. But in so far as they become conscious of and begin to struggle for their own aims, begin to play an active and not merely a passive part in the process of social change, begin to assert their own freedom, they develop their own morality in the process.

Why does freedom entail morals? It is because freedom in action is the very opposite of acting on impulse or because of external compulsion. In so far as people act on impulse or because of external compulsion, they are the very reverse of free but are constrained by chance or external causes. People act freely when they themselves, deliberately and knowingly, determine their course of action. Hence in realising and exercising their freedom people create their maxims or principles of action, which constitute their moral ideas. Their morals then correspond to the conditions and aims of their struggle, as determined on the basis of their actual conditions of material life. At the same time, they create institutions and social sanctions which, in this respect, serve as the external embodiment and defence of their morals and of the kind and degree of freedom of action which they have attained or are striving for.

The modern working class, for example, has created, and is creating, its own morality, which receives particular expression in such institutions as the trade union movement and the Communist Party—a morality of solidarity and of mutual assistance, and of putting the common struggle before the particular and short-term interests of the individual. Bourgeois morality differs from this in many ways. If many working people remain under the influence of bourgeois morality—or what this often comes to today, bourgeois lack of morality—that simply means that they remain relatively passive slaves of the capitalist system, although they may themselves think and be assured by their employers that they are behaving with great strength of mind and independence.

Thus if a worker urged to take part in his trade union

struggle replies that he will not do so because everyone should look after himself, that simply means that he has imbibed the individualistic elements of bourgeois morality, which have been pumped into him by capitalist propaganda. It also means that he does not in fact know how to look after himself, since the ideas evolved by the capitalists for looking after their own affairs are not suited to the entirely opposite purpose of assisting the workers.

In class-divided society, morality is always and necessarily class morality. It expresses precisely the requirements, the social consciousness and the measure and kind of freedom of the various classes. And when a class is going down, its morality goes down with it, and gives way to a different morality. We can say that that morality is higher which serves to advance society a step further on the road of material progress and freedom. These two things are inseparable, since in struggling for more freedom people realise their material progress, and in struggling for material progress they realise more freedom. To live more fully is the goal of all free and active life, and this alone provides the objective criterion for judging what morality is higher.

At present, no morality is higher than that which is the expression of the class struggle of the working class. If those who bemoan the decline of morals in capitalist society want to find examples of moral principle, this is where they should look. They do not do so because they are both ashamed and frightened.

"Our morality is entirely subordinated to the interests of the class struggle of the proletariat. Our morality is derived from the interests of the class struggle of the proletariat", wrote Lenin. ". . . Morality is what serves to destroy the old exploiting society and to unite all the toilers around the proletariat, which is building up a new, communist society. Communist morality is the morality which serves this struggle, which unites the toilers. . . ." (*The Tasks of the Youth Leagues.*)

When class antagonisms are abolished in socialist and communist society, then morality does become human and not class morality.

"As society has hitherto moved in class antagonism, morality was always a class morality", wrote Engels. "It has either justified the domination and the interests of the ruling class, or, as soon as the oppressed class has become powerful enough, it has represented the revolt against this domination and the future interests of the oppressed. That in this process there has on the whole been progress in morality . . . cannot be doubted. But we have not yet passed beyond class morality. A really human morality which transcends class antagonisms and their legacies in thought becomes possible only at a stage of society which has not only overcome class contradictions but has even forgotten them in practical life." (*Anti-Dühring*, Part I, chapter 9.)

Such morality expresses the principles and maxims of free action in "an association in which the free development of each is the condition for the free development of all." (Marx and Engels, *Manifesto of the Communist Party*, chapter 2.) It is deduced from nothing else than knowledge of human requirements and of how to satisfy them. And in conditions where people have deliberate, conscious control over the means of satisfying their requirements, it is the expression of their freedom and the principle guiding their free activities. The ethics of the freedom struggle of the working class, which does not reject but incorporates all that is positive and durable in the whole moral evolution of mankind, prepares the way and lays the basis.

Although human morality does not yet exist, we can perhaps guess at some of its characteristics. It is not dogmatic, but scientific and self-critical. It does not encourage self-righteousness and moral spluttering and frothing, but is calm and reasonable. For it, immoral behaviour is simply anti-social behaviour due to weakness and lack of education, and its aim is not to punish but to reform and educate. It is in all respects kind and humane, and values above everything else the free development and happiness of the human individual.

We can conclude that if we should oppose the philosophy which says that morals are decreed by heaven, we should also oppose the philosophy, no less common today in bourgeois circles, which says that judgments of good and bad are simply expressions of emotional attitudes and can have no basis in reality. If socialists are asked, why do you consider this good and that bad, they need neither preach sermons nor shrug their shoulders. Socialist morality is founded on appreciation of the real conditions and real requirements of the actual freedom struggle of mankind.

READING LIST

The following are the principal sources in the writings of Marx, Engels and Lenin dealing with problems of the theory of knowledge which have been consulted and quoted in this volume:

MARX:

Capital
Critique of Political Economy, Preface
The Poverty of Philosophy
Economic-Philosophical Manuscripts

MARX AND ENGELS:

The German Ideology
Correspondence

ENGELS:

Anti-Dühring
Ludwig Feuerbach
Socialism, Utopian and Scientific, Introduction
Dialectics of Nature

LENIN:

Materialism and Empirio-Criticism
Karl Marx
Tasks of the Youth Leagues
Philosophical Notebooks